The Kashmir Conundrum

The Kashmir Conundrum

The Quest for Peace in a Troubled Land

GENERAL N.C. VIJ

HarperCollins *Publishers* India

First published in India by HarperCollins *Publishers* 2021
Building No. 10, Tower A, 4th Floor, DLF Cyber City, Phase II,
Gurugram – 122002
www.harpercollins.co.in

2 4 6 8 10 9 7 5 3 1

Copyright © General N.C. Vij 2021

P-ISBN: 978-93-9032-741-6
E-ISBN: 978-93-9032-742-3

The maps in this book are neither accurate nor drawn to scale and the boundaries as shown neither purport to be correct nor authentic as per the directives of the Survey of India.

The views and opinions expressed in this book are the author's own and the facts are as reported by him, and the publishers are not in any way liable for the same.

General N.C. Vij asserts the moral right
to be identified as the author of this work.

All rights reserved. No part of this publication may be reproduced, stored in a retrieval system, or transmitted, in any form or by any means, electronic, mechanical, photocopying, recording or otherwise, without the prior permission of the publishers.

Cover design: Saurav Das
Cover photo: Getty Images

Typeset in 11.5/15.7 Bembo Std at
Manipal Technologies Limited, Manipal

Printed and bound at
Thomson Press (India) Ltd

❶❶❷❸HarperCollinsIn

This book is produced from independently certified FSC® paper
to ensure responsible forest management.

*Dedicated to the people of Jammu and Kashmir,
who have borne the brunt of the Pakistan-perpetrated proxy war,
and the gallant Indian soldiers who make countless supreme sacrifices
to ensure the territorial integrity of India*

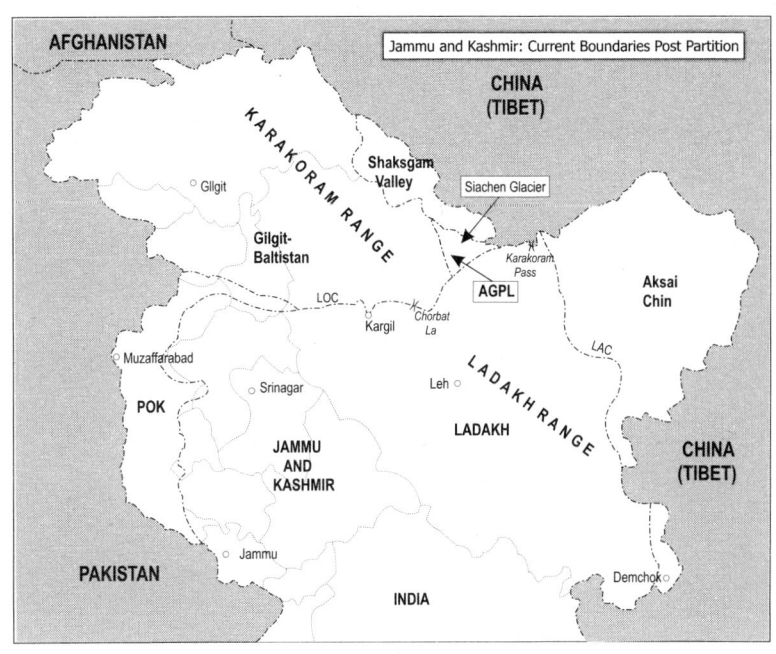

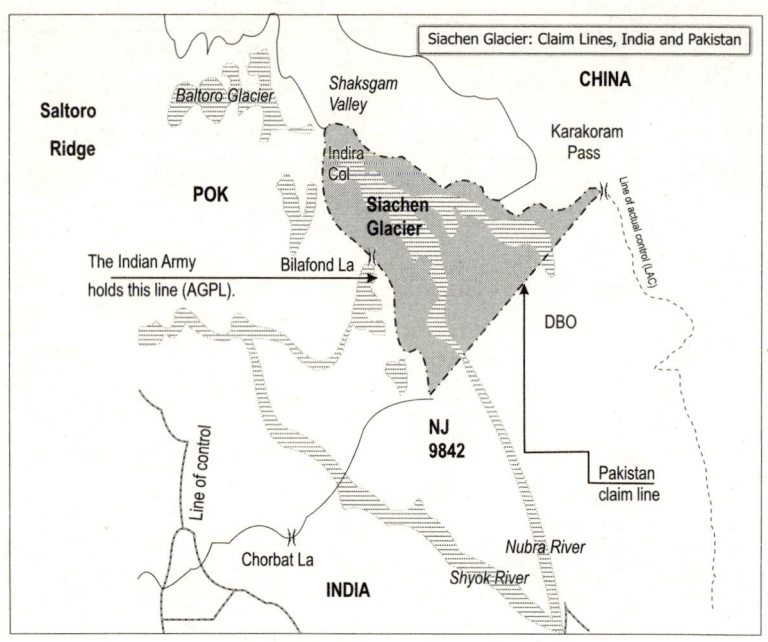

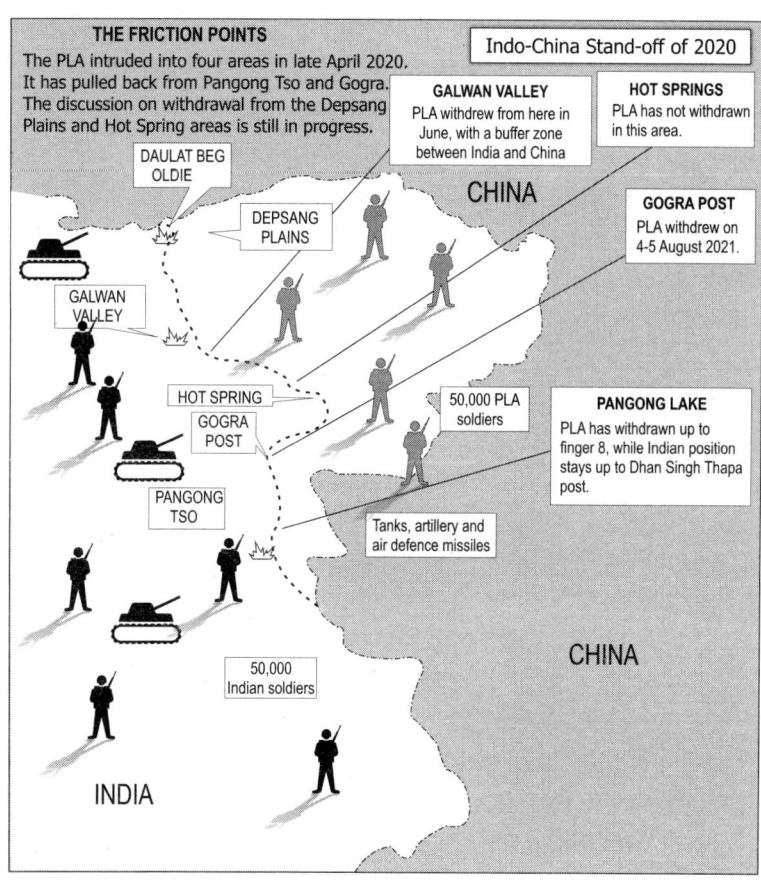

Contents

Foreword		xiii
Preface		xix
Prologue		xxv
1	The Backdrop	1
2	Invasion, Accession and Reference to the United Nations	20
3	The 1965 and 1971 Wars	68
4	Proxy War	86
5	Formulas for Settlement	128
6	Perception Management	137
7	India's Counter-militancy Strategy	156
8	The Watershed Year	176
9	Curtain Falls on Articles 370 and 35A	212

10	A Paradigm Shift	234
11	The Road Ahead	291
12	Conclusion	340

Epilogue — 349
Appendix A: Instrument of Accession of J&K State — 379
Appendix B: Ten Commandments Issued by the Chief of Army Staff — 381
Appendix C: Presidential Proclamation Abrogating Articles 370 and 35A — 382
Index — 383
Acknowledgements — 405
About the Author — 411

Foreword

Over the last few decades, hundreds of books have been written on the complex situation in Jammu and Kashmir. Authors have approached this topic from many different angles, as a result of which their conclusions have also varied sharply. A number of retired civil servants and high-ranking defence personnel have also expressed their views and given suggestions on how to sort out this highly complicated issue. This book is special because it is written by a retired army chief of staff, General N.C. Vij, who has special insights into Jammu and Kashmir.

After tracing the historical perspective of the state, he covers the invasion, accession and reference to the United Nations in some detail. Thereafter, he deals with the 1965 and 1971 wars with Pakistan and their impact on the state, and then goes on to cover the proxy war by Pakistan, which continues to the present day. After marshalling his facts, General Vij makes several valuable suggestions regarding how to deal effectively with the internal situation in Jammu and Kashmir as well as with Pakistan. He is amongst the few authors who have clearly grasped the tri-regional nature of the state and the fact that the Ladakh and Jammu regions have their own special aspirations, which must be dealt with in any overall settlement. This is in refreshing contrast to the Kashmir-centricity that most authors have adopted.

In my view, as I have expressed in Parliament, there are four clear dimensions regarding the state that must be kept in mind. First, whether we like it or not, is the international dimension. About one-third of the population of the original state of Jammu and Kashmir and one-third of its area are under Pakistan's control, out of which they have ceded over 5,000 sq. km to China in the Shaksgam Valley to facilitate the Karakoram Highway up to Gwadar Port. In addition, China has captured over 37,000 sq. km of the state's territory in Aksai-Chin. Thus, both our nuclear-armed neighbours have muscled their way into the picture. This dimension will therefore have to be tackled at some point in time.

The second dimension involves the relationship of the state with the rest of India. The Instrument of Accession, which my father signed on 26 October 1947 in the wake of the tribal invasion unleashed from Pakistan, is, of course, final and irreversible, and is exactly the same as those signed by other princes. However, there was an important difference between Jammu and Kashmir and the other Indian states. Whereas all the others subsequently signed merger agreements with the Government of India, the relationship of Jammu and Kashmir was based on Articles 370 and 35A of the Constitution, which recognized the state's special circumstances.

Subsequent to the accession, a Constituent Assembly was summoned by me on 1 May 1951 to draw up a new Constitution for the state, which came into force when I signed it on 26 January 1957. The Constitution, which clearly reiterated that Jammu and Kashmir would remain an integral part of India, also spelt out its special position. The original understanding was that the relationship would not be changed without the consent of the Constituent Assembly, but when the assembly ceased to exist, this was interpreted to mean the Jammu and Kashmir legislature. Subsequently, a large number of amendments were made by the Government of India that drastically reduced the quantum of autonomy in the state.

The dramatic constitutional developments in August 2019, when both houses of Parliament combined to abolish Articles 370 and 35A and divided the state into two union territories through an unprecedented act of constitutional legerdemain have, of course, drastically altered the situation. The relationship of the two union territories of Ladakh and Jammu and Kashmir with the Centre has undergone a sea change. Ladakh has at last achieved union territory status, which it had been demanding for decades. As far as Jammu and Kashmir is concerned, far from enjoying a special position, it is now one notch below other states of the Union. While this step has been widely welcomed in Jammu and Leh, there has expectedly been serious opposition in Kargil and the Valley, in that the last vestiges of their special status have vanished. This has already been challenged in the Supreme Court, and how the whole situation plays out in the future remains to be seen. At the time of writing, it is clear that there is likely to be prolonged unrest in the Valley, while Jammu and Ladakh will consolidate their political situation.

The third aspect, which is often overlooked but which General Vij has clearly appreciated, revolves around the multiregional nature of the state. Jammu and Kashmir was never a single integrated unit; it was brought together by a combination of diplomacy and conquest by my intrepid ancestor Maharaja Gulab Singh in the mid-nineteenth century. The Dogra empire consisted of several far-flung disparate ethnic, linguistic, cultural and geophysical units. In fact, the establishment of the multicultural state of Jammu and Kashmir was one of the major geopolitical events in the subcontinent during the nineteenth century. It extended the boundaries of India all the way up to Tibet and Central Asia, an achievement for which the Dogras have not received due credit. At the time of accession, Gilgit was, in a blatantly illegal act, given to Pakistan by the British commandant of the Gilgit Scouts, Major William Alexander Brown, while the western Muzaffarabad–Mirpur belt emerged as a separate unit after the ceasefire on 1 January 1949. As a result, only three units are now under Indian administration: Kashmir, Ladakh and Jammu.

Recent developments have fundamentally altered the situation. Ladakh has, at long last, emerged as a union territory, a step that I had publicly advocated as far back as 1965 when I was the governor of Jammu and Kashmir. This fulfils a long-standing demand of the people of Leh, while Kargil will have reservations because culturally they are very different from the Buddhists of Leh-Ladakh. Although Ladakh will not have a legislature, I presume that the Leh and Kargil hill councils will continue to function effectively and in fact be further empowered. Jammu and Kashmir are still linked together in the new union territory. With the proposed delimitation will come the enfranchisement of lakhs of west Pakistan refugees who crossed over to Jammu in 1947 but have not enjoyed permanent resident status and therefore have been deprived of all its benefits through the decades. There are also likely to be, for the first time, reservations for scheduled tribes, which would include the Muslim Gujjars and Bakarwals in the state.

As a result of all this, there may at last be a fair division of political, economic and administrative power between the two regions for the first time since the state was created in 1846. During Dogra rule, by definition the Dogras dominated, but from 1947 onwards there has been virtually Kashmiri rule, except for the short period when Ghulam Nabi Azad, who comes from Jammu, was the chief minister. This imbalance has led to continuous tension between the two regions, and if this can be balanced it would be most welcome so that both regions can enjoy a spirit of cooperation and goodwill, which will be needed if both are to prosper. Let us remember that the economy of Jammu is closely linked with that of Kashmir. Trade, commerce, tourism, especially the Sri Amarnath Yatra, all support the economy of Jammu, apart from being the mainstay of the Kashmir economy.

The fourth and final point is the humanitarian dimension. In the course of the thirty years from 1989 onwards, there has been terrible attrition and human suffering. Tens of thousands of Kashmiri youths have been killed in the conflict between militants and the security forces, many civilian lives have been lost during incidents of unrest and a large number of security personnel have sacrificed their lives. In the border areas of Jammu, thousands of families have been uprooted due to heavy shelling on the Line of Control and the international border. Their houses have been destroyed and their children's education rudely disrupted. Although some bunkers have been built in the border areas, they are still far from adequate to meet the requirements. In the Ladakh region, Pakistan's intrusion into the Kargil heights and our army's valiant reconquest of those mountain areas disrupted life in the Kargil region. Also, the gifted Kashmiri Pandit community was obliged to migrate en masse out of the Valley that had nurtured them for millennia, causing intense trauma and suffering.

As a result of all these factors, the region is facing a massive humanitarian crisis, especially in the Valley. The wails of widows and the cries of children have not received the sort of aid and sympathy that the nation gives to citizens hit by natural disasters such as floods and earthquakes. When we claim that Jammu and Kashmir is an integral part of India, we should also extend humanitarian aid and sympathy to the sufferers there, which is clearly missing. Surely our interest is not only in the geographical area but must also include a commitment to the welfare and progress of the millions of Indian citizens who reside there.

As the book was nearing publication, another serious development that took place was Chinese intrusion into Eastern Ladakh in May 2020. The Indian armed forces reacted with speed and the Chinese ingress was stopped, except a few areas wherein they had made some progress. However, after prolonged negotiations, withdrawal from both the north and south banks of Pangong Tso was commenced by both sides on 10 February 2021 and completed speedily. The discussions with regard to the other areas are still under progress. This development has very serious implications with regard to the security of our northern borders, and consequently of Jammu and Kashmir, and needs to be watched very carefully.

Many of the factors that I have mentioned have been covered by General Vij in his well-researched book. He has made several valuable suggestions with regard to the security, strategic, diplomatic and political challenges that we face in Jammu and Kashmir. Coming as they do from a former chief of army staff who hails from the state, all those concerned with the situation there, particularly those in positions of authority, would do well to take these suggestions seriously. I commend General N.C. Vij for writing this book, which will be of great interest not only to Indian readers but to those around the world who are interested in the vexed and, in many ways, tragic history of the beautiful but troubled state of Jammu and Kashmir.

Dr Karan Singh
First Sadr-i-Riyasat of J&K, 1952–65;
Governor of J&K, 1965–67
New Delhi, September 2021

Preface

I consider myself very fortunate that I was commissioned in one of the finest and most decorated infantry regiments of the Indian army, the Dogra Regiment. My journey with the army began on 11 December 1962 in the wake of the Chinese operations in Walong Sector (Lohit Division) of the Eastern Part of India. Our unit, 4 DOGRA, fought a heroic battle there as part of 11 Mountain Brigade, wherein over two days of intense fighting on 16–17 November 1962, at Tri Junction and Firm Base, 4 DOGRA sustained 206 casualties: 109 bravehearts made the supreme sacrifice, 23 were wounded and 74 taken as prisoners. In the first few years of our service in my Regiment, the focus was along India's northern and north-eastern borders. The army had taken the setback of 1962 very seriously and had pledged that such a situation would never be repeated. As young officers, we were involved in the frantic efforts to expand and upgrade the army in terms of manpower and equipment as well as training and toughening up of all ranks.

This overall upgrade and training came in handy when, in September 1965, Pakistan tried large-scale infiltration into the Kashmir Valley, though with little success. They followed this up with massive armoured thrusts into the Akhnoor–Chhamb sector, which is located 28 km from Jammu on the banks of the Chenab river. The war came to an end, with Indian troops crossing the international border and advancing right up to the outskirts of Lahore and Sialkot and threatening the very heartland of Pakistan. The subsequent war of 1971 and its outcome are far too well known to be recounted.

Despite these wars, the approach of the Indian leadership was that a 'stable and friendly' Pakistan was in India's interest. Even when in 1989-90 Pakistan launched a proxy war in Jammu and Kashmir (J&K), largely supported by their regular troops, to grab Kashmir, India's approach remained that both countries should resolve their differences amicably. This has been the steady thrust of all the Indian prime ministers since Independence. Former Prime Minister Atal Bihari Vajpayee is on record as having famously said in the Lok Sabha, 'History can be changed but not geography, friends can be changed but not neighbours. We have to live here, we live as friends or we keep fighting, making ourselves the butt of ridicule before the world.' The title of my book is thus derived from this very national approach of striving for peace with Pakistan.

As a young officer as well as in later service, I, like my compatriots, had my share of active duty in Jammu and Kashmir and had a close view of all that transpired there. And then came an opportunity to deal with the grave misadventure of Pakistan in Kargil in 1999, as director general of military operations (DGMO). A meeting with Pakistan's DGMO, Major General (later Lieutenant General) Tauqir Zia in Khasa, towards the end of this operation to coordinate the pull-out of their remaining infiltrators was an interesting experience. These deliberations showed me at first hand the degree to which Pakistan remains in denial. Over the years, I have come to the conclusion that this state of denial is very much a part of their strategy.

My experience of dealing with the Pakistani military continued when, as the vice chief of army staff, I saw terrorists belonging to Lashkar-e-Taiba (LeT) and Jaish-e-Mohammad (JeM) committing the sacrilege of attacking the Indian Parliament on 13 December 2001. Resultantly, both nations almost went to war, with the Indian army deploying fully (Operation Parakram) and awaiting political clearance to teach Pakistan a lesson for attacking the very citadel of Indian democracy. However, the clearance did not come.

Subsequently, as the chief of the army from 2003 to 2005, Kashmir (coincidentally my home state) remained one of my main areas of focus. Since I had served for several years at the 'decision-making level', I have tried in this book to give a perspective on the complexities involved in decision-making when there are always strong arguments on both sides. One of the toughest decisions that I took because of the herculean logistic effort required in the face of enemy fire was to order the erection of a 740-km-long fence along the Line of Control (LoC) from the Chenab river to the Zojila Pass. This smart obstacle system was fully manned and backed by well-coordinated rapid reaction response teams, which could be brought into immediate action on a readily available fail-safe communication system. It is to the army's credit that this herculean task was completed in the record time of just over a year. The fence considerably restricted Pakistani infiltration into Kashmir. This forced Pakistan to change their strategy in Kashmir to depend more on the Islamization of the Valley, with the youth being incited to lead the agitation, and on heavy exploitation of social media.

Over the years, the one question that has remained unanswered in my mind has been: which nation in the world, except Pakistan, would have fought four full-fledged wars in a span of seventy years and waged a proxy war against a much bigger and stronger neighbouring country (India), at such a heavy cost and with virtually no hope of success in the future? What keeps Pakistan in this permanently belligerent mood even when we have always wanted peace with them? As a nation, does it suffer from an existential threat, wherein it has not been able to reconcile to its own existence? Or is it that its dream of having a Pakistan that is equivalent to India in all respects lies shattered and it cannot get over the disappointment of failure? Or has the Kashmir issue become a 'rallying point for Pakistan to keep its national unity intact and also a mode of distraction for her people from all other national problems'? Is keeping India tied down militarily and economically the sole aim and dream of their existence? Or is it the raison d'être of the existence of their mighty army, which holds all the cards? Is there light at the end of the tunnel and a ray of hope that at some stage, our neighbour will settle for peace and friendly relations?

Since I have seen the unfolding of this sordid story in varying capacities, I feel that it is my professional responsibility to share my experiences with our soldiers and countrymen, as an offering of my deep respect and love for the Indian army. This book is not a memoir but a thematic coverage of the Kashmir imbroglio.

As far as possible, I have tried to capture all angles of the Kashmir problem and briefly run through its history. I have offered some suggestions that perhaps would not have been my preferred options while in active service. This can be attributed to changes in my perspective as a result of age and experience and now watching the developments from a distance rather than being in the midst of the confusion of a proxy war. My endeavour has been to write this book in an accessible style so that it meets the requirements of readers of all shades. I hope they find it useful. For us soldiers, such literature remains of professional interest to draw our lessons from.

This book also gives me an opportunity to pay homage to the brave officers and men of the magnificent Indian army, which I was privileged and honoured to serve and lead. They have been rock steady in their service to the nation, even at the cost of making boundless supreme sacrifices. India is indeed blessed to have the armed forces, for whom single-minded devotion and the spirit of service to the country come automatically and in whom the fire of patriotism burns unabated.

Finally, I would like to dedicate this book to the brave officers, soldiers and families of our valiant Indian army. Even as this book is being prepared for publication, our armed forces have been involved in a serious face-off with the Chinese in Eastern Ladakh, where they are putting up a glorious performance.

General N.C. Vij
New Delhi
October 2021

Prologue

'The greatest glory in living lies not in never falling, but in rising every time we fall.'

— *Nelson Mandela*

The partition of British India in 1947 was one of the bloodiest events in modern history. Millions of people on both sides of the artificially drawn border suffered, were killed, had their families torn apart and were rendered homeless. It was a tragedy of monumental proportions perhaps not clearly visualized by the main pleaders of partition. This bloodshed and mass-scale upheaval had, and continues to have, an extremely negative impact on the relations between India and Pakistan. Too many people suffered and traumatic memories on both sides have coloured their attitudes towards one another for all time to come.

Almost seven decades after Partition and Independence, the Jammu and Kashmir issue, symptomatic of the India–Pakistan rivalry, stand-off and animosity, is nowhere near resolution. Distrust is deeply embedded in the national psyche of the two countries and is showing no signs of lessening even after the passage of so much time. Whereas in India, the general view now tends to be to ignore Pakistan and focus on other pressing issues, Pakistan never misses the opportunity to raise the Kashmir issue at all regional and international forums, however unrelated this issue may be to the subject and aim of those deliberations.

Wresting control of Jammu and Kashmir from India has been the continuing Pakistani obsession since its creation in 1947. This obsession stems from their perception that they did not receive their rightful share of territory at the time of Partition.

For Muhammad Ali Jinnah – the architect of the two-nation theory – Pakistan was founded on the premise that Muslims in India were a separate nation and hence there was a need to create a separate state as a homeland for them. Of course, it can also be argued that hidden in the agenda of the two-nation theory was the ambition of creating a position of parity between Muslim Pakistan and Hindu India.[1] This was also to fulfil Jinnah's hidden desire for unchallenged personal power in the newly emergent state of Pakistan.

Pakistan, as it was formed, did not satisfy its leadership because of its small size as compared to India. Indian leaders conceded it most reluctantly, and it also hardly met the aspirations of the Muslim leaders. Jinnah is often quoted as decrying a 'moth-eaten and truncated Pakistan' granted by the British. However, in fairness

---

1   Lt Gen. H.M. Khanna, *The Kashmir Imbroglio: A Military–Operational Appraisal of J&K* (written for Chhatrapati Shivaji Chair, University of Pune, 2002), p. 3. Also, Pakistan's joining various alliances as part of CENTO–SEATO with US and China, among others, was part of that desire to create parity with India.

to India, it can be said that it has accepted Partition as a reality and moved on.

Another root cause of the problem is that the parameters governing the accession of princely states to India and Pakistan, as indicated in the Cabinet Mission Memorandum, were interpreted differently by the Congress and the Muslim League. The Congress was clear about the inherent unity of India under the British paramountcy and maintained that the rulers of the princely states had no option except to accede to India or Pakistan, based on the wishes of the people. It implied that except for the states lying within the geographical area comprising Pakistan, the rest of them must accede to India and India would inherit all the duties and responsibilities ascribed to the British Crown. The Muslim League under Jinnah aimed to not only create Pakistan but also to simultaneously prevent India's consolidation into a single entity and reduce the size and population disparity between the two countries. Based on the above premises regarding accession, the Muslim League went about enticing, cajoling and pressuring the various princely rulers to either opt for Pakistan or even remain independent.

Inciting the rulers of Junagarh and Hyderabad to not merge with India and the invasion of Jammu and Kashmir by Pakistan-sponsored tribals were all part of this design. Even today, the overriding ambition of balkanizing India is considered to be an arch strategy of Pakistan's Inter-Services Intelligence (ISI).

There is also evidence to suggest that the Muslim League's leaders tried to persuade the rulers of Jodhpur–Jaisalmer and Bikaner to opt for independence or join Pakistan.[2]

---

2 Lt Gen. H.M. Khanna, *The Kashmir Imbroglio*, p. 4.

That the British were passive supporters or perhaps even complicit in these manipulations of the Muslim League had fortunately been discerned by Sardar Vallabhbhai Patel, home minister in the interim Indian government. He realized that His Majesty's political department harboured designs to balkanize the Indian subcontinent. There was an attempt to implement Winston Churchill's Imperial Strategy, which Lord Wavell, former viceroy to India, recorded in his journal on 29 March 1949: 'He [Churchill] seems to favour partition into Pakistan, Hindustan and Princestan'.[3] This was only the tip of the iceberg. Hardly anyone could see or fathom what was being manoeuvred underneath. This is not the appropriate place to discuss the process and contribution of Sardar Patel – the iron man of India – as the unification of the rest of India, the defeat of the nefarious designs of the Muslim League and later Pakistan and also the departing British are now a reality.

However, the state of Jammu and Kashmir, which is contiguous with both India and Pakistan, posed problems which not only persist to this day but have become even more complicated with the passage of time. This state was a Muslim-majority area but ruled by a Hindu Dogra ruler, Maharaja Hari Singh. Pakistan felt entitled to Jammu and Kashmir on the basis of it being a Muslim-majority state and its contiguity with Pakistan. For India, three factors were the deciding principles for its accession to India: (i) the maharaja had signed the Instrument of Accession to India on 26 October 1947; (ii) allowing religion to be a clinching factor for a state to determine its choice would be a defeat of the principle of secularism for a state like India; and (iii) Pakistan's

---

3 R.N.P. Singh, *Sardar Patel: Unifier of Modern India* (Vitasta Publishing, 2018), p. 16.

success in attempting to force the accession of Jammu and Kashmir to Pakistan through an invasion would be tantamount to India surrendering to Pakistan.

Finally, Pakistan was defeated and Jammu and Kashmir's accession to India now remains irrevocable and final. However, as a consequence, India and Pakistan have fought four wars on this issue and the state has been subjected to unrelenting terrorism by Pakistan-sponsored and abetted terrorist organizations. These aspects are discussed in detail in this book.

1

The Backdrop

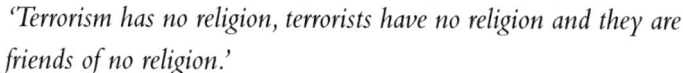

'Terrorism has no religion, terrorists have no religion and they are friends of no religion.'

– *Manmohan Singh*

The history of Jammu and Kashmir (J&K) is intertwined with the history of the broader Indian subcontinent and the surrounding regions, comprising the areas of Central Asia, South Asia and East Asia. This history of Jammu and Kashmir as a separate state starts from 1846. Till the fourteenth century, it was ruled by a series of Buddhist and Hindu dynasties. Thereafter, a number of Muslim dynasties established themselves and continued ruling the region till 1580, when it was captured by the Mughal empire, whose rule lasted till 1752. Thereafter, it passed under the control of Afghan invaders.

In the latter half of the eighteenth century, Jammu was ruled by a Dogra chief of Rajput descent named Ranjit Deo. On his death, the Sikhs turned Jammu and Kashmir and the neighbouring hill tracts into a dependency. The three great-grandnephews of Ranjit Deo, namely, Gulab Singh, Dhyan Singh and Suchet Singh, entered the service of Maharaja Ranjit Singh. Pleased with their service, in 1818, Maharaja Ranjit Singh conferred the principality of Jammu on Gulab Singh with the hereditary title of 'Raja'. Bhimber and Chibal, including Poonch, were handed over to Dhyan Singh, and Ramnagar to Suchet Singh. Both Dhyan Singh and Suchet Singh were subsequently killed in different wars.

With the death of Maharaja Ranjit Singh in 1839, Sikh power started waning. In 1846, at the close of the first Anglo-Sikh war, Gulab Singh acted as a mediator between the English and the Sikhs. At the conclusion of the negotiations, the Sikh maharaja, seven-year-old Duleep Singh, was asked to pay an indemnity to the East India Company of Rs 1 crore, in addition to ceding a large part of the territory of Punjab.

The Sikhs were unable to pay the indemnity, and as a result they ceded all the hill territories from the Indus river to the Beas river, which included Jammu and Kashmir.

However, Lord Hardinge, the then governor general, felt that this area was too large to hold and would extend the British frontiers beyond the capabilities of his military and create areas of conflict. The territory offered by the Sikh ruler included the entire area in possession of Gulab Singh, who came forward to pay the war indemnity on the condition that he was made an independent ruler of Jammu and Kashmir. A separate treaty embodying this arrangement was concluded by the English with Gulab Singh in Amritsar on 16 March 1846.

The Treaty of Amritsar marked the commencement of the history of Jammu and Kashmir as a political entity. The treaty put Gulab Singh, as maharaja, in possession of the entire hilly region between the rivers Indus and Ravi, including Kashmir, Jammu, Ladakh and Gilgit. It excluded Lahaul, Kulu and some other areas including Chamba, which for strategic purposes were retained by the English. The grandson of Gulab Singh, Maharaja Hari Singh, was the ruler of Jammu and Kashmir at the time of Partition and transfer of power.

A Historical Perspective on Kashmir

It is a well-established fact that history impacts people deeply. To understand Jammu and Kashmir and its present-day problems, it is important to take a historical perspective of the state to appreciate how it has impacted the nature, behaviour and psyche of the people.

Kashmir has the unique distinction of possessing comprehensive written records of its history. These chronicles extend from ancient times, that is, the Vedic period, to the advent of Islam, through the Mughal period, to British rule and thereafter the period after Independence.

History reveals that for thousands of years, Kashmir was dominated by a Buddhist–Brahmanical order. King Gonanda of Kashmir is believed to have attended the coronation of Yudhishthira in the Mahabharat. The Pandu empire lasted over a thousand years. The Kashmiri tradition of ascribing ancient monuments to the Pandus is reflected in their Pandavi traditions.

Kashmir also formed part of Emperor Ashoka's kingdom (272–231 BC). Ashoka is believed to have founded the city of Srinagar in the third century BC. At the height of Buddhist influence, Kashmir is said to have had one thousand Buddhist monasteries, which acted as centres of learning and spread the Buddhist religion.

There was a brief interlude in the first century AD, when the Kushans (of Turkish origin) subdued the Gonanda dynasty and extended into the heart of the Indian subcontinent. However, the Gonanda dynasty bounced back soon enough and continued to rule until the sixth century and the Hindu–Brahmanical order re-established itself as the dominant religion.

The Huns, nomadic warriors from Central Asia, gained control of the Valley in the early sixth century for a short period. The name remembered most bitterly from amongst them is that of Mihirkul, a prince as cruel as death. By AD 530, Kashmir regained its freedom and the Hindu kings returned to power. The most famous ruler during this period was Lalitaditya (AD 697–738). Another important ruler was Queen Didda, a woman of remarkable beauty, courage and strength.

This phase of Kashmir's history ended in AD 1339 when it came under Muslim rule. In 1394, an iconoclast named Sikandar inherited the throne. In his time, Hindus were offered three choices – death, conversion or exile – and all Hindu books of learning were thrown into the Dal Lake.[1] After that there was the rule of Zain-ul-Abedin (AD 1417–1469), who was tolerant, kind and a great patron of the arts, and whose rule brought new life to the tortured Valley.

Subsequently, the Chak dynasty ruled for some time, wherein Sunni Muslims and Hindus alike were persecuted, and they looked towards the Mughal empire in India for redress of their grievances. Akbar's troops occupied Kashmir in AD 1586, and the region passed under the rule of the stable Mughal empire. Jahangir visited Kashmir thirteen times during his reign. He is credited to have established the famous Mughal gardens at Shalimar, Nishat as well as Achabal and Verinag. Shah Jahan is known to have established the Chashme Shahi gardens. The Mughal period saw the development of literature, the arts, crafts, architecture, poetry and music. Subsequently, Aurangzeb's anti-Hindu zeal gradually resulted in the decline of the Mughal empire.

---

1   Sisir Gupta, *Kashmir: A Study in India–Pakistan Relations* (Asia Publishing House, published in 1966 by Council of World Affairs, New Delhi), pp. 18-19; Balraj Madhok, *Kashmir Divided* (Lucknow: Rashtra Dharma Prakashan Limited, 1949), pp. 17-19.

Mughal rule was followed by Afghan rule from AD 1752 to 1819, and it is considered the darkest chapter of Kashmir's history by way of the horrendous suffering of the people. By the early nineteenth century, Sikh power had firmly established itself in Punjab. Maharaja Ranjit Singh invaded Kashmir in AD 1819, defeated the Afghan governor and established Sikh rule, which lasted for twenty-seven years. Later, under the Treaty of Lahore (8 March 1846), the British annexed Punjab. To recover the cost of the Anglo-Sikh wars as well as to reward Gulab Singh – a nobleman of Ranjit Singh's court – for his services, the British, by way of the Treaty of Amritsar (16 March 1846), gave Gulab Singh 'all the hilly and mountainous country with its dependencies situated to the Eastward of river Indus and Westwards of river Ravi including Chamba but excluding Lahul, being part of the areas ceded to the British by the Lahore State'. This territory was sold to Gulab Singh for Rs 75 lakh. This ushered in the Dogra rule, which lasted until 1947 when India was granted independence and partitioned.

The Land

The state of Jammu and Kashmir is by no means unilingual or uniracial. In fact, it is a multiracial society, its people speaking different languages, having different religions and conforming to different dresses, traditions and customs.

It broadly consists of four distinct parts, the most populous and predominantly Muslim (Sunni) being the Kashmir Valley, which is enclosed by the Shamshabari Range to its west and the Pir Panjal Range to its south. It lies along the Jhelum river and extends up to the Uri area. To the north-west across the Zojila Range lies the Kargil area, which is dominated by Shia Muslims. The Ladakh region borders Tibet and is predominantly a Buddhist area. Jammu is the fourth prominent area. It lies to the south of Pir Panjal ranges and is predominantly a Hindu belt and also known as a city of temples, including the famous Vaishno Devi shrine. It is the winter capital of J&K. It is also contiguous with Punjab state. In the north and north-east are the sparsely populated areas of Baltistan and Dardistan encompassing the Skardu, Gilgit, Hunza and Nagar principalities, composed primarily of Shia Muslims and Ismailis. The areas of Baltistan, Skardu and others (formerly known as Northern Areas) are presently administered by Pakistan. In addition, some of the western areas of J&K, starting from Mirpur and up to Neelam Valley, were annexed by Pakistan in 1947 and are known as Pakistan-occupied Kashmir (POK).

The Jammu and Kashmir state, as constituted at present, as Balraj Madhok had said, is simply a political entity. It is a conglomeration of at least six distinct types of people who inhabit well-defined parts or zones of the state with each having a distinct language, culture, customs, manners and history.[2] These six zones are Jammu, Kashmir, Ladakh, Baltistan, Gilgit and the districts of the south-west.

The religious division is only one and not the most important of the divisions in Jammu and Kashmir. This is well illustrated by the fact that Article 48 of the new Jammu and Kashmir programme adopted by the National Conference (the major Kashmiri party at the time of Partition) in 1946 stated: 'The national languages of the State shall be Kashmiri, Dogri, Balti, Dardi, Punjabi, Hindi and Urdu.' The Preamble referring to the various constituent units reads: 'We the people of Jammu, Kashmir, Ladakh and the Frontier Regions including Poonch and Chinani ilaquas...'[3] It is indeed surprising that the state escaped trifurcation at the time of the

---

2 Sisir Gupta, *Kashmir: A Study in India–Pakistan Relations*, p. 23; Balraj Madhok, *Kashmir Divided*, pp. 16–17.

3 Ibid, p. 24.

reorganization of India into linguistic states after Independence. Perhaps the underlying idea was to keep it as a cohesive state where all religions were welcome and also to keep it economically viable. The reorganization of the state into three autonomous parts was the demand of the Jammu and Ladakh regions even at the time of Partition.

PoK and Gilgit-Baltistan

The unanimous resolution of 1994 of the Parliament of India was explicit that the entire state of Jammu and Kashmir, as it existed before Partition, belonged to India. It also resolved that the lost territories of PoK and Gilgit-Baltistan will be reacquired from Pakistan and Aksai-Chin from China.

While a great deal is written and said about PoK, much of it is without proper comprehension of its actual geographical location and the extent of the area involved. In order to get a better understanding of the area, which is most relevant, a brief description is given here.

Historically, PoK belonged to the erstwhile princely state of Jammu and Kashmir. Soon after the partition of India in 1947, the maharaja signed the Instrument of Accession, thereby formalizing the accession of the state to the Indian Union. However, part of the state, the region known as PoK, has been under the unlawful control of Pakistan ever since Pakistan's illegal invasion of Kashmir in 1947. PoK legitimately remains an integral part of India.

India calls the territory occupied by Pakistan as PoK and Pakistan calls it Azad Kashmir. Gilgit-Baltistan (formerly known as the Northern Areas) has remained an amorphous entity for over seven decades. The Trans-Karakoram Tract is a region administered by Pakistan as an administrative territory, and constitutes the Northern portion of the larger Kashmir region. This territory shares a border with PoK. More on this is covered subsequently. Pakistan ceded Shaksgam Valley illegally to China in March 1963. China struck a bargain with Pakistan wherein they promised to assist Pakistan in building the Karakoram Highway in return for control over the Trans-Karakoram Tract. This highway is presently under active construction under the China–Pakistan Economic Corridor (CPEC) or Belt and Road (formerly One Belt One Road) initiative. To the north-east of this region lies the Chinese border, further north is Kazakhstan and to the north-west is Afghanistan. The Karakoram Highway runs through this region and the Siachen Glacier commands a strategic position in this area.

PoK

PoK borders Pakistan's Punjab province to the south and Khyber Pakhtunkhwa province to the west. To the east, PoK is separated from Indian-administered Kashmir by the Line of Control (LoC), which is the de facto border between India and Pakistan, even though this remains disputed. The PoK territory also includes some border regions of old Kashmir, centred mostly around the Neelam Valley. The capital city of PoK is Muzaffarabad and the largest city is Mirpur. Other important cities are Bhimber and Poonch. PoK has ten small districts.

Out of the total area of Jammu and Kashmir (2,22,236 sq. km), about 35 per cent (78,114 sq. km) is under illegal occupation by Pakistan, and about 2 per cent (5,180 sq. km) has been handed over by it to China, which is already in illegal occupation of an additional 17 per cent in the Aksai-Chin area (37,555 sq. km). The total area of PoK excluding Gilgit-Baltistan is about 13,297 sq. km. This implies that India controls about 46 per cent (1.01 lakh sq. km) of the erstwhile state of J&K. Out of this area, about 26 per cent forms part of the Jammu division, 16 per cent the Kashmir division and the remaining 58 per cent the Ladakh-Kargil division. But the proportional distribution of the population in these divisions is 43 per cent in Jammu, 55 per cent in Kashmir and 2 per cent in Ladakh.[4] India controls 46 per cent of the land area and 61 per cent of its population. Pakistan controls 35 per cent of the land while China controls the remaining 19 per cent including the Shaksgam Valley area.

PoK (as part of the erstwhile state of Jammu and Kashmir) was nominally a self-governing area but ever since the 1949 ceasefire between India and Pakistan, Pakistan had excercised control over it without actually incorporating it. However, in 1970, major constitutional changes were introduced in Azad Kashmir. The system of adult franchise was adopted through the Azad Jammu and Kashmir Act, 1970. A semi-democratic set-up was introduced for the first time, the Legislative Assembly as well as president of Azad J&K (AJK) were elected on the basis of adult franchise by the people of AJK and the refugees of the state of J&K settled in PoK.

The assembly consisted of twenty-four elected members and one co-opted female member. The presidential system worked for about four years, after which, in 1974, the parliamentary system was introduced in AJK under the AJK Interim Constitution Act, 1974. This has undergone fourteen amendments so far.

The assembly now consists of forty-one elected members and eight co-opted members (five female, one member from Ulema-e-Deen or Mushaikh, one from amongst AJK technocrats and other professionals, and one from amongst J&K nationals residing abroad). Since 1975, the prime minister has been elected by

---

4 Y.P. Chathley, *Education, Population and Development – A Regional Perspective of Northwest India: Jammu & Kashmir, Punjab, Himachal Pradesh, Haryana, and Rajasthan* (Chandigarh: Centre for Research in Rural and Industrial Development, 1995).

members of the Legislative Assembly. He is the chief executive of the state, whereas the president is the constitutional head. Besides the executive and legislative, a full-fledged judiciary was also introduced through the 1974 Act. The Supreme Court and the high court (benches) as well as subordinate courts are now present in PoK under various laws.

All the changes have been made through executive decrees by various Pakistani governments. The prime objective was to establish a system similar to the one prevailing in Pakistan. However, the exception was that PoK would have a council, with the prime minister of Pakistan as the chairman, six elected members, three ex-officio members including the president of AJK, the prime minister of AJK or his nominee, the federal minister for Kashmir affairs and five members to be nominated from amongst the federal ministers and members of the Parliament. The council remains a constitutional body and had extensive powers under the third schedule of the 1974 Act. It could legislate on defence, security, foreign affairs, and trade and currency, among others. However, after the 13th amendment to the 1974 act, on 3 June 2018, which abolished the AJK Council's administrative and financial powers, the council has been reduced to the role of an advisory body.

Over a period of time, this system has led to complete control by Pakistan over PoK (AJK) and its continuing subjugation by Pakistan over decades, leading to an acute sense of alienation amongst the people. The case of the Mirpuris is even more pronounced, as they were forced to flee from their homes when the Mangla Dam was constructed. The construction took place despite large-scale protests. The demand for freedom from Pakistani control and abolition of the interim Constitution is gaining ground.

The question that begs an answer is what should India's stance be, given Pakistan's constant interference in the Indian-administered union territories of Jammu and Kashmir and Ladakh, while Pakistan tramples over a disturbed area that rightfully belongs to India? Should India actively support the freedom movement of the people of PoK? If so, in what manner should it be done remains a matter of debate.

Gilgit-Baltistan

Gilgit-Baltistan, formerly known as the Northern Areas, is administered by Pakistan as an administrative territory. It constitutes the northern portion of the larger Kashmir region, which has been the subject of a dispute between India and Pakistan since 1947 and between India and China from some time later.

It is the northernmost territory administered by Pakistan. It borders PoK to the south, the province of Khyber Pakhtunkhwa to the west, the Wakhan Corridor of Afghanistan to the north, the Xinjiang region of China to the east and north-east, and the Indian-administered union territories of Jammu and Kashmir and Ladakh to the south-east. Gilgit-Baltistan is six times the size of PoK. The territory of present-day Gilgit-Baltistan became a separate administrative unit in 1970 under the name of Northern Areas. It was formed by the amalgamation of the former Gilgit Agency, the Baltistan district and several former princely states, the larger ones of which were Hunza and Nagar.

On 29 August 2009, it was granted limited autonomy and renamed as Gilgit-Baltistan by the self-governance order signed by the then president of Pakistan, Asif Ali Zardari. The move was aimed to empower the people of Gilgit-Baltistan. This order was replaced in July 2018. As per the new order, all powers exercised by the Gilgit-Baltistan council were shifted to the Assembly. The role of Kashmir and the Northern Areas Ministry was abolished and some more reforms were introduced.

The order was widely criticized as it failed to address the basic question of the rights of the people and the critical issue of provincial autonomy. The order introduced elements that brought Gilgit-Baltistan closer to the structure of AJK in spirit and form but with no impact, as the strings of power rested with the Government of Pakistan. The order was rejected by political groups in Gilgit-Baltistan, the pro-independence groups and the pro-India groups. There were allegations that the order was designed to secure increasing Chinese interest in PoK.

However, it is common knowledge that the real power rests with the governor, who is appointed by the Central Government, and not with the chief minister or elected assembly. The democracy is thus only a facade. In August 2015, the Gilgit-Baltistan Legislative Assembly passed a unanimous resolution which asked the federal government to declare the region as a constitutional province of Pakistan. On 1 November 2020, Pakistan had announced its decision to grant Gilgit-Baltistan the status of a full province. Further, on 15 November 2020, elections were held in 23 of the 24 constituencies of Gilgit-Baltistan.

Gilgit-Baltistan covers an area of over 72,971 sq. km and is a mountainous region. It had an estimated population of 18,00,000 in 2015. Its capital city is Gilgit. Besides Baltistan, other prominent townships, though small, are Ishkuman, Skardu, Chilas, Astore and Burzil. Gilgit-Baltistan is home to five of the fourteen eight-thousanders (peaks over 8,000 m high) and more than fifty peaks above 7,000 m (23,000 ft). Three of the world's longest glaciers outside the polar region are found in Gilgit-Baltistan. The main business is tourism, which involves trekking and mountaineering.

A small historical narrative that would also be of interest is that Major William Brown, the commander of the Gilgit Scouts, mutinied on 1 November 1947, overthrowing the then governor of this region, Brigadier Ghansara Singh. The bloodless coup d'état was planned by Brown under the code name Datta Khel. It was also joined by a rebellious section of the Jammu and Kashmir Sixth Infantry under Mirza Hassan Khan. There was no civilian involvement in the Gilgit rebellion, which was solely the work of military leaders, not all of whom were in favour of joining Pakistan.

After taking control of Gilgit, the Gilgit Scouts along with Azad irregulars moved towards Baltistan and Ladakh and captured Skardu by May 1948, and subsequently captured Dras and Kargil as well, cutting off India's communication with Leh in Ladakh. The Indian forces subsequently mounted an offensive in the autumn of 1948 and recaptured all of Kargil district. The Baltistan region, however, remained under the control of Gilgit and thus Pakistan.

The Gilgit-Baltistan area (then known as Northern Areas) came under the direct rule of the central government of Pakistan after the Karachi Agreement of 1949. However, the region did not find mention in the Constitution of Pakistan. It was ruled directly by a joint secretary in the Ministry of Pakistan Affairs and Northern Areas (now Ministry of Kashmir Affairs and Gilgit-Baltistan).

Interestingly, in 1993, the status of the Northern Areas was petitioned in the AJK High Court and subsequently in the Supreme Court. The Supreme Court of Pakistan, in its verdict on 14 September 1994, stated that 'the Northern Areas are part of Jammu and Kashmir State but are not part of Azad Kashmir as defined in the Azad Kashmir Constitution Act 1974'.

Thereafter, the administrative arrangements underwent some changes and a rudimentary system of representative governance was introduced in the Northern Areas in October 1994 by the formation of the Northern Area Executive Council. The council had twenty-six members, who had advisory powers but no legislative powers.

On 28 May 1999, the Supreme Court of Pakistan again took note of the dictatorial and colonial system at work in Gilgit-Baltistan and directed the Pakistan government to act within six months to put in place an elected government with an independent judiciary in the Northern Areas and extend rights to the people of the region. The Pakistani government announced a package that provided for an appellate court and an expanded bench and renamed it as Northern Areas Legislative Council (NALC). Elections to the NALC were held in November 1999, but the body had few legislative and fiscal powers. However, the Pervez Musharraf government granted a few more legislative and financial powers in November 2000.

The Northern Areas were renamed as Gilgit-Baltistan in August 2009 to satisfy the long-standing demand of political parties and people for autonomy. The people rejected it as this limited action did not meet their demands. The media also called it a symbolic gesture of empathy towards the people rather than a real change.

A dispassionate analysis by some Western authors states that the region is not included in Pakistan's Constitution, meaning that there is no fundamental guarantee of civil rights, democratic representation or separation of powers. Pakistan is constantly struggling to cover up its ambivalence and injustice towards the region.

The demographic composition of the Gilgit-Baltistan region has undergone a few changes since 1947 as part of the deliberate strategy of the Pakistani government to turn the original inhabitants of the region (mostly Shias) into a minority. The issue of large-scale migration of Pashtuns has not been given its due attention by India and the international authorities.

A large number of Pashtuns live outside their traditional homeland of Pashtunistan in Afghanistan. In India also they are found in the Rohilkhand area of Uttar Pradesh. They are there in varying numbers in a large number of countries in the world.

Sectarianism has been rampant in the region since General Zia-ul-Haq's tenure, who, with the Pakistan Peoples Party (PPP), had some hold over the local population. Anti-Shia riots in Zia's time claimed over 700 lives. Both the state and non-state actors have manipulated the divisions since the 1980s, sowing the seeds of demographic divide.

The area of Gilgit-Baltistan is rich in resources. It has vast deposits of precious and semi-precious stones including the world's best rubies and high-quality marble. The Indus and its tributaries flowing through the Gilgit-Baltistan area offer huge potential for the generation of hydroelectric power with an identified capacity of around 15,000 MW in the hydropower generation sector alone. Such vast deposits of minerals and water resources have got China more interested in the region. The CPEC also passes through this area.

Pakistan has been draining the Gilgit-Baltistan area of its natural resources with no benefits to the locals. A typical example is the controversial Diamer-Bhasha Dam project. The dam will be built in Diamer in Gilgit-Baltistan, but the power plant will be in Khyber Pakhtunkhwa (formerly known as North West Frontier Province).

Finally, people in Gilgit-Baltistan have always been neglected, even more so than the area of PoK, which has also remained backward. As compared to them, the Indian side did infinitely better. As a matter of fact, a United Nations (UN) report on human rights by Emon Nicholon in the aftermath of the 2005 earthquake commends the political process in Jammu and Kashmir and compliments India on its efforts towards the socio-economic development of Jammu and Kashmir through frequent special packages for the state and also for its emphasis on job creation and measures to promote tourism in the state.

Thus, it is clear that both PoK and Gilgit-Baltistan are acutely dissatisfied with the political situation and economic development in the region. There is an ongoing agitation, especially in Gilgit-Baltistan, seeking freedom from Pakistan if their demands are not met. The Pakistan Supreme Court, on 30 April 2020, allowed Pakistan to hold general elections in Gilgit-Baltistan by amending the administrative orders. The elections were finally held in November 2020. Pakistan felt that this would satisfy the people of Gilgit-Baltistan. India had issued a demarche to protest against this move, as Gilgit-Baltistan is a disputed area.

The Strategic Importance of J&K

Briefly, the strategic importance of Jammu and Kashmir can be understood from the fact that it lies at the confluence of Islamic, Buddhist and Hindu cultures. Samuel Huntington's theory about the 'clash of civilizations' confers great strategic importance to this area, since it lies on the fault lines of three of the world's greatest civilizations and cultures.

The geo-strategic significance of this state, which shared borders with Afghanistan, the USSR, China and the emerging state of Pakistan at the time of Partition, was immense. Even the soberest of students of military history would recognize the strategic significance of J&K with respect to the Central Asian republics, with their huge proven reserves of gas and oil.

The acquisition of Gilgit-Baltistan by Pakistan in the 1947–48 war opened up several options for Pakistan. The foremost amongst these was the ability to have a direct land route to China, which today is their most important ally and all-weather friend. The strategic and operational significance of the CPEC passing through the Khunjerab Pass linking China and Pakistan cannot be overemphasized. It throws up a number of options both for Pakistan and China vis-à-vis India, besides opening up Gilgit-Baltistan itself.[5]

The acquisition of Gilgit-Baltistan also enabled Pakistan to consider Afghanistan as its own backyard, and this has been an

---

5   Lt Gen. H.M. Khanna, *The Kashmir Imbroglio*, p. 36.

essential element of Pakistan's concept of strategic depth as related to Afghanistan. This puts India geographically out of the reckoning in Afghanistan. This is also the area through which Pakistan is defending its position opposite the Siachen Glacier and was also used for Pakistan's misadventure in the Kargil area.

Hypothetically, if Pakistan were to succeed in annexing Kashmir, it would be sitting right next to both Punjab and Himachal Pradesh. Jointly with its ally China, it would acquire deep penetration capability against India. China, which is in control of Aksai-Chin and now has a corridor in the Gilgit-Baltistan area, can ill afford India gaining total control over all of Kashmir, especially as its CPEC passes through it. So China is interested in Kashmir for its own sake rather than only as an ally of Pakistan. Their strategic interests are deeply intertwined with those of Pakistan.

The People

In its more than 2,500 years of recorded history, Muslims ruled Kashmir for about 500 years. The remainder of the period, or over 2,000 years, saw Hindu and Buddhist dominance and, most recently, over a century of Sikh–Dogra rule prior to India's independence. The Greeks, the Mauryas, the Kushans, the Afghans, the Cholas and the Mirs came from outside and later also the Mughals.

Even though the Valley is predominantly Muslim, vast expanses of its territory were Hindu- and Buddhist-majority areas. Islam became the dominant religion during the Mughal period. Also, the establishment of Islam in the Valley must be credited to the influx of Sayyids from Iran and the resulting Sufi culture in the Valley. It bears no resemblance to today's gun culture inspired and driven by Pakistan-aided terrorists. During several periods of rule by foreign invaders, the Kashmiri people were subjected to brutal dispensations. So it is no surprise that they have developed a psyche of having been persecuted through the ages.

To understand today's insurgent problem in the Valley and find a solution, it will be useful to analyse the present-day Kashmiri mindset. The Kashmiris have often been described as a bundle of contradictions, 'timid yet persistent, degraded yet intellectual, mystical yet adventurous, shrewd and business-like'.[6] Towards the close of the nineteenth century, Walter Roper Lawrence, who was the settlement commissioner in Kashmir from 1889 to 1895 during the rule of Maharaja Pratap Singh, found Kashmiris to be essentially conservative but having a keen intellect. They were described as 'emotional and ruled by sentiments but very prone to give undue weightage to rumours'.[7]

A.S. Dulat, a former chief of India's Research and Analysis Wing (RAW), in his book *Kashmir: The Vajpayee Years*, has also reflected on the Kashmiri character. In a conversation with Brajesh Mishra, the principal secretary and national security advisor to Prime Minister Vajpayee, Dulat recalls him saying, 'Do you know, Dulat, the only thing straight in Kashmir are the poplars?'[8]

Another of Dulat's reflections born out of extensive dealings with Kashmiris is:

> The Kashmiri is a most complex character and not easy to fathom or engage with. He is the gentlest, kindest, most sensitive of human beings. Yet he can also be devious and prone to exaggerations. Ask any militant his life story and he will inevitably begin with the grievances of Kashmir and sighing every now and then, to express his predicament.[9]

---

6   G.M.D. Sufi, *Islamic Culture in Kashmir* (Simla: Army Press, 1925), p. 13.

7   Sisir Gupta, *Kashmir: A Study in India–Pakistan Relations*, p. 27.

8   A.S. Dulat, *Kashmir: The Vajpayee Years* (Delhi: HarperCollins, 2015), p. xv; Ashok Dhar, *Kashmir As I See It: From Within and Afar* (Delhi: Rupa Publications, 2019), p. 28.

9   A.S. Dulat, *Kashmir: The Vajpayee Years*, pp. xx-xxi.

Another one is:

> the Kashmiri rarely speaks the truth to you because he feels that you are lying to him. But it is we who have made him that way. The problem with Delhi is that it sees everything in Black and White, whereas a Kashmiri's favourite colour is Grey ... You need more than a lifetime to understand Kashmir and Kashmiris: there are layers within layers and you still may not yet get to the truth.[10]

Kashmiriyat

An important trait amongst the Kashmiri Pandits and Muslims of the Valley is 'Kashmiriyat', a term with Persio-Arabic roots. This trait is a fundamental and long-held part of Kashmir's identity and culture. It is manifested in the solidarity amongst different faiths and ethnic groups. The concept was epitomized by the patron saint of Kashmir, Sheikh Noor-ud-Din, who was born in 1375 in a Hindu family and later converted to Islam. Popularly known as Nund Rishi, he was a great unifying force between the Hindus and Muslims of the Valley. Kashmiriyat was a recipe for tolerance. The noted writer Christopher Snedden feels that this trait amongst Kashmiris partially explains why Kashmiri Muslims were ambivalent about Pakistan in 1947.[11] Alas, Kashmiriyat has become more or less extinct under the onslaught of fundamentalism in Kashmir.

---

10 Ibid., pp. xx–xxi.
11 Christopher Snedden, *Kashmir: The Unwritten History* (Delhi: HarperCollins, 2013), p. 18; Lt Gen. S.K. Sinha, *Raj to Swaraj* (Delhi: Manas Publications, 2017), p. 338.

2

Invasion, Accession and Reference to the United Nations

'Success is not final, failure is not fatal: it is the courage to continue that counts.'

– Winston S. Churchill

The Invasion and Accession

As charges and counter-charges were being made by Pakistan and Kashmir on 22 October 1947, fully armed tribesmen from the north-west of Pakistan and some other Pakistani nationals entered Kashmir from various directions in motor vehicles in a full-scale invasion to march towards the capital of the state and occupy it and decide the fate of Kashmir once again by the sword. Maharaja Hari Singh, ruler of the princely state of Jammu and Kashmir, wanted his state to remain independent, joining neither Pakistan nor India

Invasion, Accession and Reference to the United Nations

but maintaining friendly relations with both. For this reason, he offered a standstill agreement to both the countries. This, despite being told by Lord Ismay, chief of staff to Governor-General Louis Mountbatten, that both Mountbatten and Sardar Patel had said 'independence was not an option and he had to make up his mind to join either India or Pakistan'.

Pakistan immediately accepted the offer, even though no actual agreement was ever executed formally.

India never accepted the idea of a Standstill Agreement being signed by the maharaja with Pakistan and India. The maharaja's idea was to make an interim arrangement at that stage and then to take a final decision later. India was very clear that the signing of a Standstill Agreement was a plan by Pakistan to deceive the maharaja and then launch a surprise attack. In any case, the agreement with Pakistan soon came unstuck as Pakistan imposed an economic blockade to force its hand and take a decision favourable towards them, in early September 1947, stopping essential supplies and trade, resulting in heated exchanges between the two governments. The state then turned to India for help. India airlifted essential items such as salt and kerosene to Jammu and Kashmir.

During this period, the maharaja also faced a rebellion in Poonch in favour of Pakistan. Taking advantage of the situation, Pakistan started arming the rebels and, on 22 October 1947, invaded Kashmir from the direction of Muzzafrabad-Uri. One hundred and fifty soldiers of the state force under the command of the gallant Brigadier Rajinder Singh put up a stiff resistance but were pushed back. On 23 October, the raiders had occupied Chinari, and by 24 October Uri fell. The Uri bridge was destroyed by the defenders, which helped slow down the advance, but by the morning of 27 October, the raiders had reached Baramulla and unleashed their savagery. After that, they rushed in a number of columns towards Sopore, Bandipore, Handwara, Gulmarg and Badgam. It was at Baramulla that Maqbool Sherwani – a National Conference worker – gave early warning about the approaching tribesmen and was done to death. His act of heroism earned him fame for all times. Brigadier Rajinder Singh was also martyred in these operations and was awarded the Maha Vir Chakra (Posthumous), India's second-highest gallantry award.

To both India and Kashmir, this attack 'appeared as a full-fledged pre-planned invasion'.[1] There are many pieces of irrefutable evidence available to this effect. On 25 October, General Sir Robert Lockhart, the British commander-in-chief of the Indian army, read out a telegram from the Pakistan army headquarters at a meeting of the Defence Committee. The communication stated that some 5,000 tribesmen had attacked and captured Muzaffarabad and more reinforcement could be expected.[2] Further, to quote V.P. Menon:

> Why was there a demand on the Survey of India for so large a number of maps of Kashmir, what was the mysterious Operation Gulmarg, the copies of which fell into the hands of those who were not supposed to receive them?[3]

The leader of the raiders was identified as Major General Akbar Khan of the Pakistani army, who later disclosed that in 1947, 'Jinnah had ordered General Gracey to march into Kashmir with Pakistani troops but the British General had jeopardized deliberately the

---

1 Sisir Gupta, *Kashmir: A Study in India–Pakistan Relations*, p. 112.
2 Ibid, p. 112; Alan Campbell-Johnson, *Mission with Mountbatten* (London: Robert Hale, 1951), p. 224.
3 V.P. Menon, *The Story of the Integration of the Indian States* (Calcutta: Orient Longman, 1956), p. 414.

chances of liberating Kashmir'.[4] In a letter to General Lockhart, Sir George Cunningham (governor of the North West Frontier Province) had given warning of tribal infiltration and stated that the government of the province was actively helping this infiltration.[5] There are dozens of such pieces of evidence available with regard to Pakistan being involved in carrying out these operations.

The Government of Pakistan did not deny that their sympathy was for the raiders (whom they called 'liberators') – who, according to them, went to Kashmir on hearing the woes of Indian Muslims – but they repudiated the suggestions of complicity and asserted that short of war, all steps had been taken to prevent the infiltration. However, Pakistan's statements in this regard were not always consistent. As for the charge that professional soldiers were being used, it was pointed out that 70,000 troops who were on leave in Poonch might have joined the revolt.[6]

Nonetheless, the fact of aggression was there for everyone to see and it could not escape the eyes of even casual observers. The *Times* (London) reported on 13 January 1948:

> That Pakistan is unofficially aiding the raiders is certain. Your correspondent has first-hand evidence that arms, ammunition and supplies are being made available to the Azad Kashmir regular force. A few Pakistani officers are also helping to direct their operations ... and however much the Pakistani Government may disavow intervention, moral and material support is certainly forthcoming.[7]

---

4   Sisir Gupta, *Kashmir: A Study in India–Pakistan Relations*, p. 113.
5   Press Note, Ministry of External Affairs, Government of India, 6 August 1948.
6   Sisir Gupta, *Kashmir: A Study in India–Pakistan Relations*, pp. 115–16.
7   On 26 November 1947, *Dawn* reported that according to army

In the meanwhile, on the evening of 24 October, the Government of India received a desperate appeal for help from Maharaja Hari Singh to defeat the attack by the tribesmen.[8]

In the Defence Committee meeting held in Delhi on 25 October, Mountbatten was of the opinion that it would be improper to move Indian troops into Kashmir as it was still an independent state, not having yet decided whether to accede to India or Pakistan. He said that only when the maharaja acceded to India would it be possible to send troops to Srinagar. He further expressed his strong opinion that in view of the composition of the population, accession should be conditional on the will of the people being ascertained by a plebiscite, after the raiders had been driven out of the state and law and order had been restored. This was readily agreed to by Jawaharlal Nehru and his ministers.[9]

Following these deliberations, India agreed to send in its troops provided the maharaja fulfilled three conditions: he must accede to India before India could be legally empowered to accept his request; he must set up a democratic system in the state, as had been done in the rest of the country, including the erstwhile princely states; and he should take Sheikh Abdullah, the popular leader of the National Conference, into the government and make him responsible for administering the state.

V.P. Menon, who played a significant role in the integration of the princely states into India as the secretary in the Ministry of States of Independent India, was entrusted with the task of flying to Jammu and Kashmir to discuss the terms of the agreement and the maharaja's final decision.

---

intelligence, several Pakistani officers had unofficially gone on leave.

8 Sisir Gupta, *Kashmir: A Study in India–Pakistan Relations*, p. 122; V.P. Menon, *The Story of the Integration of the Indian States*, p. 359.

9 Sisir Gupta, *Kashmir: A Study in India–Pakistan Relations*, p. 122.

The maharaja accepted the conditions laid forth and signed the Instrument of Accession (see Appendix A) on 26 October 1947 and handed it over to V.P. Menon.

Menon recounts an interesting anecdote regarding this fateful meeting in his book, *Integration of Indian States*. According to Menon, after signing the instrument, the maharaja told him that before he went to sleep the previous evening, he had left instructions with his aide-de-camp (ADC) that if Menon came back, then he (the maharaja) was not to be disturbed as it would mean that the Government of India had decided to come to his rescue, and he should therefore be allowed to sleep in peace, but that if Menon failed to return, it meant that everything was lost and his ADC should shoot him in his sleep. The authenticity of this story is further confirmed by R.N.P. Singh in his book, *Sardar Patel: Unifier of Modern India* in exactly the same words as used by V.P. Menon.[10]

After signing the agreement, the maharaja sent another letter to Governor-General Mountbatten, describing the pitiable plight of the state, and reiterated his request for military help. He also informed Mountbatten that it was his intention to set up an interim government at once and ask Sheikh Abdullah to carry the responsibility of leading it in this emergency of the state.[11]

The decision to accede had the full support of Sheikh Abdullah, who was in Delhi at that time and had been pressing the Government of India on behalf of the National Conference for immediate help to be sent to resist the tribal invasion.[12]

To quote Sheikh Abdullah:

---

10 R.N.P. Singh, *Sardar Patel: Unifier of Modern India*, p. 171.
11 Sisir Gupta, *Kashmir: A Study in India–Pakistan Relations*, pp. 123–24.
12 Ibid, p. 124.

> We realized that Pakistan would not allow us any time, that we had either to suffer the fate of our kith and kin of Muzaffarabad, Baramulla ... and other towns and villages or to seek help from some outside authority. Under these circumstances, both the Maharaja and the people of Kashmir requested the Government of India to accept our accession.[13]

In the Defence Planning Committee meeting, which was held immediately on Menon's return to Delhi, it was decided to accept the accession. The accession thus became legally and constitutionally complete.[14] It was subject to the proviso that a plebiscite would be held in the state when the law and order situation allowed.

It was further decided that the necessary military support be provided to the state, and the very next day, that is, 27 October 1947, an infantry battalion be flown to Srinagar as the advance guard. The historic airlift was executed by over a hundred civilian and air force aircraft and Kashmir was saved from the raiders in the nick of time.

Lieutenant General S.K. Sinha, in his book *Raj to Swaraj*, recounts that the slogan with which the Kashmiris received the Indian soldiers was '*Hamlawar hoshiar, hum Kashmiri Hindu, Muslim, Sikh taiyar*' (Attackers, beware, we Kashmiri Hindus, Muslims, Sikhs are ready).

Relevant in this connection are the terms in which the Indian press welcomed the accession of Kashmir. Just to quote one example, the *Hindustan Times* wrote in its editorial columns: '...the accession of Kashmir to India is victory of nationalism and democracy over

---

13 Ibid.
14 Ibid.

communalism and totalitarianism. The Government and people of India should make the victory permanent and unshakable.'[15] According to the Instrument of Accession, the maharaja ceded authority over three subjects, namely, defence, foreign affairs and communication, to India. The accession document was similar to those signed by other states in the Union.

The maharaja appointed Sheikh Abdullah as the prime minister and the maharaja's son, Karan Singh, as the prince regent to act on his behalf. Jammu and Kashmir operated as a princely state until 1952. After the Constituent Assembly of Jammu and Kashmir was elected in 1952, it passed a resolution supporting the abolition of monarchy. As a result of the 1952 Delhi Agreement, the Government of India acceded to the wishes of the people of the state and the monarchy was abolished. Prince Karan Singh then accepted the post of Sadr-i-Riyasat (constitutional head of the state).

The Dispute

Regarding the subsequent dispute over Kashmir, to quote Sisir Gupta:

> The basis of the dispute was entirely a divergent understanding of the situation in the two countries as follows:
> To India, a State to which it (Jammu and Kashmir) had acceded (and even without accession, to which it had obligation) was being invaded and people being massacred by raiders from another country, with its complicity and support. The first task was to clear the soil of the invaders, the next being a reference to the people of the issue of accession. To Pakistan, a State which hoped that (Kashmir)

---

15 Ibid, p. 125.

was about to accede to her and where popular outbursts were taking place [*sic*, albeit supported from outside] had now acceded to India and the future had become a fait accompli, unless some way could be devised of keeping the issue open. Withdrawal of support from the raiders might not mean anything more than a further step towards the accomplishment of Kashmir's integration with India. To this basic difference were added numerous arguments and counterarguments in the years to follow, but the essence of the problem has remained what it was in October 1947.[16]

The degree of importance that India attached to Kashmir's accession to India can be assessed from the statements of two of India's tallest leaders of all times: Mahatma Gandhi, in one of his prayer meetings, said, 'My sole hope and prayer is that Kashmir should become a beacon of light to this benighted subcontinent.'[17]

Referring to the proposals of Pakistan, Nehru said:

We cannot treat with freebooters who have murdered large number of people and tried to ruin Kashmir. They are not a State, although a State may be behind them ... We cannot desert the people of Kashmir till the danger is passed. If the Pakistani Government is sincere, they can stop the entry of these raiders and thus accelerate the return of peace and order. After that let the people of Kashmir decide and we shall accept the decision. But if this armed conflict continues, no opportunity is given for the people to decide by peaceful means and the decision gradually takes shape by the sacrifice and power of the people in the conflict

---

16 Ibid, p. 128.
17 Ibid, p. 126.

... Kashmir and India have been bound together in many ways from ages past. These last few weeks have forged a new link which none can asunder.[18]

There were several rounds of direct talks between India and Pakistan at the top level, but the differences between the two sides continued over the withdrawal of troops from both sides, the cessation of hostilities, the release of political prisoners and forwarding a joint request to the UN to send a commission. However, the viewpoints of both sides were poles apart. On 22 December 1947, India formally complained to Pakistan that they should stop providing assistance to the raiding tribesmen, but the result was only counter-charges by Pakistan. On 31 December 1947, India formally approached the United Nations Security Council (UN Security Council) for its mediation in resolving the situation in Kashmir.

A question that is often asked, to this day, is why India referred the Kashmir question to the UN. A little background to this is necessary and after that the readers are welcome to draw their own conclusions. Sisir Gupta has explained the situation in detail in his book:

> It had become clear on the last day of 1947 – the year which saw the great liberation of the Indian subcontinent – that the politics in the region would yet not be entirely free from bitter struggles and acrimonious debates, factors which had ostensibly delayed freedom in the past and might circumscribe it in the future. It is in this context that many had criticized India's decision to refer the case of Kashmir to the UN, and had subsequently demanded its withdrawal. The principle causes for this decision, however,

---

18 Ibid, p. 134.

were (i) India's faith in the charter of the UN, (ii) Her conviction that a military decision was not always the most helpful and stable means of settling issues, (iii) Her feeling that an armed conflict in the subcontinent so soon after freedom would be infinitely worse than delay in solving the problem of Kashmir, and finally (iv) Her feeling that, in the past war, world opinion would prove to be a big enough compulsion for an aggressor to withdraw. The purpose which India had in referring the issue to the UN at this time was reflected in the opinion of the Indian press.

The *Modern Review* wrote in January 1948:

> Observers in New Delhi feel that the outcome of the reference to the Security Council would be that either Pakistan will take steps to stop the influx of the raiders in accordance with international morality or the Indian Dominion must be free to take such appropriate action as might be necessary to protect the integrity of the State and her subjects. Judging from Pakistan's usual practice of breaking every agreement arrived in with them, optimism of New Delhi that Pakistan will conform to international law and morality even under the presence of the UNO was probably not sound.[19]

Time has proved the apprehensions of the people right, and Nehru is generally held responsible for being too idealistic a politician, who was detached from the reality of the situation. Besides this, the British also perhaps did not want to leave behind a very clean arrangement so that both countries remained dependent on

---

19 *Modern Review*, 1948.

them for resolving any leftover disputes. It was the reason why the condition of plebiscite was imposed by Governor-General Mountbatten, even for those states that were clearly part of India, such as Hyderabad.

On the other hand, within India, Nehru took the matter of Kashmir under his own charge as he felt that it was related to all manner of connected issues – including international relations and military concerns – which were beyond the competence of an individual ministry. This development took place around 23 December 1947, and that is why India's referring the matter to the UN had the imprint of Nehru's decision on the matter. Perhaps the story of Kashmir would have been different, K.M. Munshi feels, if the state's affairs had been allowed to remain under Sardar Patel's jurisdiction.[20] Patel seriously doubted the appropriateness of Nehru's policy towards Kashmir and refused to share his abounding faith in Sheikh Abdullah. Even Mahatma Gandhi felt similarly and wrote to Pyare Lal: 'If Sheikh Abdullah is erring in the discharge of his duty as the Chief of his cabinet or as a devout Muslim, he should certainly step aside and give place to a better man.'[21]

In the meanwhile, Sheikh Abdullah was becoming increasingly ambitious and was determined to have total control over Kashmir. On his insistence, the maharaja was persuaded to abdicate in favour of his son, Karan Singh, in May 1949.

Nehru had asked for a plebiscite because he felt sure that with Abdullah in sole charge of the government, the bulk of the Muslim population of the state would vote for accession to India. In any case, the people of Kashmir were at that time most unhappy with

---

20 R.N.P. Singh, *Sardar Patel*, p. 181; 'Kulpati's letter' (*Bhavan's Journal*, 26 February 1967), p. 14.
21 R.N.P. Singh, *Sardar Patel*, p. 181; Pyarelal, *Mahatma Gandhi, The Last Phase* (Ahmedabad: Navjivan Publishing House, 1956), Vol. II, p. 500.

the raiders from Pakistan and their looting and destruction and would certainly have voted for India. But Abdullah did not want a plebiscite because he felt that the moment the accession to India was finalized by a plebiscite held under the supervision of the UN, he would be deprived of his importance and his trump card in dealing with the Indian government. If Kashmir had to go to India at all, then it must go as a gift from him, and he would gift it on his own terms. B.N. Mullik, then director of the IB, wrote:

> [I]f a plebiscite had been held in Jammu and Kashmir some time in 1949, there was a good chance that the majority of the people would have voted for India, because the wounds inflicted by the Pakistani raiders on the peaceful people of Kashmir were still fresh in their minds and India was held in much respect as their saviour.[22]

However, Sheikh Abdullah insisted that he represented the people of Kashmir and his decision was good enough. This left the Government of India on the horns of a dilemma, as they had opted for the plebiscite, on the support of Abdullah, and could not go back on it.

Around August 1949, B.N. Mullik spent ten days in the Valley and carried out his assessment of the situation. According to him, Sheikh Abdullah was not genuine in his intentions; he was misleading Nehru and would ultimately let down India.[23]

---

22 R.N.P. Singh, *Sardar Patel,* p. 183; B.N. Mullik, *My Years with Nehru, 1948–1964* (New Delhi: Allied Publishers, 1971), pp. 7–8.

23 B.N. Mullik, *My Years with Nehru: Kashmir,* Vol. II (New Delhi: Allied Publishers, 1971), pp. 7–8.

Invasion, Accession and Reference to the United Nations

Abdullah, in the meantime, had given an interview to Michael Davidson of the *Scotsman*, which was published on 14 April 1949 and in which Sheikh Abdullah said:

> Accession to either side cannot bring peace. We want to live in friendship with both dominions. Perhaps, a middle path between them ... and independent Kashmir must be guaranteed not only by India and Pakistan, but also by Britain, the United States and other members of the United Nations.[24]

Patel was disturbed by this, and ultimately Gopal Swami (minister without portfolio assisting in Kashmir affairs) sent a message to Sheikh Abdullah through Dwarka Nath Kachru (private secretary to Nehru), who was visiting Kashmir, to repudiate his statement, which of course was not done by Sheikh.

Before we arrive at any firm idea on Sheikh Abdullah, it is important to analyse what his thinking was after the first election was held in J&K in October 1951, and all seventy-five seats were won by his National Conference.

Sheikh Abdullah's opening speech[25] in the Constituent Assembly in October 1951 ran for a full ninety minutes. Reading from a prepared English text, he discussed one by one the options before the people of Kashmir.

---

24 R.N.P. Singh, *Sardar Patel*, p. 186; Durga Das (ed.), *Sardar Patel's Correspondence*, Vol. I (Ahmedabad: Navajivan Publishing House, 1971), p. 263.

25 Speech paraphrased from Ramachandra Guha, *India After Gandhi* (Macmillan, 2007), pp. 246–47; Sheikh Abdullah's speech is printed in extenso in Sisir Gupta's *Kashmir: A Study in India–Pakistan Relations*, pp. 367–70.

He said that the first option was to join Pakistan, that landlord-ridden and federal theocracy:

> The most powerful argument which can be advanced in her favour is that Pakistan is a Muslim State, and, a big majority of our people being Muslims, the State must accede to Pakistan. This claim of being a Muslim State is of course only a camouflage. It is a screen to dupe the common man, so that he may not see clearly that Pakistan is a feudal State, in which a clique is trying by these methods to maintain itself in power. In addition to this, the appeal to religion constitutes a sentimental and a wrong approach to the question. Sentiment has its own place in life, but often it leads to irrational action. Some argue, as a supposedly natural corollary to this, that on our acceding to Pakistan our annihilation or survival depends. Facts have disproved this. Right-thinking men would point out that Pakistan is not an organic unity of all the Muslims in this subcontinent. It has, on the contrary, caused the dispersion of the Indian Muslims for whose benefit it was claimed to have been created. There are two Pakistans, at least a thousand miles apart from each other. The total population of Western Pakistan, which is contiguous to our State, is hardly twenty-five million [sic], while the total number of Muslims resident in India is as many as forty million. As one Muslim is as good as another, the Kashmiri Muslims if they are worried by such considerations, should choose the forty millions living in India. Another big obstacle to a dispassionate evaluation of her policies is the lack of a constitution in Pakistan.

Looking at the matter too from a more modern political angle, religious affinities alone do not and should not normally determine the political alliances of states. We do not find a Christian bloc, a Buddhist bloc, or even a Muslim bloc, about which there is so much talk nowadays in Pakistan. These days economic interests and a community of political ideals more appropriately influence the policies of states.

We have another important factor to consider, if the state decides to make this [religion] the predominant consideration. What will be the fate of the millions of non-Muslims now in our state? As things stand at present there is no place for them in Pakistan. Any solution which will result in the displacement or the total subjugation of such a large number of people will not be just or fair, and it is the responsibility of this House to ensure that the decision that it takes on accession, does not militate against the interests of any religious group.

The second option was to join India, with whom the state had a kinship of ideals and whose government had 'never tried to interfere in our internal autonomy' during the last four years. Sheikh Abdullah felt that this experience had strengthened their confidence in India as a democratic state.

The real character of a state is revealed in its constitution. The Indian Constitution has set before the country the goal of secular democracy based upon justice, freedom and equality for all without distinction. This is the bedrock of modern democracy. This should meet the argument that the Muslims of Kashmir cannot have security in India where the large majority of the populations are Hindus. Any unnatural cleavage between religious groups is the legacy of imperialism, and no modern state can afford to encourage artificial divisions if it is to achieve progress and prosperity. The Indian Constitution has amply and finally repudiated the concept of a religious State, which is a throwback to medievalism, by guaranteeing the equality of rights of all citizens irrespective of their religion, colour, caste and class.

The Indian National Congress has consistently supported the cause of the state's peoples' freedom. The autocratic rule of the Princes has been done away with and representative governments have been entrusted with the administration. Steps towards democratization have been taken and these have raised the people's standard of living, brought about much-needed social reconstruction, and, above all, built up their very independence of spirit. Naturally if we accede to India there is no danger of a revival of feudalism and autocracy. Admit that certain tendencies have been asserting themselves in India which may in the future convert into a religious state wherein the interests of the Muslims will be jeopardized.

On the other hand, the continued accession of Kashmir to India would promote harmony between Hindus and Muslims and marginalize the communalists. 'Gandhiji was not wrong,' argued Sheikh Abdullah, when he uttered the words before his death, which are paraphrased: I lift up mine eyes into the hills whence cometh my help.

Sheikh Abdullah came, finally, to 'the alternative of making ourselves an Eastern Switzerland, of keeping aloof from both

States but having friendly relations with them'. This was an attractive option, but it did not seem practical. How would a small landlocked country safeguard its sovereignty? As Sheikh reminded his audience, Kashmir had once been independent of both India and Pakistan, between 15 August and 22 October 1947, when its independence had been destroyed by the tribal invasion. What was the guarantee that a sovereign Kashmir may not be the victim of similar aggression?

Thus, Sheikh rejected the option of independence as impractical and the joining of Pakistan as immoral. They would join India but on terms of their choosing. Amongst these were the retention of the state flag and the designation of the head of government as prime minister.[26]

This was not acceptable to Dr Syama Prasad Mukherjee, head of the Bharatiya Janata Party (BJP), or to the Jammu Praja Parishad. Asking for the complete integration of Kashmir into India, both parties had adopted the slogan: *Ek vidhan, ek pradhan, ek nishan* (one Constitution, one head of the state, one flag).[27]

In January 1952, shortly before Abdullah was due to speak in Jammu town, Hindu students protested against the flag of the National Conference being flown alongside the Indian tricolour. An agitation started in Jammu, and Dr Syama Prasad Mukherjee and Prem Nath Dogra, the aged leader of the Jammu Praja Parishad, were arrested. The government in Delhi, fearful of a countrywide Hindu backlash, persuaded the Kashmiri government to release the two leaders. Abdullah agreed, if reluctantly. Dr Mukherjee, however, died in custody after one month, fuelling the suspicion that he

---

26 Ramachandra Guha, *India After Gandhi*, pp. 246–47; as mentioned before, Sheikh Abdullah's speech is printed in extenso in Sisir Gupta's *Kashmir: A Study in India–Pakistan Relations*, pp. 367–70.

27 Ramachandra Guha, *India After Gandhi*, p. 247.

had been poisoned. On 10 April 1952, Abdullah made a speech in which he said his party would accept the Indian Constitution in its entirety once 'we are satisfied that the grave of communalism has been finally dug'. He, however, added: 'of that we are not sure yet'. Sheikh said that the Kashmiris feared what would happen to them and their position if, for instance, something were to happen to Nehru.[28]

This narrative would not be complete without a recounting of the full story of Sheikh Abdullah. Sheikh had given a most rational and analytical speech on the floor of the House in October 1951 and had made Kashmir's preference for India very clear. However, at some stage, he perhaps had a change of heart and deviated from the path that he had defined for himself.

In later years, Nehru was also disillusioned by Sheikh's anti-India activities. Sheikh even went to the extent of establishing contact with Pakistan through one Pir Maqbool Gilani. On 8 August 1953, Sheikh was arrested when he left for Tanmarg (near Gulmarg) to meet an emissary of Pakistan for anti-national activities. Sheikh was accused of conspiracy against the state in the infamous Kashmir Conspiracy Case and was exiled from the state and later jailed for eleven years. Bakshi Ghulam Mohammad took over as the prime minister in August 1953. Bakshi resigned under the Kamraj plan but was not removed following the disappearance of the holy relic from the Hazratbal Shrine till he left the prime-ministership in 1964.

On 8 April 1964, after eleven years, the state government dropped all charges in the Kashmir Conspiracy Case and Sheikh Abdullah was released and returned to Kashmir to an unprecedented

---

28 Ramachandra Guha, *India After Gandhi*, as reproduced from p. 247; Prem Nath Bazaz, *The History of Struggle for Freedom in Kashmir: Cultural and Political, from the Earliest Times to the Present Day* (New Delhi: Kashmir Publishing Company, 1954), pp. 569–71.

welcome by the people. After his release, he reconciled with Nehru, who requested Sheikh to act as a bridge between India and Pakistan. Sheikh went to Pakistan in the spring of 1964 and had extensive talks with then President Ayub Khan to explore various avenues for solving the Kashmir problem. President Ayub agreed to come to Delhi in mid June 1964, but then providence struck, and Nehru died three days after Sheikh's meeting with Ayub. After Nehru's death, Sheikh was interned from 1965 to 1968 and again exiled from Kashmir in 1971 for eighteen months. The Plebiscite Front, set up by Afzal Beg, one of Sheikh's close confidants, was banned from taking part in the elections in Kashmir.

However, Sheikh Abdullah again became chief minister of the state following the Indira–Sheikh Accord, signed in February 1975, and remained in office till his death on 8 September 1982. Under the accord, the state of Jammu and Kashmir, recognized as a constituent unit of the Union of India, would continue to be governed by Article 370 of the Constitution of India. Further, residuary powers of legislation would remain with the state. However, the Parliament would continue to have the power to make laws relating to the prevention of activities directed towards disclaiming, questioning or disrupting the sovereignty and territorial integrity of India or bringing about secession of a part of the territory of India from the Union or causing insult to the Indian national flag, the Indian national anthem and the Constitution. Also, where any provision of the Constitution of India had been applied to Jammu and Kashmir with adaptations and modifications, such adaptations and modifications could be altered or repealed by an order of the president under Article 370, but provisions of the Constitution already applied to Jammu and Kashmir without adaption or modification were unalterable.

Reflecting on the events that unfolded in the years following Partition and Independence, it is quite obvious that Abdullah became over-ambitious and started dreaming of an independent Kashmir, equally close to both Pakistan and India. Several events support this hypothesis.

For one, Sheikh's interview to Michael Davidson of the *Scotsman*, published on 14 April 1949, reveals his line of thinking. He held that accession to either side could not bring peace, and Kashmir wished to live in friendship with both dominions. Further, an independent Kashmir must be guaranteed not only by India and Pakistan, but also by Britain, the United States and other members of the United Nations (UN).

Then, on 8 August 1953, Sheikh was arrested on his way to Tanmarg in Kashmir to meet an emissary of Pakistan for antinational activities. Obviously, he was already hobnobbing with Pakistan.

Finally, Sheikh's statement before he convinced Nehru to agree to a separate Constitution for the state of Jammu and Kashmir, albeit as part of the Constitution of India, was: 'We shall not hesitate to secede from India if we are not assured a place of honour and dignity in terms of safeguards provided for the people of the state under Article 370 of the Constitution.'

When historians review the history of Partition, they will likely agree that Nehru was somewhat blind to the machinations of Sheikh and had a soft corner for him. India had to pay a heavy price for Nehru's poor reading of the situation.

It is obvious that Sheikh was debating a change of course around 1949–50, because his speech at the UN in 1948 was emphatically in favour of India. It is also possible that Sheikh was convinced that Pakistan would not let Kashmir live in peace, and hence felt he must develop a good understanding with Pakistan. Later, when he returned to power after the Indira–Sheikh Accord, it was based on Article 370, even though it was very much diluted. So Sheikh had, in effect, accepted limited autonomy.

However, in fairness to Sheikh, one also needs to analyse his speech to the J&K Constituent Assembly in October 1951 to fully understand that he was a visionary and under him the state's accession to India safeguarded their interests at that time.

Article 370 of the Constitution of India

The genesis of Article 370 lay in Nehru's agreeing to Sheikh Abdullah's demand to have a separate Constitution for Jammu and Kashmir. It was done because Jammu and Kashmir was a Muslim-predominant state, which was also contiguous with Pakistan.

Article 370 was introduced as part of the Constitution with the objective of giving space and autonomy (self-governance) and thus special status to the state of Jammu and Kashmir. However, it is important to remember that it was only a transitory arrangement and, seventy years after Independence, India was well justified in considering its dissolution, in my opinion.

Kashmir elected its own Constituent Assembly in September 1951. The assembly confirmed Kashmir's accession to India, abolished the office of the maharaja, replacing it with a Sadr-i-Riyasat, and decided to have a separate flag for the state. Sheikh Abdullah became the prime minister of Kashmir and Yuvraj (Prince) Karan Singh, son of Maharaja Hari Singh, was elected Sadr-i-Riyasat.

The Constitution, which finally emerged at the instance of Sheikh, kept 'Kashmir as autonomous as possible, with a tenuous bond with India through defence, communications and foreign affairs resting with India'.[29]

---

29 R.N.P. Singh, *Sardar Patel*, p. 190; B.N. Mullik, *My Years with Nehru*, p. 24.

The sum and substance of Article 370 was that with regard to Jammu and Kashmir, except for matters relating to defence, foreign affairs and communications, the Parliament of India needed the state government's agreement to apply other laws. Thus, the Parliament could make laws on all items in the Union and the Concurrent lists but only with the concurrence of the state government. This put the state of Jammu and Kashmir on a special footing, different to all other states in India.[30]

However, from 1953 onwards, numerous constitutional amendments integrating Jammu and Kashmir more intimately with India were issued. Two hundred and sixty-two Union laws were also made applicable in Jammu and Kashmir over a period of time.

As R.N.P. Singh writes in his book on Sardar Patel, the Constitution of Jammu and Kashmir was amended in 1966 to change the denomination of Sadr-i-Riyasat to that of governor and of prime minister to chief minister. Article 356 was included and the jurisdictions of the Supreme Court, the Election Commission and the Comptroller and Auditor General were formalized.[31] R.N.P. Singh further explains that from time to time, more such provisions (over twenty-eight constitutional amendments) were added between 1953 and 1975. Some of these are as follows:

- On 29 October 1951, all-India services – Indian Administrative Service (IAS) and Indian Police Service (IPS) – were introduced. The functions of the Comptroller and Auditor General were extended.
- By the 1954 presidential order, the operations of customs, central excise, civil aviation, posts and telegraph were extended.

---

30 Jagmohan, *My Frozen Turbulence in Kashmir* (New Delhi: Allied Publishers, 1991), p. 232.
31 R.N.P. Singh, *Sardar Patel*, p. 191.

- In 1959, the legislative entry relating to conducting of census of 1961 was brought under central law.
- In 1960, J&K was brought under the jurisdiction of the Supreme Court of India and the Election Commission of India.
- In 1964, Articles 356 and 357 of the Constitution were applied, making way for the introduction of president's rule and emergency.
- In 1965, several legislative entries relating to welfare of labour, trade unions, social security and social insurance were applied.
- In 1966, provisions relating to direct elections to the Lok Sabha were applied.
- Since 1953, about 337 laws relating to the Chartered Accountants Act, Coinage Act, Conservation of Foreign Exchange and Prevention of Smuggling Activities Act, Copyright Act, Dangerous Drugs Act, Delimitation Commission Act, among others, have been extended to Jammu and Kashmir.
- The visa-type permit system was abolished.[32]

Despite the aforementioned additionalities, the provisions of the Constitution of Jammu and Kashmir created several peculiarities, especially with regard to the right to hold property, the right to citizenship and the right to settlement. Citizens of India had no constitutional right to become citizens of Jammu and Kashmir. Nobody from outside the state could hold property in the state or vote in the elections. One provision that was strikingly unjust was that if a woman from Jammu and Kashmir married a person who was not a citizen of Jammu and Kashmir, she lost her property

---

32 R.N.P. Singh, *Sardar Patel*, p. 192.

and she also could not inherit property from her parents. This was highly unfair to women.

In 1954, Article 35A was incorporated into the Constitution, based on the 1952 Delhi Agreement between the then prime minister of India, Jawaharlal Nehru, and Sheikh Abdullah. The agreement extended Indian citizenship to the people of Jammu and Kashmir. This article provides legal empowerment to Article 370. Briefly, the article defines the classes of persons who are or shall be, permanent residents of the state of Jammu and Kashmir and also confers on such people special rights and privileges and places restrictions on others with respect to employment under the state government, the acquisition of immovable property, settlement in the state, and the right to scholarship and such forms of aid as the state government may provide.[33]

The article was added to the Constitution by the president of India on 14 May 1954, exercising the powers conferred by clause (1) of Article 370 of the Indian Constitution and with the concurrence of the Government of Jammu and Kashmir. Thus, Article 35A was incorporated by a presidential order and not by a constitutional amendment by the Indian Parliament. Any major change to it, when Kashmir is as troubled as at present, will provide a new grievance. On the other hand, should this be abrogated (as has been done in August 2019), it is likely to prove more beneficial to the people of Jammu and Kashmir as it will result in more jobs and growth within Jammu and Kashmir.

This article is under review by the Supreme Court of India as many legal luminaries are of the opinion that it is discriminatory and unconstitutional.

---

33 Ibid, pp. 193–94.

It is clear that Article 370 has been modified from time to time to render it that much more acceptable to India. The shape and scope of the article had really emerged as a result of the Indira–Sheikh Accord of 1975. So when one talks of autonomy to Kashmir, one can do it only with reference to the Indira–Sheikh Accord rather than the pre-1953 arrangements. This is because Sheikh Abdullah had himself accepted the limited extent of autonomy granted in the accord.

With the shift in the balance of power in the subcontinent in favour of India following India's victory in the 1971 India–Pakistan war, then prime minister Indira Gandhi's stature had risen sky-high. This had led Sheikh to the conclusion that he had no choice but to follow the terms dictated by India. Indira Gandhi had also made it very clear at the time that it was inconceivable to accept Sheikh Abdullah's demand for the restoration of the pre-1953 status, because so much time had elapsed and 'the clock could not be put back'.

The detractors of Articles 370 and 35A, and thus autonomy, felt that no other state of the Indian Union had a separate Constitution; all other states had a uniform structure as laid down in Part II of the Constitution of India. Then, why this special treatment for Jammu and Kashmir? For that reason, Article 370 was always a sore point with a great cross-section of the people in the Jammu and Ladakh regions and in the rest of the country. Prime Minister Narendra Modi is on record as having said multiple times that Articles 370 and 35A have become redundant in today's environment.

Whereas Jammu and Kashmir did indeed have a separate Constitution, certain other Indian states have special treatment in some areas of the law – for example, outsiders cannot buy land in Arunachal Pradesh, Sikkim, Uttarakhand and Mizoram. These are for specific reasons. For example, in Himachal, this restriction was put because of the poverty in the state. However, Section 118 does not put an absolute ban on sale and purchase of land and property. It restricts the transfer of land to a person who is not an agriculturist of the state, including even for the non-agriculturists of the state. Similarly, specific conditions apply to the sale and purchase of land in the other states mentioned above.

Jagmohan, the former governor of Jammu and Kashmir, has written in his book *My Frozen Turbulence in Kashmir* that, over the years, Article 370 became an instrument of exploitation in the hands of ruling political elites and other vested interests in bureaucracy, business and the judiciary.

On 21 August 1962, in reply to Pandit Bajaj's letter concerning Article 370, Nehru wrote:

> As a matter of fact, much has been done in spite of the Article in the constitution which is supposed to give a special status to Kashmir and gradually what little remains will also go. The question is more a sentimental one than anything else. Sentiment is sometimes important but we have to weigh both the sides and I think no change should be made in the matter for the present.[34]

It clearly shows that Nehru himself did not rule out future changes with regard to Article 370.

The 1947–48 Jammu and Kashmir War and Its Aftermath

The 1947–48 war was the first of the four wars fought between India and Pakistan. Pakistan precipitated the war a few weeks after

---

34 Jagmohan, *My Frozen Turbulence in Kashmir*, p. 251.

Independence by launching tribal 'lashkar' (militia) from Waziristan in an effort to secure Kashmir. The result of this inconclusive war still affects the geopolitics of both countries.

In May 1948, the Pakistani army entered the war with plans to push towards Jammu and cut off the lines of communication of the Indian forces in the Mehndar Valley. In Gilgit, the Gilgit Scouts, under the command of a British officer, Major William Brown, mutinied and illegally overthrew the governor, Brigadier Ghansara Singh. Brown prevailed on the forces to declare accession to Pakistan. They are believed to have received assistance from the Chitral Scouts of the state of Chitral, which had acceded to Pakistan on 6 October 1947.

Indian forces fought brilliantly and recaptured Uri and Baramulla and commenced operations to relieve Poonch. In the meanwhile, Kotli and Mirpur in the Jammu region were captured by Pakistani forces, but Indian forces recaptured Jhangar and Naushera. Subsequently, they also recaptured Poonch and established contact with Rajouri.

In the Kashmir Valley, Indians captured Keran and Gurez. The Zojila Pass was forced open by using tanks; Dras was recaptured and Indian forces opened the road from Kargil to Leh. Pakistani forces, however, managed to hold Skardu. At this stage, operations were halted, and a ceasefire came into effect under UN auspices on 1 January 1949. This required Pakistan to withdraw its forces, both regular and irregular, and allowed India to maintain a minimum strength of its forces in the state to maintain law and order. Importantly, only on the compliance of these conditions would a plebiscite be held to determine the future of the territory. India was the victor as it defended or recaptured almost two-thirds of the important areas of the state, and PoK had only Kotli, Bhimber, Muzaffarabad, Neelam Valley, Skardu and the Northern Areas.

Accepting a ceasefire at this stage was amongst the many strategic blunders committed by India in relation to Pakistan. Going to the UN Security Council was the first big blunder by India.

Khurshid Mahmud Kasturi, Pakistan's foreign minister under Pervez Musharraf, president of Pakistan from 2001 to 2008, has said in his book, 'the liberation of part of Kashmir and the Northern Areas became the basis of Pakistan's strategic relationship with China'.[35] This relationship between China and Pakistan has posed grave challenges to India ever since.

The Plebiscite and the UN

The UN's chosen medium for solving the Kashmir tangle was the Constitution of the United Nations Commission for India and Pakistan (UNCIP). The UNCIP made its recommendations through its resolution of 13 August 1948. This comprised three parts.

The first part related to the ceasefire, and asked the two military high commands to issue orders to this effect to their respective sides. Military observers were appointed to supervise and observe the ceasefire. This part was successful, and the ceasefire line stabilized with the passage of time.

The second part had two aspects. One related to Pakistan, and the resolution expressed the opinion that the presence of Pakistani troops in the state of J&K constituted a material change in the situation. Pakistan agreed to withdraw its troops, but exercised minimum to no pressure on the tribesmen to withdraw. Pakistan thus failed to implement this part of the resolution, which was a precondition to start the process of plebiscite. The non-fulfilment

---

35 Khurshid Mahmud Kasuri, *Neither a Hawk Nor a Dove: An Insider's Account of Pakistan's Foreign Policy* (New Delhi: Penguin Viking, 2015), p. 409.

of the precondition to pull back its forces made the issue of plebiscite redundant.

The second aspect related to India, which was to maintain only minimum forces in the state following the withdrawal of Pakistani troops and tribesmen. As Pakistan did not fulfil its obligation, India had no option but to retain its troops to safeguard its territory.

The third part related to the plebiscite. Both sides were to enter into consultations with the commission to determine the conditions for a fair and equitable plebiscite. India communicated its acceptance on 20 December 1948 and Pakistan followed on 25 December 1948; the ceasefire came into effect on 1 January 1949.

Military representatives of both sides met in Karachi from 18 to 27 July 1949 under the auspices of the UN Sub Committee. Maps were exchanged, duly marked, and a ceasefire line agreed to. This line, with minor modifications after the India–Pakistan war of 1971 and the Simla Agreement of 1972, became the LoC, the de facto border between India and Pakistan. The state of Jammu and Kashmir thus stood duly partitioned between the two sides.

Before we move on to the debates regarding the Kashmir issue in the UN, we need to have a glimpse into the British mindset at the time and after Partition. A manifestation of the trend of their opinion was the mischievous speech of Sir Winston Churchill on 28 October 1948 in the House of Commons:

> In handing over the Government of India to the so-called political classes, we are handing over to men of straw, of whom in a few years no trace will remain. The fate of India, now that the British guidance and control have suddenly and rapidly withdrawn, hangs heavy over the future of 400 million human beings. An awful tragedy has already occurred . . . no such catastrophe or anything

which approached one-twentieth part of its magnitude fell upon the helpless Indian people during the long years when they dwelt in peace safely under the British Raj and imperial crown and may I say under the constant, vigilant and humane supervision of the House of Commons.[36]

Churchill continued to hold this view until his death.

The debate in the UN commenced on 1 January 1948. India based its case on the facts that firstly, the accession of Jammu and Kashmir to the Dominion of India made India fully responsible for its defence, and secondly, they could not allow a neighbouring and unfriendly state to compel it by force to determine its internal affairs or external relations.[37] It was obvious from its approach that India was looking for the issue to be amicably settled.

Pakistan tried to make the case symbolic of Hindu–Muslim differences.

The differences in the proposals put forward by the two sides were too wide to arrive at an easy solution. They have been covered beautifully by Sisir Gupta in his book, *Kashmir: A Study in India–Pakistan Relations*. Essentially, the differences were as under:

- As far as Pakistan was concerned, the issue of accession was open, and it was an issue on which Pakistan had a better standing. For India, it was an issue between them and the people of Kashmir.
- There was also the unbridgeable difference over the role of the UN with regard to the plebiscite: Pakistan would entrust the UN with the 'authority and responsibility' as well as

---

36 Sisir Gupta, *Kashmir: A Study in India–Pakistan Relations*, p. 151.
37 Ibid, p. 142.

the functions of holding, organizing and supervising the plebiscite. India would have the plebiscite conducted by the democratically constituted government of Kashmir, under the advice of UN personnel.

- For India, the primary need was to stop the fighting and restore normal conditions. To Pakistan, it would come about as part of the preparation for the plebiscite.
- Pakistan insisted that Indian troops should withdraw simultaneously along with the tribesmen. India insisted that it would not give up its responsibility to defend and maintain internal law and order in the state, and hence Indian troops would have to be maintained within the state.
- For India, the emergent administration would be provided by Sheikh Abdullah and his cabinet. Pakistan insisted on an 'impartial interim administration' arranged by the UN commission.
- India wanted the UN to help clear out the invaders by ensuring that Pakistan stopped aiding them. Pakistan wanted the UN to take over the territory by ensuring that Indian troops pulled out.[38]

In the discussions that followed on the aforementioned proposals by the two sides, China's view initially showed greater appreciation of the Indian viewpoint. China felt that the UN Security Council should issue a directive to Pakistan to stop the fighting and secondly, that an entirely new regime in Kashmir was not necessary to secure a free plebiscite.[39]

At this stage, Sheikh Abdullah, who was also a member of the Indian delegation, intervened in the debate on behalf of Kashmir

---

38 R.N.P. Singh, *Sardar Patel*, pp. 156–57.
39 Sisir Gupta, *Kashmir: A Study in India–Pakistan Relations*, p. 160.

and stated that 'the idea of replacing the administration was reprehensible' to them. It would prevent the people of Kashmir from running their administration and 'as long as the people of Kashmir are behind me, I will remain there'. He further stated that the Indian army was essential to prevent chaos in Kashmir. The defence of Kashmir against internal disorder and external aggression was a function of the Indian army and would remain so until Kashmir withdrew from India through a plebiscite. Lastly, he said that the form of the government in Kashmir was a matter for the people of the state to decide, and while coalitions could not be ruled out, it was impossible to impose an administration there.[40]

The Chinese delegation was in favour of the Indian case and actually moved a resolution to that effect.[41] It is also relevant that India asked for a vote on the Chinese motion and declared its intention to abide by the result of the vote. However, some of the Security Council members put forth the most damaging criticism. The US found the Indian suggestion 'perfectly astonishing'.[42]

The Chinese resolution was, however, withdrawn the next day after the president, on behalf of the Security Council, announced that the Indian delegation would proceed home for consultations so that further progress could be made in the settlement of the case. However, there was great disillusionment on the Indian side, and on 15 February 1948, Nehru, while speaking at Jammu, said, 'Instead of discussing and deciding our references in a straightforward manner, the nations of the world sitting in that body got lost in power politics.'[43]

---

40 Ibid, p. 160; SCOR meetings 241 and 242 of 1948.
41 Sisir Gupta, *Kashmir: A Study in India–Pakistan Relations*, p. 163.
42 Ibid, p. 162.
43 Ibid, p. 163; *The Hindu*, 16 February 1948.

Addressing the Constituent Assembly (Legislative) on 5 March 1948, Nehru said: 'I must confess that I have been surprised and distressed by the fact that the reference we made has not been properly considered thus far and other matters have been given precedence.'[44] The *Hindu* wrote in its editorial that the non-objective attitude adopted by the power groups in the UN caused resentment in this country. The difficulty from the very beginning has been that the Anglo-American powers and their satellites in the Security Council did not have an objective attitude and identified themselves completely with the Pakistani cause.[45] This made the Government of India, thereafter, very careful of the machinations within the UN.

Even the British press seemed to have realized the gravity of the situation. Kingsley Martin wrote in the *New Statesman* and *Nation* late in February 1948 that India deserved to have its appeal 'honestly considered'.[46] The *Economist* thought that what was needed was 'action by Pakistan to put a stop to the Pathan campaign in Kashmir'.[47]

The deliberations in the UN went on without any conclusive results. However, on 17 December 1949, the UNCIP recommended that one single mediator would be better suited to tackle the problem of implementing the second and third

---

44 Sisir Gupta, *Kashmir: A Study in India–Pakistan Relations,* p. 163; S.L. Poplai (ed.), *Select Documents on Asian Affairs: India 1947–50,* Vol. II, (Bombay: Oxford University Press, 1950), p. 438.

45 Sisir Gupta, *Kashmir: A Study in India–Pakistan Relations*, p. 163; *The Hindu*, 16 February 1948.

46 Sisir Gupta, *Kashmir: A Study in India–Pakistan Relations,* p. 164; *The New Statesman* and *The Nation*, 21 February 1948.

47 Sisir Gupta, *Kashmir: A Study in India–Pakistan Relations*, p. 164; *The Economist*, 21 February 1948.

parts of the resolution. General Andrew McNaughton of Canada was nominated as the informal mediator. However, the general reported failure on 3 February 1950 when he submitted his report to the Security Council and said that his efforts were unlikely to serve any useful purpose as there were major differences between India and Pakistan. India wanted the disbanding and disarming of the Azad forces and demanded the return of the Northern Areas to India for the purpose of defence. Pakistan was totally opposed to these amendments.

On 12 April 1950, the Security Council appointed Sir Owen Dixon to continue the efforts. After the consideration of many proposals, which were rejected by either India or Pakistan, he suggested a plan whereby the plebiscite would be conducted by sections or areas and each section would be allocated to either India or Pakistan in accordance with the result of the votes therein. Further, as there were areas that were certain to vote for accession to India and others that were certain to choose Pakistan, these areas should be allotted accordingly, without taking a vote therein, and plebiscite should be confined to uncertain areas, that is, the Kashmir Valley. Pakistan rejected the proposal, but India agreed to consider the approach.[48]

India informed Dixon that it would be ready to approach the problem on the lines presented by him in light of some principles, namely, that the areas where there was no apparent doubt as to the wishes of the people should be so allotted to India and Pakistan without a plebiscite; plebiscite should be confined to those areas where there was some doubt regarding the voting results; and the demarcation must have due regard to geographical areas/features and of providing an international boundary.

---

48 Sisir Gupta, *Kashmir: A Study in India–Pakistan Relations*, p. 218.

Based on the above principles, India wanted the whole of Jammu province (the area between the Ravi river to Poonch, Udhampur, Bhadarwah, Kishtwar, and others), subject to minor corrections, and the tehsils of Ladakh and Kargil in Ladakh, except the area above the Suru river (in Kargil), towards the Valley, where a plebiscite could be held.[49]

To Pakistan, it was ready to concede Gilgit, Gilgit Agency, Gilgit Wazarat, political districts and tribal territory, Baltistan and as much of Jammu Province as was to the west of the ceasefire line as corrected. A boundary commission could apply, on the ground, the principles of the division. India also agreed not to divert or reduce the flow of the Chenab river by any artificial construction, except for irrigation within the state at the local level. India also expressed its desire to have another conference of the two prime ministers with Dixon to discuss the settlement of these lines.[50]

But Pakistan was less flexible. It came up with a red herring, which was to consider an outright partition of the state, provided the Kashmir Valley went to them. This India rejected, as indeed Dixon had anticipated.[51]

Ultimately, Dixon came to the following conclusion:

> I could not expose plebiscite conducted under the authority of the United Nations to the dangers which I believe certainly to exist. Indeed, I came to the conclusion that it would be impossible to give effect to the doctrines formulated by India in objection to my plan and at the

---

49 Ibid, p. 218 and S/1791.
50 Sisir Gupta, *Kashmir: A Study in India–Pakistan Relations*, pp. 218–19.
51 Ibid, p. 219.

same time frame a plan for partition and a limited plebiscite which I could ask Pakistan to accept.[52]

Both the prime ministers now agreed that there was nothing more that the UN representative could do in the Indian subcontinent, and Dixon left on 23 August 1950. This ended another phase of the UN mediation. After that, a proposal for the Commonwealth to lead the negotiations was also considered as an alternative but for many reasons it did not find favour with either party. On 14 December 1950, Pakistan drew the attention of the Security Council to the convening of the Constituent Assembly in the state of Jammu and Kashmir, which in their view merited serious attention. They feared that the deliberations of the Constituent Assembly would determine the future shape and affiliation of the state of Jammu and Kashmir.[53]

The issue was discussed on 21 February 1951 in the Security Council and the UN now envisaged a considerably expanded role for itself in Kashmir along with arbitration by nominees from the International Court of Justice. However, this resolution did not find favour with either India or Pakistan for different reasons, and a revised draft was attempted. Pakistan favoured further extending the Security Council's role and effecting the demilitarization of Kashmir through arbitration. India recommended onus on the parties themselves and to proceed with direct contact to solve outstanding problems. The revised draft was passed, which essentially dropped all references to the UN forces to concede a point to India, and also those to the possible division of the state to satisfy Pakistan.[54]

---

52 Ibid, p. 220.
53 Ibid, p. 230 and S/1942.
54 Sisir Gupta, *Kashmir: A Study in India–Pakistan Relations*, pp. 230–33 and

Invasion, Accession and Reference to the United Nations

The provision of arbitration was, however, retained; so also a paragraph relating to the Constituent Assembly.

India found the revised draft unacceptable. In his address to the Indian Parliament on 28 March 1950, Nehru said:

> My own feeling has been a feeling of distress that the UNO has somewhat drifted from its original conception. We went to the UN not to determine the accession issue or where the sovereignty lies ... We did not go there to seek arbitration but to complain about the aggression of another State, which was likely to lead to international complications and probably affect peace.[55]

Almost all sections of the Indian press vehemently criticized the Security Council's action in passing the Anglo-US resolution. The *National Herald* commented: 'The Anglo-US resolution on Kashmir has deeply hurt Indian feelings, justice has been sacrificed to diplomacy and mediation has been travestied for the convenience of power politics ... the Council has done irreparable damage to itself.'[56]

Hereon, Dr Frank Graham, an American diplomat, was selected to continue the effort.[57]

S/2017 RV 1.

55 Sisir Gupta, *Kashmir: A Study in India–Pakistan Relations*, p. 234.

56 Sisir Gupta, *Kashmir: A Study in India–Pakistan Relations*, pp. 234–35; *The National Herald*, 1 April 1951.

57 Sisir Gupta, *Kashmir: A Study in India–Pakistan Relations*, p. 235. As Dr Graham wrote in the *Christian Science Monitor* on 7 December 1950: 'Today the issue is more difficult to solve than it was at the outset, for in these three years India and Pakistan have formulated their points of view into positions as fixed and unyielding as the ceasefire line itself.'

In the meanwhile, there was heightened warmongering in Pakistan for jihad against India. In November, the Azad Kashmir leader, Sardar Ibrahim Khan, said: 'The only solution now lies in the revival of our war of liberation.' On 22 January 1951, Liaquat Ali Khan, the then prime minister of Pakistan, said at a press conference, 'There were only two courses open to Pakistan to settle the issue; one was to pursue the matter in the Security Council. The second, I would not tell you.' Poems in widely read Urdu dailies held out the vision of recapturing Delhi,[58] and compared Kashmir to Karbala.

It was in this context and after frequent violations of the ceasefire line that Prime Minister Nehru repeatedly declared that an attack on Kashmir would be treated as an attack on the whole of India. He also wrote to the Security Council:

> These occurrences (violations) of the ceasefire line happened in quick succession and coupled with the fanatical warmongering propaganda, that is daily growing in Pakistan, justify the suspicion that they are part of a planned programme calculated to lead, if unchecked, to the outbreak of hostilities between the two countries.[59]

It was in the face of this situation that Graham came up with his proposal, which provided for a reaffirmation by the governments of India and Pakistan that they would not make war over the question of Kashmir; an agreement that they would see that warlike statements were not made on the issue; a reaffirmation of the ceasefire line; a reaffirmation that the future of Kashmir would

---

58 Sisir Gupta, *Kashmir: A Study in India–Pakistan Relations*, pp. 235–36; *Zamindar* (Lahore), 16 June 1951.
59 Sisir Gupta, *Kashmir: A Study in India–Pakistan Relations*, p. 237 and S/2225.

be decided by a plebiscite under UN auspices; and an agreement that demilitarization would be a single continuous process. Ninety days were planned for demilitarization, which on the Pakistani side was to include large-scale disbandment of Azad troops and on the Indian side a withdrawal of the bulk of its troops. After extensive discussions, this plan also fizzled out.

Direct Negotiations: 1953–56 (Round One)

The failure of the many mediation efforts on the part of a number of UN representatives led to the opinion that it may be more fruitful to let the two parties settle the issue through direct negotiations and give the statesmanship on the part of the leaders of the two countries a chance. The discussions went on for almost two years. Finally, in January 1955, when Governor-General Ghulam Muhammad was a guest of the Government of India on the occasion of India's Republic Day celebrations, the two sides agreed to hold direct talks in Delhi later that year.

The visit by this delegation in January started with Ghulam Muhammad expressing his faith in Nehru, 'I have more faith in Nehru than you have. I am convinced that Jawaharlal Nehru desires happy relations between our two countries.'[60] Speaking at the state banquet he said:

> I think this dark period of strain has now lasted too long and the time has now come to end it completely... Let us put an end to our disputes. We owe this as a duty to posterity not to leave them a legacy of misunderstanding and bitterness.[61]

---

60 Sisir Gupta, *Kashmir: A Study in India–Pakistan Relations*, p. 287; *The Hindu*, 26 January 1955.
61 Ibid.

Finally, on 14 May 1955, a Pakistani delegation led by then Prime Minister Chaudhry Muhammad Ali and including General Iskander Mirza and Education Minister Abid Hussain arrived in Delhi. Unfortunately, the president of Pakistan, Ghulam Muhammad, who was to arrive in Delhi on 12 May to set the talks going, could not come due to health issues. Another unfortunate development was that these talks were held soon after a serious border clash at Nekowal (J&K) in which twelve Indian soldiers and one army major had been killed. The talks concluded on 18 May 1955 with a brief communiqué, but both sides stated that the talks had been constructive and declared that a new approach would be followed in subsequent discussions. No confirmed information about the proceedings was shared by the two governments except for Prime Minister Muhammad Ali saying that 'the wishes of the people might take many forms'[62] (published in the *Pakistan Standard* on 22 May). On the Indian side, a special correspondent of the *Statesman* wrote on 17 May, 'It is understood that certain new proposals relating to the basics of the plebiscite, as to whether it was possible to hold a plebiscite, may emerge from their present secrecy tomorrow.'[63]

However, the Pakistani prime minister received very hostile press and he was compelled to give clarifications on the Kashmir issue.

On 26 May at a press conference, he said that there was no question of withdrawing the issue from the UN, which was aware of all the proceedings. He also said that no government in Pakistan could take any decision with regard to Kashmir with which the people of Pakistan were not satisfied. In spite of these statements, he continued to get very negative press, especially in *Dawn*, and in August he resigned from his post and also virtually from politics.

---

62 Sisir Gupta, *Kashmir: A Study in India–Pakistan Relations*, pp. 290–91.
63 Ibid, p. 290.

It also did not help matters that Governor-General Ghulam Muhammad, who had to leave for the US for treatment in May 1955, was replaced by General Iskander Mirza. The Pakistani prime minister was replaced by Chaudhry Muhammad Ali, who formed a coalition government. Some discussions went on for over a year. Finally, after three years, the two sides went back to the Security Council. Thus ended the phase of direct contact.

In these three years, with a majority of the Security Council's permanent members, Pakistan had a political and military alliance.

Back to the Security Council

The proceedings in the UN started on 16 January 1957 with Feroze Khan Noon presenting the Pakistani case on the usual lines. V.K. Krishna Menon, who represented India, stated that 'the Kashmir problem was not a territorial dispute, the question was of aggression'. But even before Krishna Menon had completed his speech at the Security Council, a draft resolution sponsored by Australia, Columbia, Cuba, the United Kingdom (UK) and the US was circulated. The resolution reaffirmed the earlier UN resolutions as well as the UNCIP[64] resolutions and was based on the premise that the final settlement of the state's future would have to be done in accordance with the will of the people, through an impartial and free plebiscite under the supervision of the UN.

The resolution had two main aspects: the reintroduction of a UN mediator and the preference for a UN force. India had always considered the first aspect as undesirable and the second as unacceptable. Thus, it took a very strong stand and Krishna Menon

---

64 Sisir Gupta, *Kashmir: A Study in India–Pakistan Relations*, p. 316; and the resolutions of 21 April 1946, 3 June 1948, 14 March 1950, 30 March 1951, 13 August 1948 and 5 January 1949.

ended his record-setting speech – in terms of its length (eight hours) – in the UN with the words, 'My country has deliberately chosen the path of an independent foreign policy. No pressures will elbow us into an alignment in one direction or the other.'

The Soviet representative drew attention[65] to the changes in Jammu and Kashmir and the fact that the idea of plebiscite was now rejected by India. The attempt to hold a plebiscite with outside help was likely to lead to local conflicts and thereby complicate the international situation. The Soviets then vetoed the resolution, and a new and much softer resolution was adopted on 21 February 1957.

Hereafter, the emphasis once again shifted to direct negotiations between India and Pakistan.

Direct Indo-Pak Dialogue: 1958–64 (Second Round)

On 9 September 1958, the prime minister of Pakistan, Feroze Khan Noon, arrived in Delhi for talks with Nehru. On 11 September, a communiqué was issued, which indicated that they had arrived at a settlement with regard to most of the border areas in the eastern region, under which certain enclaves would be exchanged. But even before the ink could dry on the agreement, Noon was ousted by the military and a military regime was installed. Nehru called this takeover a 'naked military dictatorship'. Bakshi Ghulam Mohammad, the prime minister of J&K, commenting on the military takeover, said that it indicated the correctness of the decision of the National Conference to accede to India instead of Pakistan.

After the coup, talks between India and Pakistan eventually resumed, with the first meeting between Nehru and the president of Pakistan, General Ayub Khan, taking place in Karachi from 19

---

65 Sisir Gupta, *Kashmir: A Study in India–Pakistan Relations*, p. 320. SCOR 770 Meeting 1957.

Invasion, Accession and Reference to the United Nations

to 23 September 1960. The communiqué following the meeting stated, 'whereas [the] Kashmir issue needed careful consideration, the Indus water question presented the two Governments with an unparalleled opportunity'.

But soon thereafter, the situation became tense with President Ayub Khan declaring at Muzaffarabad on 6 October 1960 that Pakistan could not trust India until the Kashmir issue was resolved and the Pakistani army could not afford to leave the Kashmir issue unsolved for an indefinite time frame.[66] Nehru said, 'Kashmir (is) a Pandora's box which should not be opened', while Ayub Khan called it a 'time bomb'.[67]

Under these circumstances, Pakistan took the case back to the Security Council. The Western powers came up with a proposal, which was vetoed by the Soviets. In India, Nehru complained that 'the Western powers were almost invariably pitted against India on matters that created passionate feelings in the country'.[68]

In 1962, China attacked India, and India asked the US and Britain for help. These two countries, taking advantage of the situation, prevailed upon India to continue direct negotiations with Pakistan on the Kashmir issue. Resultantly, six rounds of talks took place between India, represented by Sardar Swaran Singh, and Pakistan, represented by Zulfikar Ali Bhutto, between 27 September 1962 and May 1963. Pakistan, in the meanwhile, illegally demarcated the boundary between PoK and China. This proved to India that another nexus was developing against them in the form of Pakistan–China.

---

66 Sisir Gupta, *Kashmir: A Study in India–Pakistan Relations*, p. 344.
67 Ibid, p. 345; *Pakistan Times*, 27 October 1960.
68 Sisir Gupta, *Kashmir: A Study in India–Pakistan Relations*, p. 352; Rajya Sabha, 23 June (*Foreign Affairs Record*, Vol. 8, 1962, p. 116).

At these talks, India's proposal offered to transfer the entire occupied area west and north of the Kashmir Valley and also adjust the ceasefire line by ceding some more areas. Pakistan, on the other hand, submitted a plan that would not only have it taking the Valley but also large parts of Jammu. This would have left India with less than approximately 3,000 sq. miles against the 85,000 sq. miles of the state with Pakistan. Resultantly, the sixth and last meeting terminated on 17 May 1963 regretting that no decision could be reached as the differences between the two sides were vast.

The failure of the talks led Pakistan's foreign minister to once again write to the Security Council on 6 January 1964 asking for an immediate meeting. The issue was debated over the course of six meetings in the UN between 5 and 18 May 1964, and in the end, the main suggestion to the two sides was to resolve the issue by direct negotiation.[69]

Consequent to the visit of Sheikh Abdullah to Rawalpindi, on Pandit Nehru's suggestion, on 26 May 1964, Sheikh announced that the Pakistani president Ayub Khan and the Indian prime minister would be meeting in Delhi in June 1964 to discuss the Kashmir problem. Unfortunately, on 27 May 1964 Nehru passed away and with that was lost 'another chance of reconciliation'.

Assessment of the Status of Plebiscite and Mediatory Efforts by the UN

Ever since the Indo-Pakistan war of 1965, the UN has not entertained any requests from Pakistan on the Kashmir issue. In 1972, following the Indo-Pakistan war of 1971, India and Pakistan signed the Simla Agreement, agreeing to resolve all their

---

69 Sisir Gupta, *Kashmir: A Study in India–Pakistan Relations*, pp. 358–59; *United Nations Monthly Chronicle*, June 1964, pp. 10–11.

differences through bilateral negotiations. Major powers such as the US and UK as well as other Western powers have also supported this approach. Thus, after the Simla Agreement, any mediation with regard to the Kashmir issue becomes irrelevant.

With regard to the earlier resolution passed by the Security Council, the secretary-general of the UN, Kofi Anan, during his visit to India and Pakistan in 2001, clarified that 'the Kashmir resolutions were only advisory recommendations and they should not be compared to East Timor and Iraq'. In a clear rejection of Pakistan's persistent demand to implement the UN's resolutions on Kashmir, the UN secretary-general said that these were not 'self-enforcing' and the only way out was negotiation between the two parties.[70]

On 11 January 2003, the then president of Pakistan, General Pervez Musharraf, also announced that Pakistan was willing to 'leave aside the demand for UN resolutions and plebiscite and explore alternative bilateral options for resolving the dispute'.[71]

So everybody has agreed at different times that the best way to find a solution to the Kashmir issue is through bilateral negotiations with a policy of give and take.

Why did the UN efforts to mediate between the two sides fail and why is the plebiscite no longer an option? There are several reasons. Kashmir's accession to India was legal and the then governor-general, Mountbatten, also accepted the accession as correct in all respects. On his advice, India offered to hold a plebiscite once the situation had stabilized and Pakistani aggression ended. However, the question remains as to why Nehru accepted Mountbatten's

---

70 'The only way out was negotiations between the two parties', *Rediff News*, 26 June 2004.
71 C. Christine Fair, *Fighting to the End: The Pakistan Army's Way of War* (Oxford University Press, 2014), p. 141; 'We have left aside UN resolutions on Kashmir – Musharraf', *The Hindu*, 18 December 2003.

advice to approach the UN on the Kashmir issue. This will remain a blot on Nehru's wisdom and statesmanship. There can be no doubt about Mountbatten's (British) mischief and complicity.

In all the discussions on the issue held subsequently, India was agreeable to a plebiscite provided Pakistan was first ready to end its aggression. India was also prepared to reduce its forces to the minimum to allow a fair plebiscite. Unfortunately, Pakistan never seriously considered fulfilling its own obligations.

Also, there exist powerful elements in Pakistan that do not desire peace between the two countries. The needle of suspicion can easily point towards the Pakistani army, which can retain its role of the most powerful player in Pakistan only if security problems such as Kashmir and Afghanistan remain alive.

Further, the militarization of Pakistan after they joined various security pacts such as the Southeast Asia Treaty Organization (SEATO) and the Baghdad Pact gave Pakistan the confidence to take on India militarily, which resulted in three unnecessary and horrendous wars. Pakistan also placed too much reliance on external powers, who could not effectively support a cause that was not sound on merit.

There is also the factor of time – too much time has gone by and plebiscite as an option has now became unrealistic and impractical, besides having lost its relevance post the Simla Accord. The UN has also taken the issue of Kashmir off its agenda and advised the two countries to discuss the matter bilaterally.

During the 1950s, 1960s and post-1971 India, and perhaps also Pakistan, made serious efforts to try and solve the problem bilaterally. These efforts did not succeed, partially for the reasons stated above and also because Pakistan is yet to accept that any solution to the Kashmir issue has to take into account the reality that Kashmir's accession to India is final and all solutions have to make allowance for that. A change of boundaries is not possible at this stage. Pakistan is already in occupation of 40 per cent of the total area of the erstwhile state of Jammu and Kashmir, some of which it has illegally ceded to China.

It is strongly felt in India that Pakistan has not been able to accept the fact that India has taken Partition as a reality and moved on. Also, Pakistan has not been able to give up its hidden desire of parity with India and thus harbours the ambition of breaking up India. Indeed, Kashmir is only a symptom; their problem with India is much bigger. For many in Pakistan, continuing friction with India has become a rallying point to keep Pakistan united.

There is also the fact that Pakistan unreasonably felt cheated by Partition because of the award of most of the Gurdaspur district to India, despite it being a Muslim-majority area, and the fact that Junagadh and Hyderabad joined India. The ultimate injury, of course, was the denial of Kashmir. Pakistan was thus born as an insecure state and for it, as Christine Fair says, 'partition is an unfinished business'.[72]

Finally, one is almost certain now that with or without Kashmir, Pakistan will always harbour issues with India for at least the next couple of generations. Pakistan's worry is that India is not reconciled to its existence and at some stage or the other will try to break up Pakistan.

---

72 C. Christine Fair, *Fighting to the End*, p. 65.

3

The 1965 and 1971 Wars

'There are no runners-up in war. A nation has no place for losers.'
— *Field Marshal S.H.F.J. Manekshaw*

The 1965 War and Its Outcome

In the early sixties, Pakistan's president, Ayub Khan, was doing well and was held in high regard in the country. He had resolved the water dispute with India through both sides signing the Indus Waters Treaty. Pakistan's friendship with China had started showing signs of solidity after it had signed the boundary agreement with the latter in 1963. The Indo-China war in 1962 had exposed India's weaknesses. Pakistan was also receiving sizeable military assistance from the US at this time. All in all, Pakistan felt confident enough to take on India militarily.

The loss of the Holy Relic from the Hazratbal shrine in Srinagar in December 1963 had provoked wild demonstrations and the level of protests in the Valley resembled a rebellion. Ayub

Khan felt that this situation provided him an opportunity to force a decision militarily and annex Kashmir. However, the relic mysteriously reappeared on 4 January 1964 and the situation in the Valley quietened.

Operation Gibraltar was conceived soon after the Hazratbal incident. It involved mustering and training a guerrilla force composed of thousands of army personnel, ex-servicemen and volunteers from PoK and Pakistan to start an insurrection in Kashmir. In the first week of August 1965, members of this Azad Kashmir Force began to cross the ceasefire line starting from the Rajouri sector and then across the Pir Panjal Range into Gulmarg, Uri and Baramulla. They were to occupy high grounds, fan out into the Valley and encourage a general revolt, which was to be followed by a mopping-up operation by the Pakistani regular forces. This force of guerrillas (not from the regular army) was organized and commanded by Major General Akhtar Hussain Malik, General Officer Commanding (GOC) 12 Division. The strength of the force was between 30,000 and 40,000 men. It was divided into ten task forces, with five companies each. Besides inciting rebellion, they were to destroy bridges, logistics installations and headquarters, as well as attack airfields of the Indian Air Force. Out of the ten task forces, only one, the Ghaznavi Force, managed to reach its objective in Mendhar–Rajauri.

The assessment is that Operation Gibraltar was a clumsy attempt[1] and doomed to collapse for various reasons. First of all, the Kashmiri people did not rise in revolt as expected.[2] Secondly, there was very little coordination amongst the armed forces in

---

1 Devin T. Hagerty, *South Asia in World Politics* (Rowman and Littlefield, 2005), p. 23.
2 C. Christine Fair, *Fighting to the End*, p. 142.

Pakistan; the air force was not even informed about the operation. Thirdly, the Indian army had enough intelligence about the location of the infiltrating groups and were able to effectively battle them. The locals also provided up-to-date information about the infiltrators to the Indian army.[3]

Finally, many senior officials in Pakistan were against the operation as failure could lead to an all-out war, which Pakistan wanted to avoid. As is normal with Pakistan, all their presumptions turned out to be woefully wrong and a war, of much greater intensity than they could have imagined, followed.

In August 1965, when it became clear that Operation Gibraltar was heading for disaster, Pakistan launched Operation Grand Slam to retrieve what looked like a lost cause. This was a major tank offensive in the Chhamb–Jaurian sector towards Akhnoor. The idea was to cut off the supply line to the Rajouri–Poonch sector, and contingent to success, turn towards the Jammu–Srinagar sector. This was phase two and the war was now widening. Here again Pakistan made a major strategic miscalculation.

While the Indians stiffly resisted the attack in the Chhamb sector and went into PoK on 28 August, it was obvious to them that they could reduce the pressure in the Chhamb sector if they opened another widely dispersed front.

Accordingly, early on 6 September 1965, the Indian army crossed into Pakistan in the Lahore and Sialkot sectors, across the international border. Over the next fortnight, there were ferocious tank battles and air engagements. The Pakistani armoured division's thrust (equipped with Patton tanks) was valiantly engaged in the area of Khemkaran–Valtoha by India's Sherman tanks. The so-

---

3 T.C.A. Raghavan, *The People Next Door: The Curious History of India's Relations with Pakistan* (Delhi: HarperCollins, 2017), p. 80.

called bold and strategic Pakistani manoeuvre, boasting of driving down the Grand Trunk Road to Delhi, came to a halt on the ploughed and boggy fields of the border town of Khemkaran in the famous battle of Asal Uttar. The area was subsequently called the 'Graveyard of the Patton Tanks'.

In the Jammu–Samba sector, in the area of Phillaura and Buttar Dograndi, a fierce tank battle was fought where again Pakistan suffered heavy tank casualties and losses with no progress.

In the Valley, the infiltrators were rounded up in no time, mostly based on the information provided by the local Kashmiris. The operation to Akhnoor was halted in Jaurian itself, and by the time the war ended, the Indian army advance guards were on the outskirts of Lahore and Sialkot and threatening those two strategic towns.

In the Srinagar sector, the Indian army responded with attacks across the LoC in the Kargil–Tangdhar and Uri sectors to seal off the infiltration bases. Point 13620, a major vantage point in the Kargil sector, was captured to deny Pakistan direct observation and domination over Kargil town. In the Tangdhar sector, the Bugina Bulge was captured, pushing the LoC to the Kishanganga river. And critically, the Hajipur Pass was captured, which opened up the connection between Poonch and Uri. Unfortunately, Hajipir was returned to Pakistan after the war, a move that was heavily criticized in India. The war terminated on 23 September 1965, and it can be safely concluded that Operations Gibraltar and Grand Slam turned out to be disasters.

In the overall analysis of the twenty-one-day war, Pakistan's strategy was found to be wanting in all their three major assumptions, namely, that the people of Kashmir would rise up to support the infiltrators, that the Indian army would not react violently across the LoC into Pakistan to seal off the infiltration launch pads, and that the Indian political and military leadership would lack the nerve to open the second front across the international border.[4]

Within the Kashmir Valley, the insurgency that was supposed to have been created by the infiltrators did not come to pass. E.N. Mangat Rai, the then chief secretary of Jammu and Kashmir, recalled that through the conflict, 'we had practically no internal security problem in the Kashmir Valley' and 'not a single arrest of a political nature was made during this entire period'. Another interesting and revealing remark he made was that 'we could hardly have had a clearer plebiscite from the people of the Valley'.[5]

In the final analysis, Pakistan had started a war in which they made no gains, and their plans lacked in overall strategy. All this war achieved was to set the stage for the next one, just like World War I had sowed the seeds for World War II. Reportedly, Ayub Khan was livid, proclaiming that never again 'would Pakistan risk 100 million Pakistanis for five million Kashmiris'.[6] If Pakistan had won the 1965 war, which they claim, Ayub would not have made the above remarks.

In his book, Khurshid Mahmud Kasuri, foreign minister of Pakistan from 2002 to 2007, mentions:

> The propaganda of great victory within Pakistan only produced disillusionment. Moreover, with the 1965 war, there was a striking change in Pakistan's security environment. Instead of single alignment with the United States against China and Soviet Union, Pakistan found

---

4 T.C.A. Raghavan, *The People Next Door*, p. 81; Abdul Sattar, *Pakistan's Foreign Policy, 1947–2005: A Concise History* (Delhi: Oxford University Press, 2007), p. 105.

5 Ibid.

6 C. Christine Fair, *Fighting to the End*, p. 143.

itself cut off from United States military support and on increasingly warm terms with China and treated equitably by the Soviet Union. Unchanged was the enmity with which India and Pakistan regarded each other over Kashmir. The result was the elaboration of a new security approach, called by Ayub Khan as the 'Triangular Tightrope', a tricky endeavour to maintain good ties with the United States while cultivating China and the Soviet Union. Support from the other developing nations was also welcome. None of the new relationships carried the weight of previous ties with the United States, but, taken together, they at least provided Pakistan with a political counterbalance to India.[7]

The 1971 War

The domination of the Western Wing over the Eastern Wing in Pakistan had created serious resentment amongst the Bengalis of the Eastern Wing. In Pakistan's first general election in 1970, the Bengali leader Sheikh Mujibur Rahman's Awami League won an absolute majority to form a government in Pakistan. However, there was acute reluctance on the part of the Pakistani political leadership, led by Zulfikar Ali Bhutto, and also by the Pakistani army, to hand over power to the powerful Bengali leader, who had won the election on a 'six-point agenda for provincial autonomy'.

In response, there was a military crackdown on what was then East Pakistan. The Bengalis of East Pakistan, led by Mujibur Rahman, rose in revolt against this injustice and military repression. However, as a result, over ten million refugees poured across

---

7 Khurshid Mahmud Kasuri, *Neither a Hawk Nor a Dove*, p. 413; Indo-Pakistan War of 1965, Global Security, http://www.globalsecurity.org/military/world/war/indo-pak_1965.htm.

the border into India, which resulted in a huge and unbearable economic burden on India.

Indira Gandhi, then the prime minister of India, undertook a visit to all the major powers of the world to apprise them of the scale of carnage unleashed by the Pakistani army and the great refugee influx into India, which India was unable to bear economically. The US was more concerned about Pakistan acting as a bridge for the secret visit of Henry Kissinger – at the time the assistant to the president for National Security Affairs – to China and was non-committal. The Soviet Union, however, responded positively, and the Indo–Soviet Treaty of Peace, Friendship and Cooperation was signed in August 1971. This was a unique understanding that not only epitomized the special relationship between India and the USSR, but also acted as a guarantor of regional peace. Few treaties have played such an important role in shaping the politics, history and geography of the world as the 1971 Indo-Soviet treaty.

Mujibur Rahman's arrest and the continuing repression by the Pakistani army led to the creation of the Mukti Bahini, a guerrilla resistance movement, for the liberation of East Pakistan. This was supported by India in terms of training and material support. Mukti Bahini fought valiantly for its cause and took a good toll on the Pakistani army virtually throughout 1971.

In order to reduce pressure on its Eastern Wing, Pakistan launched a pre-emptive strike in the western sector of India on 3 December 1971. This was what India wanted, and it commenced operations on both the eastern and western fronts with great intensity.

During the war, the Indian political leadership under Indira Gandhi showed great maturity and grit by not getting distracted or cowed down, even when the US moved their Seventh Fleet into the Bay of Bengal to deter India from destroying Pakistan's war machine in the western sector. The US also tried to persuade China to activate India's northern borders to distract India. Both these strategies failed. The Soviet Union also warned the US and China that they would be constrained to intervene (maybe even with nuclear weapons) should China take any hasty action.

Meanwhile, the Indian army pressed on relentlessly with operations in the western sector till the fall of Dhaka on 16 December 1971. The war had lasted for just fourteen days and with the fall of Dhaka, India declared a unilateral ceasefire all along the front with effect from the night of 16–17 December 1971.

The 1971 war was a national disaster for Pakistan. It resulted in the break-up of Pakistan and the consequent liberation of Bangladesh as an independent country.

At the end of the war, 93,000 Pakistani soldiers were left behind with India as prisoners of war. It was indeed most embarrassing for Pakistan, which had always boasted that each one of their soldiers was the equivalent of ten Indian soldiers.

The question that puzzles one is as to why Pakistan's General Yahya Khan embarked on the suicidal course of attacking India in the western sector. Perhaps it was to try and relieve the pressure on the eastern sector, but they should have known that they could not have fought on both fronts simultaneously. In this regard, the observations of T.C.A. Raghavan, till recently the Indian ambassador to Pakistan, merit deliberation. In his book, *The People Next Door: The Curious History of India's Relations with Pakistan*, Ambassador Raghavan recounts a very interesting conversation between Air Chief Marshal Asghar Khan, who commanded the Pakistani air force from 1957 to 1965, and Lieutenant General Gul Hassan, the then chief of general staff. Upon Asghar Khan asking him why Yahya Khan had started a war with India, Gul Hassan replied that the 'situation was grave (in the eastern sector) and the only answer was to start a war'. When Asghar Khan pressed him further, Gul Hassan responded: 'In order to have a ceasefire.' Asghar Khan further reflects that perhaps Gul Hassan was voicing the thoughts of the Junta and Yahya Khan. In the desperate situation they had gotten themselves into, they had begun to believe that they should open hostilities with India, and the United States would bail them out by ensuring a ceasefire.[8]

The Simla Agreement

Even though the 1971 war was predominantly fought in the east, it had direct ramifications on Kashmir. After the war, the prime minister of India, Indira Gandhi, and the president of Pakistan, Zulfikar Ali Bhutto, met in Simla along with their advisors. The outcome of this meeting was the Simla Agreement, which was signed between both sides on 2 July 1972.

The primary gains, as far as India was concerned, were that firstly, it was agreed that the Jammu and Kashmir issue would be settled bilaterally, thus making any outsider's role, including that of the UN, irrelevant. Secondly, the old ceasefire line was to be replaced by a 'Line of Control' (LoC) to indicate the demarcation between PoK and Jammu and Kashmir.[9]

Detractors of the Simla Agreement say that Pakistan was saved the humiliation of its defeat in the war, and India agreed to return the 93,000 Pakistani prisoners of war without any preconditions. They also felt that although christening the erstwhile ceasefire line as the 'LoC' did grant it more authenticity and a status of near permanence, ideally it should have been converted into

---

[8] T.C.A. Raghavan, *The People Next Door*, p. 108.
[9] Ibid, p. 117.

an international border and a commitment made by both sides to abjure the use of force. That would have ended the Kashmir problem once and for all. They feel that India lost on the negotiating table what its armed forces had won on the battlefield. Since the main players of the time have passed away, one can only draw conclusions from the written material available from them and some other authors regarding how and why the agreement was drawn up in the shape that it was.

P.N. Dhar, Indira Gandhi's economic advisor who later became principal secretary, was a close confidant of the prime minister. He was present throughout the Simla deliberations and has given a detailed account of the discussions in his book, *Indira Gandhi, the 'Emergency' and Indian Democracy*.

According to him, Bhutto, who came with a very large delegation, apologized for the size of it but explained that he was very keen on the support of all political elements in Pakistan for any agreement that was arrived at in Simla. He was also very keen on the support of Aziz Ahmed, who was the senior-most civil servant in Pakistan and had accompanied the delegation. Bhutto, in his own words, was personally inclined to accept the status quo as a permanent solution to the Kashmir problem.

Dhar says that the transformation of the ceasefire line into the LoC was the core of the Indian solution to the Kashmir problem. The de facto LoC was meant to be graduated to the level of de jure border. Aziz Ahmed vehemently objected to this and no agreement was reached after five days of negotiations. The Pakistani delegation was scheduled to leave Simla the next morning.

At that time, Bhutto asked to see Mrs Gandhi and they met alone at 6 p.m., with Dhar and Haksar waiting in the adjoining room. Emerging from the tête-à-tête with Mrs Gandhi after an hour, Bhutto looked pleased.

Dhar further writes:

> At their meeting Mrs Gandhi told Bhutto she was sympathetic to Bhutto's concerns and that she would hate to appear to be dictating terms to a defeated adversary. She agreed to the earliest possible withdrawal of troops from occupied territories in the interest of an overall agreement. On this question, India did not need the concurrence of Bangladesh as she did on the question of the return of prisoners of war who had surrendered to the Indo-Bangladesh Joint Command. At the same time she firmly reiterated the Indian desire for durable peace and stability in the subcontinent, which she thought was a precondition for economic and social development and the removal of poverty. [Bhutto used this line of argument later in his speeches in Pakistan to convince them that he had done a good job.] She had argued that this desirable state of affairs could be brought about only if India and Pakistan buried the hatchet and agreed on the settlement of the Kashmir issue along the lines suggested by the Indian side.
>
> Mrs Gandhi elaborated the merits of the Indian proposal in the following terms: it was the only feasible solution. An important feature of the proposal was that neither country was gaining or losing territory on account of war. It did not involve transfers of population from one side to the other. Kashmiris as an ethnic community were left undivided on the Indian side. The line of control was, therefore, largely an ethnic and linguistic frontier. In fact in 1947, at the time of partition, it was also an ideological frontier, being the limit of the political influence of Sheikh Mohammed Abdullah and his National Conference party.

True, there were some anomalies in this otherwise neatly etched picture, but these, Mrs Gandhi pointed out, could be removed by mutual consent.

Bhutto responded with feeling and apparent sincerity. After long reflection he had come to the conclusion that the Indian proposal was the only feasible one. But he could not agree to incorporating it in the agreement for the following reasons:

(a) His political enemies at home, especially the army bosses, would denounce him for surrendering what many in Pakistan considered their vital national interest. This would endanger the democratic set-up which had emerged after fourteen years of army rule. In this context, Bhutto repeatedly talked about his fear of what he called the Lahore lobby, though he never clearly explained what it was.

(b) He was anxious to obtain the support of all political elements in Pakistan in favour of any agreement that might emerge at Simla . . . He would, however, work towards its implementation in practice and over time.

Mrs Gandhi herself was worried that a formal withdrawal of the Indian claim on Pak-occupied Kashmir could create political trouble for her. She agreed that the solution should not be recorded in the agreement for the reason advanced by Bhutto, but it should be implemented gradually, as he had suggested.

The most important part of the agreement, sub-clause 4 (ii), says: 'In Jammu and Kashmir, the line of control resulting from the ceasefire of December 17, 1971 shall be respected by both sides without prejudice to the recognized position of either side. Neither side shall seek to alter it unilaterally, irrespective of mutual differences and legal interpretations. Both sides further undertake to refrain from the threat or the use of force in violation of this line.' The phrase 'without prejudice to the recognized position of either side' was a concession to Bhutto to save him from domestic critics. The second and third sentences were assumed to prevent the abuse of this concession and to lay the foundation for a future settlement of the Kashmir issue.[10]

Another major contribution to the narrative is that of T.N. Kaul, who was the foreign secretary at the time of the Simla Agreement and present throughout the negotiations. His views are of great interest and are reproduced from his book *A Diplomat's Diary: The Tantalizing Triangle, China, India and USA*.

> Indira Gandhi has been criticized for not getting 'a final settlement' of the Kashmir question at Simla in 1972, when India was the victor. She tried hard but Bhutto said if he agreed to a final settlement at Simla he would be overthrown and the military would take over power and increase tension with India. When I tried to intervene at the conference table, Bhutto, addressing Mrs Gandhi, said, 'Madam, I assure you that within two weeks of my return to Pakistan, I shall prepare the ground for it (a final settlement of Kashmir question)'.

T.N. Kaul further says that he left Simla for Chandigarh on the evening of 2 July 1972 to see off the Pakistani delegation because

---

[10] P.N. Dhar, *Indira Gandhi, the 'Emergency' and Indian Democracy* (New Delhi: Oxford University Press, 2000), pp. 190–94; T.C.A. Raghavan, *The People Next Door*, p. 118.

he 'did not think a settlement with Bhutto was likely'. However, he was proved wrong and Mrs Gandhi did sign the Simla Agreement on the night of 2 July 1972, after a solo meeting with Bhutto at 'the retreat'. No one else was present, but P.N. Dhar, who was outside the room in which Mrs Gandhi and Bhutto met, has said that there was a verbal understanding between Mrs Gandhi and Mr Bhutto that a final settlement of the Kashmir question along the LoC would be made.

There is no record of this and when I asked Mrs Gandhi the next day, she said, 'I do not trust Bhutto, but I wanted to make a gesture to the people of Pakistan with whom we have ultimately to settle this question and live peacefully together. I did not want to keep the 5000 sq miles of West Pakistan territory. It would have antagonized the people of Pakistan and been a millstone round our neck. Besides, we have always preached against keeping territory occupied in war.' ... I believe she was afraid of rousing criticism in her own Party, and certainly in the BJP and the Opposition, if she settled on the LoC at that time, as we had been claiming the whole of PoK as Indian Territory (Indian Parliament resolution). But she could have stood firm on a final settlement along the LoC and Bhutto would have had to give in since he could not go back empty-handed to Pakistan (as his intelligence boss told an Indian friend at Simla).[11]

---

11 T.N. Kaul, *A Diplomat's Diary (1947–1999): The Tantalizing Triangle – China, India and USA* (Macmillan India Limited, 2000), pp. 116–17.

The views of M.K. Rasgotra, who was India's foreign secretary from 1982 to 1985, also make for incisive reading. These are reproduced from his book *A Life in Diplomacy*. He wrote:

> My view was the 90,000 prisoners of war were no leverage but a huge liability. We would have to feed them and look after them under the Geneva Protocol. By handing them over to Pakistan we might earn the goodwill of their families in Pakistan's Punjab and Frontier provinces. Back home in Pakistan, they would be an embarrassment for Bhutto's government. On the other hand the areas we occupied in Pakistan were of strategic importance and should have been handed back to Pakistan only after a satisfactory peace agreement was reached, especially on Kashmir. The goal in regard to Kashmir should be recognition of the new ceasefire line as international border. Everyone agreed to the last point, but on the other two points I was overruled.
>
> Nevertheless, I do not agree with those who say we won the war and lost the peace; that in my view is only partially true. Indian leaders wanted a bilaterally negotiated peace agreement without a third party's good offices. Since the Simla Agreement, the UN and all other meddlers in Kashmir have acknowledged that the issue is now squarely for India and Pakistan to settle between them. That was some progress, even though on the question of the new Line of Control (LoC) being treated as the international border in Kashmir, Bhutto had duped our negotiations, stricken by the Versailles Syndrome.
>
> We were in a position to clinch the issue and we failed to do so for fear of a breakdown of negotiations. Haksar, D.P. Dhar and P.N. Dhar wanted to be generous to the

defeated enemy. Heavens would not have fallen if Bhutto had gone back empty-handed. He or someone else could have come back to Simla to agree to a final division of Kashmir along the LoC as the international border. The wily Bhutto agreed orally and promised he would persuade his people to support his agreement, but went back and reneged on the unwritten commitment he had given to Prime Minister Gandhi. So Simla agreement remains a story of both great gains and lost opportunity.

Many years later I asked Haksar why he had placed such trust in Bhutto's oral promise. He said Bhutto had sought a private meeting with him, fallen at his feet and begged him not to send him back to be butchered by his enemies, trust him and his word of honour about the LoC being treated as the borer; he wanted time to sell the idea to his countrymen. Haksar then persuaded Indira Gandhi that Bhutto deserved her understanding and sympathy.[12]

Irrespective of what Bhutto promised Indira Gandhi in return for the repatriation of the prisoners and also the return of Pakistani territory in the western sector, he either went back on his word or could not convert the hardliners to his view. However, he gave PoK a Constitution with a prime ministerial system, replacing its existing form of government. He also scrapped the Ministry of Kashmir Affairs.

The fatal problem of the Simla Agreement was, in P.N. Dhar's words, as given in the book *Indira: The Life of Indira Nehru Gandhi* by Katherine Frank:

---

12 Maharaja Krishna Rasgotra, *A Life in Diplomacy* (New Delhi: Penguin Books India, 2019), p. 269.

... that it was dependent upon a continued occupation of their positions of power by the two leaders who had signed it ... there was also the presumption that Bhutto would stand by the verbal assurance [that the Line of Control would evolve into an international boundary] he had given Indira Gandhi ... The possibility that his political will might weaken, or that he might lose power did not seem to bother the Indian side, and no one at this point imagined a day when Indira Gandhi would not be in power.[13]

Although Mrs Gandhi thought Bhutto untrustworthy, she felt that he had spoken honestly about his own precarious situation and believed that he wanted peace with India.

Whatever the reasons behind Mrs Gandhi's thinking, India missed a golden opportunity to settle the Kashmir issue for good. The LoC should have been converted into the international border between India and Pakistan. To allay her fears about giving away the rest of PoK to Pakistan, Mrs Gandhi could well have discussed her reservations with her Cabinet while she was in Simla and assessed whether or not such a proposition would be accepted by the Parliament and the nation. This, unfortunately, she did not do. All in all, the Simla Agreement can be taken as both a success story and a failure.

Impact of the 1971 War and Birth of Islamic Jihad

The 1971 trauma impacted Pakistan's policy towards India in several major ways. Militarily, they understood that they would never be able to defeat India in a conventional war. Thus,

---

13 Katherine Frank, *Indira: The Life of Indira Nehru Gandhi* (New Delhi: Penguin Random House, 2019), p. 347.

developing nuclear capability became the ultimate objective for them. Bhutto famously said that Pakistan would develop nuclear capability even if in the process they were 'compelled to eat grass' because of the prohibitive financial burden. Importantly, they went nuclear overtly in 1998 in response to India's nuclear tests.

Pakistan also started working towards evolving other more workable options than a war in Kashmir. Psychological war, sabotage and subversion became their major tools. The Inter-Services Intelligence (ISI) began working towards shifting the religious orientation of Kashmiris from the more secular Sufi Islam to the more radical Sunni-Salafi-Wahabi Islam. In the process, they have over the years succeeded in the Islamization of Jammu and Kashmir, especially the Valley.

They also supported Sikh militancy in Punjab in the hope that a strong subversive situation in Punjab would leave Kashmir open to Pakistan.

Most importantly, Pakistan started placing greater reliance on China for diplomatic support and also as an equipment supplier for their armed forces. The friendship between them is need-based for both sides, and hence has acquired real solidity.

With the Afghanistan venture behind them by the end of 1989, it was an opportune time for Pakistan to focus their efforts once again on Kashmir. The strategy for that had been tried and tested in Afghanistan. It was the strategy of Islamic jihad.

4

Proxy War

'Terrorism is the preferred weapon of weak and evil men.'
— *Ronald Reagan*

'Asymmetrical warfare is a euphemism for terrorism, just like collateral damage is a euphemism for killing innocent civilians.'
— *Alan Dershowitz*

Indira Gandhi–Sheikh Abdullah Kashmir Accord, February 1975

The shift in the balance of power in the Indian subcontinent in favour of India after the Indo–Pakistan war of 1971 convinced Sheikh Abdullah that he had to settle the Kashmir issue with India on its terms. In 1974, Sheikh dropped his demand for autonomy as it had existed in 1953 and the Indira–Sheikh Accord was signed on behalf of Sheikh Abdullah by Mirza Mohammad Afzal Beg and on behalf of the Indian government by G. Parthasarathy on 24 February 1975 in New Delhi.

The three most important parts of the accord are reproduced here:

- The state of Jammu and Kashmir, which is a constituent unit of the Union of India, shall, in relation with the Union, continue to be governed by Article 370 of the Constitution of India.

- The residuary powers of legislation shall remain with the state; however, Parliament will continue to have the power to make laws relating to the prevention of activities directed towards disclaiming, questioning or disrupting the sovereignty and territorial integrity of India or bringing about secession of a part of the territory of India from the Union or causing insult to the Indian national flag, the Indian national anthem and the Constitution.

- Where any provision of the Constitution of India had been applied to the state of Jammu and Kashmir with adaptations and modifications, such adaptations and modifications can be altered or repealed by an order of the president under Article 370, each individual proposal in its behalf being considered on its merit, but provisions of the Constitution of India already applied to the state of Jammu and Kashmir without adaption or modification are unalterable.[1]

This accord virtually sealed the constitutional status quo of Jammu and Kashmir existing on date with a few sops granted to them for internal functioning. Even the symbolic designations of Sadr-i-Riyasat in lieu of governor and prime minister in lieu of chief minister had already been dropped. Over a period, twenty-eight

---

1 Sumantra Bose, *Kashmir: Roots of Conflict, Path to Peace* (Cambridge, Massachusetts: Harvard University Press, 2009), p. 88.

constitutional amendments had been made and more than 300 central laws had been imposed in the state in the interim. This also made the 1953 accord irrelevant. The 1975 accord had the backing of the people and the subsequent election results are an indicator of that. In the 1977 elections, Sheikh's National Conference won forty out of forty-two seats.

Farooq Abdullah–Rajiv Gandhi Accord, November 1986

The background to the March 1987 Jammu and Kashmir Legislative Assembly election was fraught with complexities. While Sheikh Abdullah was imprisoned, his loyalists had split from the National Conference and formed the All Jammu and Kashmir Plebiscite Front, or Plebiscite Front. The remaining members of the National Conference merged their party with the Congress. It will also be relevant to note that prior to 1987 there were only two major parties in J&K, namely, the Congress and the National Conference. The Congress represented Hindus, Shias, Gujjars, Bakarwals, Buddhists and rich Sunni Muslims who had developed business links outside the state. The National Conference had its following amongst Sunnis, who were largely in the Valley, with some also settled in parts of the Rajouri–Poonch areas.

After Sheikh Abdullah's release and his accord with Indira Gandhi in 1975, he was elected as the state's chief minister with the help of the Congress. However, during the 1977 election, Abdullah revived the National Conference and ditched the Congress. He scored an impressive win in the assembly elections.

In 1981, Sheikh installed his son Farooq Abdullah as his heir apparent. Farooq became the president of the National Conference in the same year. Sheikh Abdullah died on 8 September 1982 and Farooq took over. Farooq spurned the offer of a coalition with the Congress to fight the 1983 elections. The National Conference won forty-six seats, sweeping the Valley. The Congress won twenty-six seats in the Jammu region. However, the elections became notorious for rigging and the violence during their conduct.

In the state, Farooq Abdullah played to the gallery and wittingly or unwittingly also played into the hands of the dissatisfied lobby by accepting the rapid spread of madrasas teaching fundamentalist philosophy, predominantly in the Valley.

During this period, there were internal rumblings within the National Conference and a split came about by a faction led by Ghulam Mohammad Shah, Sheikh Abdullah's son-in-law. In the assembly, Farooq lost the majority and G.M. Shah was sworn in as the chief minister, with the support of the Congress. In March 1986, however, the Congress withdrew its support and the Shah government fell, which necessitated another election in March 1987.

This led to an accord between Farooq and Rajiv Gandhi. It will be relevant to mention here that the Indira–Sheikh Accord had generated an internal struggle in Kashmir politics. The Plebiscite Front was wound up, and India got political mileage out of this development in the international forums. But in reality, politically Kashmir slipped into the hands of sympathizers of the Plebiscite Front. The pro-Pakistan forces were rehabilitated and allowed to sneak into key positions.

Rajiv Gandhi, however, failed to pick up on these signals and the situation prevailing in Kashmir. He rehabilitated Farooq, whom some members of the Parliament had described as a security risk as he was allegedly in touch with forces inimical to India.

It is with this backdrop that the Rajiv–Farooq Accord was reached in November 1986. It was an unwritten accord, 'a mere declaration to work together and form a coalition government of the National Conference and the Congress'. There was an internal understanding that power could be shared in the ratio of 60:40, with the National Conference getting 60 per cent of the seats.

Broadly, the Valley was left for the National Conference, while Ladakh, Kargil and Jammu (except Poonch and Rajouri) were left for the Congress. Seats were to be shared between the National Conference and the Congress in Poonch and Rajouri.

Jagmohan, the then governor, has in his book *My Frozen Turbulence in Kashmir* called this coalition 'another reflex of spurious democracy and the habit of nursing illusions'.[2] He felt that both parties had joined hands to serve their selfish ends and whatever good work had been done under the governor's rule was thus undone. Scholar Sten Widmalm, in his book *Kashmir in Comparative Perspective: Democracy and Violent Separatism in India*, stated that this amounted to the state's two largest parties joining hands to form an election cartel so that the discontent in the state remained invisible.

When the 1987 elections were held, the Muslim United Front's (MUF) Syed Mohammed Yusuf Shah was a candidate from the Amira Kadal constituency of Srinagar. As the vote counting began, it became clear that Yusuf Shah was a clear winner by a landslide. His opponent, Ghulam Mohiuddin Shah, lost. However, in a couple of hours, this decision was reversed, and Mohiuddin Shah was declared the winner. Yusuf Shah and his supporters were arrested and held in custody till the end of 1987.

Similarly, there were many constituencies such as Bijbehara and Shopian where MUF lost narrowly. There was no doubt in the minds of the national and international media that the elections had been heavily rigged. The total number of votes by which the National Conference and Congress candidates were declared winners far exceeded the actual tally of votes of a constituency when the winners' and losers' votes were added. The winning margins were unrealistic.

---

2   Jagmohan, *My Frozen Turbulence in Kashmir*, p. 163.

Jagmohan, in his book *My Frozen Turbulence in Kashmir* (p. 109), records, 'The coalition parties swept the poll. But the fairness of these elections was doubted by a sizeable section of the people. Because of this and many other fundamental reasons, the storm started gathering in the Valley and engulfed it with full force in the second half of 1989.'

This massive rigging shook the faith of the people in the elections and the democratic process. The 1987 election was a watershed election, sowing the seeds of a full-blown, Pakistan-sponsored insurgency. The ISI stepped in the muddy waters and started their manipulations, as they were at that time also disengaging from their involvement in Afghanistan following the Soviet withdrawal in 1989.

After the 1987 elections, Abdul Ghani Lone became a separatist leader and stated that many young people had, out of frustration with the democratic process, decided to go for an armed struggle. Hizbul Mujahideen, or just HM, was formed in 1989. It is one of the largest and oldest militant groups in Jammu and Kashmir. This group is led by Mohammad Yusuf Shah, the same person who was defeated in Amira Kadal through the rigged election in 1987. He is also known by his alias Syed Salahuddin.

Jagmohan, in his book *My Frozen Turbulence in Kashmir*, gives a detailed account of how Farooq Abdullah had lost control over the administration. A gist is presented here to indicate how the security situation was allowed to drift.

- In May 1989, the Governor recorded that the youth is sullen and angry. It is taking refuge under religion ... (p. 124 of the book).
- In April and May 1989, Jagmohan wrote twice to Rajiv Gandhi drawing his attention to critical conditions as follows: (i) The

situation is fast deteriorating. It has almost reached a point of no return ... (p. 124) (ii) In his letter of 14 May 1989: 'From May 8 to 13, there have been 14 bomb blasts and six cases of firing and cross firing ... During the Hartal period (strike) no worthwhile, activity has been visible at the political front to counter the move of subversionists ...' (p. 125) (iii) Alliance has gained in Valley (p. 337).

- In the issue of 23 November 1989, the *Times of India* commented: 'There seems to be a strange conspiracy of silence about the reign of terror, subversion and lawlessness in the once happy and now apparently helpless valley of Kashmir' (p. 337–38).
- The *Hindustan Times* in its issue of 17 December 1989 wrote: 'The all-powerful National Conference, which claims to have cadre in every village of the valley, has miserably failed to fight terrorism ... (p. 338).
- There were numerous such write-ups in the media about the spread of terrorism in the countryside.

Farooq Abdullah's coalition government lacked legitimacy, and the Valley sank into a 'morass of frustration and radicalization'. A cycle of violence and protests took hold, steadily rising in tempo. In January 1990, the Farooq Abdullah government was dismissed and governor's rule imposed. This spell of governor's rule lasted till 2007. This closed the chapter on the Rajiv–Farooq accord.

The Launch of Militancy in J&K

Five major developments took place internationally that helped in the launch of a proxy war and it taking root first in the Valley and later progressively in other parts of the state.

Firstly, the Soviets invaded Afghanistan in 1979. This gave Pakistan a golden opportunity to offer its services to the US as a frontline state that could provide launch pads from where the US could initiate irregular warfare to defeat the Soviets. For this, Pakistan's ISI used mercenaries from all over the Islamic world. By the time the Soviets finally pulled out from Afghanistan in May 1988, Pakistan had mastered the art of irregular/hybrid warfare. From thereon, Pakistan regarded Afghanistan as its strategic depth in case of an Indian offensive. On the withdrawal of the Russians, Pakistan was gifted large quantities of sophisticated arms and equipment by the US, including MI-16 armoured personnel carriers, and guns and radars.

Secondly, in 1977, General Zia-ul-Haq took over as the president of Pakistan. Zia aligned with Saudi Arabia and in return got recognition in the Islamic world and also financial support from Saudi Arabia. Pakistani military engagement started when its special services participated in the operation to eliminate fundamentalist elements that seized the Grand Mosque in Mecca in 1979. Later as part of defence cooperation with Saudi Arabia based on a 1982 bilateral protocol, troops have been deployed in training and advisory roles. Tens of thousands of Pakistani troops remained in Saudi Arabia during the Iran-Iraq war. Most were recalled after the war ended in 1988. The two countries' close ties were tested in 2015 when the Pakistani parliament unanimously rejected a Saudi request for Pakistani troops to support its Yemen campaign.

Thirdly, in the late seventies, Pakistan sowed the seeds of militancy in Punjab through the supply of arms and drugs as well as financial support. It is indeed surprising that a community as patriotic as the Punjabis could be misled by religious zealots. Ultimately, this movement died down, but India paid a heavy price. Pakistan's ISI was now doubly reassured of its capabilities.

Fourthly, Zia-ul-Haq became certain that through an Islamic jihad, Pakistan would be able to beat India in Kashmir and take revenge for the 1971 debacle. To start the proxy war, he had mercenaries from other Islamic countries available. They believed, though erroneously, that with the help of dissatisfied Kashmiris, they would be able to create enough unrest to spur the breakaway of Kashmir from India.

Finally, with the development of nuclear weapons in 1999, Pakistan meshed their 'strategy of proxy war (which was started in 1989) with a nuclear overhang'. This meant that India was denied the advantage of its conventional superiority as Pakistan threatened to use nuclear weapons in response to the use of any conventional force by India across the LoC in reaction to acts of proxy war. Since then, they have also introduced tactical nukes, which have added another dimension to the situation.

Pakistan has been at war with India ever since its creation. Parity and security were the pillars of the flight of fancy of Jinnah and the Muslim League at the time of Partition. From the time Bhutto signed the Simla Agreement, it became clear that militarily, Pakistan would never be able to annex Kashmir. They had to evolve another strategy and be prepared for a long-drawn struggle.

Soon they came up with a plan that was based on a few key strategies. The first was attaining nuclear capability, which was the highest priority. Second was to launch a proxy war in the Valley and other parts of Kashmir to generate local disturbances and a demand for secession from India. The experience gained in Afghanistan would be a big help in this plan, which was to provide the Pakistan deep state a 'low-cost option'. This strategy was further strengthened with the development of nuclear weapons. Thirdly, Pakistan was to be militarily prepared to deter Indian conventional designs. The development of nuclear capability would also act as a cover for both the conventional forces and the proxy war. And finally, Pakistan would work to turn the Sufi Islam of the Valley into radicalized Islam, which would be a great force multiplier.

Operation Topac

In 1984, General Zia-ul-Haq had tasked the ISI with evolving a plan, which was to exploit the political space in the valley. This operation was to commence in 1990. This was given the code name 'Operation Topac'. The strategy had three phases. Under the first phase, Pakistan was to spur militancy in Kashmir, which India calls a 'proxy war' because of the total involvement of the Pakistani state. The intensity of this militancy was to be regulated such that the state government continued to function and was not removed by the Centre. The subversion of the police force, financial institutions and educational institutions, among others, was also to be attempted. These actions would serve to create overall unrest of the kind wherein there was youth-led rioting, which would bring the Valley to a point where it would be ready for secession.

As part of the second phase, Pakistan would start exerting pressure along the LoC when the state was already deeply infected by terrorism and there was a state of unrest. At this stage, they were to start engaging the Indian army and divert its attention to the LoC, to defend its own establishments, thereby reducing the army to a fortress mentality and tying it down on the ground. When the situation became ripe, Pakistan would take some major military action to deliver a final push. The timing of the Kargil misadventure in May 1999 was perfect for Pakistan for that final push.

In the final phase, Pakistan hoped to create a mini-Islamic state and cleanse the Valley of the Kashmiri Pandits and other Hindus.[3] In the final analysis, the cleansing was achieved in 1990, a little over a year after the start of Operation Topac. It speaks poorly of

---

3 Maroof Raza and Iqbal Chand Malhotra, *Kashmir's Untold Story: Declassified* (New Delhi: Bloomsbury, 2019), p. 139.

India that Pakistan succeeded so quickly. This failing really needs to be closely examined as a lesson for the future.

The Siachen operation was also a part of Pakistan's masterplan but was pre-empted by India when its troops occupied the glacier on 13 April 1984. The Kargil operation was ultimately a disaster for Pakistan and brought shame on them when they were reduced to disowning the bodies of their soldiers from the Northern Light Infantry battalions, which had taken part in the Kargil operations.

The Kashmir problem today is a manifestation of Zia's plans and ambitions. Where Pakistan's strategy has been a big success is that it has kept the militancy dynamic in nature. It has constantly changed its aims and goalposts in accordance with the need of the day.

Three major problems that are the direct consequence of Operation Topac are the start of militancy in the state, the ethnic cleansing of the Valley, and the deep radicalization of the Valley and the snuffing out of Sufism.

Once Pakistan had evolved its strategy of fuelling militancy in the Valley, it decided to use the mercenaries with them. They were to be infiltrated across the LoC with the assistance of the Pakistani army. In the Valley they had already established links with members of the Jamait (a fundamentalist group), who were to assist these infiltrators. The necessary groundwork had already been done. Thus began the onslaught of the Pakistan-perpetrated proxy war in J&K.

The Beginning: 1989–93

Consequent to the introduction of the Resettlement Bill by Sheikh Abdullah in 1982 (this bill has not been accorded consent by the President or decided upon by the Supreme Court, which stayed its operation; also, this bill is among the 153 state laws and Governor's

Acts abolished under the J&K Reorganization Act 2019), it is believed by the people of J&K that around 2,500 Kashmiris from PoK were allowed to return to the Valley by Farooq Abdullah when he became chief minister of J&K in 1982. Some of them may have been selected and trained by the ISI for subversive activities, including religious purification, meaning poisoning the minds of Kashmiris and infecting them with Islamic fundamentalism.

It is a historical fact that from day one after Independence, Pakistan had been focused on grabbing J&K by all possible means. The ISI had opened a large number of camps to indoctrinate and poison the minds of Kashmiris with Islamic fundamentalism. Various wars fought from 1947 onwards and long history of proxy war bear testimony to this.

However, the present situation is that using the J&K Reorganisation Act 2019, the central government has scrapped this old law that permitted the return of J&K residents who fled to Pakistan between 1947 and 1954. Abdur Rahim Rather, a senior National Conference leader and former J&K law minister, has said that since the Resettlement Act has been abolished, the doors have been shut for the return of any J&K refugees from Pakistan, and it is a closed chapter now.

From 1989 onwards, a large number of terrorists were infiltrated across the LoC by the ISI with the full support of the Pakistani army. There was open defiance of the government's authority in the Valley. Youth with Kalashnikovs on their shoulders were a common sight. The year 1990 was the time when the proxy war gained substantial ground. The state government machinery and the private sector were terrorized and had virtually stopped functioning. The terrorists followed a systematic approach, destroying infrastructure, telephone and telegraph offices, schools and colleges and looting banks. Television and radio stations had stopped functioning regularly. The police were targeted and were demoralized.

The terrorists also burnt cinemas, beauty parlours and video libraries. The idea was to create a breakdown of law and order. Furthermore, the political turbulence because of the botched elections of 1987 had provided a god-sent opportunity for the spread of general discontent. At this time, some prominent leaders who had a saner voice, such as Maulana Madodi, the Mirwaiz-e-Kashmir; Maulvi Farooq, chairman of the All Jammu and Kashmir Awami Action Committee; Dr Qazi Nissar, the Mirwaiz of south Kashmir; and Dr Abdul Ahmed Guru, the vice chancellor of Kashmir University, were assassinated.

Things really came to a head when Dr Rubaiya Sayeed, the daughter of Mufti Mohammad Sayeed (from Kashmir), the home minister of India, was kidnapped at 3.45 p.m. on 8 December 1989, about 500 m from her home near Naugam when she was returning from the hospital in a local minibus. Her release was obtained four days later through the exchange of five militant leaders. Hereafter, the militants recognized this form of coercion to be an effective tool because of the capitulation by the government.

Another major development that took place with traumatic effect was that the Hindus of the Kashmir Valley, a large majority of whom were Kashmiri Pandits, were forced to flee the Valley in 1990. This was the result of their being targeted by the Jammu Kashmir Liberation Front (JKLF) and Islamist insurgents during late 1989 and early 1990. Almost 4,00,000 Kashmiri Pandits were dislodged. They were initially housed in camps in Jammu and its surrounding areas. Most families were resettled in Jammu, the National Capital Region (NCR) and other neighbouring states. This development was indeed a blot on the prestige of the national and state governments. The Pandits have not returned to the Valley even after thirty years, and it is unlikely that they will return in the foreseeable future, if at all.

A fear psychosis was generated by the killing of many Pandits in the Valley and their exile. Militants had thus gained ascendancy by the early nineties, with the all-out support of Pakistan, and the insurgency was brought to a high pitch.

Armed Forces Special Powers Act (AFSPA)

As a result of this wave of terror in the Valley, the Armed Forces Special Powers Act (AFSPA) was enacted in J&K in September 1990. The intensity of the violence had reached such a crescendo that the law-and-order machinery collapsed in the Valley and was unable to tackle the rising armed militancy. There was no option left but to induct the army in the state to restore law and order.

The AFSPA gives the armed forces special power to maintain law and order in a state or areas declared as 'disturbed areas' under the provisions of this act. According to the Disturbed Areas Act, 1976, an area once declared disturbed has to maintain status quo and it cannot be revoked before three months.

The Jammu and Kashmir AFSPA 1990 is an emergency law that gives legal cover to the armed forces operating in disturbed areas from prosecution. The act, however, has had its share of controversies, and thirty-one years after AFSPA was enforced in J&K, it remains a bone of contention in the militancy-hit state. There is a demand for its abrogation.

However, it is essential to get the correct perspective on this act before taking a call on whether it should be abrogated or not in J&K.

Section (3) of the AFSPA empowers the governor of that state or the administrator of that union territory or the central government to issue an official notification in the Gazette of

India to declare the area as disturbed, following which the Centre has the authority to send in the armed forces in aid of the civil administration.

The Constitution of India empowers state governments to declare a state of emergency due to one or more of the following reasons: a failure of the administration and the local police to tackle local issues; the de-induction of (central) security forces leading to a return of miscreants/erosion of the 'peace dividend'; or if the scale of unrest or instability in the state is too large for local forces to handle.

In such cases, it is the prerogative of the state government to call for central help. AFSPA can be enacted only when a state, or part of it, is declared a 'disturbed area'. Continued unrest, as in the cases of militancy and insurgency, especially when borders are threatened, are situations where AFSPA is resorted to.

The AFSPA has come under intense criticism. Some people allege that it violates fundamental rights.

Some of the objections include that Section 4 (a), under which the army is authorized to shoot-to-kill to protect itself and prevent the destruction of national property, violates the right to Article 21, the right to life. Section 4 (b), 'search without warrant', violates the right to liberty and Article 22. The dispersion of civil assembly by armed forces under Section 121 violates the right to assembly. The fact that the permission of a judicial magistrate is not required to make an arrest violates Article 22. Finally, the special powers of AFSPA also override the Code of Criminal Procedure (CrPC). It is agreed that the handling of insurgent and extremist activities in disturbed areas needs special powers and these special powers are also to preserve country's integrity and uphold law and order.

On the other hand, the army insists on AFSPA because if the troops do not have the legal protection offered under the act, the state would fail to protect its own army from the legal cases that can arise as a result of the discharge of legal and legitimate duties by the armed forces.

Further, it is important to know that AFSPA was legislated as an act of Parliament. It has been approved by the Supreme Court, and the army has issued 'dos and don'ts' for the guidance of troops in the conduct of operations. The chief of army staff has issued directions for operations based on the guidelines from the Supreme Court in the form of the 'Ten Commandments' for troops to follow. Any failure to follow these is severely punishable. (The dos and don'ts and the Ten Commandments are given at Appendix B.)

If AFSPA is repealed or diluted, the armed forces will no longer have legal protection when operating in the proxy war environment. It would be wrong to deploy the army under such circumstances as the morale of the armed forces would be gravely affected and they may even shy away from engagements. Even now, the Supreme Court's directions are to investigate each encounter. It is demoralizing for soldiers to be required to answer for their actions in the courts (instead of the command structure of the army and the government) when carrying out operations in the interest of the state. Already, there are around 700 cases of officers and men who have gone to the Supreme Court with regard to the limitations imposed on the discharge of their duties in case of removal of AFSPA. There can be no denying the fact that this trend of men fighting for their rights, rather than the organization doing so for them, will undermine the discipline and morale of the armed forces.

The armed forces are very conscious of the fact that they cannot afford to fail when called upon to safeguard the country's integrity. Proper legislation to protect them is a must; otherwise their efforts may fall short and the terrorists may seize the initiative.

The AFSPA is not an anti-people act and does not provide the army the licence to act with impunity. Fake (non-genuine or unjustifiable) encounters, extra-judicial killings and rape and sexual assault are all punishable crimes.

Further, armies all around the world thrive on discipline. The Indian army is acknowledged the world over as one of the finest and the best. The record of the Indian army as part of the UN peacekeeping forces is a testimony to the above statement. In addition to this, the army's own disciplinary mechanism is of very high standards. To illustrate, in 2017–18 the army started court martial proceedings against six personnel, and these have since been finalized and the guilty punished. There is a constant effort to improve discipline in the force. This is obvious from a marked decline in allegations, which dropped from 1,170 between 1990 and 1999, to 226 between 2000 and 2004, then to six in 2010 and to only four in 2011. As per an *Economic Times* report of 20 October 2010, quoting the Brigadier General Staff of Northern Command, as many as 1,514 FIRs had been been registered against army personnel for alleged human rights violations in the past 20 years of militancy, of which 97 per cent were found false. Only 35 cases (2.3 per cent of total cases) were found true and the guilty punished. No authentic figures are available for the subsequent period at this stage. It also needs to be understood that many a times public interest litigations (PILs) can also serve as a stratagem to dissuade the army from acting. Indeed, false allegations of human rights violations may sometimes be made against security forces.

It has always been the army's recommendation that as soon as the security situation starts improving in the state, AFSPA should be withdrawn gradually from those areas and the army disengaged. To illustrate, the situation could be considered to have improved sufficiently for the removal of AFSPA when tourism picks up in the state and it sees, say, over 6–8 million tourists a year, over and above the pilgrims for the Amarnath Yatra. The second acid test could be that violence in the Valley drops to such a level that the Kashmiri Pandits feel confident enough to return to their homes. The return of the Pandits should be the objective and a final indicator of normalcy having returned to the state.

Notwithstanding the controversy surrounding the AFSPA, the army was able to alleviate the situation in the state, and by the end of 1993, the security forces had regained significant control and put the militants on the defensive.

Pakistan had initially utilized the JKLF to help realize its aims, but by this time it had started depending heavily on the Hizbul Mujahideen, and the JKLF's prominence reduced considerably.

Launch of a Full-blown Proxy War: 1993–96

In terms of religious status, Srinagar's Hazratbal mosque, which houses what is believed to be a hair of Prophet Muhammad, is to the Kashmiri Muslims what the Golden Temple is to the Sikhs. On 15 October 1993, information was received that forty terrorists had entered the mosque and were in the process of opening the locks of the room where the Holy Relic was placed. There were 120 civilians inside the mosque at that time. They were taken hostage by the terrorists. Their tactics were obvious; they wanted the security forces to attack, take possession of the mosque, release the hostages and, in the process, damage the mosque. The security forces did not fall into the terrorists' trap and instead laid a siege. Subsequently, food was supplied to both the hostages and the terrorists under a court order. Telephone lines were restored inside the shrine for the hostages, but these were also used by the terrorists for massive propaganda, to great effect. In the meanwhile, negotiations with the terrorists were in process, and on the fifteenth day, the siege ended with safe passage granted to the terrorists, but without their weapons. This operation brought out the lack of coordination amongst various security and government agencies.

The rise of terrorism in the Valley was obvious. Consequently, governor's rule, which had been imposed in January 1990, continued till October 1996, when the democratic process was restored in the state. The situation had been brought under reasonable control by then.

Also in 1990, additional paramilitary forces such as the Central Reserve Police Force (CRPF) and the Border Security Force (BSF) were inducted in the state along with the army. Gradually, the security grid was extended south of the Pir Panjal, initially towards Bhadarwah, Kishtwar and Doda, and subsequently to the entire Jammu province as militancy spread in those areas as well.

A major step that was taken to ensure better control and coordination amongst various security and administrative agencies was the setting up of the Unified Headquarters in mid 1993 for the areas north of the Pir Panjal. Subsequently, it was also set up for areas to the south of the Pir Panjal. It was headed by the chief minister (initially by the governor because of governor's rule up to 1996). The other members of the Unified Headquarters included the chief secretary, the respective corps commanders as security advisors, select personnel from civil intelligence agencies and heads of the CRPF, BSF and civil police. The corps commanders were designated as operational group commanders. The Unified Headquarters also provided a platform to share intelligence and lay down broad operational guidelines for counter-insurgency (CI) operations. It also helped to establish civil authority in the cities and rural areas. The Unified Headquarters has worked successfully, even though there are areas where further improvements could be made.

By the middle of 1994, an effective CI grid was functional in the areas both north and south of the Pir Panjal. The security forces had regained control of all cities and rural areas. However, infiltration across the border continued, and in a year, between 2,500 to over 3,000 terrorists were crossing over the LoC and operating inside the state. The major challenge for the security forces was to check infiltration. By 1995–96, however, the security forces had regained reasonable control and the civilian population was somewhat disillusioned with the terrorists because of their blatant abuse of human rights.

By 1995, the central government had started thinking of restoring the political process in the state. In May 1995, in a desperate bid to delay the political process and prove their own relevance, the foreign terrorists took control of another holy shrine, that of Hazrat Sheikh Noor-ud-Din at Charar-e-Sharief, in Budgam district, approximately 40 km from Srinagar. Hazrat Sheikh Noor-ud-Din is a revered poet-saint of the fifteenth century. He was popularly known as Nund Rishi and was worshipped by both Muslims and Hindus alike.

Security forces laid siege to the shrine while the terrorists were holed up inside. Unfortunately, because of the terrain, a close cordon, as was done at the Hazratbal shrine, was not possible. The terrorists, led by the notorious Mast Gul, set the shrine on fire on the night of 10 May 1995 and tried to escape. Twenty militants were killed in the ensuing fight. Some, including Mast Gul, managed to escape. The shrine, which was mostly a wooden construction, was, however, gutted. Not allowing the media access to the shrine was a blunder, as it gave way to lots of damaging rumours.

It was during this period (1993 onwards) that a splinter group of the erstwhile Plebiscite Front and twenty-seven other such groups joined together to form the All Parties Hurriyat Conference (APHC). The APHC has been a staunch pro-Pakistan group. It claims to be fighting for the Kashmiris' right of self-determination with the populist slogan of 'azadi' or freedom. It essentially draws its support from the Jamaat-e-Islami and its mentors in Pakistan.

APHC has had varying degrees of importance at different stages. However, it has never had the confidence to join the electoral process and fight elections.

Another important aspect is that more and more foreign terrorists with first-hand experience in Afghanistan were inducted to boost the turbulence in the state. Hizbul Mujahideen, the largest indigenous terrorist group, had suffered the maximum casualties and its morale was low. The ISI also started giving greater importance and financial support to groups such as Lashkar-e-Taiba (LeT), Harkat-ul-Mujahideen (HUM) and Harkat-ul-Jihad-i-Islami (HUJI). In this period, however, a large number of surrendered militants were won over by the intelligence agencies and they began to assist the security forces. The foreign terrorists changed their tactics and started avoiding direct confrontation with security forces. They started placing more reliance on improvised explosive devices (IEDs). However, the security forces were quick in their response and started acquiring and deploying electronic jammers, thus rendering the IEDs largely ineffective.

Return to Near Normalcy: 1996–99

In May 1996, parliamentary elections were conducted successfully. These were followed by state elections in J&K. Farooq Abdullah's National Conference won the elections, which were internationally regarded as fair. The establishment of a credible civil government was a dampener for the militancy. Farooq's government managed to increase its tally during the 1998 parliamentary elections, with the help of arrangements with some smaller political parties and independents. Farooq also joined the National Democratic Alliance (NDA) that had come to power in the Centre. Around this time, the Peoples Democratic Party (PDP) also emerged on the political scene. It was led by veteran politician Mufti Mohammad Sayeed, the former home minister of India.

Overall, militancy steadily declined during 1997–98, even though Pakistan's propaganda machinery continued to paint a rosy picture. The kill ratio between militants and the security forces was around six militants to one soldier. The General Headquarters (GHQ) of the Pakistani army and the ISI must have seen intense discussions to find some method to give a fillip to the proxy war, which was not going the way they would have liked. Thus was born the strategy of launching the Kargil offensive, which was to cost them dearly in due course.

Another noteworthy development during this time was the publishing of the State Autonomy Commission's report. A little backdrop to the 1996 elections would be in order to understand the issue of the *Autonomy Report*. No election had been held in the state between 1987 and 1996. Without the participation of the National Conference, the elections would not have been meaningful and without Dr Farooq Abdullah, the National Conference would not have participated. So Dr Abdullah was brought back from England, where his family was living, but with a tacit understanding. According to Dr Abdullah, the understanding was that after the elections 'the state could carry out a study on their demand for autonomy', which the Centre would consider. The National Conference fought the election with autonomy as its election plank, as according to him this was part of the understanding. The study was carried out and it advocated 'a series of constitutional and legislative measures to restore the political autonomy which they claimed that Jammu and Kashmir was guaranteed at the time of its accession'. In 2000, Dr Abdullah had a resolution passed in the assembly for the restoration of autonomy to the pre-1953 status for the state in accordance with the *Autonomy Report*, pending approval from the president of India.

This report, which was approved by the state legislative assembly, drew harsh reactions from mainstream political parties in India. The BJP declared itself to be 'totally against' the demand for autonomy for J&K, and insisted that it be rejected outright. The then BJP president, Kushabhau Thakre, also warned that any return to a pre-1953 status for Kashmir would lead to disintegration and instability in the country, because in addition to J&K, various other states were bound to seek autonomy. The Rashtriya Swayamsevak Sangh (RSS) denounced it as 'a step short of actual secession' and demanded that the Vajpayee government should keep all options open, including the dismissal of the state government. Shiv Sena supremo Bal Thackeray characterized Dr Abdullah's advocacy as 'traitorous', in fact a move towards 'another partition of India'. The Congress (I) also rejected the report. The report received limited support only from the Left parties. Within the state, the Jammu and Ladakh regions were not at all in agreement with this proposition.

The adverse and aggressive response that this report got in the national media and from the various political parties discouraged the central government from even discussing it, leave aside advancing it. This created a fair amount of distrust between Dr Farooq Abdullah and the central government, which Dr Abdullah never got over. Farooq's failure to secure the progress of the *Autonomy Report* led to certain political developments in the state in due course. In April 2001, K.C. Pant, a renowned political leader, was appointed by the Government of India to talk to people of all shades in Kashmir.

The Kargil War: 8 May 1999 – 26 July 1999[4]

The success of the security force's operations and the flourishing of the democratic process in the state were a cause of great worry to the ISI and the GHQ of the Pakistani army. The planning in the GHQ must have been based on the appreciation that there

---

4   Author's note: In another book being planned by the author, there will be a detailed chapter on the Kargil war. Here only those details are given that had a direct impact on the militancy.

was an urgent need to draw away the bulk of the Indian army from the security and CI grid in the Valley to reduce pressure on the militants. This was necessary for them to regain initiative. The operation that was planned as a result of these calculations, however, turned out to be only a momentary gain but with huge international embarrassment for Pakistan in the subsequent period.

The operation – Operation Badr – was thus launched by the Pakistani army at a time when the insurgency was somewhat flagging in Jammu and Kashmir. The militants were losing confidence in the Pakistani army as they felt that the latter's contribution was limited to exchanging fire across the LoC to assist in the militants' infiltration. There was thus pressure from the militants on the Pakistani army to play a more active role.

In their operational planning, the intruders tried to copy the Indian model of occupying the Siachen heights, from which they could not be dislodged by Pakistani forces. Their plan was to move through the adverse terrain in bad weather conditions and occupy the heights along National Highway 1A, from Zojila to Kargil and Batalik. From there, they would be in a position to interfere effectively with the traffic on the road from Dras to Kargil and thereby stop movement along this lifeline of logistic support for the Indian troops deployed in the Kargil–Ladakh sector. The other supply route along Rohtang Pass in Himachal Pradesh was not yet fully functional. Over and above this, both these routes remained closed during the winter months. Pakistan surmised that this closure of logistic support would render Indian positions in the Kargil sector untenable and impact even Ladakh adversely.

They had also assessed that the Indian army was tired and would hardly be in a position to dislodge them from these tortuous heights even if they took the risk of moving out large numbers of troops from the CI grid in the Valley for these operations. And, with the

Valley's CI grid unsettled, it would fall easily with the support of the locals. This was another huge miscalculation on Pakistan's part.

The Pakistanis had perhaps overlooked the fact that India had raised and deployed a large number of Rashtriya Rifles (RR) battalions in the Valley to hold the CI grid and provide continuity. When 8 Mountain Division was moved to Kargil, it was relieved by 6 Mountain Division, which had been immediately inducted from the hinterland on the discovery of Pakistani soldiers on the Kargil heights. The Indian army started preparing for a full-fledged war against Pakistan in Kashmir, and 6 Mountain Division was retained in the Valley, predominantly as a 'threat in being' against Pakistan. The director general of RR was deputed to handle militancy in Kashmir and relieve GOC 15 corps so he could look after the main operations in the Kargil sector. Pakistan's strategy to unsettle the CI grid had failed. Very soon, 8 Mountain Division, under a brilliant commander, Major General (later Lieutenant General) Mohinder Puri, laid their plans and rehearsed drills to dislodge the Pakistani troops from the Kargil heights. It certainly took some time for the army to switch from insurgency mode to operational mode, both psychologically and physically. The entire operation, named Operation Vijay, lasted from 3 May to 26 July 1999 (two months, three weeks and two days). The Indian army learnt the important lesson that the operational grid should never be disturbed to make troops available for insurgency operations as Pakistan could never be trusted. In case of necessity, an alternative arrangement should be made.

In the final analysis, the Dras–Kargil–Batalik hills were recaptured by India, and Pakistan suffered huge international embarrassment. The biggest gain was that the battle displayed India's resolve to the entire world that it would never allow Pakistan or any other power to meddle in its internal affairs. Pakistan's control over the mujahideen and their direct involvement in fomenting the proxy war in Kashmir was also exposed to the world.

Pakistan's then prime minister, Nawaz Sharif, had to make a dash to the US to seek then President Bill Clinton's intervention to get India to agree to the withdrawal of the terrorists to Pakistan's side of the LoC. Ultimately, the Kargil misadventure also set the stage for the overthrow of Prime Minister Nawaz Sharif in a military coup and General Musharraf assuming power on 12 October 1999. Altaf Gauhar, a renowned Pakistani journalist, was indeed expressive when he called the operation a 'panga', meaning an uncalled-for risky adventure that was likely to backfire on the initiator.

Back to the Proxy War: 1999–2003

Pakistan's response to the failure of Operation Badr in Kargil was to revert to its time-tested tool of cross-border terrorism with renewed vigour. The escalation of the militancy involved both the qualitative and quantitative upgrade of the equipment, manpower and tactics used by the terrorists operating under Pakistan's control. The Pakistan- and PoK-based terrorist organizations such as LeT and HUM were given ascendency over the indigenously predominant 'tanzeems' such as Hizbul Mujahideen and JKLF. Frequency-hopping radio sets capable of coded burst transmissions were introduced to prevent interception and monitoring of important terrorist links. More sophisticated radio-controlled IEDs, capable of defeating the IED-neutralizing devices in use, were introduced along with the greater use of claymore mines.

Its activities focused on suicide attacks by fanatical elements on isolated security posts and , government institutions and offices. These created a greater psychological impact. It also targeted suspected informers and counterterrorist groups (Ikhwans). It carried out select killings of politicians and other renowned personalities who spoke against them. Finally, it resorted to periodic civilian massacres to spread fear and despondency.

No narrative of the insurgency in Kashmir would be complete without mentioning Mohammad Yusuf Parray, better known as Kuka Parray, and his role and efforts towards the restoration of peace in J&K.

Parray was a former member of the legislative assembly (MLA). He was a pioneer of the counter-insurgency movement in Kashmir and the founder of the Jammu and Kashmir Awami League. He established a pro-India militant outfit, Ikhwan-ul-Muslimeen, which targeted top pro-Pakistani militants. By 1994, a section of JKLF militants who felt marginalized by the ISI's favouring of Hizbul Mujahideen and other groups were seeking alternative avenues. They were also disillusioned by the approach of the ISI.

Besides Ikhwan, other groups were operated by Javed Ahmed Shah (who had the backing of the state police's Special Operations Group) and Liaquat Ali Khan (who operated in Kashmir's Anantnag district). By the end of 1994, all three groups had merged into one entity known as Ikhwan-ul-Muslimeen.

Ikawans were a great challenge to the militants and helped the security forces to break the back of militancy during the late 1990s and first few years of the 2000s. However, Parray was killed in an attack by militants on 13 September 2003. His death was considered a major blow to the security forces' efforts against terrorism in Kashmir. The then chief minister of J&K, Mufti Mohammad Sayeed, described his killing as 'a setback to the peace process'.

It would also be appropriate to narrate the role played by Abdul Majeed Dar in attempting to restore some normalcy in the state. He was a leader of the people of Kashmir and a former operational chief commander of Hizbul Mujahideen in Jammu and Kashmir till 2001.

A politician by profession, Dar was from Sopore, where he had worked with the Muslim League during the 1970s. In this period, he was involved with Syed Ali Shah Geelani, the separatist leader, and went to jail several times. In the late 1980s, after the rigged 1987 elections, Dar became a militant along with his friend Fazl-ul-Haq Qureshi. By 1990, he was the leader of an organization called Tehreek-e-Jihad-e-Kashmir (TJK). In 1991, Dar merged with Hizbul Mujahideen, bringing in several thousand followers.

In the following years, rivalries developed within Hizbul Mujahideen, culminating in the killing of twenty-one people in an Azad Kashmir village near the LoC in 1998.

Parveen Swami, an author, citing friends of Dar, said that he went for hajj and had a revelation about the suffering that a decade of terror had inflicted on Jammu and Kashmir. This had a serious impact on him. Eventually, after the Chittisinghpura massacre of March 2000 – in which terrorists massacred twenty-seven Sikhs in Chittisinghpura village in south Kashmir and then escaped – several voices within the Hizbul Mujahideen joined Dar in seeking a return to a more peaceful approach. At that time, Dar said, 'We want to show to the world that we are not hardliners and are reasonable people who are in search of a peaceful solution.' If this effort had succeeded, the Hizbul Mujahideen would perhaps have converted into a political organization and then fought elections.

In July 2000, Dar, along with four other Hizbul commanders, declared a unilateral ceasefire in a statement made from the outskirts of Srinagar. The ceasefire was ratified by the PoK-based Hizbul Mujahideen commander, Syed Salahuddin. This was strongly criticized in the Pakistani media. Under intense pressure from ISI, Salahuddin withdrew the offer of a ceasefire.

This led to deep divisions between the followers of Dar and Salahuddin. In May 2002, Dar was expelled from the Hizbul Mujahideen along with two of his associates, Assad Yazdani and

Zafar Abdul Fateh. In March 2003, as he was coming out of his house in Sopore, Dar was shot dead by two gunmen. No one claimed responsibility for the attack. However, it was obvious that it could only have been carried out with the approval of Syed Salahuddin, supported by the ISI.

It was widely rumoured that Dar was in touch with the Indian intelligence agencies, the RAW and IB. With Dar's death, another golden opportunity to strike a peace settlement in the state slipped away.

On the international front, in the fight against the Taliban regime and Al-Qaeda in Afghanistan, the US once again enrolled Pakistan as its frontline ally. Consequently, the US decreased its pressure on Pakistan to shun terrorism in J&K. Also, with this development, Pakistan's fear of being declared a terrorist state evaporated. With this assurance, Pakistan pulled out all the stops in promoting terrorist activities in the Valley, and embarked on a no-holds-barred fight.

Another notable incident during this period was the hijacking of IC-814, the Indian Airlines flight from Kathmandu to Delhi, to Kandahar on 24 December 1999. This hijacking removed any doubts in the minds of the international community regarding the Taliban's active involvement in Pakistan-sponsored proxy war in Kashmir. After negotiations, the Indian government conceded to the hijackers' demand to hand over three important terrorists who were in custody in Indian jails in return for releasing all the passengers. The released terrorists included Maulana Masood Azhar, the notorious terrorist who founded the Jaish-e-Mohammad (JeM) – the 'Army of Muhammed', a Pakistan-based Deobandi jihadist terrorist group – by poaching militants from LeT, HUJI, HUM and Hizbul Mujahideen cadres. This capitulation by India remains a blot.

Perhaps one of the worst attacks yet of the proxy war came on 13 December 2001, when terrorists attacked the Indian Parliament. As a result, India and Pakistan almost went to war. The Indian army mobilized and was prepared for full-scale operations (Operation Parakram).

In 2002, in the state elections, the Congress withdrew support from the National Conference and Mufti Mohammed Sayeed, the founder of PDP, became the chief minister. My tenure as army chief from December 2002 to February 2005 coincided with his chief ministership. The Indian army, which was in the process of erecting an anti-infiltration fence during this period, maintained heavy pressure on the Pakistani army across the LoC through intense artillery fire and mortar barrages.

In April 2003, Pakistan announced a unilateral ceasefire along the LoC. Besides the intense pressure built up by the Indian army, there were concerted backchannel discussions between the two countries during this period. India agreed to observe the ceasefire and also asked for it to be extended to Siachen, which was done. The ceasefire was also extended to the international border of J&K, which Pakistan calls a working boundary. This resulted in a dramatic drop in militant activities. An India–Pakistan 'composite dialogue' was also started following a joint statement issued by then Prime Minister Atal Bihari Vajpayee and General Musharraf. On 2 May 2003, India and Pakistan restored diplomatic ties.

The ceasefire of 2003 held for a number of years along the LoC. However, during this period, suicide attacks also took place in Kaluchak and the Sunjuwan army camp (both in Jammu province), as well as in Tanda (Akhnoor army workshop area), despite the ceasefire. In a first of sorts, the terrorists carried out an IED explosion in Katra village on 21 July 2003, killing seven pilgrims and wounding thirty persons who were on their way to Vaishno Devi temple.

Getting Control of the Situation: 2004–07

In mid 2003, during my tenure as army chief, the fencing of the LoC from Chenab to the Zojila Pass was started to check infiltration. It was a herculean task, but the army proved that it could surmount any challenge, completing the project by November 2004. It was a complete package in terms of a wire obstacle in three strands, lighting along the fence up to Poonch, and booby traps to give early warning of approaching terrorists. In the Valley, the lighting was done away with because of the adverse weather conditions. Further, the fence was linked by a fail-safe communications system to platoon headquarters located near the fence. Numbers were marked along the fence to indicate the exact location where infiltrators were spotted. The fence was covered by patrols, and there were also quick reaction teams to respond to terrorists spotted along the fence. The idea behind the fence was to channelize the terrorists, delay them at the fence while they tried to negotiate it, and in that period neutralize them along the fence or near it. This system has been a great success and helped to reduce infiltration substantially.

The level of violence and terrorism in the state was perceptibly lower during this time. This is evident from the fact that over three and a half lakh tourists visited the Valley, and the Amarnath Yatra once again picked up in numbers. However, odd incidents of suicide attacks and encounters continued throughout 2004. The most notable was the attack on members of the village defence committee in Surankote on 25–26 June 2004, in which twelve civilians were killed.

The fence started impacting the terrorists' operations in a marked manner by mid 2004. Terrorist-related incidents came down by 22 per cent, civilian deaths by 21 per cent and security force casualties by 33 per cent in 2005 as compared to 2004.

During 2006, the number of incidents dropped by 16 per cent, civilians killed by 30 per cent and security forces killed by 20 per cent. This trend continued every year because the rate of infiltration dropped appreciably. In 2006, only 573 terrorists could infiltrate as compared to over 1,500 in 2004–05. Also, the fence seriously hampered the movements of terrorists who were crossing over to Pakistan to train under the ISI and then returning to the state to operate as hardcore terrorists. It was no longer safe for anyone to negotiate the fence twice. So, the training of Kashmiri militants in Pakistani camps virtually stopped.

It may be seen from the following chart that the number of incidents and casualties reduced progressively and the situation in the state improved considerably. The number of infiltrators also dropped considerably, year by year.

Year	Incidents (resulting in kills)	Security forces killed	Civilians killed	Terrorists killed
2003	3,401	314	795	1,494
2004	2,565	281	707	976
2005	1,990	189	557	917
2006	1,667	151	389	591
2007	887	82	131	358

The Pakistani traders and visitors from PoK who visited India's part of Kashmir often expressed surprise on the degree of improvement on India's side of the LoC.

With militancy on the wane, the time was right to attempt to normalize relations between India and Pakistan. In a big step to this end, the historic bus service between Srinagar and Muzaffarabad was flagged off at a special public function organized at the Shere-Kashmir stadium in Srinagar on 7 April 2005, and the bus was cheered all along its route. The then prime minister, Dr Manmohan Singh, also held discussions with a five-member delegation of the All Party Hurriyat Conference on 5 September 2005.

That the democratic process in J&K had taken deep root and was not adversely affected by militancy was evident from the voter turnout in various elections held over the years. These were the parliamentary elections of 1996, 1998, 1999 and 2004; the assembly elections of 1996 and 2002; and the panchayat election of 2005. The election to the urban civic bodies held in 2005 also witnessed a very high voter turnout despite terrorists' threats. Similarly, the by-elections to four assembly constituencies held in 2006 witnessed an all-time high voter turnout.

The government continued its endeavours to find a peaceful solution within the state. The third round of round-table conferences with citizens, which were started in 2005, took place on 24 April 2007 under the chairmanship of the prime minister. The Hurriyat separatists, however, stayed away from this conference.

Some Semblance of Law and Order: 2008–10

By and large, violence levels in Kashmir at the beginning of 2008 were low. However, the situation deteriorated when on 26 May 2008, the state government of Jammu and Kashmir reached an agreement to transfer ninety-nine acres of forest land to the Shri Amarnathji Shrine Board in the Kashmir Valley to set up temporary shelters and facilities for pilgrims in the Sonamarg area. This caused a huge controversy, with demonstrations in the Kashmir Valley against the land transfer and protests in the Jammu region supporting the land transfer. Six people were killed and more than a hundred injured when the police fired into a crowd in Srinagar. The opposition to the land transfer was ostensibly due to concern for the environment, but what really weighed on Kashmiri minds were religious reasons.

The following year, 2009, was a relatively good one for Kashmir. The locals enthusiastically participated in the 2009 general elections. However, there were disturbances over the Shopian rape and murder case, wherein two women were alleged to have been murdered in mysterious circumstances between 29 and 30 May by security forces in Bongam, Shopian.

Also in 2009, Shah Faesal, a Kashmiri doctor, topped the IAS examination and became a youth icon and role model overnight. His success story inspired Kashmiri students to excel in civil services examinations thereafter. However, in 2018, Shah Faesal resigned from the IAS and launched a political party of his own.

The year did see its share of violent mob protests and agitations, organized at the grass-roots level by anti-national elements, and a sizeable number of civilians lost their lives due to various law-and-order disturbances including stone pelting, stampedes and blasts.

The year 2010 witnessed pan-Valley unrest, which resulted in a series of violent protests and riots. These started in June 2010, after the army claimed to have killed three Pakistani infiltrators, which was later revealed to be a case of a fake encounter. In this incident, it was alleged that soldiers of the Territorial Army and a former special police officer had lured three young men from Nadihal village in Baramulla district and then killed them in an encounter at Sona Pindi. The army later convicted two officers and seven soldiers and sentenced them to life imprisonment for the staged killing of these three Kashmiri civilians. The protests turned into a movement spearheaded by the All Party Hurriyat Conference led by Syed Ali Shah Geelani and Mirwaiz Umar Farooq, who called for the complete demilitarization of Jammu and Kashmir. The APHC put out a call to strike, citing human rights abuses by the security forces.

Rioters shouting pro-independence slogans defied curfew, attacked the police with stones and burnt vehicles and buildings.

The agitation later also targeted the US following the 2010 Quran-burning controversy. In July 2010, Terry Jones, the pastor of the Dove World Outreach Center in Gainesville, Florida, had announced that he would burn 200 Qurans on the ninth anniversary of the 9/11 attacks.

The Jammu and Kashmir police and central police forces fired tear-gas shells, rubber bullets and also live ammunition on the protesters, resulting in a large number of deaths, including that of many teenagers. The protests subsided after the Government of India announced a package of measures in September 2010, aimed at defusing tensions. These protests were termed as the 'battle of stones versus bullets' and were one of the deadliest mass protests, wherein the youth fuelled the agitations locally and achieved a sense of collectivism against the security forces. The measures taken by the Government of India appeared to go down well with the public, and towards the end of 2010, the environment appeared to be improving, which ushered in a very encouraging 2011.

Relative Peace Returns: 2011–13

As the situation in the Kashmir Valley improved following the implementation of the package of measures announced by the Government of India in September 2010, terrorism also appeared to be on the wane. This was evident from the fact that in 2011, more than ten lakh tourists visited Kashmir, the highest number in the past two decades. These numbers were over and above those of the pilgrims who visited Vaishno Devi's shrine and devotees who undertook the Amarnath Yatra. Violence in the state dipped by approximately 60 per cent and terrorism-related incidents were reported to be the lowest in twenty-two years.

The summer of 2011 was quite peaceful. The stones that had earlier been used as potent weapons against the security forces were now put to better use for construction activities.

The year 2012 was also calm, but politically a semi-dramatic one. The much-awaited and talked-about reports of interlocutors on Kashmir appointed by the Government of India carried out parleys at different levels. The then chief minister, Omar Abdullah, sought the partial revocation of AFSPA. Pakistan, surprisingly, took a soft stand on the Kashmir issue. This year is also known for the return of Bollywood to Kashmir after a long gap, which was an encouraging development for local artists and tourism in the Valley. However, the year also witnessed considerable violence in the form of the killing of panchayat members, which disturbed the political process at the grass-roots level. A welcome initiative by the state government was to organize the return of some youth from Pakistan under the government's rehabilitation policy.

The following year, 2013, saw some violence in the wake of the hanging of Mohammed Afzal Guru, a Kashmiri separatist who was convicted for his role in the 2001 attack on the Indian Parliament. His hanging was played up as hurting the sentiments of the Kashmiris. Afzal Guru had received the death sentence for his involvement in the attack, which was upheld by the Supreme Court. Following the rejection of a mercy petition by the president of India, he was executed on 9 February 2013, and his body was buried within the precincts of Delhi's Tihar Jail. The burial was carried out without the family's knowledge and without any public announcement. Protests flared up near Sopore, Afzal's home district, despite various preventive measures, and heavy violence took place.

The year 2013 also had the unique distinction of seeing the ratio of terrorists killed to casualties amongst security forces to be near identical. The terrorists had changed their tactics and commenced suicide attacks, mainly in the Jammu region. The attacks on army camps in Hiranagar and Samba in September 2013 were the most notorious ones.

Through 2013, while Kashmir Valley appeared to be calm for the most part, J&K as a state saw a renewed phase of armed insurgency. The incidents were sparse but deadly, especially with terrorists catching security and intelligence agencies off guard. Infiltration attempts along the LoC increased, and terrorists adopted a new strategy of pushing in large numbers of infiltrators from multiple points, surprising security forces, though not with any great success.

Floods and Political Vacuum: 2014–16

In 2014, the Kashmir Valley witnessed devastating floods caused by the overflowing of the Jhelum river. For years there had been warnings that humankind's encroaching upon and vandalizing of rivers, lakes and forests would not go unpunished and one day these ecosystems would reclaim their original borders. That is exactly what happened. Heavy rains in the Kashmir Valley led to floods, which brought devastation, shock and trauma to this beautiful land of meadows, rivers and lakes. The floods claimed over 200 lives and led to the loss of crores of rupees in terms of damage to government infrastructure, business and private property. People say that the Dal Lake had swollen in anger to reclaim its original boundaries and the Jhelum in fury had again demarcated its flood basin, sending out a devastating warning to Kashmiris not to mess with its majesty. Once again, it was the valiant Indian armed forces that came as saviours to rescue the Kashmiris.

The floods gave a temporary pause to the violence in Kashmir. During November–December 2014, the Jammu and Kashmir Legislative Assembly elections were held, wherein the voters elected eighty-seven members to the assembly. Before this election, the Indian National Congress broke its alliance with the National Conference and contested all assembly seats. As usual, the hardliners boycotted these elections. More than 65 per cent of voters turned out for the elections. Following the elections, a new PDP–BJP government was formed in March 2015, after the two parties ironed out their ideological differences, with veteran Mufti Mohammed Sayeed as the second-time chief minister. It was decided that contentious issues such as Article 370 and AFSPA would be referred to a high-powered committee comprising representatives from both parties and civil society.

The newly elected government generated some positive political activity in Kashmir. However, the prevailing social factors such as the youth bulge, unemployment, the high-handedness of the police, radicalization and Pakistan-sponsored subversion were not addressed appropriately. Over the years, these factors had led to the extinction of Kashmiriyat and had been exploited by anti-India elements to generate anti-establishment feelings through regular propaganda and agitations. Various local players with anti-India sentiments, including some leaders/members of mainstream regional political parties, the bar association, traders' associations and the local media, continued to vitiate the environment regularly.

Gradually, separatist activities increased. Regular calls to strike were given by the Hurriyat whenever terrorists were eliminated or there was an inadvertent occurrence during sponsored agitations on issues such as a well-meant proposal for separate Pandit and Sainik colonies. In fact, the separatists had been given this strategy by Pakistan. These were obviously well-planned efforts to keep the Valley on the boil. The state government and the police and gradually the army were subjected to stone pelting as a pattern.

The effort of the state government should have been to ensure that life in Kashmir remained normal. However, the political compulsions of the PDP did not let this happen. The terrorist and separatist protests continued to adversely affect schools, government offices and markets, and normal life was increasingly disrupted.

The demise of the chief minister, Mufti Mohammed Sayeed, in January 2016 created a temporary political void. This was a period of disquiet and was a stepping stone to the intense terrorist activities from 2016 onwards.

Violence Returns: 2016–19

July 2016 witnessed a watershed event in the recent history of Kashmir in the form of the elimination of a Hizbul Mujahideen divisional commander, Burhan-ud-din-Wani, by security forces in the Anantnag district of south Kashmir.

Burhan, a young man, was the poster boy of terrorists and a youth icon, mostly due to his social media exploits. He was propped up as the face of militancy in Kashmir and was the longest-surviving Hizbul Mujahideen terrorist. He had been regularly receiving weapons and financing from Pakistan and had effectively utilized these resources to create his network and recruit young boys as terrorists.

After the elimination of Burhan, a precarious security situation erupted in the Kashmir Valley. The initial protests were largely attributed to the youth support for Burhan and their emotional outburst over his killing. Various misinformation campaigns added fuel to the fire. The law enforcement agencies could not have imagined the intensity and scale of the protests. What followed was heavy stone pelting, damage to schools and government property, firing from the mob, widespread 'chalo' (join us) calls, violent protests, attacks on security forces, looting of weapons, arson and the targeting of government officials and suspected informers. The poor handling of the security situation by the Jammu and Kashmir police during the initial few days led to a proliferation of protests and agitations. These were further fuelled by the large number of civilian deaths, which led to the spread of the disturbance to a larger area and eventually to the entire Kashmir Valley. All this presented an ideal opportunity for the separatists, anti-India elements and Pakistan to create a subversive environment, spread hostile propaganda and give a new dimension to the dynamics of the agitation. The prevailing sentiments were played up by the separatists, local media, radical and religious groups at the local level, while Pakistan played its part at the international level. The anger of the locals increased with the increase in the death of civilians during the agitations and crossed manageable limits within a few weeks.

All this created the impression of an uprising. Having seen the effect of the mobilization of the masses during the Arab Spring in Tunisia, Libya, Egypt, Syria and Yemen, Pakistan could not have asked for a more cost-effective method to keep the Kashmir issue alive. To that end, Pakistan guided the anti-India elements to mobilize the people. However, the strength of secularism in India was such that there was no adverse reaction from the Indian Muslims, and Pakistani propaganda was not effective outside the Valley.

The media played its role in further inflaming tempers. Almost the entire local media was critical of the actions of the security forces and gave maximum coverage to the civilian casualties. Social media was full of propaganda, including the circulation of photographs of individuals killed and injured. Most of these social media posts were engineered in Pakistan.

There was a collapse of the civil administration, especially in the hinterland. The political and administrative presence in the Kashmir Valley, especially in southern Kashmir, was negligible. It took almost five months of intense and well-coordinated operations by all the security forces to normalize the situation in the Kashmir Valley. By the end of 2016, the anti-national elements had realized that the option of azadi did not exist, even though violence continued in the subsequent years.

Violence levels in Kashmir increased manifold in 2017. Attempts to infiltrate terrorists across the border increased, though without any noticeable success. Terrorist groups such as JeM gained in presence. The security forces too increased its strength and the tempo of operations to prevent a repeat of the 2016 scenario.

All this while, developmental and political activities and the welfare of the people lost priority, which increased the alienation of the people. Education, business, tourism, in effect everything, suffered. The attack on pilgrims going on the Amarnath Yatra in July 2017 brought in a reminder of the situation prevailing in 2001–02, and the landscape of violence in Kashmir took a drastically grim turn.

Nothing much changed in 2018. New terrorist groups such as Ansar Ghazwat-ul-Hind (AGuH; an Al-Qaeda affiliate) emerged, while old groups such as Al Badar and Tehreek-ul-Mujahideen attempted a revival. In addition, the Islamic State also tried to make its presence felt in the Kashmir Valley in the form of the Islamic State of Jammu and Kashmir, of course without any success.

In a departure from the norm and against the wishes of the security forces, after almost seventeen years, a unilateral Ramadan ceasefire in the form of non-initiation of combat operations was declared by the Mehbooba Mufti government in May–June 2018. This temporarily reduced the violence levels against civilians but resulted in a marked spurt in attacks against security forces. Because of this adverse turn of events, the ceasefire was not extended.

In June 2018, the BJP withdrew its support to the state government and Mehbooba's government fell. The main reason behind this withdrawal of support was that the BJP wanted a more muscular approach to militancy, much against Mehbooba's policy of a soft and patronizing approach. Governor's rule was imposed, which brought stability to the security situation. Development projects also restarted.

Local recruitment reached an all-time high during 2018, which was a serious cause of concern. The prevailing situation adversely impacted tourism, business and the Amarnath Yatra.

State of Militancy Post August 2019

In recent times, along with the leadership elements, the SFs have also eliminated a large number of terrorist cadres, resulting in a decline in overall cadre strength. According to a 14 January 2021 report in South Asia Terrorism Portal (SATF), there were around 270 active terrorists in J&K, as against an estimated 300 in 2020 and 421 in 2019. The decline in the number of active terrorists is also the result of the fact that the anti-infiltration grid has been strengthened and the number of successful infiltrations has gone down. About 50 militants infiltrated in 2020 as against 138 in 2019 and 143 in 2018. Declining infiltrations have also resulted in a shortage of arms and ammunition. Recruitment of local militants has declined by 40 per cent.

Further, strong action has been taken against alleged Over Ground Workers (OGWs) of various terrorist groups. The police detained around 625 alleged OGWs in J&K in 2020. Most of the OGWs arrested were booked under stringent sections of the law, including the Arms Act, for possession of weapons, which increases the possibility of their confinement for longer periods.

In addition, a decline has been seen in terrorist-related incidents, killings of civilians and so on. These strong anti-terrorism measures have resulted in a general improved security situation in J&K.

5

Formulas for Settlement

'Life itself is really simple, but we insist on making it complicated.'
— Nelson Mandela

'Conciliation failing, force remains. Force failing, no further hope of reconciliation is left.'
— Edmund Burke

Over the last seventy years of India's independence, serious attempts have been made to find various formulas to settle the Kashmir issue amicably. There have been quite a few of them, and appreciatively, the leadership on both sides has taken the initiative at various points in time. The merits and demerits of these formulas are touched upon briefly here.

UN–Dixon Partition Plan, 1950

Shortly after Independence, India took the issue of Kashmir to the United Nations in the hope of finding an amicable solution. There followed a series of protracted discussions conducted under the auspices of the United Nations General Assembly and Security Council and the United Nations Commission for India and Pakistan (UNCIP). In 1950, the UN Security Council appointed Sir Owen Dixon as the UN representative to the two countries to assist with hammering out a solution to the Kashmir issue. During a conference of the prime ministers of India and Pakistan with him in 1950, Dixon proposed a plan whereby a plebiscite would be conducted by sections or areas and each section would be allocated to either India or Pakistan in accordance with the result of the vote therein. Further, as certain areas were sure to vote for accession to India and some were certain to choose Pakistan, these areas should be accordingly allotted, without the need of a vote, and the plebiscite should be confined to uncertain areas, that is, the Kashmir Valley.[1]

Based on the above principles, India wanted the whole of Jammu province, subject to minor corrections, and the tehsils of Ladakh and Kargil in Ladakh, except the area above the Suru river in Kargil, where a plebiscite could be held.

To Pakistan, India was ready to concede Gilgit, Gilgit Agency, Gilgit Wazarat, the political districts and tribal territory of Baltistan and as much of Jammu province as was to the west of the ceasefire line after correction.

However, as was quite normal in discussions between India and Pakistan, no issue could be taken to the final conclusion, and this proposal came to naught.

Ayub Formula, 1959

The India-China war of 1962 brought India closer to the United States. Soon after the war, the British minister for commonwealth relations, Duncan Sandys, and W. Averell Harriman, US assistant

---

1 Sisir Gupta, *Kashmir: A Study in India–Pakistan Relations*, p. 218.

secretary of state for eastern affairs, travelled to the region to propose India–Pakistan discussions on Kashmir without any preconditions. Ayub turned down the idea of direct dialogue with Nehru but accepted a meeting between cabinet-level representatives from both countries.

Averell Harriman has noted that he had made it plain to the then president of Pakistan, Ayub Khan, that Pakistan's demand for plebiscite in Kashmir could not be fulfilled and that the Vale of Kashmir, controlled by India, 'could not be transferred to Pakistan', but the Indians understood that they had to make certain concessions beyond the existing ceasefire line.[2]

Ayub said that for his part, he was prepared to find a solution to Kashmir if three elements of the problem were taken fully into account, namely, that the people of [Jammu and] Kashmir had a stake in their future; that Pakistan had a stake in Kashmir; and that India had a stake in the area.

Ayub had told President Dwight D. Eisenhower in 1959 that a plebiscite would be fine, but if that was not possible, he was prepared to consider any alternative that would satisfy the three points.[3] However, with Pakistan's attack on India in 1965, all these efforts came to a standstill.

Rajaji–Abdullah Formula, May 1964

Another formula for a settlement of the issue was evolved between Rajaji (Chakravarti Rajagopalachari was the first and last Governor-

---

2 Husain Haqqani, *India Vs Pakistan: Why Can't We Just Be Friends?* (New Delhi: Juggernaut Books, 2016), p. 52.

3 Husain Haqqani, *India Vs Pakistan*, pp. 52–53; memorandum of conversation between President Eisenhower and President Ayub Khan, Karachi, 8 December 1959, FRUS 1958–60, Vol. 15, pp. 781–92.

General of India as soon as India became a republic in 1950) and Sheikh Abdullah in May 1964. In Sheikh's words, he and Rajaji 'had worked out an honourable solution which would not give a sense of victory either to India or Pakistan and at the same time would ensure a place of honour to the people of Kashmir'.

The proposal was discussed by Sheikh with a team of officials deputed by the then Prime Minister Jawaharlal Nehru. All kinds of alternatives were mooted. These included a plebiscite for the entire undivided state of Jammu and Kashmir, as it existed before 1947; the maintenance of the status quo; and a fresh division of the state, such that the Jammu and Ladakh regions went to India, PoK including northern Kashmir went to Pakistan, and a plebiscite was held in the Valley alone to decide its future.

The basic terms of reference given to an analysis team comprising legal experts, nominated by Nehru, was that they should work out the specifics of the solution so as to ensure that it promoted Indo-Pakistani friendship, did not weaken the secular ideals of the Indian Constitution, and did not undermine the position of minorities in either country.

Abdullah told the officials that while he entirely agreed with the specifics given by Pandit Nehru, he asked them to give him more than one alternative, which he could carry with him to Pakistan. Sheikh Abdullah's conditions more or less ruled out a plebiscite, as he felt that it would leave one country dissatisfied and the minorities on both sides vulnerable.

The Rajaji formula was for Kashmir to be an Indo-Pakistan condominium, with defence and external affairs being the joint responsibility of the two governments (the model here was of Andorra, a tiny but autonomous enclave whose security was guaranteed by its two large neighbours, France and Spain). Another possibility in his mind was of creating a confederation amongst India, Pakistan and Kashmir.[4]

Rajaji wrote to Shiva Rao, a parliamentarian:

> Any plan should therefore leave the prizes of war untouched ... Probably the best procedure is for Sheikh to concentrate on the valley leaving Jammu as a counterpoise to Azad Kashmir (PoK), to be presumed to be integrated to India without question. This reduced shape of problem is good enough, if solved as we desire, to bring about an improvement in the Indo-Pakistan relationship. And being of reduced size, would be a fitting subject for UN trusteeship partial or complete.[5]

As regards Nehru's position, his papers are closed to scholars, but a letter written by his foreign secretary (one of the three officials who discussed various formulas with Sheikh) gives a clue to his thinking at that time. The prime minister had apparently asked legal experts to explore the implications of a confederation between India, Pakistan and Kashmir as a possible solution. Such an arrangement would not imply an 'annulment of Partition', as India and Pakistan would remain separate, sovereign states. Kashmir would be part of the confederation, with its exact status to be determined by dialogue. There might be a customs union

---

4 Ramachandra Guha, *India After Gandhi*, pp. 355–56; 'Kashmir—Talk with Sheikh Abdullah on 8 May 1964' at PM's House, Object File 4, Y.D. Gundevia Papers, NMML (Macmillan, 2007).

5 Ramachandra Guha, *India After Gandhi*, p. 356; Shiva Rao to Rajaji 10 May 1964, Rajaji to Shiva Rao 12 May 1964, both in subject file 92, C. Rajagopalachari Papers, fourth installment, NMML.

of the three units, some form of financial integration and special provisions for the protection of minorities.[6]

As can be seen from the above, no one formula was evolved, but several ideas were toyed with for discussion between Pakistan and India, should such an opportunity arise. Due to the untimely death of Jawaharlal Nehru in May 1964, there was no further progress on these ideas.

Efforts by Prime Minister A.B. Vajpayee and President Pervez Musharraf

On New Year's Day 2001, Prime Minister Vajpayee promised to seek a lasting solution to the Kashmir problem. He assured that in this quest, both in its internal and external dimensions, the beaten tracks of the past would not be traversed.

During the Agra Summit between Vajpayee and Musharraf in July 2001, Vajpayee certainly had some discussions with the president of Pakistan to resolve the Kashmir issue. Most probably, some form of a mutually acceptable formula was reached between the two leaders. However, this was not found acceptable by the other members of the delegations on both sides. The details of that have remained classified. Khurshid Mahmud Kasuri, the former foreign minister of Pakistan, also makes a mention of this in his book, *Neither a Hawk nor a Dove*. According to him, Musharraf enunciated the four points he had made at the summit in the press conference at Agra, in the breakfast meeting with the press, on 16 July 2001, at the end of the Agra Summit. However, the Indian media claimed that no such formula was claimed by him and

---

6 Ramachandra Guha, *India After Gandhi*, pp. 356–57. Y.D. Gundevia to V.K. Chari (Attorney General Madras) 13 May 1964; both in subject file 4, Y.D. Gundevia Papers, NMML.

echoed the official Indian line that Musharraf had been belligerent.[7] Internally, however, it is learnt that Musharraf's formulation was uncannily similar to that of Ayub in his conversation with Eisenhower in 1959. Musharraf spoke predominantly of fashioning the compromise 'through a process of elimination' to do away with anything not acceptable to India, Pakistan and the Kashmiris.

Pervez Musharraf–Manmohan Singh Formula, 2004–07

When Pervez Musharraf offered a four-point formula between 2004 and 2007 to resolve the Kashmir issue, his formulation was more or less similar to what Ayub had offered Eisenhower in 1959.

As Husain Haqqani, Pakistan's former ambassador to Sri Lanka and the US, explains in his book, 'Ayub had enunciated the need for the deal to reflect the interests of Kashmiris, Pakistan and India. Musharraf spoke of fashioning the compromise, as he had done with Vajpayee, to eliminate anything not acceptable to India, Pakistan and Kashmiris.'[8]

Another formulation of Musharraf's solution is given by T.C.A. Raghavan in his book *The People Next Door*. This is based on the same formula explained by Haqqani, as given earlier. In Raghavan's words, the main approach was focused on:

> ...firstly, identifying the geographic regions of Kashmir that need resolution. At present the Pakistani part is divided

---

7 Khurshid Mahmud Kasuri, *Neither a Hawk Nor a Dove*, p. 298; A.G. Noorani, *Frontline*, July 2005, 'The Truth About Agra and Musharraf'; Pervez Musharraf, *In the Line of Fire: A Memoir* (New York: Free Press, 2006), pp. 299.

8 Husain Haqqani, *India Vs Pakistan*, p. 62; Pervez Musharraf, *In the Line of Fire*, pp. 299–303.

into two regions: Northern Areas and Azad Kashmir. The Indian part is divided into three regions: Jammu, Srinagar [sic], and Ladakh.

Secondly, demilitarizing the identified region or regions and curbing all militant aspects of the struggle for freedom. Thirdly, introducing self-governance or self-rule in the identified region or regions.

Fourthly, and most importantly, having a joint management mechanism with a membership consisting of Pakistanis, Indians and Kashmiris overseeing self-governance.[9]

To elaborate on the above formula, the premise was that Jammu and Kashmir could not be made independent. There could be no redrawing of borders, but they could be reduced to 'just lines on a map'; travel and trade across the LoC could take place effortlessly. J&K and PoK could work out the mechanisms for cooperation between themselves.

In an interview with British journalist Jonathan Power shortly after being sworn in for the second time (22 May 2009), Prime Minister Manmohan Singh articulated the parameters of a possible Kashmir solution by stating, 'Short of secession, short of redrawing boundaries, the Indian Establishment can live with anything. Meanwhile we need soft borders – the borders are not so important.'

Kasuri says that for Pakistan, this was sadly not enough because besides satisfying the Kashmiris, the people of Pakistan also needed

---

9 T.C.A. Raghavan, *The People Next Door*, pp. 279–80; Pervez Musharraf, *In the Line of Fire*, p. 303.

to be convinced that Pakistan was not accepting a status quo solution.[10]

Dr Manmohan Singh also expressed the view that the two governments were on a common track to reach some understanding along the above lines. Accordingly, there were discussions taking place on Jammu and Kashmir between designated representatives of both countries. That these backchannel talks were happening was well known, even if their substance was not.

These efforts on the part of both leaders and frantic activity via Track II diplomacy gave a lot of hope, but finally they did not fructify because there was a change of government in Pakistan and with that, these proposals faded away.

Although ultimately none of these proposals were adopted, one must note the uncanny similarities amongst all the formulas suggested over time, thereby accepting that possibly that there has always been some merit in these approaches.

Even if the process of dialogue comes to a standstill at the level of the two governments, the dialogue through backchannels and amongst the various think tanks of the two countries must continue.

---

10 Khurshid Mahmud Kasuri, *Neither a Hawk Nor a Dove*, p. 298 and p. 302.

6

Perception Management

'Miscommunication is the number one cause of all problems: Communication is your bridge to other people. Without it, there's nothing. So when it is damaged you have to solve all these problems it creates.'

– Earl Sweatshirt

'Social media is not a media. The key is to listen, engage and build relationships.'

– David Alston

We have seen the genesis of Pakistan-sponsored terrorism along with successive political developments in previous chapters. However, today India is faced with another facet of the ground situation, the deep radicalization of the youth who have all but forgotten the observations that Vajpayee made at a rally in Srinagar in 2003 – 'Kashmiriyat' (eclectic Kashmiri culture), 'jamhooriyat' (democracy) and 'insaniyat' (humanity).

And while there are real or imaginary grievances in Kashmir, equally so there is dissatisfaction in Jammu and Ladakh, where the people feel that they are being discriminated against vis-à-vis Kashmir. The pattern of voting in successive elections bears this out. In fact, it is being openly voiced in various forums.

The lives of Kashmiri people and security forces are being lost at the hands of terrorists from Pakistan and the radicalized Kashmiri youth of the Valley. Each lull is followed by renewed levels of militancy. Some of these youths are self-radicalized, while others have been radicalized by their peers and yet some more, who follow the same path, via social media and the internet. The radicalization of youth by ISIS (Islamic State of Iraq and Syria) in several Western countries is an example where the people feel they are being discriminated against.

India is aware that social media is being used against it by promoting the views of religious zealots, but it is yet to formalize its approach to combat it. The legends of Burhan Wani and Zakir Musa, who were extremist leaders, were extensively propagated by social media. (This has been covered in detail later in the book.)

The unending cycle of violence, bandhs (shutdowns), agitations, curfews and unrest have paralysed the life of the silent majority (farmers, boatmen, taxi operators, local craftsmen, among others). On an average, Kashmir has suffered the loss of up to three months of working days a year during the past twenty-five years. The common man denies any hand in this. They say that they are the victims of the machinations of the terrorists. The induced socio-economic suffocation sparks unrest, which has been most pronounced in the districts of south Kashmir (Pulwama, Anantnag, Shopian, Kulgam and Budgam), which account for nearly 63 per cent of the violence in the Valley. With the physical space to voice opinions and demonstrate dissent reducing continuously due to the muscular internal security response, cyberspace is being increasingly exploited as an effective alternative by several forces, including the ISI, the Pakistani army and the terrorist–jihadi combine. Threats have diversified and increased exponentially due to the involvement of the Pakistan deep state and the innovative exploitation of social, visual, print and vernacular media for recruitment, radicalization, communication, intelligence sharing, coordination, propaganda and perception management. Consequently, the situation has been catapulted into the cognitive domain, necessitating an innovative approach by security forces and involving the exploitation of technology and information to create a favourable situation on the ground.

There is an urgent need to understand the role and characteristics of social media, the mindset of terrorists and the impact of technology in perception management. India's leaders and commanders will have to be trained and equipped to operate in the cognitive domain along with other options to create trust and confidence amongst the people of Kashmir. This calls for a strategy for effecting a change in mindset of the people and those handling perception management.

India today has 700 million internet users, the second-largest number of internet users in the world, and almost a billion mobile phone users, next only to China. Fifty per cent of these are smartphone users and the number is increasing by the hour.

For many connected users in India, the internet is used primarily for accessing social media networks. According to the Internet and Mobile Association of India (IAMAI), 66 per cent of internet users in urban India and 33 per cent of users in rural India regularly access social media platforms. Popular activities on social media include maintaining one's virtual profile on the likes of Facebook and Twitter, posting, sharing and loading applications as well as replying to something a friend has posted. While over 75 per cent of people in Kashmir use social media, 72 per cent are youth below the age of thirty (these figures do not include the large number of users on the dark net or those operating in the deep web and thus are the priority targets of the security forces and the intelligence agencies).

Socially and culturally, India is a land of diversity with different ethnic, religious, caste and linguistic groups. While this is its strength, India also suffers from a lack of inclusive growth, which is still a work in progress. Add to these the aspirations of the youth accentuated by the vision of the developed world available through the internet. Additionally, Indian society is going through a major transformation with people moving from the agricultural to the industrial and information domains. The people from the Valley and especially the youth are hyperactive in moving towards the information domain. The challenge is to manage this environment and ensure proactively that the situation is not exploited by Pakistan and militants through social media.

Social media platforms such as Facebook, Twitter, YouTube and LinkedIn have emerged as powerful tools for perception management by way of social engineering, psychological operations, cyber deception and open-source intelligence. Indeed, social media has emerged as a major instrument for waging 'asymmetric operations' through the exploitation of various leverage points such as the aspirations of people, differential development, varying religious beliefs and cultural leanings.

Social media is the preferred mass media method of kinetic operations by most jihadis and terrorists. It has also become an attractive means for recruitment and radicalization by terrorist organizations.

Social media has affected the art, methods, weapons, tactics and narratives used in the cognitive domain today. It influences a large audience and is a weapon of 'mass instruction' and 'disruption' that can impact targets in the real world.

The ability to rapidly disseminate graphic images and ideas to shape the public narrative on any endeavour or issue of national interest transforms social media into a strategic resource in the hands of those engaged in conflict. There are several reasons why social media is such an attractive and powerful medium. It operates at both the physical and cognitive levels, so the minds and hearts of a population can be targeted. Its impact is almost instantaneous. It is low cost, being an audio-visual mass media, and its conversational style, output and power to reach act as force multipliers in increasing networking and intelligence capabilities. It has a very high penetration level, as millions of people are connected through the principal global platforms by virtue of sharing experiences, pictures, documents and media. It is also a paradise for anti-national elements due to the low level of awareness of the people, resultant vulnerabilities and the ability to hit a large number of users at the same time.

Thus, it is clear that social media platforms have a tremendous impact on both the individual and society, which makes them interesting for governments, terrorists and intelligence agencies, particularly in the formulation of cyber strategies. Indeed, social media and proxy wars are becoming increasingly intertwined. Social media was used extensively in the propagation of the 'government's narrative' during the civil war in Libya. The ongoing conflict between Ukraine and Russia illustrates the role of social media in achieving multiple objectives.

We are well aware of how events such as the Arab Spring were initiated on social media, albeit to overthrow largely dictatorial regimes, or those where the democratic process did not have free reign. In Kashmir, the people have not been denied the democratic process. On the contrary, it has always been encouraged. But even a freely elected political system has failed to bring about stability and growth except in patches because Pakistan has continued to fuel insurgency by pumping in armed terrorists from across the border. Wahabi religious teachers have added to the problem as they seem to have found a fertile base for their ideas to flourish. India is a secular country and has the second largest number of followers of Islam in the world and more than 300,000 active mosques. These assets could be used by the mischievous insurgents to propagate extremism and many innocent people could be misled; consequently, Sufism could be threatened. The impact of this has been felt in the Valley where radicalization has taken deep roots and Sufism is virtually extinct. Moderates are vanishing under the fear of the guns of the terrorists, who are being further aided and abetted by Pakistan-sponsored use of cyberspace. To add to this, propaganda spread through social media has found ready listeners. Ironically, this is happening in a state that is far ahead of many others in India in terms of socio-economic parameters.

Historically, the people of Kashmir were generally peace-loving. Successive invasions notwithstanding, they were quite happy to lead peaceful lives. It was when the Kashmiris felt let down by the rigged electoral process in the 1987 elections that their local political leaders shifted to militancy. That was when Pakistan seized the moment and stepped up its interference in Kashmir in a big way. Pakistan had by then lost three wars to India and seen itself halved after the war of 1971. They commenced a low-cost induction of terrorists into Kashmir and established linkages with the disaffected locals in Kashmir. A doctrine based on Wahabi and Deobandi literature and maulvis steeped in this hardcore Islam were introduced into the Valley. Mosques proliferated. Under the effect of such philosophies and the constant media barrage from Pakistan, the unemployed and idle youth of the Valley could not remain unaffected. This, combined with Pakistan's creation of anti-India terrorists within the state as well as the infiltration of terrorists from Pakistan, has led to the present situation. Whenever there is a lull in insurgency in the Valley, Pakistan ups the ante. It should be clear that any dialogue with Pakistan must first address the issue of terrorism. Otherwise whatever India does, the dialogue will go nowhere in the presently charged and radicalized atmosphere.

Cognitive Dimensions of the Conflict

Let us for a moment look at the dynamics in J&K. Pakistan is waging a dirty proxy war primarily through terrorists, directly supporting their activities, training and arming them, and providing them with transit facilities and finance. This is backed by a complementary strategy to internally subvert Kashmir both physically and cognitively.

Kashmiri youth are being indoctrinated to become irrational, and irrationality does not care if the means do not justify the ends. An entire generation of youth has grown up under the shadow of the gun and perceive the Indian security apparatus to be an occupational force. The perceptions of these youth will have to be changed with concurrent and integrated information operations, which would encompass the complete information environment comprising psychological, intelligence, deception and information manipulation on multimedia. It is a big challenge, but doable. The solution to the Kashmir problem thus substantially lies in the 'information sphere' where the use of cognitive tools and the agility of minds are the determining factors.

To summarize, the Pakistan factor, a lack of jobs, a poor economic situation, failed governance, a feeling of being exploited and neglected, an identity crisis, poor leadership, a fear psychosis, confusion with regard to a value system, varied cultural leanings and religious beliefs, frustration due to unfulfilled aspirations, differential development, and the attitude of common citizens towards them are some of the factors that govern the psychology and mindset of Kashmiri youth today. To this add and re-emphasize the indisputable Pakistan factor and we have an explosive situation that can best be resolved through perception management.

Extremism is thus filling the cognitive domain of the youth of J&K by falsely portraying and amplifying victimhood, trauma, memories and events. It is done scientifically through social, political and religious layers, of which the religious layer is the most potent. Social media is playing an important role in the spread of folklore, myth-making and propaganda through Facebook, Instagram, YouTube, WhatsApp and such. The national media is contributing to the humiliation in Kashmir by creating a social sanction for aggressive rhetoric. The rapidly escalating effect on the cognitive domain can be gauged from the fact that social media access in Kashmir grew from just 23 per cent in 2010 to 75 per cent in 2016.

Systems Approach for Contesting and Winning the Perception Battle

Kashmir is a very complex issue with a number of hard and soft elements impinging on it concurrently. A 'systems approach' is required to provide a holistic, unbiased perspective and suggest strategies to manage the problem.

To this end, India's approach to handling this issue should start with recognizing that Kashmir is a 'system of systems'. To understand this complex set-up, a causal loop analysis of the prosperity and perception subsystems in Kashmir would be helpful. (A causal loop analysis is the process of analysing the interactions of reinforcing and balancing loops and the possible effects of loops and delays on the dynamic behaviour of the problem.) Finally, based on the analysis, recommendations can be made.

Jammu and Kashmir: A 'System of Systems'

There can be no disagreement with the classification of Jammu and Kashmir as a 'complex unitary system', considering the political, geographical, demographic, socio-economic, internal security and psychological dimensions of the prevalent situation. It is 'complex' because these dimensions have a large number of subsystems that have their own interplay amongst themselves, the outcome of which is difficult to determine. It is 'unitary' because the affected participants of the system – people, politicians, governments, security forces – all have the common aim of achieving peace and prosperity.

The people or the 'awaam' are the centre of gravity of this system in the state of J&K. This system is densely populated by disparate elements. Internally, there are the local population residing in distinct demographic segments, the youth, jammaitis (fundamentalists), state government, security forces, local media, secessionists, Kashmiri Pandits, local terrorists, among others. Externally, the system is driven by influences such as external abetment to terrorism, radicalization influences, fake Indian currency and hawala, mainland India attitudes and policies, the central government and most importantly, the cyber element, which is a typical example of both 'externally generated but internally influenced' and 'internally generated but externally influenced' elements.

All these elements have a complex interplay amongst themselves, forming subsystems that at times reinforce each other and at times draw negatively on each other. Unlike 'hard systems', which require linear problem-solving – that is, identification of the problem, followed by the evaluation of alternatives and finally the development of a solution and its implementation – complex soft systems require non-linear understanding of multiple subsystems (parallel processing) leading to the designation of multiple leverage points and their address by different agencies. The agencies attempting problem-solving by addressing leverage points need to cater for unintended consequences of the approach. So, Kashmir as a complex soft system comprises the interrelated subsystems of popular perceptions, people, youth, prosperity, heritage and culture, security forces and operations, politico-administrative machinery, media, social media, terrorism and the external Pakistan and central government factors that influence the system.

Only two of these subsystems are being illustrated with the causal loop to highlight the complex interplay of elements and then show how these subsystems effect, have influence on and interplay with the system of perception.

Causal Loop Analysis

The Prosperity Subsystem

It is well understood that economic activity is the main driver of the prosperity subsystem. It requires central support in the form of favourable policies, investments and infrastructure to propel industrial growth and generate economic activity. This loop is influenced by the effectiveness of governance and a conducive security environment, in itself a factor of security force operations and popular aspirations. Should these influencing subsystems drive economic activity favourably, employment will be generated, the engagement of youth in livelihoods will induce a negative effect on the terrorism/radicalization subsystems and the aspirations of the people will be positively influenced. Concurrently, state capacity for governance will increase, driving investments. These are thus reinforcing loops. But the moment the terrorist-radicalization factors start bearing down heavily on drivers of prosperity and the security force operations escalate to contain them, negative spirals are generated in the perception and popular aspiration subsystems. The clearly evident leverage points are therefore the security environment, infrastructural investment, industry and management of perceptions.

The Perception Subsystem

This subsystem is driven by factors such as people (demography, literacy, social mobility indices, unemployment, among others), radicalization, media (print, audio-visual and cyberspace, social media, among others) and the internal security environment, to name a few.

People: As mentioned earlier, contrary to popular perception, J&K compares favourably with the rest of India in most social mobility and development indices. The state has a high per capita income of Rs 92,800 in FY 2019–20 (up 44 per cent since 2011), a high literacy rate (67.1 per cent against the national average of 65 per cent) and a young population (larger than the rest of India in the 17–30-year age group). However, it also ranks in the bottom 5 per cent of the most corrupt and business-unfriendly states. Unemployment, ineffective governance, underdevelopment and a large youth bulge are thus fuelling the alienation felt by Kashmiris.

Radicalization: A conflict zone provides radical influences and recruitment-permissive environments. Unfortunately, Kashmir has already become such a conflict zone, where jihadi movements have grown as local groups adapted to fit their needs. Realizing the crucial role of cyberspace in stimulating a global Islamist identity amongst Kashmiri Muslims, radical and jihadi organizations have been trying to create a cyber Islamic environment in Kashmir, which would provide them with a psychological platform to transmit their messages for indoctrination and recruitment to ever-expanding audiences. Besides the easy availability of the internet – another key factor responsible for the growing Islamic radicalization – there has been a decrease in the practise of Sufi Islam, the traditional form of religious practice in this region, and the spread of Wahabi ideology through various Ahl-e-Hadith factions (Ittehad-e-Millat, Jamaat-e-Islami, among others). All this indicates a larger political shift in the Valley and the Indian government is yet to fully grasp the dangerous potential of this change.

Print media and cyberspace: There is a need for both the regional vernacular media and the national media to present nuanced reporting of events in Kashmir. A strident tone (whether negative or positive) has its own implications in the complex mindscape of Kashmir. Cyberspace and social media are generally unregulated environments where anonymity provides more opportunities than ever to disseminate extreme views. It makes it possible to create hoaxes without revealing the person or organization responsible for creation of the content. Despite the sustained efforts of security agencies, according to an internal communication of the Jammu and Kashmir police in 2014, terrorists and separatists were able to maintain uninterrupted communication through Voice over Internet Protocol (VoIP) and other social media platforms such as Skype and WhatsApp. Pakistan's state and non-state actors are conducting aggressive intelligence against Indian security personnel in Kashmir using specially developed applications to access strategic information. It can be argued that the cyber dimension has become prominent in escalating protests and political violence in Kashmir in recent years. The most extreme and catastrophic expression of this trend was seen following Burhan Wani's death in 2016. Government buildings were targeted as usual, but violence this time was not confined to government symbols alone; the security of families and civilians seen as 'collaborators' also increasingly came under attack. The large-scale protests benefited from the newfound ability of protesters and insurgents to send and receive information on platforms that were not controlled by the establishment they were up against. Clearly, social media has offered insurgents a unique platform for preparation as well as after-action deliberation. The unconstrained circulation of videos and pictures allows the perpetuation of a certain narrative that, in turn, fuels further unrest.

Recommendations: Balancing the Perception Subsystem

There is an urgent need to change the discourse in favour of the common people. To effectively challenge Pakistan and its terror propaganda and lies, the following measures are considered imperative.

Change the Narrative

There must be a strategic narrative with a compelling storyline and the Kashmiris must be made aware of it. The 'heart is my weapon' narrative is one such example. Sporadic media bursts in the wake of untoward incidents serve no purpose. The three Cs of messaging, namely, clarity, conciseness and comprehensiveness, are essential.

Strategic Communication

The driving force behind communication with the people must change from 'management' to 'engagement' – a shift to a progressive narrative, with an openness to talk. Comprehensive, multi-themed, segment-directed and sustained campaigns are needed to nullify Pakistan's Inter-Services Public Relations (ISPR) propaganda through identifying, fact-checking and posting-back the factual responses, to overcome any apprehensions and doubts so created by malicious posts. Providing regular and correct updates through official accounts and posting creative messages on official accounts and web portals is critical. Calling out inaccurate narratives, themes and distortions on the internet is essential.

Information Engagement

As cyberspace and social media are generally unregulated environments, they are used for the unconstrained circulation of videos and pictures to fuel unrest. There is a need to counter this deluge both qualitatively and quantitatively. Since the objective is to dissuade Kashmiri youth from joining e-jihad, it is important to find more effective strategies to discredit Islamist radicals in cyberspace. To this end, the Government of India needs to analyse and outline the full scope of 'information engagement' in its counterterrorism policy. The government, administration and security forces in Kashmir must assertively employ all available social media platforms as well as all traditional media to present an accessible, professional, efficient and accountable image.

Counter Radicalization

The religious extension of the separatist's mindset is the attempt to radicalize the Valley, especially the youth. The concerted effort to replace Sufism with the radical Deobandi/Wahabi philosophy is evident in the free flow of Wahabi literature. This is a very potent threat with irreversible implications. It must be met at different levels, from madrasas to mosques to society at large. Religious heads, leaders and people will have to be employed in strengthening the Sufi system and Kashmiriyat culture. A dedicated campaign to change the mindset of the people through the application of each component of perception management in an integrated manner is an urgent necessity.

Upgrade Sadhbhavna (Good Intentions) to Yakeen (Trust)

Operation Sadbhavana, also known as Operation Goodwill, was launched by the army in J&K to ameliorate living conditions and has proved to be a great success. The pattern followed is to discuss with the locals, living in the areas where the army is deployed, what their needs are. The demands of the villagers are generally the same as those of any others in India. They range from the construction of a school, a vocation centre or a playground to laying of water pipes, and so on. The construction and inauguration of these facilities in quick time has the maximum impact.

These projects are run purely by the army and funds allotted are vetted at successive levels and audited by the Competent Financial Authority (CFA).

Often, the locals do not hesitate to join in the work. They freely interact with the army and gradually a rapport develops. So much so that they become the best 'feeders' of information to the army, whom they start seeing as protectors and assistance-givers. The army also ensures that the locals, particularly the youth, are taken on tours to places in India that many of them have never seen.

Given the success of the initiative, an upgraded scheme based on this concept must be envisaged at the state level. The state government and the civil administration could expand such projects to a larger scale using both state resources and those allocated by the Centre. These projects (as mentioned earlier) could be the construction or setting up of schools, waterworks, vocational centres, playgrounds, entertainment centres, clinics and so on, based on the requests of the locals and identified by the district administration and the state government.

A dedicated team of officers from the civil administration, civil engineers and the police could start these projects. The army can advise and assist by way of incidental protection but cannot be expected to construct and maintain the projects. The state or Centre can decide on suitable names such as 'ashwasan' (assurance) or 'yakeen' (trust). If such projects take off and are set up in good time, they will have a huge impact in Kashmir.

Cyber-Mobilization

In today's fast-changing socio-political scenario in Kashmir, it is not sufficient to focus on organizational and doctrinal changes in the military domain alone. In the long run, what really counts is the large-scale mobilization of people. Cyber-mobilization has emerged as a crucial element not just in recruiting fighters but, more importantly, in inspiring violence and struggle. Thus, the government needs an effective cyber strategy for counter-insurgency in Kashmir, turning more attention to analysing, influencing and countering the mobilization tactics of the insurgents.

A Dedicated Organization for Perception Management

Perception management is a challenging issue, and it requires time and synergy amongst all stakeholders. Perception management cannot help in solving the problem on its own but can help in 'managing' the problem in the immediate and medium term. Solving the problem will require a consistent, determined policy and, most importantly, political will with a clear understanding of the physical, virtual and cognitive domains and information operations. It has to be addressed at the national level with a clear and dynamic strategy based on a national policy, a national doctrine assisted by security forces, state leadership and the administration.

To win the perception battle, a dedicated organization for information management and continuous monitoring of the information environment is required. This organization should work under the Unified Headquarters and be located in Srinagar as an immediate operational requirement. It should have a wing each in Jammu, Srinagar, Leh and Delhi. Its members should include the finest minds in the country from the academic, bureaucratic, diplomatic, military, police, cultural and religious domains, who are capable of understanding the issues in depth and creating a counternarrative that is more convincing than that of the terrorists.

The organization's mandate should include monitoring social media for information on a regular basis, and receiving, storing, processing and transmitting it to concerned agencies, ensuring the integrity of information throughout. Thus, this ought to be a high-technology organization provided with the requisite funds. It must have high-speed, secure and resilient connectivity with intelligence organizations across the nation.

The responsibilities of the organization should cover the generation of content for perception management for different groups in the vernacular and in different formats in consonance with the 'narratives'. It should aim at providing highly skilled human resources; research and development for installation of sensors and subsystems; planning and executing information operations; ensuring the availability of information systems in the field for early warning, full-spectrum monitoring and exploitation of contemporary technologies such as big data, analytics and bots; establishing a simulation laboratory for network components, sensors and the conduct of information operations; and monitoring both the dark net and deep web overtly and covertly.[1] Sensors are the eyes and ears of the system. These are of different types and are meant to collect information and pass that on to the designated organization/agency. For planning and implementation of information warfare, operators require a skill-set consisting of hardware, software, content generation, language expertise, information processing, information integrity and management of network in real time. Integration of information, technology and highly skilled manpower are the very essence of conducting Perception Management Operations.

The internet revolution in the Kashmir Valley is not just altering the way local people think but is also changing the way they resist the establishment. Although jihadi guerrillas are not going to be replaced by cyber insurgents operating in a virtual battlefield, cyber dominance in Kashmir may well make the difference between success and failure. India has to contend with a restless Kashmir, which has been exposed to incessant online provocations. New Delhi must assume control of this narrative. Contesting the war of narratives is as vital as restoring normalcy. As a matter of fact, this will greatly help in bringing about normalcy. To dissuade the Kashmiri youth from joining the e-jihad, it is important to find more effective strategies to discredit Islamist radicals both on the

---

1 Dark net is an umbrella term for those parts of the internet that are purposefully not open to public view or hidden networks whose architecture is superimposed on that of the internet. Not many are aware of the existence of the dark net, and it is used for illegal activity. It can be accessed through special software such as Tor – software that allows one to browse a network anonymously – and I2P – Invisible Internet Project, an anonymous network layer that enables censorship-resistant communication. The deep web is an umbrella term for websites, overt and covert message boards and other digital services that are not intended to be easily found.

battlefield and in cyberspace. This is a mission that can best be carried out by thinkers and practitioners with intimate knowledge of the magnitude of the problem. India can ill afford to lose any more time in creating this organization. To my mind, this lack of a concerted effort to create and manage a conducive perception, favourable to India, remains a gaping hole in its strategy for handling the Kashmir situation.

7

India's Counter-militancy Strategy

'Extremism thrives amidst ignorance and anger, intimidation and cowardice.'
— Hillary Clinton

'I have never advocated war except as a means of peace.'
— Ulysses S. Grant

The Indian army has been engaged in counter-insurgency operations in one part of the country or the other ever since Independence. These operations have been conducted in varied terrain ranging from the jungles of the north-eastern states of India to the Kashmir Valley. The Indian army was also involved in peacekeeping operations in Sri Lanka, which very soon turned into CI operations. In Punjab, the army primarily looked after the exterior lines (outer peripheries in relation to the centre of gravity with the ability to encircle the enemy) with the police operating along the interior lines (closer to the centre of gravity like towns and population centres). All these areas and operations had their own peculiarities and posed their own challenges. While it would not be prudent to impose any one model on another, the lessons learnt in all these situations were certainly useful and were applied selectively to other situations. Thus, CI models are constantly evolving and remain a work in progress.

Since 1989, the state of J&K has been mired in a deadly insurgency that has changed its character several times in the last three decades, akin to the Greek monster Hydra. It is also true that while the people of J&K have by and large stood by India's side, there have always been some radical elements who have supported Pakistan. Ever since India's none-too-friendly neighbour started fomenting unrest amongst the local populace, exploiting the religious angle to wage a proxy war, India has been watchful of its nefarious intents. Between 1947 and 1971, Pakistan also fought three wars with India with the aim to annex Kashmir but failed miserably. The 1999 Kargil war was also a consequence of Pakistan's effort to revive the flagging insurgency. Post 1989, after it became free from its commitments in Afghanistan, Pakistan once again turned its full attention on Kashmir. The aim was to constantly bleed India. Pakistan also hoped to engineer a rebellion supported by the trained terrorists that it infiltrated into the Valley so that the Valley would slip out of India's control and fall into Pakistan's lap.

In its efforts to control the situation and bring back normalcy, India initiated numerous steps such as raising Rashtriya Rifles battalions (manpower taken from the army on deputation for three-year tenures) and creating Ikhwans (CI militia comprising surrendered terrorists). However, the most effective initiative that contributed to reducing violence levels in the state was the installation of an anti-infiltration obstacle system in the form of a fence along the LoC. It not only prevented groups of foreign mercenaries from crossing the LoC uninhibited but also prevented the influx of weapons and ammunition into the Valley. This game changer brought about a steady decline in the numbers of terrorists infiltrating the Valley and forced India's adversary to look for other options to keep the pot boiling.

Before going further into the contours of the Pakistan-sponsored proxy war in Kashmir, it will be useful to recapitulate the salient lessons learnt from India's experiences in CI operations in different parts of the country and also in Sri Lanka.

Nagaland

To understand the evolution of the Indian army's CI doctrine, one has to go back to its experience in Nagaland from the 1950s onwards, which has been the cornerstone of its CI programme. The army learnt several major lessons from its operations there. For one, it is essential to define a clear-cut political aim. A unified command structure is also required. Segregating the local population from the insurgents is another useful strategy. As an analogy, if one considers the local population to be water and the insurgents fish, the fish will not be able to survive if the water (support of the local population) dries up. To help achieve this, it is important to win the 'hearts and minds' of the people and use minimum force. The army also followed the principle of area domination in Nagaland. Finally, it is important to maintain the superiority of forces at all times.

Mizoram

In the mid 1960s, the Indian army was deployed for CI operations in Mizoram. It was during this period that a specialized CI warfare school was established in Mizoram. As part of its modernization plan, the Indian army also created special CI battalions (later on, this experiment was abandoned) and modernized the Assam Rifles (a paramilitary force for the north-eastern sector, but its officers were taken on deputation from the army). Some of the operational measures instituted included launching 'village grouping schemes', which primarily hinged on area domination by physical occupation of forward-operating bases at the platoon level in select villages. Continuous cordon and search operations were also instituted. The army also relied on heli-borne operations. Finally, civil–military synergy in the conduct of operations was important.

Operation Pawan, Sri Lanka

The Indian Peace-Keeping Force (IPKF) was deployed in Sri Lanka as a consequence of the Indo-Sri Lanka Peace Accord of 1987, to assist the Sinhalese government in brokering peace with the warring Tamils led by the Liberation Tigers of Tamil Eelam (LTTE). However, the peacekeeping mission was quickly transformed into a CI campaign as the LTTE refused to surrender arms. This took the IPKF by surprise. CI operations were launched against the LTTE, who were hardened guerrilla fighters. The IPKF suffered heavy losses initially. This was the first CI operation launched by the Indian army in a foreign country. Notwithstanding the political indecisiveness and lack of local support, the IPFK soon improved the situation, albeit at a heavy cost. By the time the IPKF departed from the island in 1990, the Indian army had been successful in significantly cutting down the size of the Tamil Tigers. The methods employed during the CI operations included the use of attack helicopters, special forces operations, intelligence-based operations with small teams, working in close coordination with the civil administration, and launching operations along the coast.

Punjab

The anti-militancy campaign in Punjab was unique as the Punjab police and the paramilitary forces rightly took the lead role. The Indian army carried out CI operations only in the worst-affected regions of Punjab. For the most part, it operated along the exterior lines. The army's presence in large numbers was a great morale booster for the Punjab police. The army also remained available for any critical operations on short notice. The biggest factor in support of the forces was that a large cross-section of the people did not support the militancy, and within a short span of time, Punjab regained normalcy. This was despite the fact that this insurgency also had Pakistani support, although not as intimately as in J&K. The reasons for the success of the CI operations in Punjab were political will, quality of leadership at the political and operational levels coupled with complete confidence in the unified command mechanism, a lack of popular support for the militants, and intelligence-based surgical operations by the security forces.

The Strategy of the Security Forces in J&K

Of all the counter-insurgency campaigns conducted by the Indian army since India's independence, none were against an insurgency that had such intimate and direct support of another nation as the proxy war in J&K. The unrest has persisted for over three decades at full throttle. One of the main reasons why the proxy war has sustained itself since 1989 is that it has run a dynamic course, constantly changing and evolving to adapt to the circumstances. There have been peaks and troughs, but the insurgency has persisted. The following paragraphs outline the course of the Pakistan-sponsored proxy war and the dynamic measures taken by the Indian army, the paramilitary forces and the local police to counter it.

Phase I – 1980–89: From Discontent to Insurgency

The build-up of dissatisfaction during the eighties on various accounts, including the heavily rigged elections of 1987, resulted in discontent amongst the Kashmiri populace. Pursuing its policy of a 'thousand cuts', Pakistan fuelled an internal struggle for freedom by providing training and infrastructural support to misguided youth from the Valley. In the wake of alleged irregularities in the 1987 elections, disillusioned Kashmiri youth started sneaking into PoK to receive training in arms. On their return, their agitation took the form of clashes with the local police, carrying out assassinations of local politicians and finally, gaining enough confidence to take on the other security forces. A number of foreign mercenaries and Pakistani nationals infiltrated the state and took to inciting mobs in the name of jihad and confronting the Indian security apparatus. When the situation started getting out of hand, the state government declared certain severely affected areas as 'disturbed areas' and the AFSPA was imposed to provide suitable legal cover for army operations. Simultaneously, Pakistan started spreading a radicalized form of Islam, with the Ahl-e-Hadith school of thought making inroads in the Valley.

Phase II – 1990–98: Eruption of Insurgency and Proxy War

In the early nineties, a number of tanzeems (extremist organizations of varying numbers) were formed in the Valley, which were either pro-azadi (freedom) or pro-Pakistan. There was large-scale infiltration across the LoC, into J&K. The insurgency initially spread to urban areas and then to rural areas as well. Terrorists gradually established control over civil administration and the population. In 1992, Sopore notoriously became a liberalized zone, which was free from the control of the security forces because of intense activities of the extremists, but security forces gradually regained control by 1993. In March 1993, the ISI engineered the formation of the All Party Hurriyat Conference (APHC). The APHC is an alliance of 26 political, social and religious organizations formed on 9 March 1993, as a united political front to raise the cause of Kashmiri separatism in the Kashmiri movement. The APHC is a proxy tool of the ISI, on whom they are heavily dependent for funds for supporting terrorism. Syed Ali Shah Geelani has been the most influential and pro-PoK leader of this group. A large number of its members were from the erstwhile Plebiscite Front. The police revolted at Batamaloo in 1993, but the army quickly regained control in an operation which took the revolters with complete surprise. The Hazratbal mosque incident was another major landmark event, and the arc of terrorism spread. The Special Task Force (STF) and Special Operations Group (SOG) were formed. By 1996, the army and other security forces had regained reasonable control and successful elections to the state legislative assembly and Parliament were held to build the political process in the state. In 1998, Operation Sadbhavana, a very successful civil action scheme, was launched by the army.

During this period, the focus of the army and the allied security forces was initially restricted to bringing back a semblance of control and order in J&K. The army carried out a reorientation of the counter-infiltration and counterterrorist grid along the LoC and the exterior lines. The police and the paramilitary forces operated along the interior lines. There was a concerted effort to increase coordination amongst the army, police and other government agencies. Several large-scale joint operations were carried out to neutralize militants. There was heavy deployment of army personnel; the AFSPA, which had been enforced in the

Valley, progressively spread to the rest of the state as the arc of insurgency spread.

Phase III – 1999–2004: Kargil Misadventure and Continuing Terrorism

In May 1999, Pakistan infiltrated the Kargil sector, but the Indian army reacted admirably to Pakistan's aggression and ejected all the invaders from the Kargil heights within three months, that is by 26 July 1999. Pakistan suffered a large number of casualties and also huge embarrassment internationally. However, Pakistan was able to take advantage of the inevitable disturbance in the counter-insurgency grid in the Valley as a result of some fighting formations being pulled out to be redeployed in the Kargil sector.

Terrorist activities such as the hijacking of Indian Airlines flight IC-814 on 24 December 1999 and the consequent release of three terrorists by India to secure the release of the passengers were a big setback. Incidents such as the attack on Amarnath yatris and the massacre of thirty-six villagers in Chittisinghpura by terrorists further aroused passions.

In 2003-04, the security forces carried out a reorientation of the counter-infiltration grid based on a fence – anti-infiltration obstacle system – supported by quick reaction teams. This helped to significantly reduce militancy in the Valley. Army camps and garrisons were strengthened, but without getting into a fortress mentality. People-friendly operations intensified. Operation Sadbhavana, launched to alleviate the hardships of the local population, started paying dividends.

Phase IV – 2005–12: Intermittent Normalcy

With the improvement in the security situation, reconciliatory notes were heard from various quarters, and the prospects of a peaceful solution looked bright till the first half of 2008. Various parliamentary and civic body elections were held with high voter turnouts. However, the Mumbai terror attack in November 2008 by LeT operators changed the equation and diminished all hopes of a settlement with Pakistan. The Pakistani hand in the attack was identified and accepted by the international community.

Mass uprisings and violent agitations in 2008 and 2010 added a new dimension to the Kashmir imbroglio. The agitations of 2008, which were fuelled by the Amarnath Shrine Board land dispute incident, increased the polarization of the two regions, that is, the areas north and south of the Pir Panjal, thereby increasing the religious divide between the Jammu region and the Valley. Pakistan realized that sustaining external support was becoming a difficult and expensive option and thus focused on neutralizing Kashmiriyat as well as the secular Sufism traditionally practised in the Valley by exploiting the 'rising Islamic fervour'. This was a brilliant strategy. More importantly, taking a cue from events in the Middle East, it started focusing on agitational dynamics.

The unrest in 2010, after the alleged killing of innocent Kashmiris, added fuel to the fire and the security situation deteriorated even further. After the unrest of 2008 and 2010, Kashmiris felt that their identity was being threatened and innocents were being targeted, which prompted large numbers to take up arms against the state with renewed vigour. Although protests, bandhs and minor stone pelting had been going on in Kashmir for decades, the sheer scale of this unrest reflected the rage of the masses. The inept handling of the unrest and a large number of civilian casualties provided an ideal opportunity to the propaganda machinery to crank up the hoopla over the atrocities and oppression. The narratives of 'colonization', 'occupation' and 'exploitation' were thrown up by the terrorists and their sympathizers once again, which resulted in preparing the ground for a new type of terrorism to take root. Agitational terrorism gained impetus, with the separatists and Hurriyat cadres gaining prominence.

However, a package of welfare measures was announced by the Government of India in September 2010 to defuse tensions, which created a positive effect. As a result, 2011-12 were relatively calm years, and more than a million tourists visited the Valley over and above the yatris for the Amarnath pilgrimage.

Army operations were guided by a strategy that saw the cordon and search operations which were becoming an irritant in the army's relations with the civil populace replaced by intelligence-based pinpoint operations, which yielded better results with far less inconvenience to the people. Additionally, the army exercised maximum restraint while carrying out operations. The people-friendly attitude that had been introduced as part of the operations was further cemented and has come to stay as a policy. The army also adopted a policy of zero tolerance towards human rights abuses and dealt severely with defaulters. Close coordination with the civil administration improved the functioning and general environment in the state. The Unified Headquarters continued to be of immense value.

Phase V – 2013 Onwards: Era of Stone Pelting and Social Media

During this period, a new breed of terrorists started surfacing and violence levels picked up gradually. Pakistan also gingered up its terror apparatus, and a large number of terrorist camps mushroomed in the areas close to Muzaffarabad. However, a stable security grid and intelligence-based targeting of the top leadership of terrorist groups reduced violence in the state, resulting in a reduction in the support base for terrorists and hardliners. Tourism witnessed an upward swing, and the locals started enjoying the dividends of peace. The assistance provided by the army during the devastating floods of 2014 helped increase its popularity to an all-time high, albeit temporarily.

During this period, increased internet and mobile connectivity led to an increase in social media users, who were exposed to venomous ideologies from around the world. Radical preachers and extremists were also able to reach out to the Kashmiri youth much more easily. The new-found tool of social media provided an impetus to radicalization on both sides of the LoC. The youth, in the absence of any other form of entertainment, gravitated towards the inflammatory videos spewing anti-India venom. Besides generating hatred for the Indian state, these videos encouraged the impressionable youth to wage jihad against the 'kaffirs' (non-believers), who were projected as an occupying force.

The success and effectiveness of the counter-infiltration grid had weakened the strength of terrorists (especially of terrorist leaders and foreign terrorists) operating in the state. To make up the numbers and to maintain the critical mass necessary to sustain the so-called 'Kashmiri freedom movement', Pakistan provided an impetus to infiltration on the one hand and encouraged an increase in local recruitment in Kashmir on the other. This was aided by the proliferation of smartphones, social media platforms, turbulence in West Asia and the dramatic rise of the Salafi hardcore jihadi group ISIS.

The results of the state assembly elections which were held in November-December 2014 and the consequent political dispensation of the BJP–PDP combine further increased the polarization effect. The Pakistani deep state, besides providing a fresh impetus to the infiltration of foreign terrorists, also started proactively exploiting the power and reach of social media. This led to a state of uncertainty and apparently calm instability in Kashmir. This period also witnessed the convergence of terrorism and mass protests wherein locals were seen coming out in large numbers to pelt stones and assist terrorists cornered during encounters to escape. This new trend and the astronomical emergence of raducak youth icons such as Burhan Wani and Zakir Musa not only added worrisome dimensions to the problem but also resulted in neutralizing the gains that had been made in the drive against terrorism.

The unrest triggered after the killing of Burhan Wani on 8 July 2016 (in part by Pakistan-supported instigators) was very violent, and the outburst of the locals manifested in the form of heavy stone pelting, intense sloganeering, burning and damaging of government property and the beating and threatening of government employees. The protests were characterized by a sudden build-up of crowds and the increased participation of women and children. Traffic was not allowed to ply on most roads and shops were shut forcibly by miscreants. Lanes and bylanes witnessed running battles between the infuriated protesters and security forces. Besides violent agitations and stone-pelting incidents, the protests in 2016 also witnessed the use of petrol bombs and firing from crowds. Weapon snatching, attacks on police stations, burning of schools and damage to government property were seen. Twenty-eight schools were burnt down and numerous banks were looted. Aerial firing to infuse fear amongst people who had opened their shops was also resorted to. Taking advantage of the deteriorating internal security situation, terrorists intensified their activities and provided a new impetus to recruitment.

Unlike the situation in 2008 and 2010, the mass uprising in 2016 was against the elimination of a terrorist, who was commemorated as a martyr while the families of policemen and army personnel were targeted. This resulted in more gullible youth joining the ranks of terrorist tanzeems. These developments, combined with the new trend of tanzeems joining hands and operating together, made intelligence gathering a herculean task and security force operations even more difficult.

The security situation deteriorated rapidly following the unrest of 2016, especially in south Kashmir. The protesters became more audacious and it became increasingly difficult to control locals, who came out in large numbers to join the protests. Social media was increasingly used as a very effective tool. Societal dynamics underwent a transformation, and large numbers of sympathizers pelting stones to disrupt the counterterrorist operations of security forces became the norm. Pakistan intensified its efforts to vitiate the situation by orchestrating numerous high visibility terror strikes and, at the same time, ISPR was finding innovative ways to influence Kashmiri minds. The uncertain political situation further complicated the issue. Youth icon terrorists such as Zakir Musa began openly endorsing shariah and the rule of the Caliphate and refused to call the Kashmiri movement a political struggle but instead adopted the radical religious objectives of Al-Qaeda.

Kashmiri society saw decreasing levels of religious tolerance. Misinformation spread by inimical elements on either side of the LoC polluted the minds of the locals and vitiated the security situation. The emergence of educated and young terrorist leaders as well as skilled speakers of the Jamaat-e-Islami filled the void created by the lack of mainstream political as also Hurriyat leadership. The propagation of the narrative of the oppression of Muslims and irresponsible media activism added further fuel to the simmering discontent.

The targeting of army and policemen while on leave also intensified as a strategy. There was also an increase in the subversion of police and civil administration. However, the militancy was really active in only five districts of south Kashmir. The remaining seventeen districts of Kashmir were reasonably quiet, although susceptible to flare-ups at any moment.

In June 2018, the BJP withdrew its support from the PDP and governor's rule was imposed. Thus ended the rule by an unsatisfactory and mismatched coalition. The state of militancy post the abrogation of Article 370 has briefly been dealt with in an earlier chapter.

The Poster Boys of Militancy

Burhan Wani

Burhan Wani was born in the affluent and educated family of a school headmaster in Tral in Pulwama district. He had a dashing personality. When he was in class ten, he went out with his brother one day for a ride on his brother's motorbike. While they were out, they were stopped by a police patrol and frisked. In the process, they got into a scuffle with the policemen and were beaten up. It is said that it was then that Burhan decided to take up arms.

He rose swiftly up the ranks of the Hizbul Mujahideen and soon came to be called the 'poster boy of the militancy'. He is known to have recruited over a hundred boys from Kashmir for the Hizbul Mujahideen and used social media extensively to influence the minds of the youth.

Burhan was one of the first militants to reveal his face and identity on social media. Those Kashmiris who believed that Kashmir should be allowed to separate from India had found a face in him. YouTube was full of videos of Burhan Wani with militants, giggling, cracking jokes and occasionally humming and playing cricket. He had turned into an icon for enraged Kashmiri youth.

His appeal also lay in the fact that he discarded his mask, took ownership of the path that he had chosen and disclosed that he was from Tral and a well-educated family.

He was killed in an encounter with security forces on 8 July 2016 in Tral. Over 50,000 people congregated to mourn his death and joined his funeral procession.

Zakir Musa

On 12 May 2016, an audio recording by one Zakir Bhat went viral on the internet. Zakir was at that time the divisional commander of the Hizbul Mujahideen for south Kashmir. After the clip went viral, he was touted as a successor to Burhan Wani. Zakir had taken the name 'Musa' in honour of Prophet Moses, who is celebrated for having delivered his people from slavery through miracles.

Musa's audio clip emphasized that the militants were fighting to establish an 'Islamist system based on shariah law'. He described voting and democracy as 'haram' (religiously unacceptable in Islam). He expressed anger at those who described Kashmir's struggle as a 'political' one. He strongly rejected nationalism as the basis of the struggle, whether it was Kashmiri nationalism, Pakistani nationalism or any other nationalism. He demanded that the Hurriyat stop referring to the movement as a 'political' one. He went on to declare that he would slit the throat of any Kashmiri leader who called Kashmir's struggle a political one and string him up in Lal Chowk, the centre of Srinagar.

This part of his recording sent shock waves through the region and Pakistan's ISI handlers immediately swung into action. Musa also disassociated himself from the Hizbul Mujahideen. As a concession, he clarified that he had not criticized Syed Ali Shah Geelani, leader of the All Parties Hurriyat Conference, who wanted

Balidan Stambh in Jammu is a unique memorial which was conceived, and its foundation stone laid, during my tenure as Chief of Army Staff, in 2005. The underlying theme was to pay homage to all the martyrs from among the armed forces, paramilitary, police forces and civilians who have made the supreme sacrifice to uphold the territorial integrity of India. The obelisk is over 196 feet high, is shaped like a bayoneted rifle, the universal sign of a martyr, and symbolizes soldiers who have fought bravely in wars. The obelisk is visible from all places in the city and is a big tourist attraction.

A road was named after me on my superannuation in 2005, at a civic function organized by the state government. It runs along the main arterial route from the state assembly hall to Kachhi Chawni radio station in Jammu. My ancestral home is also located along this road.

All photos in this section courtesy of the author

At the pooja ceremony for the naming of General N.C. Vij Road: (from left to right) Governor Lieutenant General S.K. Sinha, Mrs Sinha, I and my wife Mrs Rita Vij.

To counter the menace of Pakistan-sponsored infiltration, a 740-kilometre-long anti-infiltration fence, from Chenab river in Jammu to Zojila Pass in the Kashmir Valley, was conceived and erected during my tenure as Chief of Army Staff in a record time of eighteen months. It is not only a complete physical barrier but also a system that integrates sensors, radars, night-vision devices, fail-safe communication and assured quick response reaction teams. This photograph catches one small portion of the fence from Chenab to Poonch.

The entire anti-infiltration fence up to Poonch is lit up at night.

A portion of the anti-infiltration fence in a snowed-in area in Tangdhar in the Kashmir Valley.

Soldiers patrolling in difficult terrain and conditions in Gurej Sector in the Kashmir Valley.

President of India Dr A.P.J. Abdul Kalam and I being briefed by the Brigade Commander, Brigadier (later Major General) V.K. Lalotra, along the Line of Control in the Rajouri-Poonch Sector.

To win the hearts and minds of the people, a welfare project by the name of Operation Sadbhavana was launched by the army around three decades back in J&K. Over the years it has become very popular with the locals. Here, President Dr A.P.J. Abdul Kalam meets with the head boy and head girl of Pine Wood school, being run by the army under this operation, along the Line of Control in the Rajouri-Poonch Sector on 3 May 2004.

A medical camp being run by the army as part of Operation Sadbhavana in South Kashmir.

Defence Minister (later President) Pranab Mukherjee being briefed by the Divisional Commander at Rustam Top view point in the Hajipir Pass area in Uri-Tithwal Sector: (from left to right) Divisional Commander Major General (later Lieutenant General) R.K. Mehta, Defence Minister Pranab Mukherjee, I and Lieutenant General Nirbhay Sharma, the Corps Commander.

Defence Minister (later President) Pranab Mukherjee with some of the command element of Northern Command at Rustam Post: (from left to right) Lieutenant General Nirbhay Sharma, GOC, 15 Corps; I; Lieutenant General Hari Prasad, the Army Commander; Major General R.K. Mehta, the Divisional Commander, and the Defence Minister.

Meeting the troops over a cup of tea: (from left to right) Lieutenant General Tippy Brar, 16 Corps Commander, and I.

My wife, Rita, and I.

On 31 December 2002, the day I took over as Chief of Army Staff: (from left to right) our son, Nalin; my wife, Rita; our daughter-in-law, Maneerath; and I.

Kashmir to be a part of Pakistan based on the fact that Pakistan was Islamic. Musa had, however, felt that Pakistan had 'betrayed Kashmiri jihad'.

Musa shot to popularity amongst Kashmiri teenagers for making that aggressive statement. He appeared at the funeral of another militant by the name of Sabaz, and there was a frenzy to touch his face, hair and clothes. He had become famous for having taken the extremist Islamist line to a higher level. While he was particularly popular amongst the youth, not all in the older generation shared his views.

David Devadas, in his book *Rage of Kashmir*, explains that Musa's image had developed over the decade from 2007 to 2017. At the time, there was a radical shift in the way young people treated and practised religion. There was also a general rejection of liberal democracy as a legitimate system. The romance of an Islamist regime based on shariah law and the traditions of an early Caliphate became immensely popular with the youth. Another trend was a generational shift to 'mass rage'. Musa was in his early twenties when he became the divisional commander. Burhan was only twenty when he was elevated.

Later on, the Hizbul Mujahideen distanced itself from Musa and he was declared as chief of the AGuH, a newly created cell of Al-Qaeda, which caught traction on social media. Today, most of Musa's associates have been eliminated, and there are reportedly only four people left in his group. He himself was eliminated on 24 May 2019 in an encounter with the police in Tral. Musa is as relevant as Burhan Wani in the narrative of Kashmiri terrorism wherein any resistance to the government and a rebellious attitude are very much appreciated.

Challenging Times

There is little doubt that these were very challenging times. However, the security forces rose to the challenge admirably and constantly re-tailored their own strategy. As a result, the army carried out more and more joint operations with the police and paramilitary forces. The security forces evolved effective strategies to combat the increasing stone pelting, wherein the police and CRPF played important and effective roles. The army continued to exercise tremendous restraint in the face of massive provocations. There was increased emphasis on the coordination of pinpoint intelligence-based operations with police and paramilitary forces. The army also took severe disciplinary action in all cases of grave violation of human rights, which has been appreciated by all.

Many senior officers in the Valley at the level of divisional and corps commanders have stated on record that the Kashmir issue is a political problem. Thus, ultimately, the answer to the militancy lies in finding a political solution, but one that keeps national interest uppermost in mind. It has to be made clear to the agitators that J&K is a part of India and freedom is not an option. These were the two most important parameters of any mutually arrived at solution with the Kashmiris. The problem is that Kashmiri leaders are unwilling to negotiate a solution. Perhaps they were aware that if they negotiate with the central government, they will lose their standing and will be rejected by the people of the Valley.

The Prime Pillars of Pakistan's Strategy

There are some key assumptions that Pakistan always takes into consideration when planning anything against India.

Firstly, there is the persistent belief that India is a weak nation because of its heterogeneity. Secondly, Pakistan believes that the

India's Counter-militancy Strategy

Kashmiri Muslim population remains completely outside the realm of integration with India, so much so that the Kashmiri Muslims have not integrated even with the Indian Muslims. Thirdly, even though the Shia Muslims of Kargil, who constitute 12 per cent of the Muslim population in J&K, have no separatist inclinations, they are segregated by the Zojila Pass and thus are largely inconsequential. The five Sunni-dominated districts of south Kashmir in the Valley are solid proponents of azadi. Geographically also, the Valley constitutes a distinctly separate and independent entity, which facilitates the struggle. Fourthly, the provinces of Jammu and Ladakh stand alienated from the Valley, so the Valley goes its own way and adopts courses of action by itself and for itself. Fifthly, while most Kashmiris may be against joining with Pakistan, the fervour for azadi is strong and can definitely be exploited by Pakistan. Finally, Pakistan has succeeded in radicalizing the Valley, which has become the single-biggest factor of concern.

It can be clearly understood from the above-mentioned issues that Pakistan considers the merger of Kashmir with it as an unfinished agenda of Partition. Even at the time of Partition, plans to annex the serene Valley were hatched and executed in October 1947. In 1965, the same strategy was once again adopted to wrest control of the state from India. The drive to stage and support the secession of Kashmir from the Union of India received revengeful impetus after the humiliating defeat of Pakistan and its partition in 1971. Pakistan's dictator, General Mohammad Zia-ul-Haq, Islamized Pakistani society, including its army, and constructed numerous madrasas and mosques along the entire frontier straddling Pakistan and Afghanistan. He used these jihadi factories to produce terrorists in the hundreds, sending them to Afghanistan to fight the Soviets, and diverting them to Kashmir, Chechnya and Bosnia to spread terror. The portrayal of Pakistani army regulars as mujahids in the Kargil conflict of 1999 was part of the same strategy.

What is more disconcerting is that just when India's strategies to counter the proxy war were beginning to bear fruit, Pakistan changed gears, and the earlier policy of a 'thousand cuts' propagated by General Zia-ul-Haq was replaced by the policy of a 'thousand revolutions', propounded by former chief of army staff, General Raheel Sharif. This new strategy was fuelled by highly effective information warfare, which India found problematic to keep pace with.

The seeds of militancy were sown in the Valley in the late nineties and since then it has witnessed various shifts from indigenous to proxy war and from a demand for freedom to an ideology-driven strife. These changes were primarily due to strategic transformations orchestrated by Pakistan. The constantly changing contours of the militancy in accordance with developing situations has been the prime reason for its survival for so long.

The continued success of the militancy is thus dependent on factors such as the promotion of the idea of separatism, cultivation of the media, the continuous flow of finances including counterfeit currency from Pakistan and the Gulf countries, the radicalization of the Muslim population, street turbulence, exploitation of social media and the curtailment of government initiatives. Fortunately for the militants, whenever their efforts began losing ground, they were innovative enough to find triggers to reignite the militancy.

Pakistan's endeavour is that the worldwide Islamic community sides with them to put pressure on India regarding the Kashmir issue. To this end, Pakistan has been pleading the case of Kashmir at meetings of the Organisation of Islamic Cooperation (OIC), an influential group of fifty-seven Islamic countries. Pakistan's efforts elicited a favourable statement from the OIC. However,

India made notable gains in this sphere when the then foreign minister, Sushma Swaraj, was invited as a guest of honour to the OIC meeting on 1 March 2019. This was the first time that India was invited to a meeting of the OIC. In protest, Pakistan boycotted the session.

One aspect that is, however, laudable in Jammu and Kashmir is that despite its best efforts, Pakistan has not been able to engineer Hindu–Muslim riots in the state, and that is why the Jammu and hill belts of the state have been stable and under the firm control of the administration. This, however, does not mean that Pakistan has been deterred by its failures and is likely to give up its efforts in the immediate and mid-future. India must be prepared to live with the proxy war for the foreseeable future.

8

The Watershed Year

'Men never do evil so completely and cheerfully as when they do it from religious conviction.'
— Blaise Pascal

'Fundamentalism isn't about religion, it's about power.'
— Salman Rushdie

The Pulwama Attack

On 14 February 2019, a suicide attack took place on a CRPF convoy moving from Jammu to Srinagar in the Pulwama area in south Kashmir. It was a big convoy of seventy-eight vehicles carrying approximately 2,500 CRPF personnel. A car suddenly appeared on the highway near Pulwama, emerging from a village road. It was driven by a young man and turned out to be loaded with explosives. He drove parallel to the convoy for a short while and then detonated his device next to the fourth vehicle in the convoy. There was a massive explosion and the fourth and fifth vehicles were hit. As a result, forty CRPF personnel were killed and a large number injured. The Pulwama bomber was identified as Adil Ahmad Dar, a school dropout. He was a deeply radicalized fanatic, who was fully prepared to blow himself up along with the CRPF personnel. The intelligence agencies had never considered him to be a high-grade security risk.

The JeM immediately claimed responsibility for this incident. Their leader is Masood Azhar, a notorious fundamentalist, who was one of the three militants released in January 2000 by India in exchange for the hostages on Indian Airlines flight IC-814 that was hijacked and taken to Kandahar. The group's primary aim is to separate Kashmir from India and merge it with Pakistan. This, they feel, will open up the gateway to the rest of India for their jihad. Since its inception in 2000, this terror outfit has carried out several notorious attacks. These include suicide attacks at the J&K legislature complex, the army's 15 Corps headquarters in Badami Bagh in Srinagar, the Sunjuwan army cantonment in Jammu, the Uri brigade headquarters in Kashmir and the Indian Parliament. JeM operates at two levels: one is infiltrating terrorists into J&K and the second is masterminding major terror attacks both within J&K and outside.

A detailed enquiry into the Pulwama incident has now been concluded, but the details have yet to be declassified for reasons best known to the government. However, *The Lover Boy of Bhawalpur: How the Pulwama Case Was Cracked*, a book by counterinsurgency journalist Rahul Pandita, published in 2021, clearly establishes the involvement of Adil Dar, a local terrorist, and Umar Farooq, nephew of Masood Azhar. Preliminary findings indicated that anywhere between 100 and 200 kg of explosives was used, which included approximately 50–70 kg of the high-grade military explosive RDX. It was also established that one highly trained Jaish bomb maker travelled to Kashmir to assemble the bomb with a full trigger mechanism. This bomb maker was subsequently eliminated in an encounter with security forces within three days of the Pulwama incident.

The nation was aghast and angry at this dastardly attack on the CRPF convoy. Every time such an attack takes place, there is a huge clamour in the country and questions are raised as to how India has allowed the problem in Kashmir to linger on politically and administratively for over three decades. The real problem is that there has never been any well-defined consistent national strategy to handle the Pakistan-sponsored terrorism in the state. As a result, there has been no consistency in India's approach to the problem. At times, it appears that we drift from one high-profile incident to another. The decades-old approach of fighting terrorism from inside Indian territory has hardly helped. Another drawback has been that India has never made Pakistan, the abettors of this terrorism, pay the price for its misadventures, and hence it has pressed on with impunity.

India's Response

The anger in the country following the Pulwama incident was so intense that it was obvious to one and all that mere condemnation of the incident would not assuage the feelings of the people. The punishment meted out to the terrorist group JeM would have to be of such magnitude that it would serve as a stark warning to all other terrorist groups and also equally to Pakistan. The prime minister announced that he had given a free hand to the armed forces to respond at a place, time and manner of their choosing.

It was assessed that the military options short of war ranged from intense artillery shelling and missile attacks on terrorist camps to ground-based attacks and the capture of some weak Pakistani posts in PoK. Precise and well-calibrated air strikes against non-state actors in PoK was also considered amongst the most effective options to serve a warning and not only instil fear into the terrorists but also embarrass Pakistan. This would define a new 'red line' for Pakistan and clearly indicate that incidents of this kind would draw a serious Indian response, and the responsibility for any escalation would lie squarely on Pakistan's shoulders.

Ultimately, the Indian response went many notches higher and surprised everybody. On 26 February 2019, twelve Mirage 2000 jets of the Indian air force carried out a precision attack on a JeM camp at Balakot, 80 km inside Pakistani territory in Pakhtunkhwa. Following the strike, India's foreign secretary, in a joint press statement along with the air force, clearly stated the Indian stand that the action was a 'pre-emptive non-military air strike on a JeM training centre facility, based on credible intelligence to thwart another possible attack on India which was under planning by the JeM'.

Pakistan conceded the violation of its air space and the engagement of, what it called, a Jaish madrasa at Balakot. It also asserted that their scrambling fighters had forced the Indian jets to retreat hastily and drop their payloads in vacant fields and forests, as a result of which no casualties or infrastructural damage had been suffered. This response from Pakistan was along expected lines. The Indian strike force had used SPICE laser-guided Israeli missiles, which had hit the targets with great precision. The satellite pictures of the target have subsequently proved the genuineness of the Indian strike and the possible damage inflicted and disproved the Pakistani assertion of no damage. The most critical aspect of the strike was that Indian air force fighters had not only crossed the LoC for the first time since the war of 1971 and also since both sides had become nuclear powers, but had also gone 80 km inside Pakistan. Even during the Kargil war, the Indian air force had been severely restricted and had not been allowed to cross the LoC. This was clearly a departure from how India had responded in the past. It was now ready to call Pakistan's bluff.

On the morning of 27 February, the day after the air strike on Balakot, twenty-four Pakistani F-16 jets came close to the LoC in the Rajouri area and were chased by India's alert air defence aircraft, which were a combination of Sukhoi 30, Mirage 2000 and MiG-21 Bison jets. The Pakistani fighters, to avoid being engaged by the Indian fighters, hurried to make an exit and just emptied their payloads, thus widely missing the targeted brigade headquarters and a petrol dump. In the dogfight, the Pakistanis lost one F-16 to a MiG-21 Bison, which was chasing it. In its forward momentum, the MiG crossed the LoC and was shot down by ground fire. The pilot, Wing Commander Abhinandan Varthaman, ejected and landed in the Lam valley area and survived. History had been created wherein a MiG-21 Bison had shot down the much-vaunted F-16. The Indian pilot was repatriated to India at the Wagha border near Amritsar after forty-eight hours due to immense Indian and international pressure. Pakistan's prime minister called it a peace move and also made empty offers of reconciliation, which were ignored by India.

The Implications

The Indian air strike not only left Pakistan and the rest of the world surprised but also drew certain red lines for Pakistan. It had emphatically created a new first. There were, however, both positives as well as uncertainties that emerged.

First the positives. For one, it was made clear to Pakistan that India would retain the right to respond to terrorist attacks in the manner it deemed most appropriate. The LoC in such scenarios would henceforth have no significance and would be crossed at will to punish terrorists. They would not be allowed to live and sleep in peace. The nature of the punishment would vary from incident to incident and the mode could range from artillery fire to drone, missile or even ground attacks and the capture of Pakistani posts in PoK.

Going forward, India's self-imposed restriction on the use of its air force for an offensive operation would no longer be applicable and terror targets would be engaged even inside mainland Pakistan. If Pakistan were to retaliate and engage military targets, as they did after the Balakot strike, it would be deemed as launching war against India and they would be held squarely responsible for the escalation and not India, who would have justifiably gone after only the terror targets. Pakistan has no such targets inside India and hence there is no justification for a military response by them.

Covert action by India could also be an option, but the Government of India has not given any such indication, nor has any such action been carried out. There are clearly defined fault lines in Pakistan's own backyard that India has refrained from exploiting. In any case, the details of such operations, if ever carried out, are never revealed.

An important factor that has generally been glossed over or not understood by analysts at large is that Pakistan had quite successfully adopted a strategy of what they termed 'full-spectrum deterrence'. This helped Pakistan pursue a sub-conventional war (proxy war) under the umbrella of a nuclear overhang, thus denying India the option to use its conventional might to punish the terrorists inside Pakistan for their misadventures. One of the biggest positives resulting from the air strikes following the Pulwama incident was that India punctured and shattered this strategy of full spectrum deterrence. It now stands established that controlled escalations and controlled wars of this kind, wherein the targets remain only the terrorists, are very possible. This will help India grievously hurt the jihadis anywhere inside Pakistan and thus reduce their efficacy. This should also seriously discourage Pakistan from engineering any rash incidents inside J&K or anywhere across the international border.

The Pulwama attack also focused the world's attention on the jihadi groups in Pakistan that are promoting terrorism in India. In fact, India's robust reaction in using its air force for an anti-terrorist strike in mainland Pakistan won understanding from key countries. Surprisingly, even China's response was very carefully formulated.

As a result, Pakistan is now under severe pressure to act against these terror groups and has made moves against Jamaat-ud-Dawa (JuD) and JeM. However, these are only demonstrative actions and easily reversible and thus not of any consequence.

A joint resolution was moved by the US, the UK and France in the Security Council to declare and ban JeM as an international terrorist organization and declare Masood Azhar a global terrorist. Russia also supported the resolution, but China blocked it in a discussion in the UN Security Council on 13 December 2019.

However, another resolution moved by the US on this issue and supported by France and the UK came up before the Security Council on 1 May 2019 and this time China withdrew its so-called 'technical blockade'. Masood Azhar has now been declared a global terrorist. This was a big political victory for India and a vindication of its stand against terrorism.

India also initiated certain political actions such as withdrawing Pakistan's 'most favoured nation' status and increasing the excise duty on Pakistani merchandise to 200 per cent. In Kashmir, the security cover for separatist leaders was withdrawn and so also for over a hundred other politicians and leaders with dubious backgrounds. Over a hundred battalions of paramilitary forces were inducted in the Valley to further strengthen the security grid. On the flip side, even though Balakot was a strong message from India to Pakistan, whether it has been seriously registered by them or not is not clear. India's strong response and subsequent actions are unlikely to dissuade the Pakistani deep state from pursuing their low-cost strategy of a proxy war. There may be temporary and intermittent lulls, but the proxy war is unlikely to be abandoned by the Pakistani military establishment. Indeed, for the Pakistani military to stay in power and relevant, the Kashmir problem must persist, and so they are not going to let go of this strategy.

In the final analysis, it is clear once again that India will have to fight terrorism on its own. India has shown that it has refined its strategy to combat terrorism on multiple fronts, including diplomatic, economic and military. Pakistan, which is already in a financially precarious situation, cannot afford to be drawn into an uncontrolled escalation, which would be ruinous for it both militarily and economically. It is already under the close scrutiny of the international Financial Action Task Force (FATF) and any terrorist actions would be counterproductive for it. The FATF is an intergovernmental organization founded in 1989 on the initiative of the G7 to develop policies to combat money laundering. In 2001, its mandate was expanded to include terrorism financing. The recent Saudi bailout will only help its financial condition in the short term. In the long run, Pakistan has no financial staying power.

While the security forces in India will continue to do their best to fight the menace, the answer to this long-drawn battle lies in a multipronged approach along the diplomatic, economic and military fronts. The world is very concerned by the rise of terrorism as it has spread to Europe and the US. South Asia and the Middle

East are already engulfed in a protracted war. So Pakistan must be pressured to give up this path. However, despite their concern regarding India–Pakistan relations, it is most unlikely that America and its allies will downgrade Pakistan to Blacklist (America needs Pakistan's help to get out of Afghanistan) as was done in the case of Iran, North Korea and even Russia. Imran Khan's discourse of a 'naya (new) Pakistan' is only a chimera, as Kanwal Sibal, India's distinguished former foreign secretary, has called it.

In the long run, Kashmiri radicals may come to realize that they are pursuing an impossible mission and that Pakistan cannot help them. However, the deeply ingrained radicalization has made the radicals blind to logic, and they may take quite some time to understand this. India must thus be prepared for a long struggle in the interim.

The Situation as of July 2019 – Before Abrogation of Articles 370 and 35A

The level of militancy in J&K could broadly be judged from the data provided below.

Between 1990 and 2007, the number of active foreign terrorists in the Valley hovered around 2,000 to 2,500. By 2013, there were only 70–80 active militants in the Valley. The number of foreign terrorists has dropped to just three-digit figures. The main reason for the drop in the number of foreign militants has been the failure on the part of Pakistan to infiltrate large numbers of terrorists into J&K due to the fence along the LoC being closely and effectively guarded. As a result, there has been a change in Pakistan's strategy and a major drive towards local recruitment since 2008. The data given subsequently is compiled from the records of the J&K police.

A police report of early August 2018 revealed that 337 militants were active in the Valley, of which 211 were locals and 126 were foreigners. Of the listed militants, 181 were active in 2018 in the volatile south Kashmir districts, which have been on the edge ever since the killing of Burhan Wani in 2016.

In four districts of south Kashmir, namely, Anantnag, Kulgam, Pulwama and Shopian, there were 166 local militants in 2019. Out of the 129 militants active in the north, ninety-four were foreign terrorists and thirty-five were locals. There were reportedly only seventeen militants in central Kashmir's districts of Srinagar, Budgam and Ganderbal.

Another set of figures available from the Rajya Sabha's question-and-answer sessions of 27 March 2017 and 12 December 2018 are given below.

Year	Infiltration attempts	Net estimated infiltration	Number of youth joining the militancy
2013	277	97	16
2014	222	65	53
2015	121	33	66
2016	371	119	88
2017	419	136	126
2018	284	128	164

It is clear that Pakistan's ability to infiltrate foreign terrorists into India in large numbers has been severely compromised. The related trend of an increase in local militants is obvious.

Even the local militants are largely confined to south Kashmir, which has become the centre of gravity of the militancy. However, it is important to understand that the situation in the Valley can flare up at the smallest instance and engulf the entire Valley, including north Kashmir.

The situation, though not stable, was nowhere near as grim as it was earlier up to 2005–06, when foreign terrorists played a major part, or even post-Burhan Wani's elimination. However, the emphasis had clearly shifted to local militants.

A new set of figures, provided by the J&K police and the army on 24 April 2019, is given below.

Terror Attacks

From May 2004 to May 2014 (ten years): 1,771
From May 2014 to April 2019 (five years): 1,708
(This shows the increased intensity of militancy)

Terrorists Killed

From May 2004 to May 2014 (ten years): 471
From May 2014 to April 2019 (five years): 945
(Terrorists suffered almost 200 per cent more attrition in the 2014–19 five-year period than in the preceding ten-year period)
In 2018: 257
In 2019, up to 28 June: 113

A new area of concern was the increasing number of suicide attacks and car bombs. Another matter of concern is that most of the terrorists are using steel bullets, which can pierce through the security forces' bulletproof jackets. Such bullets and the explosives used for car bombs are likely sourced from the Chinese. The security forces will have to accordingly readjust their tactics and standard operating procedures to counter these threats.

The security forces have an upper hand in the operations, and the operational lifespan of a terrorist is rather limited, from six to nine months. Most of the terrorist leadership has been eliminated. India is, however, losing out badly in the domain of social media and perception management. Deep radicalization of the Valley and alienation are the major reasons for that. India has to overcome weaknesses in these areas at the earliest. Despite such heavy casualties in the last five years from 2016 to 2020 and especially during the last one year, the terrorists have not realized that they are only cannon fodder. This is the impact of radicalization wherein they feel that their getting killed gives them a passage to heaven.

A Comparison with 1990

A perception that was being created by the separatists was that the situation in 2019 was akin to that in 1990–92 when the proxy war commenced and was quite grim. At that time, the pro-Pakistan faction of the Kashmiris believed that Kashmir would attain azadi overnight. This incorrect conclusion needs to be better explained and clearly understood.

In 1990, the strength of terrorists in Kashmir was extremely large, between 2,000 and 3,000, and the LoC was virtually open with little efficacy in deployment to stop infiltration and exfiltration. Pakistan had also established training camps in the far reaches of the hills surrounding the Valley and had gradually built up large caches of arms, ammunition and explosives. (Today, hardly any such catches exist.) Furthermore, the J&K police were largely inexperienced and in some cases their loyalty had also been eroded. The SOG had not yet been raised, and a few hastily rushed BSF battalions, which were not trained well enough, were fighting the hardcore terrorists. Also, the army had not yet been deployed, and the AFSPA was enacted in Kashmir only in 1990 to provide the legal empowerment for their deployment.

In contrast, over forty battalions of the RR controlled the counterterrorist grid deployment in the Valley, as of 2019, and the regular army formations have a well-coordinated counter-infiltration grid based on the fence, which runs from the Chenab river to Zojila Pass. One big advantage of the RR battalions is that they remain in the security grid and hence their institutional memory becomes a reservoir of information.

Further, a set of dedicated Special Forces battalions support the army's operations, acting as force multipliers. The CRPF had over sixty battalions on active duty in the region as of 2019 (the number of CRPF battalions increased to 80 in 2020–21). The J&K police have the capable SOG supporting their operations.

Another advantage is that the AFSPA has been operative for a long time now and the army troops are well aware of its implications.

The intelligence today is also of a much higher quality and that has enabled the security forces to pinpoint targets. However, there are still gaps in the intelligence and there is considerable scope for improvement. A striking example of this lacuna is that it has not been able to identify and neutralize the terrorists' leadership.

The success of the operations by the security forces is obvious from the fact that the number of foreign terrorists in the Valley has come down to less than 100, as against the 2,000 to 3,000 that was the case in the nineties.

The problem is that the youth, which has grown up under the shadow of the gun and bears antipathy towards the security forces, has been trying to bring about a new type of militancy since 2016. The youth is deeply radicalized and alienated and ever more willing to experiment with the use of extreme violence. Stone pelting has become the new normal. Pakistan is instigating street turbulence through an invisible leadership and employing social media, other means of information warfare and clandestine financing.

But what causes even greater worry is that, as mentioned before, there are still definite gaps in the efficacy of India's intelligence gathering, even though it has improved by leaps and bounds in the last five years. The fact that the intelligence agencies did not have a clue that JeM was planning the Pulwama attack for months and even smuggled an expert into the Valley to assemble a bomb is a serious lapse. How did they not find out that such a large quantity of explosives, which even more worryingly included a large quantity of RDX, had been collected? And how is it that they did not know that the suicide bomber, Adil Ahmad Dar, who was already under suspicion, had turned into a hardcore terrorist? In any counter-insurgency operation, intelligence forms the nerve centre. Till the intelligence improves to near perfection, such incidents will be unavoidable. But in fairness to the intelligence set-up, it must be clarified that they are almost there and moreover, no intelligence agency can perhaps achieve perfection in intelligence gathering.

The other major failure has been in terms of relaxing the tried-and-tested standard operating procedures. Otherwise, the simultaneous movement of civil vehicles on the same segment of the road on which the military convoy was moving would not have been permitted. This lapse resulted in a grim tragedy.

However, broadly, it can be concluded that the security situation in the Valley is much better than in 1990 and has also somewhat improved from what it was following Burhan Wani's elimination. With a tight anti-infiltration posture, the number of foreign terrorists in the Valley has reduced considerably over a period. Pakistan is now focusing more on maintaining the heat along the LoC, smuggling in fake money and keeping the noise over Kashmir alive internationally. There has also been a constant effort to create high-profile incidents, such as the attack in Pulwama.

Although the security situation may have improved, there are other worrying trends and forces to contend with. The high degree of radicalization and assumption of leadership of the militancy by the deeply radicalized and alienated youth poses an altogether new type of challenge. From the pulpits of the mosques to social media accounts, it is obvious that the Valley is turning Wahabi with a fierceness that has never been seen before. The power of the mosques continues to remain high. This radicalization is also the result of having jobless and idle youth in the Valley.

Stone pelting is being carried out by children between the ages of eight and fifteen, and this is being exploited as a major tool by mischievous elements, who are doling out money to these children. If educational institutions remain closed for long periods, as it happened after Burhan Wani's death, more and more of these children will be available in the streets.

It is unfortunate that India could not take advantage of the periods of relative peace during the time of the Vajpayee government (1998–2004) and then between 2008 and 2012 (even though there were interludes of violence during the period) to improve the quality of governance. The government should have gone all out to bring about major development in the state, started meaningful dialogues at several levels and thus made progress. Instead, it wasted those hard-earned years of peace and India is now paying for it. But did the fault lie with the government or with the self-serving leaders and the people of the Valley who were blinded by deep radicalization?

As it stands today, there is no dialogue at any level. This lack of dialogue creates a 'pressure cooker' kind of a situation, which is tense and undesirable.

The fall of the BJP–PDP state government in June 2018 also contributed towards a sense of insecurity amongst the people, more so in the Valley. The Kashmiris were very suspicious of this alliance from the very beginning.

Similarly, rumours that the central government was likely to remove Article 35A and possibly also do away with Article 370 generated a lot of disquiet and unrest (this was announced on 5 August 2019 and is covered in detail in later chapters). This added to the ever-increasing degree of insecurity in the state.

Various political parties were competing with each other to take advantage of this situation.

Unfortunately, rather than help each other ease the situation, all three major provinces of the state, namely, Jammu, Ladakh and Kashmir, had become increasingly estranged from one another. The time had come for the grievances of the people of Jammu and Ladakh to also be looked at seriously. If not done, it would further deepen the divide. The unprecedented strikes in Jammu in 2008 in connection with the dispute over the transfer of land to the Shri Amarnath Shrine Board left a lot of bitterness in the minds of the Kashmiris. At the same time, it led to the realization in Kashmir that Jammu can be an effective bottleneck to choke their logistics in case of serious differences of opinion. Alienation between Jammu and Kashmir is not in anybody's interest and is also detrimental to national interest.

People were losing faith in governance and resultantly the political process was faltering. In the 2014 assembly elections, the percentage of voter turnout was 65.23 per cent, which was a spectacular achievement. Contrast this to the 2018 by-election in Srinagar for the parliamentary seat wherein Dr Farooq Abdullah was elected and barely 7 per cent chose to exercise their franchise. This is in itself a barometer of the people's lack of faith in the government. The panchayat elections in October 2018 also saw a very low percentage of votes being cast and what is more, many seats were not even contested. Even the percentage of voting in the April-May 2019 parliamentary elections hovered between 7 to 18 per cent in different segments of the Valley.

A New Government at the Centre in May 2019

In early 2019, Home Minister Amit Shah visited J&K. His visit aroused a lot of interest and also hopes in some segments that the government was serious about solving the Jammu and Kashmir issue. Following his visit, the Ministry of Home Affairs presented in the Parliament an analysis of the status of militancy as follows:

- Decline in terror incidents: 28 per cent
- Reduction in infiltration: 43 per cent
- Decline in local recruitment: 40 per cent
- Increase in neutralization of terrorists: 22 per cent

These certainly presented encouraging indications. This was, however, not the first time that such a situation had existed. But the governments of the time failed to seize the initiative because their efforts were mostly unidimensional rather than all encompassing.

The new government at the Centre realized that Pakistan was indulging in hybrid warfare, which is a military strategy that employs political warfare and blends conventional warfare, irregular warfare and cyber warfare with other influencing methods such as fake news and diplomacy. Hybrid warfare is most commonly used in conducting militancy. Hybrid conflicts in J&K are being boosted by five major parameters, namely, the total number of terrorists as a sum total of infiltration plus members out of local recruitment; financial resources and the availability of wherewithal such as weapons; over-ground workers; ideology/radicalization; and the alienation of the youth.

The government is focusing its efforts on neutralizing the above parameters. The over-ground workers (people who help militants with logistical support, cash, shelter, etc.) have been rounded up over the past few years and charged under stringent acts of the law. Other parameters assisting hybrid warfare, like human and financial resources, are also being taken care of by the intelligence and security agencies. But two parameters that would require a humongous effort are combating radicalization and addressing the alienation of the youth. This would be a long-drawn process stretching over several years, maybe 3–5 years.

India should also not forget that Pakistan's ISI will leave no stone unturned to reignite the flashpoints in the Valley. The government should focus on a 'whole of the government' approach and for once take advantage of the emerging positive situation so that this opportunity is not wasted as before.

One is now left wondering if fighting a proxy war in the state will ever lead to a solution. India has countered the insurgency during the last thirty years in various intensities, but with no dramatic results. Has the time come to carry out some major changes which may create difficulties in the beginning but ultimately lead to a permanent solution? This is a question that has been on many minds, especially of the central leadership, which is not prepared to allow this kind of situation to drift for too long. Their response can be seen in the subsequent sections.

Kashmir vis-à-vis PoK and Gilgit-Baltistan

The issue of Kashmir has always been a bone of contention between India and Pakistan. PoK is the area occupied by Pakistan through an illegal invasion after the Instrument of Accession was signed by the maharaja of Jammu and Kashmir with India.

With regard to Gilgit-Baltistan, in 1930 the maharaja gave this area to the British under a sixty-year lease to look after the frontiers. When Independence was announced, all earlier deeds were treated as cancelled and the maharaja sent Brigadier Ghansara Singh as his governor to take over the area. Legally, Gilgit-Baltistan became part of the Instrument of Accession, but the local British contingent commander (not to be mistaken for the British government) incited a revolt and took over the area and later handed it over to Pakistan.

Both PoK and Gilgit-Baltistan legally belong to India, and it was made clear after the abrogation of Articles 370 and 35A on 5 August 2019 that it has a genuine claim over these areas. It will be of interest to make a comparative study of these two areas that are with Pakistan vis-à-vis Kashmir on the Indian side, to gauge the progress made by both sides. This is being attempted in two parts. The first is a statistical comparison, which establishes clearly how well-off the Kashmiris on India's side are as compared to those in Pakistan. The second explains how poorly adjusted the Kashmiris are with Pakistan. For this part, I have relied on some interesting excerpts from a book written by Dr Sudhir Bloeria, a former chief secretary of J&K, and eight articles written by a Kashmiri, M. Zafar Chaudhary, who wrote these after his visit to PoK in 2011.

Subject	Jammu and Kashmir (India)	Pakistan-occupied Kashmir (Azad Jammu and Kashmir)	Gilgit-Baltistan
Budget	Rs 1,01,428 crore (2020–21) (USD 13,514.35 million)	Rs 54,890 million (2019–20) (USD 333 million)	Rs 33,000 million (USD 205 million)
Health and medical services	Rs 1,268 crore (USD 168.95 million)	Rs 750 million (2019–20) (USD 4.55 million)	Rs 587 million (USD 3.56 million)
Population	1,25,41,302 (2011 census)	40,45,366 (2017 census)	14,92,000 (2017 census)
NSDP per capita income	Rs 92,800 (2019–20) (USD 1305.27)	USD 1,201 (2017–18)	USD 268 (2017–18)

Subject	Jammu and Kashmir (India)	Pakistan-occupied Kashmir (Azad Jammu and Kashmir)	Gilgit-Baltistan
Education	Rs 2,392 crore (USD 318.7 million; 12 per cent of the state budget)	Rs 670 million (2019–20) (USD 4.06 million)	Rs 1.26 billion (USD 7.6 million)
(a) Institutes of national importance	• Indian Institute of Technology, Jammu • Indian Institute of Management, Jammu • National Institute of Technology, Srinagar • National Institute of Fashion Technology, Srinagar	• University of Science and Technology, Mirpur • University of Azad Jammu and Kashmir • Mohi-ud-Din Islamic University • University of Kotli	• Karakoram International University • University of Baltistan
(b) Number of prominent colleges	• Kashmir: 50 colleges • Jammu: 27 colleges	• 6 colleges	• 4 colleges

Subject	Jammu and Kashmir (India)	Pakistan-occupied Kashmir (Azad Jammu and Kashmir)	Gilgit-Baltistan
(c) Medical colleges	• Government Medical College, Srinagar • Government Medical College, Anantnag • Sher-i-Kashmir Institute of Medical Sciences, Srinagar • Government Medical College, Baramulla • Government Medical College, Jammu • Government Medical College, Kathua • Government Medical College, Rajouri • Acharya Shri Chander College of Medical Sciences, Jammu	• Mohtarma Benazir Bhutto Shaheed Medical College, Mirpur • Azad Jammu Kashmir Medical College, Muzaffarabad • Poonch Medical College, Rawalakot • Mohi-ud-Din Islamic Medical College, Mirpur	• Abaseen Institute of Medical and Modern Sciences, Gilgit

The Watershed Year

Subject	Jammu and Kashmir (India)	Pakistan-occupied Kashmir (Azad Jammu and Kashmir)	Gilgit-Baltistan
Infrastructure			
(a) Airports	• Jammu airport • Srinagar international airport • Advanced landing ground, Kargil (used for helicopters and flights for civilians to Leh and other areas • Poonch airport Used for • Rajouri airport. Helicopter flights.	Nil (Both the Muzaffarabad and Rawalakot airports have been closed since 2016)	• Gilgit airport (small) • Skardu airport (proper airport)
(b) Railway stations	Jammu region: • Kathua, Hiranagar, Samba, Vijaypur, Bari Brahmana, Jammu, Bajalta, Ramnagar, Udhampur, Chak Rakhwal, Katra and Banihal	• Hanapur railway station • Muzaffarabad railway station is proposed for construction	The reconstruction of the Khunjerab railway line is proposed, from Abbottabad to Khunjerab Junction passing through Gilgit, Hunza, Khunjerab Junction, China

Subject	Jammu and Kashmir (India)	Pakistan-occupied Kashmir (Azad Jammu and Kashmir)	Gilgit-Baltistan
	Srinagar region: • Hiller Shahabad, Qazigund, Anantnag, Bijbiara, Panzgom, Awantipura, Pampur, Srinagar, Badgam, Pattan, Sopur and Baramulla • More railway stations will come up when the railway line from Jammu to Srinagar is completed.		

Subject	Jammu and Kashmir (India)	Pakistan-occupied Kashmir (Azad Jammu and Kashmir)	Gilgit-Baltistan
(c) Highways	Vikas Yojana • Budget: Rs 42,000 crore (USD 5.51 billion) • Chenani–Reasi tunnel • Length: 9.2 km • Height: 1,200 ft • Mughal Road (completed): Rs 4,000 crore (USD 0.52 billion) • Ring Road, Srinagar: Rs 2,002 crore (USD 0.26 billion) • Ring Road, Jammu: Rs 2,000 crore (USD 0.26 billion) • National highway in north India that connects the Kashmir Valley to Jammu and the rest of India.	• The China–Pakistan Economic Corridor is being constructed by China. It will run through the Khunjerab Pass from China through northern Pakistan, Lahore, Karachi and Gwadar Port. • The construction cost projected for the corridor was USD 62 billion in 2017.	

Subject	Jammu and Kashmir (India)	Pakistan-occupied Kashmir (Azad Jammu and Kashmir)	Gilgit-Baltistan
	• Old National Highway 1A to Leh runs through some treacherous terrain and is closed down during the winter months because of avalanches or landslides. • Jawahar Tunnel, which connects Jammu with the Kashmir Valley across the Pir Panjal Range.		

Subject	Jammu and Kashmir (India)	Pakistan-occupied Kashmir (Azad Jammu and Kashmir)	Gilgit-Baltistan
	• New tunnels are being constructed to reduce the distance between Jammu and Srinagar by 82 km and the travel time by two-thirds. Most of these tunnels, such as the Dr Syama Prasad Mookerjee Tunnel and the new Banihal Qazigund Road Tunnel have been completed and commissioned.		

Subject	Jammu and Kashmir (India)	Pakistan-occupied Kashmir (Azad Jammu and Kashmir)	Gilgit-Baltistan
(d) Dams	Jammu region • Baglihar dam • Dul Hasti hydropower plant • Pakal Dul dam Kashmir region • Kishanganga hydropower plant • Salal hydropower station • Uri hydropower station	Mangla dam, a multipurpose dam on the Jhelum river in Mirpur district	The Diamer-Bhasha hydropower project, being undertaken jointly with China, is under construction for about Rs 1,406.5 billion (USD 8.51 billion USD). It might be completed in 2028.
(e) Roads/bridges	• 511 bridges are planned • 78 major bridges were to be completed by 2019 • The 1,315 metre Chenab bridge is under construction in Reasi. It will be the tallest rail bridge in Asia.	The 474-metre-long Earthquake Memorial Bridge on the Jhelum river in Muzaffarabad (constructed in 2014)	• Danyor suspension bridge on the Hunza river, which connects to the Karakoram Highway • The Hussaini suspension bridge on the Hunza river

Subject	Jammu and Kashmir (India)	Pakistan-occupied Kashmir (Azad Jammu and Kashmir)	Gilgit-Baltistan
	• Anji Khad bridge, the Indian Railways' first cable-stayed bridge, will connect Katra and Reasi. • The Z-Morh tunnel on National Highway 1, which will provide year-round connectivity between the Kashmir Valley and Ladakh.		• The Kanchey bridge on the Gilgit river

Since 5 May 2020, the Indian Meteorological Department (regional office) has started including meteorological reports for PoK and Gilgit-Baltistan in their forecasts. This has created a lot of worry and unrest in the Pakistani establishment because they perhaps suspect that this is yet another step taken by the Indians towards annexing PoK and Gilgit-Baltistan.

The effort of successive governments in Jammu and Kashmir has been to ensure that democracy prevails and there is a popular government in the state that enjoys the mandate of the people. This has been India's biggest strength. Pakistan has always tried to create disturbances in the state and unfortunately, ever since the proxy war broke out in 1989–90, there have been some disruptions and governor's rule had to be imposed. However, it goes to the credit of the central government and the people of J&K that governor's rule was imposed only for a total of eleven of the seventy-three years since India's independence in 1947. Since the proxy war began in 1990, governor's rule was imposed for ten out of the last thirty years, which is quite creditable because Pakistan has spared no effort to heighten the tempo of problems in the state.

It has also been the effort of successive Indian governments that the state progresses economically at a rapid pace. To fulfil this goal, they have given preferential treatment to J&K, far beyond what they have done for other states. To illustrate this point, it may be noted that Uttar Pradesh (UP), which is fourteen times bigger than J&K, gets only 8.2 per cent of the central government's grants whereas J&K receives 10 per cent of the central grants. Also, J&K comprises only 1 per cent of the national population.

The central government has also paid a great deal of attention to enhancing educational facilities in the state, as is evident from the preceding table. Also, a disproportionately high number of seats have been earmarked in a large number of universities in the country for students from J&K.

Even during natural calamities, the Government of India has gone beyond the set precedents and systems to assist the state in all respects. For example, during the 2014 floods in the Valley, not only were a huge number of forces deployed to help the state government tide over the problem, but a big financial package of Rs 80,000 crore (over USD 11 billion) was allotted to the state. During the Pakistan–Kashmir earthquake on 8 October 2005, villages on India's side of the LoC were rebuilt to the great satisfaction of the local people at a very rapid pace. Apart from allocating funds for such emergencies, from time to time other sops have been allotted to the state, over and above the standard financial grants to the state. For example, Rs 24,000 crore (USD 3.5 billion), Rs 16,000 crore (USD 2.3 billion) and Rs 1000 crore (USD 1.3 billion) were allotted between 2004 and 2010.

PoK and Gilgit-Baltistan

Dr Sudhir Bloeria has made a very sound observation in his book:[1]

> The Pakistani government and its leaders don't tire of shedding crocodile tears over the so-called plight of their 'Muslim brethren' in 'Hindu India', forgetting that more Muslims live in India than in Pakistan. Pakistan's representatives raise a din in every international forum about the right of self-determination of the people of Jammu and Kashmir. It would be interesting and relevant to look at how Pakistan has been treating their area of Jammu and Kashmir, illegally occupied by them since 1947.

PoK

Although PoK has been projected as a country with a president, prime minister and legislature, underneath, these institutions are moth-eaten, devoid of any power and at best of cosmetic value. PoK is in fact being treated as a colony of Pakistan.

Sardar Muhammad Ibrahim Khan had declared the formation of the Azad Kashmir government on 24 October 1947 in Plandhari town of Poonch district. On 28 April 1949, the Karachi Agreement

---

1 Sudhir Bloeria, *Pakistan's Insurgency vs India's Security* (New Delhi: Manas Publications, 2000).

was signed between Mushtaq Ahmed Gurmani, who was a 'minister without portfolio' in the central government of Pakistan and in-charge of Kashmir affairs (later he was interior minister of Pakistan and Governor of the one unit of west Pakistan) and Sardar Muhammad Ibrahim, the President of Azad Kashmir (PoK). By virtue of this agreement, Pakistan got control of all matters relating to defence, foreign affairs, rehabilitation of refugees and the affairs of Gilgit and Baltistan, under the control of a political agent at Gilgit. This agreement turned PoK into a subservient state of Pakistan. The president and the prime minister of PoK have enjoyed only titular powers since then. In October 1952, Rules of Business were formulated by the Pakistani government, which made the Government of PoK totally subservient to the Ministry of Kashmir Affairs. When General Ayub Khan took over the presidency of Pakistan, all political activity was banned in PoK. In 1961, Ayub Khan extended his Basic Democracies Act to Azad Jammu and Kashmir (AJK) also, which legislated party-less elections of local bodies, circumventing the provincial government. These reforms further divided the country into 80,000 wards (single-member constituencies of 1,000 to 1,200 people each) to elect a 'Basic Democrat' on a non-party basis. The AJK president and a newly created AJK Council were indirectly elected in 1961 by various directly elected local bodies through the 'votes of basic democrats'. This Council consisted of 12 members elected by the people of Azad Jammu and Kashmir, whereas 12 members were elected by the refugees of Jammu and Kashmir State settled in Pakistan. The Council, however, remained a mere advisory body. K.H. Khurshid was the first president of PoK who was democratically elected and was dismissed in 1964 because he had begun asserting himself.

Subsequently, there were several changes in the system as regimes in Pakistan changed from Yahya Khan's to Bhutto's to that of General Zia-ul-Haq. Just how illusory the independent existence of PoK is becomes clear with a reading of the following provision of the PoK Constitution: 'No person or political party shall be permitted to propagate against or take part in activities prejudicial or detrimental to the ideology of the State's (Jammu and Kashmir) accession to Pakistan (Paragraph 2 of Section 7 – under Section 5(2)(vii) of AJK Legislative Assembly election ordinance 1970, a person would be disqualified for propagating any opinion or acting in any manner prejudicial to the ideology of Pakistan, the ideology of State's accession to Pakistan or the sovereignty and integrity of Pakistan).'

In June 1991, Pakistan's prime minister, Nawaz Sharif, dissolved the Government of PoK under Prime Minister Mumtaz Hussain Rathore for developing pro-independence tendencies.

There was strong unrest in PoK over the way Pakistan has handled them in 1996 after the Legislative Assembly elections. At one time, as many as thirty-four electoral candidates refused to sign the declaration calling PoK's accession to Pakistan an article of faith. *Dawn* stated that the candidates not only struck down the declaration of the state's accession to Pakistan but also refused to sign the 'allegiance to the sovereignty and integrity of Pakistan'. After seventy-three years of independence, Islamabad had realized that PoK's politicians could not be taken for granted.

Pakistan has not only maintained an ironclad control over PoK but has also been milking the area, taking full benefit of the resources available there. Hardly any federal assistance is given to PoK. If we look at what has been done for the Indian Kashmiris in comparison, we can understand the vast disparity that exists between Indian Kashmir and Pakistan-held Kashmir.

The complete hold of the rulers of Pakistan over PoK has been expressed by K.N. Daruwala, 'Each executive head of Pakistan, be it Ayub, Bhutto or Zia, did exactly what he wanted in PoK, brought in martial law or the form of government which he desired, suspended political activities when he chose and sacked the President/Prime Minister he disliked.'

The deprivations of the people of PoK have been aptly summed up by Hashim Qureshi in an article titled 'Why "Azad Kashmir" be [sic] called POK?', published in the *Daily Excelsior* in Jammu on 22 November 1998: 'Azad Kashmir had no medical colleges or engineering colleges or a poly-tech institute or a forestry college. None. A university for name's sake merely runs classes in four or five towns. On the other hand, in Kashmir on the Indian side, whomsoever you meet is either a doctor, engineer, professor, technocrat or a scientist, etc.' The difference is glaring.

Gilgit-Baltistan

Gilgit-Baltistan is a huge land mass of over 72,000 sq. km of Jammu and Kashmir territory occupied by Pakistan in 1947. The people of this area have been subjected to central rule from Islamabad, which is harsher and more degrading to human dignity, life and property than the regime's control over PoK. Successive governments have followed a policy that has left Gilgit-Baltistan's inhabitants with no political identity, civil rights or even constitutional status. For a long period of time, they did not have the right to vote, had no legislature and no access to justice in the form of appeals to a high court or supreme court. They have been treated as second-class citizens by all Pakistani governments.

When Pakistan's relations with China were strengthening, Gilgit-Baltistan, which borders China, became a prized territory. In view of this and to assuage the feelings of the people, the first major step towards the political empowerment of the region was taken through the Gilgit-Baltistan Empowerment and

Self-Governance Order of 2009, wherein Gilgit-Baltistan was granted self-governance to an extent. A good measure of federal control, however, continued in the form of the Gilgit-Baltistan Council.

In 2018, the Gilgit-Baltistan Order issued by the Pakistani government replaced the 2009 order of self-governance. The new order changed the nomenclature of the Gilgit-Baltistan Legislative Assembly. All powers exercised by the four provincial assemblies under schedule IV of the Constitution of Pakistan were granted to the Gilgit-Baltistan assembly. The assembly has the right to pass legislations regarding the mineral, hydropower and tourism sectors. The area is rich in minerals and its hydropower potential is estimated to be 40,000 million MW. The Gilgit-Baltistan Order of 2018 included some changes in the judiciary as well. Another improvement was that whereas the last empowerment order (2009) guaranteed only seventeen basic rights limited to the Gilgit-Baltistan territory, the 2018 order allowed citizens of Gilgit-Baltistan to demand their rights with access to all apex courts of the country.

It is believed that what hastened Pakistan's acceding to the demands of Gilgit-Baltistan was the subtle pressure exerted by the Chinese. The Chinese, given their massive investments, were not comfortable with the unsettled political status of the region.

In November 2020, Pakistan went still further and declared its intent that Gilgit-Baltistan shall be a full-fledged province, implying thereby that it would be its fifth province. India voiced strong opposition to this reported move. India's Ministry of External Affairs made it clear in November 2020 that India 'firmly rejects' the attempt by Pakistan to bring material changes to a part of Indian territory which is under Islamabad's 'illegal and forcible occupation'. Any attempt by Pakistan to change the legal status would thus have no basis whatsoever. India also called upon Pakistan to vacate all occupied areas.

Interestingly, Pakistan's move to make Gilgit-Baltistan its fifth province triggered widespread protests across PoK and Gilgit-Baltistan. The people, led by lawyers in both regions, have said that Pakistan is selling a part of Kashmir to China just like it accepted the grab of Aksai-Chin by China and gave away Shaksgam Valley to China. According to the protesters, the Pakistani government wants to carve out the region from the state of Jammu and Kashmir to make the land available to the Chinese government for the China–Pakistan Economic Corridor. Some echoes of this may be discerned from the Chinese intrusion in the Eastern Ladakh region in May–June 2020.

From all the above, it is obvious that there is really no comparison between the two halves of Kashmir, one with India and the other with Pakistan. Both are qualitatively, materially and democratically far apart. In Pakistan, where apart from Punjab no other state matters, PoK and Gilgit-Baltistan stand no chance to get a fair deal.

The fact is that there is no information available in the public domain on life in PoK. Even the census data is not published by the government. No one really knows the basic social and economic status of the people living there. There was virtually no press in PoK and Gilgit-Baltistan till President Musharraf came on the scene and thirty-two newspapers started operating, of course with limited freedom.

The reality is that neither in PoK nor in Gilgit-Baltistan do the people have any love for Pakistan. In the entire area, Mirpur is perhaps the most prosperous. In Pakistan, people feel that Mirpur is a mini Bradford or Birmingham of the UK or vice versa because economically they are prosperous and lots of these refugees have settled in the UK. Mirpur's political elites, however, still seek to identify with Jammu and not Bradford or Birmingham, because identifying with Jammu is hitting Pakistan and Muzaffarabad where it hurts the most. Mirpur is one of the prominent places in PoK where '*Kashmir banega Pakistan*' (Kashmir will become Pakistan) has no currency. But Mirpur is not the only place in PoK where people are opposed to the idea of integration with Pakistan. The common refrain in PoK has been that 'every decision in matters of Azad Kashmir is the sole prerogative of the Kashmir Council and the decision, if taken in Muzaffarabad, has to be approved by Islamabad. In warrant of precedence, the Kashmir Affairs Minister in Pakistan is superior to the president of Azad Government of Jammu and Kashmir.' People therefore really feel that they do not control their own affairs and destiny like they should in a democratic country.

Another important aspect is that a life around the military and intelligence agencies is the dominant culture in PoK and Gilgit-Baltistan, just as in the rest of Pakistan. This is illustrated by the following example: four words that are commonly used in their interactions are *farishte*, *babe*, *pape* and *mame* (angels, wise people, fathers and uncles). Upon asking, the locals will explain that farishte refers to ISI spies, babe are the other intelligence men, pape are the military men and mame are the militants or mujahideen.

Thus, one can safely deduce that PoK and Gilgit-Baltistan are not on the route to progress. They are the tools available in the hands of Pakistan to meet the huge ambitions of China in the region and for the Pakistani military to maintain its pre-eminence.

9

Curtain Falls on Articles 370 and 35A

'We do not create terrorism by fighting the terrorists. We invite terrorism by ignoring them.'

– George W. Bush

The Birth of a Naya (New) Kashmir

Was Article 370 a bridge that linked Jammu and Kashmir with India or a chasm that prevented the full integration of the state with the nation? This is the question that has rankled in the nation's mind since the article was introduced in 1949. While there may have been different answers and different solutions to the question, nobody doubted the fact that Kashmir was an integral part of India.

There can also be no doubt that India spent more than seventy years attempting dialogue, promoting cultural exchanges, setting up democratic processes and even taking on the rehabilitation of militants and separatists in order to move towards the final goal of the full integration of Jammu and Kashmir with India. Yes, there was always a minority view that Kashmiris should be given a semblance of autonomy under the umbrella of the already much-diluted Article 370. Within the state, perhaps some political parties would have accepted this view, but it would have found very little favour and perhaps even hostile reactions from other political parties outside the state in mainland India.

Readers might also recall that a draft autonomy bill was prepared by a State Autonomy Committee during the tenure of J&K's chief minister Farooq Abdullah in 2000. This report, which was approved by the J&K Legislative Assembly, drew harsh reactions from India's mainstream political parties. Except for some Left parties, all others rejected it outright, with differing degrees of condemnation. As a matter of fact, this episode left lingering doubt about Farooq's loyalty to India. Obviously for Indians, accepting a solution that proposed anything less than the total integration of Jammu and Kashmir with India was just not palatable.

Going further back in history, at times many may have scoffed at what they termed the Nehruvian liberal weakness of granting a special status to the state, or called the act a historic blunder. But the fact is that it served the purpose at the time of India's independence. It was important for India at that time to secure the loyalty and unstinting support of Sheikh Abdullah, the unquestioned leader of the Kashmiri masses. It served its purpose as a temporary arrangement, but having it in force for over seventy years was a bit too much. If the retention of Article 370 was considered so important, one can rightly question why it was not turned into a permanent arrangement. The answer is that it was never meant to be a permanent arrangement. Even Nehru had no such intentions as he used to say quite often that the act would keep getting diluted until it disappeared altogether.

The Jammu and Kashmir Reorganization Act 2019, and the Days Thereafter

A bold and historic decision was thus taken by the Narendra Modi government on 5 August 2019. With the home minister's presentation of the Jammu and Kashmir Reservation (Second Amendment) Bill, 2019, and the J&K Reorganization Bill, 2019, the die was cast. Many things changed with the stroke of the President's pen and the proclamation, not only in Jammu and Kashmir but also in India. The Rubicon has been crossed and there is no going back, irrespective of the outcome. India will have to negotiate the difficulties that may arise successfully; failure is not an option. The government not only scrapped Articles 370 and 35A (some legal experts have even opined that Article 370 has not been abrogated but only diluted) but went further and bifurcated the state into the union territories of Jammu and Kashmir and Ladakh–Kargil. The union territory of Jammu and Kashmir would have a legislature. Both the union territories would come under the direct control of the Centre and once the situation improves, the Centre promised to recreate the Jammu and Kashmir state, less the Ladakh–Kargil regions.

Bifurcating rather than trifurcating the state and keeping Jammu and Kashmir together was a rational move. The link between Jammu and Kashmir is traditional and very strong. They are indeed interdependent in their traditions and customs. The strategic all-weather roads to Ladakh and Kashmir also pass through Jammu. There is heavy routine trade between these two areas. Most importantly, separating the two would have reflected a thought process of splitting the region based on faith. That would have been self-defeating because India strongly believes that Kashmir being a part of the nation reflects her strong secular beliefs. Lieutenant

General Syed Ata Hasnain in one of his articles has rightly observed that the 'route to the prosperity and mainstreaming of Kashmir passes through Jammu'. Article 370 allowed the state a certain degree of autonomy, its own Constitution, a separate flag and the freedom to make laws. Foreign affairs, defence and communication had, however, remained the preserve of the central government. Later, under pressure from New Delhi in December 1964, Article 356 was incorporated by G.M. Sadiq, the then chief minister of J&K. This catered for President's Rule and amending the state's Constitution to convert the office of the elected Sadr-i-Riyasat to that of a governor appointed by the central government. Under the Indira–Sheikh Accord of 1975, the autonomy of the state was further whittled down, and what remained of Article 370 was only symbolic. Yet it gave the Kashmiris a great degree of comfort as the real impact of the article was psychological: Kashmiris had always liked to believe that they were a separate island in the big land mass of India. Former governor of Jammu and Kashmir, Jagmohan, has written in his book, *My Frozen Turbulence in Kashmir*:

> One of the strongest roots of Kashmiri separatism and alienation lies in Article 370 of the constitution of India, which gives special status to the State of Jammu and Kashmir. It is an issue which involves not only historical, constitutional, political, social and economic considerations of far-reaching consequences, but also psychological and emotional ones. A fierce nationwide controversy has often been raised about it. Its deletion or retention has been advocated with equal vehemence. But one fundamental aspect has always been lost sight of that pertains to its misuse by vested interests.

There is little doubt that Articles 370 and 35A were anachronistic and out of tune with the times. They had to be scrapped to bring Jammu and Kashmir on the same footing as the rest of the country and thus integrate it fully with India.

The scourge of militancy and terrorism unleashed by Pakistan as part of the proxy war it launched in Jammu and Kashmir has taken a heavy toll on the state. Over 40,000 people have lost their lives. Thousands of soldiers have made the supreme sacrifice in the line of duty to contain this proxy war. This cycle of violence had to be checked. That time had come, even though the abrogation of the articles has left 7–8 million angry and alienated people in the Valley. Over the years, they have been exposed to Pakistani propaganda and politicians who enjoyed all the benefits of the Indian state without any quid pro quo. The politicians cleverly played to the galleries on both sides and survived. In the process, some people fell prey to Pakistani propaganda to the extent that they took up arms as local militants. They seemed to be secure in the belief that Articles 370 and 35A would never be revoked. This has now happened and has left them discomfited, not understanding the near- and long-term benefits that will accrue on becoming a genuine part of the larger Indian state.

Other issues, such as Shia Muslims' fear that they may be discriminated against by Ladakhis in the Kargil sector, are normal apprehensions in the wake of territorial changes. They are of a temporary nature and will be ameliorated by a more even distribution of resources between Ladakh and Kargil. The Jammu and Ladakh regions have been demanding this measure for a long time and indeed are celebrating.

Ideally, the government should have first built consensus and then moved in this direction. But that would not have been practical for various reasons. In my assessment, any such debate would have been unending and thus fruitless. The government tried to make up for the shortfall in consensus-building through the way the bill was manoeuvred in Parliament by the home minister, Amit Shah. Even though they did not have a majority in the Rajya Sabha, the government managed to garner more than two-thirds of the votes in the Rajya Sabha and four-fifths in the Lok Sabha. So, while there was no prior consensus-building, the subsequent voting pattern showed that the lawmakers across different parties were in agreement with the bill.

Mission Kashmir: How Did the Events Unfold?

Jawaharlal Nehru, India's first prime minister, gave a historic speech to the Indian Constituent Assembly in the Parliament on the eve of India's independence, towards midnight on 14 August 1947. It is considered to be one of the greatest speeches of the twentieth century. It began with the famous words, 'Long years ago we made a tryst with destiny, and now the time comes when we shall redeem our pledge, not wholly or in full measure, but very substantially.'

On 5-6 August 2019, seventy-two years after that famous speech, the stage was being set for another tectonic shift in the history of independent India through the revocation of Articles 370 and 35A of the Constitution of India and the simultaneous bifurcation of the state of Jammu and Kashmir. Another tryst was made with destiny in completing the task leftover from the time of Independence and ensuring the complete integration of the erstwhile state of Jammu and Kashmir with the Union of India.

The abrogation of Articles 370 and 35A had been on the agenda of the RSS since 1952, when it passed its first resolution at a meeting of its Kendriya Karyakari Mandal (central executive). In this they condemned the 'Pak-American Pact' of February 1954 when President Eisenhower announced that the US had decided to give military assistance to Pakistan as an 'open aggression on Kashmir'. The following year they ran a massive campaign of the Bhartiya Jana Sangh, which was a political arm of RSS and a right-wing political party. Syama Prasad Mukherjee, who was a minister in Nehru's interim cabinet, was its first president. He entered the state to stage protests in May 1953 with the '*Ek desh, ek vidhan, ek nishan*' (one country, one constitution, one flag) slogan. He was arrested and put in solitary confinement by Sheikh Abdullah, where he died after over a month, some say of poisoning. There were massive protests in Jammu against the suspected killing of Mukherjee but with no result; such was the standing of Sheikh Abdullah.

In 1964, the highest decision-making body of the RSS passed a resolution which said that Article 370 was a temporary provision and must be repealed and the State brought in line with the other States. The RSS had maintained this stand and repeatedly said that Article 370 was being misused to fan communal and separatist feelings. Thereafter, the abrogation of Article 370 remained in the political manifesto of the BJP (the political wing of the RSS) all along.

When the Modi government came back to power with a massive majority (354 seats out of 545) in the Lok Sabha in the parliamentary elections of May 2019, it was expected that a major initiative would be taken with regard to Jammu and Kashmir, and the clock started ticking for the state from then.

Part of the reason the central government moved quickly to abrogate Articles 370 and 35A, soon after assuming power for the second time, was that J&K assembly elections were due soon after the Amarnath Yatra was to commence on 1 July and conclude on 15 August 2019. The government was not very sure of getting the strong mandate in the state assembly that would enable it to enforce the radical changes it had in mind.

The Modi government had also calculated that after unrelenting terrorist attacks, the attitude of the Indian people to such a drastic action would at worst hover between resignation and irritation but would not be explosive. US President Donald Trump's repeated offers of mediation between India and Pakistan at the end of July 2019, even though strongly rejected by India, also confirmed the need for speed.

India's response following the Pulwama attack had displayed the determination of a new India to the world, which had quietly appreciated it. The world had lost patience with terror. India was thus confident of handling the world's response to the revocation, which has been proved right.

The central government went about its mission with determination and in accordance with a well-orchestrated plan.

During his 2017 visit to Jammu, Home Minister Amit Shah had invoked the death and sacrifice of Syama Prasad Mukherjee for repealing Article 370. The die was cast then.

The BJP was also at that time in a coalition government in the state with the PDP. They utilized this time to fully understand the various administrative aspects of the state and how to implement their plan when the time came.

The countdown to the revocation began when the BJP withdrew its support from the coalition government in J&K, as a result of which Mehbooba Mufti resigned as chief minister and governor's rule was imposed on 19 June 2018. The Centre then hand-picked B.V.R. Subrahmanyam, an IAS officer who had a reputation for being very firm and efficient, as chief secretary of the state on 21 June 2018. It also identified eight other bureaucrats at different levels and posted them to the state.

The government next made exhaustive lists of all economic offenders and over-ground workers who were sympathetic to the militancy. All these individuals were rounded up and placed under preventive custody in different places in India from March–April 2019 onwards to deprive the militants of sympathetic leadership. This was a big setback for the militancy. The exact number of people rounded up is anybody's guess as the figures have not been revealed, but these were possibly between 300 and 500. Some rumours even say that the number was between 1,500 and 2,000.

Earlier, the Jamaat-e-Islami, a cadre-based socio-religious–political extremist organization had been legally debarred for five years under the Unlawful Activities (Prevention) Act for allegedly supporting extremism and militancy in the state. The underlying idea was to remove this support base which was promoting the secession of Kashmir from India for the militants.

The National Investigation Agency (NIA) filed a charge sheet against the JuD chief, Hafiz Saeed, and also named Salahuddin (the head of Hizbul Mujahideen) in it. The NIA named ten other major leaders, including several separatist leaders. Sources in the home ministry said that the idea was not only to discredit antinational forces but also to stop them from using their money power to engineer fake protests, stone pelting and attacks on security forces. The NIA and the Enforcement Directorate (ED) intensified their investigations into terrorist financing, slapping cases on the leaders of the Hurriyat and other separatist organization leaders such as Yasin Malik, Asiya Andrabi, Shabir Shah and Masarat Alam. They also went after some prominent businessmen who were sympathizers.

Panchayat elections had been held in the state between 17 November and 11 December 2018, much against the advice of the state leadership, who did not want this institution to be strengthened. Surprisingly, the elections went off quite peacefully. The government then set about the task of building up its machinery from the grass-roots level.

The house arrests of Hurriyat leaders Mirwaiz Umar Farooq and many others on 22 June 2019 were pre-emptive actions taken ahead of the third anniversary of the killing of Burhan Wani. Some sources close to the establishment termed these as the start of the government's 'Mission Kashmir'.

The first hint that something big was afoot came on 20 July 2019, when a senior IB officer told an organization (identity not revealed) to postpone an important programme that was to be held in Srinagar.

By late July 2019, the government had finalized its plan. The number of people who were in the loop regarding what was afoot was limited to less than two dozen. These included the chief secretary and the director general of police of J&K, the chiefs of the RAW and the IB, the defence chiefs, the army commander northern command, the principal secretary to the prime minister, the home secretary and the cabinet secretary in New Delhi. Besides the prime minister and the home minister, those who were deeply involved in planning the move were the national security advisor, the defence minister and the foreign minister. The law minister and the attorney general of India were also later taken into confidence.

The scene then shifted to the ground of action. Over 10,000 CRPF personnel were inducted into the Valley in the last week of July, after the visit of National Security Advisor Ajit Doval to carry out an on-the-spot study of the security situation.

On 2 August 2019, the corps commander of 15 Corps, Srinagar, held a press conference with senior police officers in attendance. The corps commander displayed a sniper rifle and a landmine made in Pakistan and said that he had information that there was a serious threat to the Amarnath Yatra. Under the circumstances, the yatra could not be allowed to continue. The pilgrims were instructed to return home immediately. Similarly, all the yatras across the Banihal Pass in the Bhadarwah–Kishtwar areas were also cancelled.

The Centre also issued instructions for all tourists, which included over 600 foreigners, to leave the state immediately. Special flights were flown by the airlines. The Indian air force's Globemasters, which are transport aircrafts, were pressed into service to carry passengers out of the Valley. A large number of buses were also pressed into action.

Meanwhile, there was heavy firing by Indian forces all along the LoC to keep Pakistan engaged and distracted from Kashmir and prevent infiltration. For the first time, 155 mm howitzers (Bofors) were fired by India along the LoC.

From 3 August onwards, reportedly over 40,000 more CRPF personnel were airlifted into the Valley to provide extra security. The might of the Government of India was on display.

Adjustments were made in the security grid, with the army focusing on the LoC and the hinterland being taken care of by the Rashtriya Rifles battalions. The police and the CRPF were to handle the civilian population.

In preparation for the planned communications shutdown, the police were equipped with an alternative wireless system to ensure uninterrupted communication when the internet services would be removed. Hospitals were also quietly stocked with extra medicines.

Rumours were afloat that some big announcement was in the offing, that maybe Article 35A was to be revoked. The governor gave a few interviews but disclosed nothing.

Curtain Falls on Articles 370 and 35A

On 4 August, an all-party conference was called at Farooq Abdullah's house, which was heavily attended. They counselled peace and advised the central government not to take any reckless steps. They also reiterated their earlier warning that if Article 35A were to be revoked, it would invariably lead to bloodshed and affect the relationship of the state with India.

Earlier, at the prime minister's residence, Home Minister Amit Shah, Defence Minister Rajnath Singh and National Security Advisor Ajit Doval had held several rounds of discussions and were convinced that they could handle whatever the fallout was after the announcement.

On 4 August, it was declared that the home minister would make an important announcement in the Rajya Sabha on 5 August. On the morning of 5 August, Amit Shah announced in Parliament that the government was revoking the provisions of Article 370 of the Constitution, which granted special status to Jammu and Kashmir. He also said the state would be bifurcated into two union territories – Jammu and Kashmir with a legislature and Ladakh–Kargil without a legislature. This took the opposition parties by surprise.

In Parliament, the home minister reiterated the charge that only a few families had gained from Article 370 and that both articles, 370 and 35A, were harmful for the good of the people of Jammu and Kashmir. He also talked of the Modi government's decision to rectify a historical blunder and their commitment to bringing the two newly created union territories onto the path to prosperity.

Even opposition parties such as the Aam Aadmi Party (AAP), Telugu Desam Party (TDP) and Bahujan Samaj Party (BSP) supported the bill. There were fissures in the Congress party as well. Ultimately, when the votes were counted, the bill had secured more than two-thirds of the votes in its favour in the

Rajya Sabha. The following day in the Lok Sabha, the bill secured a four-fifths majority. BJP members chanted the slogan '*Ab desh me hoga ek vidhan, ek samvidhan aur ek nishan*' (there will now be one legislation, one constitution and one flag in our country).

In Jammu and Kashmir, all state flags were quietly removed. The president signed the bill on 9 August 2019 and with that the erstwhile state of Jammu and Kashmir was fully integrated with India. (A copy of the presidential proclamation is attached in Appendix C.)

The people of Ladakh were happy that at long last their demand had been fulfilled and with the promised help of the central government they would soon be on the path to prosperity. And even though the demand of the people of Jammu for separate statehood had not been met, they were happy that they would now be equal to the Kashmiris in all respects and not their junior partners.

In his address to the nation on 9 August 2019, the prime minister explained the rationale behind this historic step. He charged that Articles 370 and 35A had acted as tools to spread terrorism and violence in the Valley. Their abrogation would open the route to the unprecedented development of the region in a short span of time as by scrapping them, the government had removed an impediment to the development of Jammu and Kashmir. Hospitals such as the All India Institute of Medical Sciences (AIIMS) and educational institutions such as the Indian Institutes of Management (IIM) and Indian Institutes of Technology (IIT) would be set up soon, and the Centre would do its very best to ensure employment for all the youth in Jammu and Kashmir and Ladakh–Kargil. Further, all government employees of J&K would get the same benefits as central government employees.

Laws were made for the entire country, but J&K had not benefited from these progressive laws; this would now change.

He also stated that assembly elections would be held in J&K as soon as the situation permitted, and the people would choose their representatives of their own free will.

People who had migrated to India after 1947 could not contest polls in J&K. They had rights everywhere else, but not in Jammu and Kashmir. With the scrapping of Article 370, the rights of those who had migrated would be restored.

The prime minister also announced that a conclave of corporate leaders would be held in Srinagar to discuss investments in Jammu and Kashmir and Ladakh.

The Aftermath

There are essentially three areas in which the impact of this announcement was and will continue to be felt: the international reaction, the legal battle in the Supreme Court for the consideration of petitions by aggrieved parties challenging the abrogation of Article 370 by a five-judge bench, and the challenge in the Valley in the aftermath of the revocation. (The last part about the challenge in the Valley is discussed in Chapter 10.)

The International Reaction

From the way the world responded, it was obvious that Kashmir was now much less of a priority globally. Pakistan desperately wants to keep the issue alive. Yet, for most major powers there is little to gain from wasting political capital in pressuring India on the Kashmir issue, or in promoting a quasi-independent inevitably Islamist territory at the intersection of South and Central Asia. Today, this would be a nightmare. Moreover, the world is now more focused on the adverse situations building up in Hong Kong, the Middle East and even Syria.

Secondly, India's stock in the international arena is high and most countries would rather have good relations with India than please Pakistan. India's rising economic might and its incomparable market demand are two other critical factors.

However, on the recommendation of Pakistan's all-weather friend, China, this issue of the revocation of the special status of J&K was taken up in a closed-door meeting of the Security Council. There is no official record of the proceeding, nor did the informal exchange result in any outcome document. The only consensus that had the backing of the majority of the members was that India and Pakistan should resolve the matter bilaterally. This procedure is followed when discussions are to be taken up informally. Such meetings are at the lowest end of the spectrum of importance in UN Security Council meetings. China (understandably) and the UK (because of its strong Muslim lobby and the impact of this lobby on British electoral politics) tried to give this representation by China a little wind but were outmanoeuvred by strident opposition from the US and France. Russia took a careful middle path. But there was no doubt that in case of any difficulty, they would have come out strongly in favour of India. Prime Minister Modi visited Russia in September and ensured that their support would be sealed in the future.

China, however, was hostile to India, even talking of human rights violations. They conveniently overlooked their own house where millions of pro-democracy people in Hong Kong came out on the streets to protest against their repression day in and day out. Also, they seemed to have overlooked the genocide of the Tibetans and the Uyghurs in Tibet and the Xinjiang region. Thus, they really did not carry any credibility when they talked of human rights violations. China has a deeper motive behind wanting a simmering Kashmir, which is that it fits into its strategy of India being kept bogged down by Pakistan. It also has a deep interest in the CPEC and the Shaksgam Valley and Aksai-Chin areas. Thus, its national interest also aligns with that of Pakistan.

Ultimately, the Security Council discussed the issue behind closed doors, notes were neither made nor kept. The issue was declared to be a bilateral one in which the Security Council had no role to play. For Pakistan, this was a huge setback.

What was most upsetting for Pakistan was that even the OIC countries declared Kashmir to be a bilateral issue, as did countries nearer home, including Bangladesh, Nepal, the Maldives, Bhutan and Sri Lanka.

Overall, it was a resounding win for India. To understand Pakistan's frustration, one must look at their foreign minister Mahmood Qureshi's statement in their Parliament. Qureshi warned that even traditional supporters of Pakistan who had always used their voting rights in international bodies to support Islamabad – such as China – and friendly Islamic countries – such as Saudi Arabia and other Gulf countries – had turned away from Pakistan. The Pakistani establishment had come to understand well that these countries only acted when it suited their national interests or when they received the appropriate signals from Washington to do so.

Qureshi's candidness was also because it had become clear that the three permanent members of the Security Council, namely, the US, Russia and France, were pro-India thanks to military and business links and India's growing stock in the world. Whatever hope, if any, for Pakistan would have evaporated after seeing the repeated handshaking and backslapping between Modi and Trump during the G-7 meeting in Paris on 26 August 2019. Trump declared that he was confident that India and Pakistan would be able to resolve the bilateral issue of Kashmir between the two of them. He did not mention his offer of mediation during this meeting. Even the Biden administration is friendly with India and has not taken sides.

Finally, after the drubbing in the Security Council meeting, Qureshi told his countrymen that nobody was waiting with garlands at the Security Council Headquarters in New York to welcome Pakistan's bid to reverse India's decision on Jammu and Kashmir. Pakistan's foreign minister had admitted that his country's ability to agitate global superpowers and Islamic nations in its support was dwindling.

President Xi Jinping of China visited India on 11–12 October 2019 primarily for an informal meeting with Prime Minister Modi to revive the Wuhan spirit. The six-hour-long discussion between the two top leaders was called the 'Chennai Vision'. Despite all the sympathy that China has for Pakistan, the Kashmir issue was neither raised nor discussed by the Chinese president, and this is especially important given the fact that his visit to India was right after Imran Khan's visit to China.

It would, however, be worthwhile to take note of an observation by Ashley J. Tellis, senior fellow at the Carnegie Endowment for International Peace. He said that the critical issue that worried him was that having gone to the UN, there is now precedent for UNSC discussions on J&K. And depending upon what happens within the state in the months ahead, it could create more opportunities for the Pakistanis, Chinese and others to return to the UNSC. India would have to guard against such possibilities.

Further, there are two issues on which India should never lose focus. First, for the next 15–20 years, China may be happy with a bipolar world. Thereafter, they will be satisfied only with a unipolar world and the impact of that will be very visible. And second, similarly in Asia, they will be satisfied only with a unipolar Asia, because for them, there cannot be, as the Chinese saying goes, 'two tigers on one hill'.

Pakistan has generally been rebuffed by the world at large. The UN Security Council rejected Pakistan's appeal and declared Kashmir to be a bilateral matter. Not even the OIC countries supported Pakistan in this.

Also, the FATF started considering whether to include Pakistan on its public statement of high-risk jurisdictions, often referred to as the 'blacklist', after assessing its efforts to combat money laundering and terrorist financing. Pakistan started looking for support from China, Malaysia and Turkey to prevent it from being placed on the blacklist. According to the rules, Pakistan needed a minimum of three votes to avoid the blacklist.

Besides the FATF, the International Monetary Fund (IMF) also posed another problem for Pakistan. Pakistan has taken loans from IMF more than twenty-two times. This is a record of sorts. If Pakistan's links to Al-Qaeda are established, it is likely to lead to the country being blacklisted by both the FATF and the IMF.

Financially, Pakistan is in dire straits. The US cut down their aid to Pakistan in 2018 owing to its inability to curtail homegrown terrorist network in the region and gave financial support of only USD 40 million for the maintenance of Pakistan's F-16 fleet. With more loans from China for the CPEC and power generation to the tune of USD 62 billion, Pakistan will be more than neck-deep in debt.

India has also warned Pakistan that since Kashmir is an integral part of India, future talks with them will be only about PoK and Gilgit-Baltistan, which also belong to India. This has added to Pakistan's concerns.

Indeed, the abrogation of Articles 370 and 35A by the Government of India has left Pakistan nonplussed. Their responses have been like those of a person who is rattled and bound to make blunders. To begin with, Pakistan's prime minister threatened war with India, going so far as to say that it could even be a nuclear war. This was hardly a sensible approach. Pakistan also immediately downgraded diplomatic relations with India. It cut off all trade with India and closed Pakistani air space for all flights leaving and entering India. It warned India that 30,000 to 40,000 Talibans/jihadis were training in Pakistan to enter Kashmir. These include elements from Al-Qaeda. Further, terrorists such as Hafiz Saeed of JeM and Maulana Masood Azhar of LeT would be given a free hand to carry out their missions.

However, one area where work continued uninterrupted was the construction of the Kartarpur Corridor between India and Pakistan. Pakistan did this to win the support of the Sikhs and also to show to the world that they are reasonable in their dealings with India despite the abrogation of Article 370 and Article 35A in Kashmir. The corridor connects the Sikh shrines of Dera Baba Nanak (located in Punjab, India) and Gurudwara Darbar Sahib Kartarpur (located in Punjab, Pakistan). Completed in November 2019, the corridor allows religious devotees from India to visit the gurudwara in Kartarpur, which is 4.7 km from the Pakistan–India border on the Pakistani side, without a visa.

Pakistan has decided to charge USD 20 per pilgrim visiting the Kartarpur Gurudwara from India. Captain Amarinder Singh, the chief minister of Punjab (India) until September 2021, labelled this charge as jazia, which used to be a per capita yearly taxation historically levied on permanent non-Muslim (male) subjects of a state governed by Islamic law in order to fund the public expenditure of the state. Pakistan is expected to get approximately

Rs 21.6 crore (USD 3 million) each month through this charge. India snubbed them by deciding not to charge any such reciprocal tax. The corridor is presently closed due to Covid restrictions.

The Legal Battle in the Supreme Court

On 5 August 2019, when Home Minister Amit Shah rose in the Rajya Sabha, he did not move a bill to amend the Constitution. Instead, he took the indirect route of a presidential order (C.O. 272). This order, which came into effect immediately, removed the special status accorded to the state of J&K under Article 370 of the Constitution of India. By extension, Article 35A was also repealed, as it flows from Article 370, having been introduced through a presidential order in 1954.

The resolution moved by the home minister in Parliament sought to invoke the authority that flowed from the effects of Presidential Order C.O. 272 to recommend that the president abrogate Article 370 and also approve the Reorganisation Bill, which broke up the state of Jammu and Kashmir into the Union Territories of Ladakh (without a legislature) and Jammu and Kashmir (with a legislature).

Perhaps the most important part of Article 370 was the proviso to clause 3, which authorized the president to pass an order removing or modifying parts of Article 370. The proviso stated that the recommendation of the Constituent Assembly of the state referred to in clause (2) shall be necessary for the president to issue such a notification. In other words, therefore, for Article 370 itself to be amended, the recommendation of the Constituent Assembly of Jammu and Kashmir was required. The Constituent Assembly of the state had ceased functioning in 1957. This, thus, had led to a long-standing debate about whether Article 370 had effectively become permanent and could not be modified.

The presidential order, however, took an entirely different path. It used the power of the president under Article 370(1) to indirectly amend Article 370(3) via a third constitutional provision, that is, Article 367, which provides various guidelines about how the Constitution may be interpreted. The presidential order added to Article 367 an additional clause providing for 'Constituent Assembly of the State' to be read as 'Legislative Assembly of the State'. In other words, the presidential order – with the concurrence of the Government of Jammu and Kashmir – could amend or modify various provisions of the Constitution in relation to Jammu and Kashmir. This triggered the resolution that recommended to the president the removal of Article 370 as the approval of the J&K government (the governor) was already in place.

Extensive legal opinions were taken by the central government over a period of time, and this process was found to be in order as, at the time, Parliament (through the governor) was performing the role of the state assembly.

The Supreme Court, while hearing an appeal filed by a petitioner against the Delhi High Court's order dismissing a plea seeking that Article 370 be declared temporary in nature, had ruled on 3 April 2018 that Article 370 was not a temporary provision. The bench comprising Justices A.K. Goel and Rohinton Nariman had further observed that despite the fact that the head note said 'it is a temporary provision, it is not'. In its ruling the apex court also invoked its earlier verdict of 2017 in the SARFESI case, wherein it had been already held that Article 370 was 'not a temporary provision', and it had never ceased to be operative.

Whether the government's action was legal is the question before a five-judge constitutional bench of the Supreme Court.

There have been objections raised about the role of the presidential order. The first is that Presidential Order C.O. 272

amends Article 367 but not Article 370. The Supreme Court has held on multiple occasions that you cannot do indirectly what you can do directly. There is a second important point, in that the presidential order states – as it must – that the concurrence of the Government of the state of Jammu and Kashmir has been taken. However, Jammu and Kashmir had been under president's rule for many months. Consequently, it implies that the consent of the governor, who is a representative of the central government, was accorded. In effect, therefore, the presidential order amounts to the central government taking its own consent to amend the Constitution. Thirdly, it is argued that president's rule is temporary since it is meant to be a stand-in until the elected government is restored. Therefore, decisions of a permanent character – such as changing the entire status of a state or its constitution – taken without the concurrence of the elected legislative assembly, but by the governor, are inherently problematic. The matter shall therefore be considered by the Supreme Court.

Post the Reorganisation Act, the Supreme Court heard the cases and refused to intervene in the J&K bifurcation issue. The five-judge bench led by Justice N.V. Ramana met on 1 October 2020 and wound up the hearing shortly after realizing that the Centre and the J&K government had not yet filed any response to the series of petitions challenging the revocation of Article 370. The case has not yet come up for hearing thereafter.

I am no legal expert and have compiled the views presented above from various sources, including the print media and discussions on television. Legal opinion is sharply divided over this legal manoeuvring and we will have to wait a considerable time before any final judgement is proclaimed by the Supreme Court.

10

A Paradigm Shift

'Fighting terrorism is like being a goalkeeper. You can make a hundred brilliant saves but the only shot that people remember is the one that gets past you.'

– Paul Wilkinson

The Modi government took the world by surprise when on 5–6 August 2019 it moved the Jammu and Kashmir Reorganization Act in both houses of Parliament and secured thumping majorities. Law and order was brought directly under the control of the Centre.

The general perception in the mind of the common man in India is that with the abrogation of Articles 370 and 35A, the Jammu and Kashmir issue is done and dusted. India now only needs to move ahead from the stage of post-integration to evolving new systems for the two newly created union territories. It is certainly not as simple as it looks.

India has brought about a situation wherein J&K has been firmly integrated into the nation. It is as much a part of India in all respects as any other state. It also ceases to be a bilateral issue with Pakistan wherein India does not accept that Pakistan has any stake in Kashmir. In fact, India is now laying stress on a long-pending issue with Pakistan, that of India's rights to PoK and Gilgit-Baltistan, which are in Pakistan's illegal possession. The rationale is based on the principle that Maharaja Hari Singh signed the Instrument of Accession on 26 October 1947 for the entire state of Jammu and Kashmir as it existed at the time of Partition. It is Pakistan who, through a mixed force of lashkars and army, illegally captured PoK and Gilgit-Baltistan after Partition. These continue to be India's territories.

The Indian Parliament's action gave great satisfaction to a large segment of the country's people as it stemmed from years of frustration at the failure of all efforts to establish durable peace in Jammu and Kashmir. The widely held perception was that granting the state special status was a historical blunder.

However, India's action has left Pakistan rattled. Kashmir has been the bedrock of Pakistan's nationalism for the last seven decades, as evidenced by slogans and statements such as 'Kashmir *banega* Pakistan' (Kashmir will be part of Pakistan), Kashmir is the unfinished agenda of Partition, Kashmir is Pakistan's jugular vein, and others. Pakistan has always felt insecure or even somewhat dwarfed by India's size. With the creation of Bangladesh, this fear of Pakistan being further cut down in size or being broken up, was even more accentuated. Pakistan has always felt existentially threatened even though India has never had any such designs. Pakistan thereafter started talking of 'Nazaria-i-Pakistan' (ideology of Pakistan) of which Kashmir was an integral part. They have kept coining slogans to keep pace with the changing times and in the process keeping their people occupied and misled.

As Lawrence Ziring, professor, political scientist and expert on Pakistan, put it, all of Pakistan was made hostage to the Kashmir conundrum. The terrorism in Kashmir has become a full-fledged industry in Pakistan. There are vested interests that would like the issue to thrive rather than die down. Kashmir has enabled the Pakistani army to dominate the national political scene, because with the Afghanistan and Kashmir issues on the boil, the Pakistani army will remain the lead players in the nation. The three-year extension to General Bajwa, chief of the Pakistani army, and the army rule earlier in the country for more than half of its independent life are rock-solid proofs of Pakistan being a country that has yet to find its moorings, in my opinion. According to the Government of Pakistan, the extension to General Bajwa was given in view of the regional security environment. It is a known fact that Prime Minister Imran Khan is so much dependent on Bajwa that he had taken him along to meet President Trump at the White House in 2019. The Pakistani army continues to play a predominant role in politics and running of Pakistan.

Pakistan has been obsessed with Kashmir since the time of its independence. Zulfikar Ali Bhutto, the late prime minister of Pakistan, explained this obsession when he said, 'If a Muslim majority area can remain a part of India, the raison d'être of Pakistan collapses.' In short, he linked the existence or survival of Pakistan with its annexing of Kashmir. For the same reasons, Pakistan must continue to struggle for the Kashmiris' right to self-determination. Tilak Devasher, member of the National Security Advisory Board, has aptly said that it should not surprise anybody that Pakistan has spent last 70 years trying to grab Kashmir.

With the jingoistic and nationalistic narrative that Pakistan built over this entire period lying shattered, it was no wonder that Pakistan bordered on brinkmanship, talking of the possibilities of conventional war (which could be a limited/sectoral war in Kashmir itself) and even stretching it to the option of a nuclear war. One conclusion is safe, that irrespective of what the risks are to it, Pakistan will not give up its efforts to grab Kashmir.

Kanwal Sibal, India's former foreign secretary, wrote in his article 'A Rebuttal of Pakistani Propaganda' that 'India has made it clear that the change in the constitutional status of J&K within the Indian Union does not change India's present external borders with Pakistan or affect the Line of Actual Control with China in Ladakh'. As a matter of fact, it is the Chinese who, by setting up the CPEC, have effected a major geopolitical change in the status quo by making the Chinese presence permanent in PoK. This is besides bringing Chinese civilian and military personnel closer to the Indian border. China is unlikely to agree to any future settlement of the Kashmir issue that might mean it losing control over CPEC and influence over Pakistan.

Pakistan has understood that India needed to scrap Article 370 to correct the problems within India. But they fear that it is not India's final solution. India will now strive to capture PoK, and that will be its final solution. The prospect of losing PoK is causing Pakistan endless worry. Losing PoK will mean that their control over CPEC will be lost and they will lose their linkage with China in this sector. Pakistan thus will have no border with China. It will also negate the ambiguity on the part of China that India has no legal presence in Kashmir.

Once PoK is taken, irrespective of when, India will gain direct access to Afghanistan, which will drastically reduce Pakistan's influence over the US. India can then have direct access to Afghanistan, Russia and other countries in the region and will not have to depend upon Pakistan for access to Afghanistan. An indirect offshoot would be that the hyphenation between India and Pakistan would automatically disappear.

Pakistan understands well that a determined India is capable of achieving all this. That is why they are so badly rattled. What are Pakistan's options? They could fight a conventional war, but they have no hope of winning it. It would also ruin them financially. They cannot afford to be drawn into a war with such heavy loans hanging over their head and with them being under the close scrutiny of IMF and FATF. The fear of being blacklisted by FATF is like the sword of Damocles hanging over Pakistan's head.

What Factors Can Keep the Militancy Going Post Reorganization?

Before India moves on to evolving its ground-level strategy to deal with the security scenario developing post the revocation of Article 370, a close look is warranted to assess what kind of militancy could erupt in Kashmir after all the restrictions have been removed.

There have always been five important movers of militancy in Kashmir. The first has been the infiltration by Pakistan of a large number of hardcore terrorists into the Valley. Lately, this figure has dropped dramatically because of the tight and alert counter-infiltration grid maintained by the army. The infiltration figures have remained appreciably below 100, as has been highlighted in the preceding sections. In the winter months, it becomes even more difficult to infiltrate.

Second, the pushing in of arms, ammunition and explosives is as important as infiltrating terrorists. There have been reports that

Pakistan is trying to smuggle weapons and ammunition into the Valley through small (mini) drones. This strategy could somewhat work because the drones are unlikely to be easily picked up on radars.

Third, local recruitment has been a major source of militancy in view of the drastic reduction in infiltration. However, local recruitment since 2019 has remained low. But, if Pakistan manages to smuggle weapons and ammunition into India using drones, they will be able to recruit more young men.

Fourth, deep radicalization in the Valley, especially of the youth, has been the greatest success story for Pakistan. In today's scenario, this is their greatest asset and poses the gravest threat to the region.

The fifth factor is relatively new. In south Kashmir, the trend is that new recruits are joining AGuH rather than the Hizbul Mujahideen, LeT or JeM. AGuH believes in an Islamist Kashmir governed by the shariah and is the ideological face of mother terrorist organizations such as Al-Qaeda and Islamic State in Kashmir. AGuH marks an ideological shift from the idea of political struggle for azadi to the establishment of an Islamic caliphate. This is seen as the early onset of a phase of intense radicalization that is likely to precipitate enhanced militancy in Kashmir in the future. This process has already started and an Islamic State-styled caliphate mindset has started taking root in parts of Srinagar and central Kashmir. The recent incidents of violence indicate its entrenchment in Shopian and Pulwama also.

Thus, while the role of Pakistan will remain crucial, the recent emergence of a staunch Wahabi organization such as AGuH is likely to pose an even greater danger in the years to come. This is the organization to which Zakir Musa also belonged.

The Likely Shape and Nature of Militancy after the J&K Reorganization Act

The problem in J&K has festered for far too long for any one decision to stabilize the issue even for a short while. There are numerous dimensions to the problem and multifarious actors involved in this imbroglio. Pakistan, which has been the main promoter of terrorism, has far too much at stake. The separatists, the jammaitis, the political leaders, the clergy, all have vested interests. They will not want this problem to wither away easily.

Appreciably, the Government of India carried out its preparations for the Reorganization Act well, commencing months in advance, as described earlier in the narrative. The entire terrorist support and financial ecosystem was brought under the security dragnet and control of the government. The mobile network, which is the mainstay of the terrorists' communications, was made inoperative. The political leadership, the Hurriyat, jammaitis and prominent over-ground workers were put under detention. Complete surprise was attained.

The thoroughness of the preparations and the suddenness of this action left everybody perplexed. People in the state remained indoors for the first few days as curfews and Section 144 were imposed, wondering and discussing what had struck them and what awaited them. After a few days, life slowly returned to what they were used to leading, as in the times when the Hurriyat gave calls for indefinite strikes. The shops used to open from 7 a.m. to 11 a.m. and then from 5 p.m. to 8 p.m. due to threats from militants. Initially, after 5 August 2019, they were permitted for a very limited number of hours by the militants. Timings also varied from place to place.

However, it would have been naive or even wishful thinking on the part of the handlers of Kashmir's affairs to have assumed any prolonged absence of violence. The government drew satisfaction from the fact that in the first ninety days of the restrictions having been imposed, not one civilian was killed due to firing from security forces. The administration's approach was that the perspective of stability would in itself generate tranquillity, which would allow the gradual lifting of more controls. Yes, unlike in the past, they were able to prevent any major security challenge by controlling street turbulence and rabble-rousing. But, the violence has returned as could only be expected, at the hands of the terrorists who are victimizing innocent civilians, though it has generally remained low. This has led to armchair strategists and human rights activists questioning what was achieved by imposing restrictions.

Civilians have never been the victims of the fire of India's security forces. The absence of fire by security forces in the three months following the abrogation was to prove to the world that India has never held any animus towards its Kashmiri brethren. Kashmiris are well aware of the realities but are blinded by the mist of Islamism. The culprits have always been the terrorists, and civilian casualties took place either at the hands of terrorists or as a result of being caught in the crossfire between terrorists and security forces.

On the other hand, the government's strategy should have been to educate people that the violence was likely to continue as before, or would perhaps even increase as Pakistan's deep state was likely to leave no stone unturned in its efforts to unleash violence. For Pakistan also, this has become a last-ditch battle. This angle perhaps escaped the decision-makers, or they weighed the pros and cons differently.

Following the abrogation of Articles 370 and 35A, the Kashmiris have been confronted with altogether new and monumental questions. Their biggest rallying point was likely to be an intense degree of radicalization, which may help drag terrorism on for a little while longer. It cannot survive for too long, however, because the chief manipulator, Pakistan, is struggling for its own survival. The spread of fundamentalist Islam was very much a part of proxy war launched by Pakistan. But it took real firm root during Musa's time when the militants were fighting to establish an Islamist system based on shariah law. Describing voting and democracy as '*haram*' (unacceptable), Musa expressed anger at those who described Kashmir's struggle as a 'political' one. Musa even went to the extent of threatening to cut the throat of any leader who called Kashmir's struggle a political one.[1]

The fact is that fundamentalism has taken firm root in Kashmir and radicalization poses the greatest challenge to peace and security. By and large all fundamentalists are separatists because they consider India a Hindu majoritarian state, of which they cannot be a part. It is this cross-section of fundamentalists who are pushing the narrative in Kashmir. This number may not be very large but the fact is that this minuscule minority is driving the narrative.[2]

This aspect is discussed in detail subsequently.

What is most relevant here is that whereas the world has accepted the striking down of Article 370 as an internal matter

---

1 David Devadas, *The Generation of Rage in Kashmir* (New Delhi: Oxford University Press, 2018), pp. 80–81.

2 Refer to the book *Kashmir's Untold Story* by Maroof Raza and Iqbal Chand Malhotra, last paragraph, p. 173. It is not possible to make a well-informed estimate of this hardcore element but it is generally assessed to be around 30 per cent or so.

for India, there is a lot of clamour about what they are terming as a 'clampdown' in the Valley. Unfortunately, these restrictions, especially those related to the Internet and mobile connectivity, even though as a temporary measure, internationalized the Kashmir issue. These restrictions were removed subsequently.

According to the government, within two months of the abrogation of Article 370, Section 144 was imposed in only six of the 196 jurisdictions of the police stations and life was slowly returning to normal. Along the LoC, the army maintained an aggressive posture. Only sixty terrorists were reported to have infiltrated into the Valley during the three months from August 2019, and a number of them were eliminated. Thereafter, infiltration was unable to pick up momentum because of the strong vigil maintained by the security forces. Local recruitment was abysmally low. A check on hawala transactions indicates that black money was virtually out of circulation. Post-paid mobile connectivity was restored in the region. Though prepaid connectivity was still restricted to 2G, Internet facilities were restored. Railway services within the Valley resumed. This would put a lid on the interest of the outside world, which would be in the interest of India.

There should now be two premier goals for the government. First, India must concentrate and move full steam ahead on developmental parameters, as the prime minister had promised. This will be the best weapon against terrorism. This is also the time to rectify the regional imbalances and resolve other internal matters that have been the source of acrimony amongst the three regions of the erstwhile state. The second goal ought to be to develop, from amongst a saner cross-section of society, a new rung of leadership that understands the changed realities and can bring about honest and efficient governance.

Following the removal of the partial restrictions, the militancy could have followed one of the paths or combinations thereof, as given below. However, since two years have passed, the activities on ground show that the chances of option 1 still remain, though at a reduced level; the possibility of option 2 materializing has become virtually extinct.

Option 1: Mass Non-violent Civil Disobedience

To start with, this appeared to be the most lucrative and viable option. Militants could organize a mass non-violent civil disobedience movement in the Valley through the closure of shops, schools and government offices. However, it seemed that the militants were now worried that the Centre might take some strong actions to subdue their movement. Consequently, such an option was not resorted to nor were signs of it apparent at any stage as militant groups avoided any direct confrontations or escalation. Also, they would have required a heavy flow of money from Pakistan to sustain a prolonged agitation. India had focused on blocking this type of funding, especially through hawala transactions, and had been reasonably successful.

Notwithstanding the above, this option is always open to militants, and Indian security forces and intelligence agencies must keep themselves abreast of developing situations and trends to be able to take all anticipatory, preventive and curative measures.

Option 2: Mass Rebellion

There could possibly have been a mass rebellion, wherein hundreds of thousands of protesters could have turned up on the roads and streets and carried out protests. Invariably such rebellions lead to violence, as any government is left with no option but to use force to control mobs. This would have been a worst-case scenario for India, as the resultant casualties could have precipitated and aggravated further violence.

Four factors were important to counter such a scenario. First, good technical and human intelligence to learn of the protesters' designs well in advance. This is how the Israelis operate. Second, denail of the option of assembling en masse by resorting to selective curfews, imposing Section 144 and such other measures. Third, handling of protests by the local police and CRPF. The army should invariably not be involved in such operations. And fourth, the cardinal principle of the application of minimum force. For that, the government should have enough state-of-the-art crowd-dispersal equipment, which is effective and yet does not result in mass casualties, which must not occur under any circumstances. India, therefore, must acquire the required sophisticated crowd-dispersal equipment, which is not sufficient presently. Pellet guns, which India has, are the worst kind of weapon systems and must be discarded. Some of the equipment that is available in the world market and that India could consider buying is discussed at the end of this chapter.

In short, the key to success in pre-empting and controlling such mass rebellions lay in excellent prior deciphering of intent through technical and human intelligence, preventing mobs from gathering and, if they did, breaking up the crowds through minimum use of force. Intelligence is the key point, which fortunately India has built up appreciably in the Valley today.

If the administration and the security forces continue to operate in cooperation with each other, as they do presently, the government should be in a position to handle such contingencies effectively.

It is my assessment that the time for this kind of rebellion by Kashmiris has already passed, at least for the present. If they had any such inclination, they would have perhaps resorted to this option within two to three days of the revocation of Article 370. That they did not do so was perhaps the result of the factors of surprise and shock over losing statehood, a new worry of the possibility of being reduced to a minority within their own state, and also perhaps disappointment with Pakistan, which did not give them any prior warning. However, the government should still be prepared for such an eventuality. One should not rule it out altogether.

Option 3: 'Normal' Violent Activities

Violence in the Valley has shown considerable decline since 2019. There was a concern that regular violent activities, on the same lines as those following Burhan Wani's death, may commence, with a large support base amongst the people, when restrictions are fully lifted and the Covid-19 situation abates. There was also the worry that this problem may extend to the entire length and breadth of the Valley, in differing intensities, rather than being limited to only south Kashmir. However, this also did not come about when the restrictions were subsequently lifted.

There could also be a change of tactics with regard to violent activities on the ground. These may now take the shape of sporadic incidents of human bombs and car bombs, both of which are high-profile activities resulting in greater impact and casualties. There are likely to be enough volunteers for such suicide missions among the youth. Throwing hand grenades in crowded areas is also likely to be common as they create a significant impact. Street turbulence and stone pelting could continue at a moderate level of intensity as and when the opportunities arise. It, however, is to the credit of the Indian state that none of these activities have materialized significantly so far.

March 2020 onwards, Covid interfered with all regular activities. However, people's basic necessities continued to be more than met and life more or less returned to normal. To make ends meet, the main occupation of handicrafts could be carried out in homes; in any case, shops continued to open intermittently, depending on the lockdowns. The sale of apples was facilitated by the UT administration by procuring the produce straight from orchards. Terrorists threatened the owners of the orchards and killed or wounded some to pressure them into not selling through arrangements made by the the security forces and the state, but without much success. Schools and colleges remained shut because of Covid restrictions, as in the rest of the country.

Handling of the Situation

Combatting any of the above scenarios going forward will require accurate and precise intelligence and preventing unhindered assembly. The selective imposition of curfews and Section 144 in different, non-contiguous localities to curtail assemblies, and the use of drones to observe the situation from the air, would be useful methods. What shape the reactions from militants will take will largely depend on Pakistan's ability to support them. For the present, their ability has been severely curtailed by India. India, however, should be in no doubt that such protests can take place even without the help of Pakistan, yet it is also true that this could happen only for short periods.

Once again, it merits stressing that protests or violence in the erstwhile state of J&K will continue for quite some time. Militancy has raged there for thirty years and will not die down suddenly. But it is my opinion that India has taken the wind out of the sails of the militancy and it cannot last far too long. In the meantime, India should continue to deal with the militancy as before. India's success will lie in controlling the areas of disturbance and the tempo of the protests or conflict. The initiative presently lies with India and it should not let that pass into the hands of terrorists. The government's priority should remain on saving lives. The law-enforcement agencies have to secure a psychological victory over the terrorists.

The strategy, as suggested above, should be that the police and the CRPF handle protests, if any, and deal with civilians while the army is kept along the exterior lines and the LoC. The Rashtriya Rifles should continue to maintain the counter-infiltration grid. It will also be the right optics for the rest of the world.

The central government and the two new union territories should establish good communication channels with the people to remove their misgivings. Such dialogue with the people must be aimed at allaying their fears and reassuring them. They are India's people and everything possible must be done to put their minds at ease. The local police should be gradually given more and more responsibility instead of the armed forces. This step will also be important in denying any space to propaganda by terrorists and Pakistan. This process is already in full swing.

Overall Strategy to Counter Terrorism in Jammu and Kashmir and Kargil–Ladakh

While India continues to counter Pakistan's efforts in the international forum on the one hand, on the other, the tactics and operational-level strategy on the ground will be crucial. These should result in the least number of casualties amongst innocent civilians and yet create maximum impact. This is likely to be a fairly long haul.

In the following paragraphs, I have outlined a recommended approach to countering the militancy. These efforts should be carried out without prejudice to provide good administration and developmental activities to build a new Jammu and Kashmir. This strategy should originate from the Centre, after which consultations with all the stakeholders and then go down to the last man in the Valley as all of them are equally important players.

Strategy at the National Level

A National Policy and Security Doctrine

India has fought an active proxy war in J&K for over three decades. Dozens of agencies at both the national and state levels, besides security forces in a large quantum, have been involved in this effort, but all this is without having a formal national policy, doctrine and security strategy in place to fight this menace. As a result, India's approach and responses to this problem have been incident-centric, and depend heavily on the attitude and approach of the government in power and how they choose to react.

The only aspect that remained constant was that India was defensive in its approach and never took its response across the border. It never opted to punish the abettors of this problem, that is, Pakistan, nor did it go after the terrorist groups that were safely lodged inside Pakistan. India was tied down at the operational level from crossing the LoC to raid the Pakistani army's border action teams, or even their vulnerable posts. These actions would have posed a real threat to the terrorists and even the Pakistani army. It is a fact that India's political leadership allowed themselves to be deterred by Pakistan's bogey of using nuclear weapons to neutralize India's conventional superiority.

After the Pulwama incident and the Balakot air strike, India's response paradigm underwent a complete change. From thereon, Pakistan and the global community have had to contend with India's newly defined red lines. These are that firstly, the sanctity of the LoC or the international border will no longer be restricting factors for India to decide on the punishment to be inflicted on terror groups. Secondly, India is prepared to hit terrorist organizations and their training camps even inside mainland Pakistan. And finally, there will be no restriction on the type of response, which could range from air strikes to the use of heavy artillery or missiles on terror targets anywhere inside Pakistan or even the capture of Pakistani posts in PoK, which act as facilitators to the terrorists as firm bases. India reserves the right to even go beyond all these. This has been a huge paradigm shift.

Pakistan had thus far followed a low-cost strategy in terms of military hardware, manpower and economic burden to keep the fire burning in J&K, but that strategy is unlikely to work any more. The cost of persisting with this approach is likely to be prohibitive and risky. India also successfully exhibited its ability to handle this problem on multiple fronts, that is, diplomatically, economically and militarily. There is immense merit in this approach, and it has already paid dividends.

The abolition of Articles 370 and 35A and the reorganization of the state into two union territories has brought about a completely new scenario and a change in the security metrics. India now needs to clearly redefine and crystallize its strategy, which has already been put into motion, both within J&K and extending to and including Pakistan. Irrespective of which government is in power at the Centre or in the UTs, there ought to be consistency in India's approach to handling this problem.

It is therefore important that a policy and doctrine on the proxy war in J&K are issued by the central government for clarity at all levels. These should also lay down the guiding principles for the UT government. The national security strategy should be derived from the national policy. In turn, the security doctrine should evolve by carrying out an inter-departmental, inter-agency and multidisciplinary strategic review of the dynamics of the state/ UT. This doctrine must be all-encompassing, covering all facets from security aspects, job opportunities, economic development of the state and all administrative issues besides the crucial perception management aspects.

The doctrine must thus be aimed at increasing the credibility of the Indian state in the eyes of the people of all the three regions of the state, especially in the eyes of the Kashmiris. The Kashmiris' apprehensions must be removed and they must be reassured that they are part and parcel of the country. Articles 370 and 35A were repealed to bring them into India's embrace rather than push them away or punish them. To this end, the Kashmiri people, especially the youth, must be convinced that the Indian state cares for their aspirations and they are as important as the geographical territory of Kashmir.

India should also start simultaneous dialogues with the people of all regions of the state to understand the regional perspectives and their problems and aspirations. This is a critical aspect and should be dealt with at the highest priority.

India must also accord a high priority to deradicalizing the youth of the Valley as they pose the gravest danger to peace and stability in the region. Reviving Kashmiriyat and the Sufi culture will go a long way in ensuring this. Also, Kashmiri youth love sports. An effort must be made to provide extensive sporting facilities within the state. These can prove to be game changers.

The state must be provided with able administration and corruption must be weeded out. Sufficient employment opportunities have to be created urgently as employment will usher in development at a fast rate.

Corporates must help optimize the assets of the state such as tourism, handicrafts, the apple and saffron trade, the houseboat business, mountaineering and trekking, among others.

The return of the Kashmiri Pandits to the Valley should remain the ultimate goal. That would be the litmus test of India's success. This will definitely take some time to materialize, perhaps 5–8 years.

Single-point Handling of the Proxy War at the Centre

It was always a matter of discussion as to which central ministry should handle the J&K conflict. As a result, there was little coordination amongst the various ministries and agencies, for example, the coordination between the ministries of home and defence needed improvement. A notable example of this weakness is the measures announced by the central government after the 2014 floods in Kashmir. These left the people in the Valley very dissatisfied because of the lack of expeditious follow-up and coordination on the part of the Centre in the allocation of funds and other necessary actions. Even though it was recognized that the high level of corruption in the state was a regressive factor, better coordination and guidance from the Centre would have helped immensely.

Now, the home ministry has taken a clear lead on the Jammu and Kashmir issue and under the present dispensation should handle it with the support and coordination of all other relevant ministries and agencies. It has already been decided to set up a core group of a few relevant ministries to expedite all desired activities.

Setting Up a Perception-Management Body

After the repeal of Articles 370 and 35A in August 2019, Pakistan launched an all-out war on social media to malign India internationally. Their story was that India had imposed severe restrictions in the Valley by way of curbs on the internet, and imposed curfews to prevent people from coming out onto the streets to express themselves.

These measures were imposed by India to prevent loss of life, which was achieved. Moreover, all these restrictions have been lifted progressively.

Pakistan, however, is doing its best to keep the rumour mills going. There are two levels at which India needs to counter this malicious propaganda. One is at the international level and the other is within the state.

At the international level, India has done well and Pakistan has been rebuffed at the UN Security Council, the United Nations Human Rights Council (UNHRC), and even by the European Union. Pakistan met the same fate when they raised this issue at the United Nations General Assembly on 27 September 2019. Despite this, Pakistan has been propagating that they have the support of sixty Muslim countries, which is again false, because the only Muslim countries that have stood by them are Malaysia, to some extent, and Turkey.

India needs to counter this narrative of Pakistan at the international level. To this end, a number of tours have been undertaken by the international media and the diplomatic staff of various countries to the Valley.

The other and most important aspect is to build a positive narrative within Kashmir. This internal effort has always been weak in the absence of an expert professional body dedicated to perception management. This is a critical area and deserves the highest priority.

A good part of the battle for mind space in Kashmir can be won if India has a suitable 'Kashmir narrative'. The Hurriyat has a narrative and so do the other terror outfits. All of them push their ideas, day in and day out, quite effectively. And India, which has the truth and the legal accession of the state on its side, has not been able to create a narrative that tells Kashmiris its side of the story convincingly. There are lots of fence-sitters who may overtly support the terrorists but in their hearts hate them. They need a counter-narrative so powerful that it blows everything apart and brings them firmly on India's side.

Social media and cyberspace are undoubtedly critical in this endeavour. It has to be ensured that both the vernacular and national media have a nuanced approach to the Kashmir issue in the interest of the country. This can be achieved through regular official briefings.

Perception management is also necessary to overcome the scars of the internal conflict. Efforts have been made by the army through Operation Sadbhavana, which, as mentioned earlier, has had great effect. But this is not good enough for the changed scenario. What India has long needed is a high-level empowered body of professionals from a range of fields, including diplomats, bureaucrats, academics, soldiers, economists and artists, to comprehensively study the environment of Jammu and Kashmir. They should study the diplomatic, political, socio-economic, military and psychological aspects. This perception management body must have inputs from intelligence agencies, academia, captains of the industry, think tanks, among others. This body must also have easy access to the decision-makers at the highest levels, both at the national and state levels, besides adequate financing. They should develop a comprehensive plan that covers both the state and national levels and should be responsible for implementing it with the central and state administration.

Perception management is undoubtedly not only one of the most crucial, but perhaps the most important tool in India's efforts to counter the proxy war, other than the kinetic aspect. The false imprints in the hearts and minds of the people have to be replaced by more positive messaging. An effective counter-narrative and an efficient and credible dissemination system are the keys to success. India cannot afford to lose any more time in this effort.

Countering Radicalization in the Valley

As far as India is concerned, J&K was never an issue. India's view all along has been that after Partition happened in 1947, India has moved on and so should Pakistan.

Pakistan, however, could not bring itself to see the reality, and for them J&K has always remained an unfinished agenda of the Partition. As a result, in the seventy years after Partition, they fought four wars and unleashed a proxy war on India for thirty years. In the process, they have inflicted countless miseries on the people of the state. They have radicalized the people of Kashmir, the same people who were proud of their Sufi culture not too long ago.

For a Kashmiri, the ethnic aspect of being a Kashmiri is important, but there has also developed a strong and overriding Muslim aspiration. However, it may still be true that if a Kashmiri Muslim and a Kashmiri Pandit meet each other outside the Valley, they may hug each other. This is because being a Kashmiri takes precedence over being a Muslim or a Hindu. Yes, there is a political divergence, but ethnicity cannot be ignored. Similarly, when we talk of radicalization, some people are of the view that there has been a political radicalization in the Valley and not necessarily a religious radicalization. They also feel that radicalization in Kashmir is not a cause of the conflict but rather an outcome or an effect of it. Whichever way one may look at it, the fact is that the Islamist radicalization in Kashmir is a major threat today. There should also be no doubt that radicalization of the Kashmiri populace has come about because of Pakistan's concerted efforts in this direction.

When one looks at various survey reports, it is obvious that the Kashmiris are being radicalized by the Wahabi, Barelvi and Salafi ideologies. Perhaps this shift has also to do with how the global

Islamist revolution is working. How does one otherwise explain the fact that just before he joined the militancy, Zakir Musa was an engineering student in Chandigarh, enjoying a secular life. He belonged to a prosperous family, with a father who was an engineer with the Public Works Department and a brother who was a doctor, both working with the government. And yet Musa became a staunch radical overnight. It is for scholars to study this aspect, but the fact is that fundamentalism in Islam has already acquired a central place and the entire world is trying to come to grips with it. The killings in Christchurch (New Zealand) on 20 March 2019 in two mosques are another example of how seriously the world is affected by Islamophobia. Kashmir is thus no exception.

India must therefore take all the necessary steps to curb this radicalization so as to ensure that this menace does not spread to the rest of India, where the Muslims appreciably are quite moderate. The solution for this radicalization/Islamization can only be found through wise political process, dialogue and all-round development. There must be ample educational facilities and jobs available for the youth in Jammu, Kashmir and Ladakh. And last but not the least, since they are India's youth, even when misguided, we ought to have compassion for them. They have to be treated like family members who have gone astray. A feeling of security amongst Kashmiri students in mainland India must be ensured. They should be India's ambassadors in Kashmir.

People of Kashmir Are India's People – Maintain Dialogue with Them

The people of Kashmir are India's people and it must make them feel that it is genuinely interested in their well-being, which in fact very much is a reality.

A Paradigm Shift

India should remember that Prime Minister Vajpayee won the hearts and minds of the Kashmiris when he said in Srinagar in 2003 that he would like to deal with the Kashmiri brethren with an approach of *'Kashmiriyat, jamhooriyat* and *insaniyat'* (Kashmiriyat denotes amity and cordiality, jamhooriyat denotes democracy and insaniyat denotes humanism).

The people of Kashmir are as much at the centre of the issue as is the geographical territory of Kashmir. They are the most affected by the situation and hence they are the most important players. Dialogues with representatives of the people of all shades and opinions in the Valley, Jammu and Ladakh must be commenced at various levels without any preconditions.

It is important to instil a sense of belonging in the hearts of the people of the erstwhile state. India's security forces also, when dealing with the Kashmiri people, have always kept this aspect uppermost in their minds. All the propaganda about human rights violations is the handiwork of the Pakistani deep state.

As a matter of fact, it is to the credit of India's security forces that they have accepted casualties to themselves many a times just to avoid collateral damage. No country in the world takes as many precautions in this regard as does India. If the people realize this fact and cooperate, then gradually the security forces present in the Valley can be reduced.

Strategy at the International Level

Following the abrogation of Articles 370 and 35A, the world stood by India. The international opinion is that J&K is a bilateral issue between India and Pakistan. India's efforts to isolate Pakistan diplomatically as a state sponsor of terrorism had also yielded tangible results. Following the Pulwama attack, the diplomatic pressure on Pakistan from the US, European Union countries and the OIC, especially UAE and Saudi Arabia, is a good example of these efforts. These have been fruitful because of India's financial might and the strong diplomatic ties that it has with these countries. Today, the world stands with India, but maintaining this status will have to be an ongoing effort. India cannot afford to be complacent on this account.

Diplomatic Initiatives

The work by India's diplomatic missions abroad to promote a positive perception and negate the propaganda by the separatists and Pakistan are not being given the salience that they merit. The Pakistani government's diplomatic missions and diaspora score over India in maintaining a high pitch of continuous rhetoric and projecting their viewpoint. India needs to clearly and proactively convey its threshold of tolerance for Pakistan's active promotion of terror in Kashmir. Pressure has to be brought on Pakistan from the US, European Union countries, Russia and even OIC to shun the path of terrorism. India must even try and persuade China. India has to convince these countries of its concerns regarding terrorism. This should not be difficult as the world is convinced that Pakistan is an epicentre of terrorism.

India's Relations with Afghanistan and Iran

India has traditionally had great relations with both Afghanistan and Iran. As a matter of fact, India has invested over USD 3 billion in Afghanistan and earned their appreciation. Their Parliament building and a hospital in Afghanistan are just two of the many monuments that stand in testimony to India's friendship with them. All this assistance has been financial and developmental in nature. India has always enjoyed maximum credibility with the people of Afghanistan. It must build on that.

The proposed American pullout from Afghanistan by September 2021 went totally haywire as, by 15 August 2021, the Taliban had already entered Kabul because of the absence of any resistance whatsoever. With the sudden collapse of state forces, then President Ashraf Ghani fled the country to the UAE, which gave him amnesty on humanitarian grounds. The entire American plan of a peaceful transfer of power lay in tatters. A rebellion did erupt in Panjshir Valley under the leadership of Ahmed Massoud (son of the former lion of Panjshir Ahmad Shah Massoud) and former Vice President Amrullah Saleh but it was soon crushed by the Taliban with the close help and guidance of the ISI. The Taliban is thus in full control of Afghanistan. The developments in Afghanistan will have grave implications on the entire region. India would have liked to continue to work in close coordination with Afghanistan, but now, with the Taliban regime in Kabul, the first question that arises is whether India will have an official relationship with Afghanistan or not. A decision on this is yet to be made, and it may be some time before a final call is taken.

India conducts extensive trade with Iran and used to import almost 30 million metric tons of oil annually from it. US sanctions against it resulted in these imports being halted for a short while, but Iran will continue to be India's friend in the long run. It has borders with Pakistan and a constant problem on that account by way of terrorism. Both India and Iran suffer from the same menace from Pakistan. All these are factors in India's favour, but it has yet to take advantage of them.

India must continue to maintain its traditionally strong relations with Iran, even when the sanctions against it by the US continue.

Indus Waters Treaty

While India hopes that better sense will prevail in Pakistan, certain pressure points must be built up on them alongside, such as discussions on the World Bank-brokered Indus Waters Treaty of 1960. Given the sensitivity of this issue in India–Pakistan relations, even a measured distancing from this treaty will send a strong signal to Pakistan and resonate positively in J&K. This treaty has been exceptionally generous to the lower riparian Pakistan, which has repeatedly misused its provisions to obstruct permissible projects in J&K. There are also strong sentiments in J&K against the treaty.

On 3 April 2002, the J&K Legislative Assembly had even adopted a resolution seeking a review of this treaty. As an immediate step, India could consider withdrawing its commissioner from the Permanent Indus Commission, making it non-functional, and convey that it is suspending its participation in the dispute-settlement mechanism under Article IX of the treaty. India should also announce that it will not only proceed vigorously with the implementation of the Baglihar and Kishanganga projects, which have overcome the objections raised by Pakistan, but also resume work on the Tulbal project to address the pressing needs of the people of J&K. This project is on the mouth of the Jhelum river but has been suspended since 1987 (because of Pakistan's obstructionist attitude).

While indicating its readiness to continue to provide data and abide by other obligations under the Indus Waters Treaty for the time being, India could state that it will consider withdrawing from the treaty unless Pakistan abandons state sponsorship of terrorism in India.

BIMSTEC, BBIN and IORA

In parallel, India can actively promote regional/subregional cooperation minus Pakistan under the aegis of the Bay of Bengal Initiative for Multi-Sectoral Technical and Economic Cooperation (BIMSTEC), the Bangladesh, Bhutan, India, Nepal (BBIN) initiative and the Indian Ocean Rim Association (IORA). India should shed its traditional reluctance to take the lead in such forums; instead, it should vigorously set the agenda of these organizations, which have the potential of developing into India-led platforms. The BRICS (Brazil, Russia, India, China and South Africa)–BIMSTEC outreach summit in Goa a few years ago was an excellent initiative. Likewise, an IORA summit could be organized by India, while keeping Pakistan out of the organization. All these steps when combined together will create a significant impact. It is a positive signal that India is engaging in many such dialogues with its neighbours in multiple forums. These measures will hit Pakistan hard economically and isolate them diplomatically.

Building Deterrence

India needs to take a series of steps to deter Pakistan from striking at targets in India through its proxies. These could include both long-term and immediate measures. To begin with, enhancing India's defence preparedness, including an appreciable increase in the defence budget, plugging the gaps in its military capabilities and structural reforms in the defence ministry are urgently required.

The 26 February 2019 air strike at Balakot defined India's new red lines. These should go a long way in deterring Pakistan from indulging in nefarious activities and promoting terrorism inside Kashmir. The strike established that controlled escalations are very much possible and Pakistan's strategy of 'full spectrum deterrence' has come into serious question.

India should also conduct a limited review of its nuclear doctrine of 'no first use' with the clear caveat that pre-emptive actions can be taken should India get prior indication of an impending nuclear attack by Pakistan. Especially because Pakistan has second-strike capability despite India's strategy of 'massive retaliation to cause unacceptable damage'. In such a case, why would India want to accept two strikes, one initially by Pakistan and the second in response to its retaliation? It would be unwise and suicidal. This necessitates serious reconsideration. I was relieved to hear India's defence minister, Rajnath Singh, giving a clear hint of possible suitable readjustments in India's nuclear deterrence policy. This information is, however, based on open sources.

India should also consider developing low-yield battlefield nuclear weapons to address the gaps in its nuclear arsenal against Pakistan, which is constantly threatening India with the possible use of tactical nuclear weapons and has a stated policy of using them in the field against India. No ambiguity should be left in this regard, especially so with adversaries where unstable non-state actors abound. This would further strengthen India's nuclear deterrence in the face of the never-ending nuclear brinkmanship by Pakistan.

A successful deterrent patrol by Indian Naval Ship (INS) *Arihant* on 6 November 2018 completed India's nuclear triad and was a positive step towards its defence preparedness.

The reinforcement and upgrade of the fence along the LoC into a 'smart' fence is a high priority operational requirement. This should include state-of-the-art surveillance technologies such as thermal imagers and infrared and laser-based intruder alarms that form an invisible land fence. Aerostats, drones and unmanned aerial vehicles (UAVs) for continuous aerial surveillance; unattended ground sensors that can help detect intrusion bids through tunnels; radars; sonar systems to secure some riverine portions; fibre-optic sensors; and command and control systems that receive data from all surveillance devices in real time are also important. All these need to be backed by quick response teams available in the close vicinity of the obstacle system at all times. Most of these already exist.

India must also harden security at vital military and civilian installations to prevent attacks by Pakistani proxies (studies have already been done to estimate the manual effort required and the financial cost). The Lieutenant General Philip Campose Committee report in this regard is relevant. This process must be judiciously arrived at and restricted to the minimum essential so that Indian troops do not develop a fortress mentality.

Long-term adherence to a policy of inflicting punitive measures such as the surgical strike in 2016 and the air strike on 26 February 2019 is essential. The terrorists should not be allowed to live and sleep in peace anywhere, even deep inside Pakistan. There should be no let-up in this aggressive strategy.

Financial Strangulation of the Terrorist Network

It is well known that no terrorist network can survive without financial support. Unfortunately, India had long failed to choke financial support to the terrorist network in Kashmir. However, before the 5 August 2019 declaration, India gave this aspect great importance and today the financial ecosystem of the terrorist network is reasonably under India's control. The petrodollars supporting the spread of Wahabism in the Valley must be dried up. This is the single-biggest source of funding and is routed through Pakistan. Demonetization, and the more active use of the ED,

NIA, among others, have been steps in the right direction. India also needs to ensure that all conduits such as Pakistan's diplomatic mission in New Delhi, terrorist funding through the apple and walnut trade and other hawala networks are blocked to starve the financial ecosystem of the terrorists. However, more work is required to completely eliminate the hawala network operating in Kashmir. Lately, there has been encouraging progress in this direction.

Dialogue with Pakistan

Under the present situation in Kashmir, Articles 370 and 35A have ceased to be relevant. Also, importantly, what has become irrelevant is the LoC between J&K and Pakistan. This should now be treated as an international border between J&K and Pakistan. Any dialogue with Pakistan regarding Kashmir can now only be on India's claim on PoK and Gilgit-Baltistan. Pakistan will have to come to grips with this changed reality, rather than keep threatening war, including (most irresponsibly) a nuclear conflict, which would be a suicidal option for them.

Before I discuss this aspect further, I must emphasize that even though Pakistan has always been a perpetrator of terrorism and the proxy war in J&K – despite their denials – India has always remained open to talks with them. All the past Indian governments, such as those of prime ministers Atal Bihari Vajpayee and Dr Manmohan Singh, kept the dialogue going with Pakistan but with no success. Pakistan remained rigid and unidimensional in its approach, their eyes shut to the reality on the ground. They were not prepared to change their stance. So, for the last five years plus, India's approach changed and it demanded that the terrorism in J&K must first stop before any dialogue could take place.

Here I must recount an interesting story to elucidate how deeply and irrationally the Kashmir issue has been ingrained in the Pakistani psyche. This narration is borrowed from Arun Shourie's book, *Will the Iron Fence Save a Tree Hollowed by Termites?* He recounts that for the *India Today* conclave of 2003, President Musharraf was invited to give the keynote address via satellite from Islamabad. In eighty minutes, Musharraf mentioned Kashmir seventy times. His message – incessantly reiterated – was simple: Kashmir was a dispute between India and Pakistan. It was the key dispute. In fact, so central was it that if it were solved, no other dispute would survive, and if it were not solved, no other dispute could be resolved. And the only solution to the Kashmir dispute was for India to give up its 'rigid' stand and accept Pakistan's position.

Today, the government of Imran Khan is no different. As a matter of fact, it is possibly even more irrational and unpredictable, as shown by its rhetoric post 5 August 2019. In all probability, Pakistan's responses even in the future will continue to reflect their irrational thought process, in spite of the fact that the present Modi government has given ample proof of its sincerity in wanting to maintain a dialogue with Pakistan. Firstly, Modi invited Pakistan's then prime minister Nawaz Sharif to his oath-taking ceremony on 24 May 2014. Secondly, on his way back from Afghanistan in December 2015, Modi made an unscheduled stop in Lahore to extend personal greetings to Nawaz Shariff on the occasion of his granddaughter's wedding.

Another important issue is that India can never be sure whether Pakistan's civilian government is in full control. It is well known that it is the Pakistani army that rules the roost. The policies on issues such as Kashmir, the proxy war and relations with the US,

China and Afghanistan are all areas that are under the direct watch of the Pakistani army and the ISI. An illustration of this is the fact that Prime Minister Imran Khan was accompanied by the chief of Army Staff of the Pakistani army and the director-general of the ISI when he met then US president Trump. Any civilian government that has not followed the army's diktats, especially with regard to Kashmir affairs, has been thrown out. If any dialogue is to take place with Pakistan, it may be worthwhile to consider whether a parallel dialogue with the Pakistani army can take place simultaneously. The problem for India, a democratic country, is that it is not a desirable and practical proposition for the Indian army to interact directly with the Pakistani army, and yet some way has to be found. A back-channel dialogue could be an option. This could be over and above a formal dialogue with the Pakistani government at the political level.

Another factor is that terrorist groups such as JeM, LeT, Hizbul Mujahideen and now even the Taliban, which have the power to act in concert with and even independently of the civilian government, must be rendered defunct by the Pakistani government before India commences any talks with them. These groups have to be brought to proper judicial trials and their funds confiscated. This also necessitates that the military and the ISI be on the same page as their government. Even now, Pakistan has taken permission from the Security Council to allow Hafiz Saeed, a declared global terrorist, to draw a hefty pension. Can there be any bigger hypocrisy than this? This clearly shows their intent and close linkage with terror groups.

Can these terrorist groups also act independently of the army? Two attempts on President Musharraf's life by the JeM throw up this question. He held dialogues with prime ministers Vajpayee and

Manmohan Singh to find an amicable solution to the Kashmir problem. It is possible that these dialogues spurred the attempts on his life; one cannot be very sure of this because there are wheels within wheels in Pakistan's set-up.

The plea by Pakistan that they themselves are victims of terrorism can no longer be accepted. For too long, India has granted them that excuse. Hillary Clinton, the erstwhile US secretary of state, had famously and bluntly remarked in Islamabad on 21 October 2011: 'If you promote terrorism you will definitely be affected by it yourself to a great extent. You cannot keep snakes in your backyard with the hope that they will bite only your neighbours. Eventually these snakes are also going to turn on whoever has them in their backyard.'

So, while talks are an option, they must be only on terror first. And from there on only about PoK and Gilgit-Baltistan.

A related issue is the question of plebiscite in J&K, which Pakistan keeps pushing. They refuse to accept that plebiscite as a solution never became a practical option as Pakistan never fulfilled the conditions that were prerequisites. Even the UN has removed the dispute regarding J&K from its agenda and advised both countries to handle it bilaterally. Furthermore, and importantly, the Simla Agreement clearly laid down that 'the Kashmir issue would be handled bilaterally'. No third-party intervention would be acceptable under any circumstances. It does not talk of plebiscite as an option.

The Musharraf–Manmohan Singh formula and even the Musharraf–Vajpayee formula (which was never disclosed but was reportedly very close to being signed at Agra) can no longer be on the table for consideration. They are now irrelevant. There can now be talks only on the changed ground reality. When the situation improves, the aspects of better neighbourly relations and trade can also be discussed. India has always been open to such ideas.

For those amongst us who tend to be pessimistic, if East Germany and West Germany, China and Taiwan, South Korea and North Korea, the US and North Korea could talk to each other, then why can't India and Pakistan? If Pakistan convinces India of their sincerity and honesty of purpose and there is irrevocable proof of their shutting down terrorist camps, and they stop their proxy war, then India and Pakistan can certainly live as good neighbours.

A Back Channel Is Always a Plus

This has been included here only as a concept. At present, when Pakistan is not inclined to accept the reality of the changed circumstances in J&K post 5 August 2019, there is little possibility of a backchannel operating between the two countries.

However, as and when it is considered appropriate to start a dialogue or even consider the possibility of starting a dialogue, a backchannel contact may be useful to discuss the options and modality of the proposed dialogue itself.

Backchannel politics was not very common in the case of Pakistan and India, in view of the troubled nature of the relationship and the trust deficit. In the past, there have been periods of sustained dialogue between India and Pakistan followed by a long period of silence, during which the two sides would mull over what they had discussed. If this interlude was not taken advantage of, then the trail went cold. Had a backchannel system been operating at those meetings, the two sides would have had a reasonably well-crafted draft on the table to rely on during subsequent discussions. It was only during the era of Prime Minister Atal Bihari Vajpayee, after his visit to Lahore in 1999, that backchannel dialogues were initiated. It was then that R.K. Mishra and Niaz A. Naik started talking to each other via the backchannel as special envoys of their prime ministers.[3] The medium was found to be somewhat useful even during the Kargil war.

The fact is that backchannel talks have always been in vogue in the world of diplomacy. During the Cuban missile crisis, President Kennedy always referred to the messages coming through the backchannels and ignored the negative ones from Nikita Khrushchev.[4] Henry Kissinger, in his book *Years of Renewal*, has also referred to the advantages of backchannel diplomacy. He felt that backchannel negotiations helped President Nixon impose coherence on various departments of the government that were trying to 'thwart his policy'.[5]

Presently, there are at least half a dozen reputed think tanks in both India and Pakistan that are in constant dialogue with one another. While the Indian think tanks on their return from these parleys submit feedback to the government, they are generally not the beneficiaries of structured guidelines before going for such parleys. Nor do they often get feedback from the government, even informally. It would be far more beneficial if some think tanks were to be nominated, even confidentially, by the two governments to talk on their behalf. It is recommended that a number of suitable backchannel talks between India and Pakistan be kept going even when formal talks may not be taking place and irrespective of how bad the relations between the two countries are.

---

3 Sartaj Aziz, *Between Dreams and Realities: Some Milestones in Pakistan's History* (Karachi: Oxford University Press, 2009), p. 275.
4 Steven R. Weisman, 'The World; Secret Diplomacy: Rules of the Road', *New York Times*, 19 January 2003.
5 Henry Kissinger, *Years of Renewal* (London: Simon & Schuster, 1999), pp. 79–81.

Strategy at the State Level

Unified Headquarters

The Unified Headquarters was set up in J&K in 1993, on the model of a similar organization in Assam established during Operation Rhino. The aims of the Unified Headquarters are to lay down objectives for the state and security forces and to coordinate operational and intelligence plans. One of the major advantages of the Unified Headquarters is that it brings bureaucrats, the army, police, central police organizations and intelligence agencies on the same platform for sharing intelligence and planning the broad parameters of operations. This is also the best place to discuss the broad policy directives for the state. The biggest advantage lies in having the chief minister, the elected head of the government (or the head of the UT till statehood is restored), chairing these meetings and taking the lead in issuing directions to the multiple agencies. This brings in the ownership aspect and thus the backing of the head of the government.

In the post-5 August 2019 dispensation, in the absence of a chief minister, the lieutenant governor assumes an important and lead role and has overriding powers in matters of security. This will be essential in order for the Centre to have complete control over security matters. However, (when statehood is restored) the chief minister would continue to chair the meetings of the Unified Headquarters. Also, equally importantly, plans for people-friendly schemes and perception management can be finalized in the Unified Headquarters in consultation with all important agencies.

Whereas the Unified Headquarters has brought about a good amount of unity in the conduct of operations and the sharing of intelligence, there are still areas where improvements are required. The biggest lacuna is that the army commander is not part of the Unified Headquarters. This is because both corps are geographically separated in the north and south of the Pir Panjal and are responsible for their respective corps zones. Their approaches and tactics are also different because the dynamics of the insurgency are different in these two parts of the state. Therefore, the governments prefer to deal directly with the corps commanders, thus leaving out the command headquarters. This weakness, however, is addressed by the army's mechanism of regular briefings at the command headquarters at the level of corps commanders and the staff. Army commanders, however, have full authority and get due deference from the chief minister and the governor (now lieutenant governor), whom they meet frequently to discuss and render advice on issues concerning the state (now union territories).

The second major weakness is that the Unified Headquarters does not have a dedicated secretariat/staff with a chief of staff to ensure follow-ups on the decisions taken. In its absence, the staff from the respective corps headquarters try to bridge the gap. However, at best they can only partially cover this shortcoming because each service – the police, paramilitary forces, bureaucracy – jealously guards its own independent identity, domain and status.

Despite these drawbacks, the Unified Headquarters continues to discharge its responsibilities effectively and is a big asset.

Dialogue Within the State

Unfortunately, the psychological barriers amongst the three major regions of the state, that is, Kashmir, Jammu and Ladakh, have grown immensely over time. This factor was always underplayed by the political leadership of the state because of vested interests in the Valley. There was a tendency to forget that the name of the state was 'Jammu and Kashmir' and not Kashmir alone. These different regions have their own aspirations, which are critical. Now this issue will acquire new dimensions because the state has been divided into two union territories. On the one hand, there are huge differences between Jammu and Kashmir and, on the other, in the second union territory of Ladakh, people from Kargil are worried that the Ladakhis will take all the benefits.

Basically, the differences emerged from the fact that the non-Muslim belts felt that they were not getting their fair and proportionate share from the developmental and financial resources of the state. They complained that they were getting a smaller share of government jobs and fewer seats in professional colleges and vocational institutes. No government tried seriously to resolve these issues and, as a result, these differences grew and have now also acquired religious overtones. The divide between Jammu and Kashmir became most apparent from the results of the 2014 elections in the state, wherein the BJP won all their seats in Jammu province and PDP won in Kashmir. So a clear political divide had emerged between the two sides of the Pir Panjal.

This does not augur well for the new union territories. There is thus a need to start a dialogue amongst all the major regions of the state on priority. This dialogue will have to have the backing of all the major political parties. Unless these differences, which have already become very sharp, are resolved expeditiously to the satisfaction of the people of all three provinces, the political and geographical cohesiveness of these union territories will be at risk. The remedy would lie in rectifying the imbalances that have developed over the years. Everybody will have to be given their fair share in financial allocations, commerce, employment, development and administration. This is the ideal time to rectify these problems, as the new procedures and systems are being evolved in the union territories and before J&K (without Ladakh) is restored as a state.

Deradicalization of the Valley Youth

The biggest success that Pakistan has secured in Kashmir is the radicalization of the Valley, especially the youth. This indeed poses a real long-term danger. Kashmir watchers are of the view that the rise of radicalization could have unpredictable social consequences. The unparalleled popularity of militant commanders like Burhan Wani and Zakir Musa is a good indicator of the extent to which that process of radicalization has already succeeded.

What exactly does radicalization mean and how does it impact society? There are no easily found definitions of the term religious radicalization. Lieutenant General Syed Ata Hasnain, who has intimate knowledge of the Valley, as he has served there in all ranks from brigadier onwards including as lieutenant general when he was the corps commander in the Valley, has defined the term radicalization very well (*Times of India*, 14 May 2018). He has said that 'more than a precise definition it needs to be understood that those who believe in the universal application of only their faith, belief and ideology without the right of others to exist, are clearly radical. It goes a step beyond – those willing to adopt extreme violence to pursue a path towards eventual domination of their belief and ideology indeed classify as radicals.'

This process started in the nineties but did not draw much attention at that time. However, thirty years down the line, it stares India starkly in the face as a very large percentage of the youth is affected deeply, especially in south Kashmir. And who are these youth? Mostly those who are educated but not employed. They spend most of their time in mosques discussing religion and giving vent to their frustrations. Pakistan has thus been successful in radicalizing the youth of the Valley to the extent that they no longer need any motivation from Pakistan. Journalist Bashir Assad, in his book *K File*, writes that 'the extremist and deadly Islamist ideology has made them hardcore in their approach to violence. This current breed only needs weapons and expertise to sustain. In my assessment, the biggest problem that we are confronted with today in the Valley is the aspect of radicalized youth'.

The deradicalization strategy will be a battle of hearts and minds. Hasnain suggests that first of all, research must be carried out to identify how to counter the causes of radical belief. India needs to look at successful models of countries such as Malaysia, with whom India has had consultations to learn from their experience in deradicalization, and Singapore, which has a small Muslim population. Singapore identified educational institutions, clubs and prisons where radicalization could take place. It placed them under surveillance and instituted a deradicalization programme. Although the Valley is far too big to be covered effectively by this measure, it can be one of the measures instituted. Secondly, the government will need to run contact programmes to inculcate counter-radical beliefs. The trusted pluralist clergy will play a key part in this. The government will also need to enlist the support of important seminaries such as the Darul Uloom Deoband. Thirdly, all sermons and lectures in Friday mosque programmes should be recorded. Fourthly, the political leadership of Jammu and Kashmir will have to play a responsible part in curbing separatism.

The strategy will also have to include efforts to revive Kashmiriyat and Sufism, prevent the misuse of religious places, modernize madrasas, start a massive employment drive, choke terrorist funding, and mainstream Kashmiri youth through more educational facilities. Ingenuity and flexibility in this counter-radicalization strategy will be the key to success. Both the central and the state/union territory governments will have to make a concerted effort in this direction. A just and wise political solution to problems will hopefully go a long way towards deradicalization as it is likely that the majority of the population does not support extremism. But today, one can only wonder if such an assumption really holds.

Some experts feel that a political solution to the Kashmir problem may also decrease radicalization. Perhaps this will be possible when backed by other measures suggested in this section. But what kind of political solution is India looking for? The demand for azadi cannot even be considered. It is no more an option, as the final solution to the Kashmir issue has already been sealed. The deradicalization models will have to be developed within the limits of this final solution.

Mainstreaming J&K into the National Discourse

Nobody can question the salience of mainstreaming J&K into the national discourse. This must be approached holistically, involving multiple facets such as the political, social, economic and psychological.

India should stop looking at J&K as a border state that is detached from the rest of the country. The media, especially the national media, should help in this process.

The people of Jammu and Kashmir will have to have faith in the policies of the Government of India. That will be possible only if the Centre and the state work in harmony and take an all-encompassing approach. The smooth functioning, weeding out of corruption, clean administration and rapid development of the union territories will help bring them closer to the people of India.

That there is a huge unemployment issue should be obvious from the fact that for only, say, one hundred vacancies in the central police forces or the army, thousands of Kashmiris line up even when the situation in the Valley is tense. This is in itself proof that given the opportunity, Kashmiris will join government services and merge into the mainstream, should it serve their material purpose.

The government's efforts should be focused on getting more and more businessmen and students to merge into the national mainstream. Creating jobs for them is important because in the state, in the absence of a corporate sector – because of Articles 370 and 35A and violence – there are no jobs outside the government. Many Indian corporate heads have promised to come forward and join the efforts of the Centre to create employment opportunities. But for such economic development, peace in the union territories is a prerequisite.

Economic and Social Development

It needs to be understood that the economy plays a major part in the prosperity and development of social index in any state, and which in turn has a major role in controlling unrest due to the frustration of the youth. Therefore, ensuring the economic and social development of the erstwhile state is of critical importance. Jammu and Kashmir's economy is predominantly dependent on tourism, agriculture and allied activities.

While Jammu and Kashmir compares favourably with other states, with a high per capita income of Rs 92,800, it is not enough. The lack of infrastructure, industry, and educational and medical facilities are obvious shortfalls. J&K is generally at fifteenth place in most of the developmental indices in the country. But, for a state with the potential of J&K and given the amount of money invested, it is performing much below par. It can do far better.

The Government of India has been keen to turn J&K into a fast-developing economy in keeping with its potential, with a focus on good governance, the socio-economic development of the people, infrastructure building and generation of employment. The two budgets since the abrogation of Article 370 have seen provisions of beyond Rs 1 lakh crore. The budget of FY 2021-22 had a provision of Rs 1,08,000 crore, an all-time high (Rs 39,817 crore for revenue while Rs 68,804 crore has been earmarked for capital expenditure). This means 63.7 per cent of the earmarked budget shall be spent on development and infrastructure projects. Further, the Centre allocated a grant of Rs 30,757 crore for the UT of J&K in FY 2021-22, besides a proposed gas pipeline project.

The Gross State Domestic Product (GSDP) has increased by 8.51 per cent between 2015-16 and 2020-21 to reach Rs 1.76 trillion. Total exports from J&K till January 2021 stood at $125.65 million.

The Indian government had allocated Rs 80,000 crore under the Prime Minister's Development Package in 2015 for a major push for infrastructure development in J&K. It included 54 projects with an outlay of Rs 58,627 crore for Jammu and Kashmir, while the rest was for Ladakh. Twenty projects have since been completed, while 34 are ongoing. The New Industrial Development Scheme 2021 has been announced by the administration, which includes benefits and incentives up to the year 2037.

However, the Covid-19 and security imperatives have slowed down the plans to not only revive but boost the economy at the grass-root level. The most severe challenge to the economy is unemployment, and the lack of tourists and associated avenues for the sale of agri products. Various schemes have been introduced to help on this front.

Kashmiris excel in studies and many of them would like to pursue higher education. Here I would strongly recommend that comparisons with other states should not be made. Rather, exceptions should be made for J&K as it is a troubled state. First-rate educational facilities must be set up in J&K. Initially, the people of the erstwhile state must also be given a disproportionately high number of seats in professional and vocational colleges all over the country. This will help develop a deeper sense of belonging, and there cannot be any better ambassadors for the state and India than students. The government must also aim to set up several medical facilities like AIIMS in Jammu, Srinagar and Leh. Similarly, IITs and IIMs should be opened in these cities. More engineering, medical, law and other vocational colleges must also be opened as quickly as possible. The students of Kashmir need to be weaned away from centres of Wahabism and Salafism, and that will only be possible if they are provided with more educational facilities and jobs.

Kashmiris are very fond of sports but have limited sports facilities. Their recent entry into cricket and football at the national level as a result of the opening of football and cricket clubs in Srinagar are positive stories. Playing and coaching facilities for cricket, football, hockey, volleyball, basketball and other sports should be established in all three parts of the erstwhile state.

In order to ensure that interprovincial rivalries are not aggravated, all these provisions mentioned above must be made available for both Jammu and Srinagar and also proportionately for Leh and Kargil. Jammu and Srinagar have already been included in the list of smart cities. Leh must also be included in that list.

Another avenue for bringing about development in the region is expanding the army's successful Operation Sadbhavana. This scheme should be financially upgraded so as to carry out bigger projects at the local level. It should be handled together by the Centre, state, army and police. There is no doubt that it will be a roaring success if it is executed vigorously.

Better Connectivity to Bring Hearts and Minds Closer

Physical connectivity is the best medium to bring people psychologically closer to each other. In this regard, India's performance so far can at best be termed as average. Resultantly, the people of Jammu and Kashmir have generally remained somewhat isolated. There can be no excuse for this, and it is inexplicable that even after over seventy years of independence, there is still no rail connectivity to the Valley. Construction of a state-of-the-art road between Jammu and Srinagar is at an advanced stage but is likely to take up to a year more. Similarly, the train connectivity is also being developed at a rapid pace. A new semi high-speed train by the name of Vande Bharat Express has been started from New Delhi to Jammu–Katra. This covers the distance between the two cities in eight hours instead of the 12–13 hours previously taken.

Air connectivity is at present expensive. The government should look into this. Maybe the airports in the new union territories can also be covered under the Ude Desh Ka Aam Nagrik (UDAN) scheme, which offers subsidized air travel.

Thus, to develop better harmony between J&K and the rest of the country, India must accelerate physical connectivity of all kinds – rail, road and air. Better connectivity brings the hearts and minds closer.

FM Radio Channels Must Supplement the Mobile Network

In the absence of jobs and good educational facilities, the permanent companions of the youth are their mobile phones. In the last five to seven years, the spread of social media has gone up from a meagre 18 per cent to 75 per cent. Mobiles are the main conduits for malicious propaganda. This has to be countered effectively. There is thus a need to develop popular TV channels for J&K with the guidance of professionals and provide FM channels as an alternative to the onslaught of malicious social media. In the absence of that, the youth watch Pakistan TV or BBC. The help of experts from all over the country, including Bollywood and Prasar Bharati, must be taken in this direction.

Corruption

Jammu and Kashmir has been one of India's most pampered states. It received Rs 1.14 lakh crore (approximately USD 16 billion) in grants over a sixteen-year period from 2000 to 2016. It received 10 per cent of all central grants given to states, despite having only 1 per cent of the country's population. By comparison, India's most populous state, that is, UP, got only 8.2 per cent of central grants. In November 2015, following the devastating floods in 2014, Prime Minister Modi announced a whopping allocation of Rs 80,000 crore, calling it a gift and saying that it was just the beginning. Out of this, Rs 37,700 crore has been released to the implementing agencies concerned, even though the utilization so far has been low – just 37 per cent in the past four years, as per latest estimates.

The standard of living of a state can also be judged by taking stock of certain developmental factors. About 99.3 per cent of all households in the state have electricity (the national average is 88.2 per cent). Further, 57 per cent of J&K's households have access to clean fuel for cooking (the national average is 43.8 per cent).

However, for all the central assistance and positive developmental indications, it must be noted that the state's finances are weak. It is common in the Valley to not pay electricity and water bills and avoid even income tax and GST. As per the budget of 2018–19, Jammu and Kashmir's outstanding liabilities were worth 45.6 per cent of its gross state domestic product. It fared worse than some other special category and even non-special category states.

Since development in the state is much below its potential despite such large grants, all the parties that have ruled the state at different times must be held accountable. There is definitely a need for better governance and removal of corruption in the state for optimal and honest utilization of funds. For this, the ideal solution would be by way of the public demanding accountability. In addition, the NIA, the ED and the Income Tax department need to work in close coordination to root out corruption. The best IAS and IPS officers should be posted to the state, especially to far-flung areas, to improve the quality of administration. Corruption is one of the major ills of the state and must be weeded out. Only then will it progress.

Neutralization of Over-ground Workers

Over-ground workers are the people in various white-collar professions, such as teachers, doctors and lawyers, who provide support to terrorism and separatism. They are deeply radicalized and are generally great supporters of the jamiat. Because they are passive supporters, they are not easily identifiable, and the police generally do not have any evidence against them. They keep an eye on society and identify those who are not active supporters of the militancy and are also possible informers for the police. Many of the targets for elimination by terrorists were indicated by over-ground workers. Constant pressure had never been applied against these elements.

But now the government has realized the degree of damage being caused by this segment and has decided to act against them. Prior to 5 August 2019, they were all detained to help minimize law and order problems at the time of the changeover resulting from the reorganization bill. Their being pinned down is a big blow to terrorists.

Security of Policemen and Their Families

This problem is becoming a burning issue because a number of policemen and their families have been killed. Army and police personnel have become preferred targets while on leave. This problem is even more acute in the case of policemen because they live in civil areas all over the cities. Maybe the solution lies in developing police colonies near police stations. All that one can say at this stage is that this problem can no longer be brushed under the carpet. An answer to this has to be found by the governments of the union territories and the police department in close consultation with each other.

The Armed Forces Special Powers Act (AFSPA)

The AFSPA is being decried as a symbol of the oppressive face of the state, and calls for its removal have become a constant chant. More than anything else, politicians are trying to gain popularity by maintaining an anti-AFSPA posture. They have projected the AFSPA as a draconian law that gives the armed forces licence to carry out atrocities against innocent people. This is untrue, unfair and distant from reality.

In the army, the use of minimum force is a cardinal principle and anyone violating that invites harsh punishments from within the army's own system. The Indian army's human rights record is far better than that of any other force in the world. Unfortunately, because of the deep involvement of Pakistan's ISI, separatists in the state have created an environment of distrust, because of which people in the Valley are not prepared to look at the truth. The fact that not using heavy weapons against the militants is a self-imposed restraint on the part of the army needs to be appreciated by everyone. India is the only country in the world that fights insurgency without using heavy weapons, attack helicopters, and such.

People need to remember that the AFSPA was enacted through an act of Parliament. Subsequently, the Supreme Court has examined it and issued exhaustive dos and don'ts. The Chief of Army Staff has also issued 'Ten Commandments' based on the guidelines of the Supreme Court, and there are elaborate standard operating procedures. For example, in areas more than 15 km away from the LoC, the army can operate only when a policeman accompanies their columns. In an operation where women may be affected, a female constable is required to accompany the army columns.

One issue that needs understanding is that the army and other security forces have always operated in these areas with their hands tied. Preventing collateral damage is like an act of faith with them. They have taken many uncalled-for casualties in order to ensure that they do not default on this score. To illustrate, on 14 February 2019 in Pulwama, to eliminate just three hardcore terrorists of the JeM, one army brigadier, one colonel, one captain and one DIG CRPF were injured, and one major and four soldiers were killed, all in order to avoid collateral damage. This is just one of the hundreds of such examples.

Army operations today are more intelligence-based and they are going for pinpointing targets rather than the erstwhile cordon and search operations. Thus, the inconvenience caused to civilians is minimal. But even then, the locals get involved in stone pelting at encounter sites because of the money being doled out to them by terrorists and over-ground workers. Soft handling by the security forces also encourages this behaviour by the locals.

Having said this, I would like to stress that the fear and respect for the army should not be lost. I say this with a sense of responsibility. If that happens, it is likely to result in more violence and hence exponentially more casualties. Photographs of an army truck, with all its windows closed and militants/protesters climbing all over it, which appeared in a national weekly in 2018, is bad in effect and optics. Such a situation is not acceptable. The protesters must be well aware of the limits that cannot be crossed. Stone pelting must also be made a serious offence. The effort to avoid civilian casualties must be genuine but never amount to counterproductive softness on the part of the army and security forces.

If the AFSPA is withdrawn, the army will not be able to operate in the J&K region as there will be no legal cover for them. The logical approach to this issue is to analyse whether the army has fulfilled its role in the state or not. This should be taken up at the Unified Headquarters. If the answer is that the task is as yet unfinished, then the army cannot be withdrawn. If the answer is that the task is finished in a certain area, then the army can and must be withdrawn from that area to the exterior lines (closer towards the LoC), and the CRPF can take over the responsibility for counter-insurgency operations besides the maintenance of law and order. The AFSPA can then subsequently be withdrawn from that part of the state and the army presence thinned out. This decision needs to be taken by the state/union territory government and the lieutenant governor with the utmost care and in consultation with the army at the levels of corps, command and army headquarters, and also finally have the approval of the central government. A hasty and populist decision will result in a higher number of casualties and effort to restore the situation if it deteriorates and these forces are required to be brought back. I must stress that at present, the situation is not conducive to the moving out of the army.

Given the choice, the army itself would not like to be deployed for even one additional day once their task has been accomplished. As a matter of fact, the most detestable responsibility for the army is to operate against their own countrymen. They look at the Kashmiris as Indians and thus their brethren, even though somewhat misguided and pressured by the pro-Pakistan elements in the Valley.

It is thus recommended that as and when the situation improves in some areas of the state, those areas can be declared as non-disturbed and AFSPA removed from there. For example, to begin with, in Jammu province, the areas of Samba and Kathua can be declared non-disturbed and the army withdrawn from there. Gradually, this process can reach the areas of Udhampur and Bhadarwah and maybe some parts of the Valley, when the situation improves. This would be a better strategy than trying to dilute the AFSPA to serve narrow political interests. Having said this, I agree in principle that a reduced presence of the army, should the situation so permit, will give the impression of improved law and order and lessen tension.

Finally, the Government of India must seriously consider whether the army will be able to fulfil its responsibility if unworkable restrictions such as 'proportionate use of force' are imposed on them in their handling of terrorists, who suffer from no such disadvantage. While one cannot propagate the disproportionate use of force, sometimes force has to be used. The decision with regard to the degree of force to be used must be left to the commanders in the field. Defaulters can always be taken to task. The principle of proportionate use of force is presently under discussion in the Supreme Court. With due deference to the wisdom of the highest court in the country, this is one aspect that unfortunately is not presented rationally in the court. I think the military should be allowed to present their case themselves along with defence ministry officials in the court, just as air force personnel were called in to 'establish operational necessity' for the Rafale fighter aircraft.

India cannot as a nation take steps that put the security of her own troops at risk, and order them to carry out tasks in an undesirable legal environment. The AFSPA should never be allowed to be brought into the realm of politics (which unfortunately is being attempted) because on it depend the lives and morale of India's soldiers.

There are already two unprecedented cases of individual groups of officers approaching the Supreme Court to safeguard the interest of soldiers, a responsibility that should have been assumed and discharged by the army headquarters and the central government. That such a situation has arisen is very worrisome.

The Public Security Act

A measure that has drawn much criticism is the imposition of the Public Security Act (PSA), which has led to the wrongful detention of thousands of young people without charge or trial, including minors branded as stone-pelters. This act was originally enacted during Sheikh Abdullah's chief ministership in 1978 as a safeguard against timber smugglers in the state. Under it, a suspect can be detained for a period of up to two years without trial. This act has been retained in the J&K Reorganisation Act 2019 despite numerous acts being repealed from the erstwhile J&K constitution. The act is very harsh and has only resulted in people hero-worshipping the stone-pelters. The government needs to revisit this act to make it more humane and also subject it to a judicial review.

Anti-national Indoctrination and Propaganda

For the jobless and disgruntled youth, mosques and madrasas have become attractive places to spend their time. The maulvis in the Valley are mostly from Bihar and UP and are the biggest conduits for the Wahabi and Salafi brands of Islam. This is taking the Valley further and further away from Kashmiriyat, which stands for amity and cordiality amongst different religions.[6] The late Lieutenant General S.K. Sinha made a concerted effort to promote Kashmiriyat during his tenure as the governor of J&K. He set up an autonomous institute of Kashmir studies within the University of Kashmir. He also organized a successful seminar on Kashmiriyat in Srinagar to which the state invited both Indian and foreign scholars, including from Pakistan. Incidentally, perhaps for purposes of propaganda, the University of Lahore in Pakistan also has a department for Kashmiriyat.[7]

In order to remove the suspicion and bias in the minds of the Muslim community against non-Muslims, countries such as the US are trying to create a cadre of maulvis who are broad-minded, well-educated and well-informed about all religions. They are being called 'internet maulvis'. Developing such maulvis over a period of 3–5 years and deploying them in Kashmir would be a productive step towards rejuvenating Kashmiriyat and reducing

---

6   Lt Gen. S.K. Sinha, *Raj to Swaraj*, p. 338.
7   Ibid, p. 339.

radicalization in the Valley. They should replace the present fundamentalist and uneducated brand of maulvis in J&K, who should be eased out within 2–3 years. This is a crucial requirement and should be seriously worked upon expeditiously.

Also, in order to ensure that madrasas prepare their students for professional careers, it is essential that their curriculum includes the study of physics, chemistry and mathematics. At the very least, these madrasas should help develop vocational skills such as carpentry, masonry and electrical work. This will help wean the youth away from the repositories of separatism and militancy in J&K. The Chinese have made vocational education a mandatory requirement for all the madrasas in Sinkiang and elsewhere in China. India must also ensure that these measures and vocational training are made mandatory everywhere in the country, including Jammu and Kashmir.

Juvenile Management

There is a need to open a large number of reform centres for the management of juveniles. Their management at schools should be left to the school administration. Also, strict action should be taken by the state administration against teachers who misguide and instigate the students. Keeping the children occupied in various activities and sports will help keep them away from militancy.

Moving Political Prisoners Out of J&K

It is essential that political prisoners are moved out of the state to faraway places such as Rajasthan and Tamil Nadu so that there is no interaction between them and undesirable elements within J&K. Keeping them in local jails becomes counterproductive as these jails turn into safe houses for the terrorists with instant communication throughout the state.

Proper Crowd-control Equipment

Two major occurrences that alienated the Kashmiris in general and the youth in particular were the killing of Burhan Wani and the loss of eyesight by over a hundred young students during the protests in the aftermath of his death. This was due to the use of the unsuitable pellet guns. It is sad that the paramilitary forces do not have proper non-lethal weapons for crowd control. The pellet guns have generated huge resentment in the Valley. The youth who lost their eyesight will always carry tell-tale signs of what they will propagate as the atrocities of the security forces. There is an urgent need for India to procure better crowd-dispersal equipment. There is a plethora of 'softer' equipment available off the shelf in world markets. These need to be evaluated by India's security forces with specific reference to J&K. To expedite this, empowered teams can be sent abroad to identify and facilitate the purchase of the technologically advanced equipment.

Some Suggested Equipment for Crowd Dispersal

It is difficult to understand why, despite being in a proxy war for decades, India has not been able to provide its security forces with suitable equipment. Any equipment, such as pellet guns, which leaves permanent marks is certainly undesirable and must be replaced immediately. Some suggestions are given below, only to point out that there are alternatives available to replace pellet guns. By no means are these the only options; there are many more which must also be considered and then a final decision taken.

Long-range acoustic device (LRAD): Emits a concentrated, 150-decibel high-energy acoustic wave that retains a level of 100 decibels over distances of 500 m. The wave is focused within a 15- to 30-degree 'beam', allowing the LRAD to be aimed at a specific target. Its effect is like standing in front of a jet engine. It can induce headache, panic and deafness. Used by the New York Police Department.

Electrolaser: An electroshock weapon that forms an electrically conductive laser-induced plasma channel. A powerful electric current is sent down the plasma channel to incapacitate targets. The weapon functions as a long-distance version of the taser, which can cause temporary paralysis. Developed for the US military.

Dazzler: Employs intense visible light, usually generated by a laser, to cause temporary blindness or disorientation. Used by the US military in Iraq.

Active denial system: Emits electromagnetic radiation at a frequency of 95 GHz towards the subject. The waves deter individuals by causing an intense, painful burning sensation without actually burning the skin. Developed by the Department of Defense's Joint Non-Lethal Weapons Directorate of the US.

Sticky foam gun: Fires multiple shots of sticky material that entangles and impairs individuals. Provided to the US Marine Corps for Operation United Shield (code name for the UN operation in Somalia in 1995).

LED incapacitator: Resembling a large flashlight, this weapon uses light emitting diode (LED) lights flashed at several frequencies with multiple colours and random pulses that the brain cannot process. The result is that the suspect becomes physically ill. Developed for the US Department of Homeland Security.

11

The Road Ahead

'The spirit of democracy cannot be established in the midst of terrorism, whether governmental or popular.'

– *Mahatma Gandhi*

The Road Traversed

Right at the beginning of this book, it has been stated that a certain amount of confusion and indecisiveness have always existed in the minds of the Kashmiri people. This psyche has developed over the course of their long and sometimes tragic history. Sudden and swift changes in their moods are a result of this psyche. It is also a fact that no government has been able to take advantage of the periods of relative peace in Jammu and Kashmir and build on that. Two-thirds of the present population of Kashmir was born after the militancy began in 1989. They have lived with death and destruction and the overpowering presence of a large number of counter-militancy forces. The problem has become more pronounced because the culture of Kashmiriyat has given way to more hardened attitudes and a greater leaning towards fundamentalism. The fly in the ointment remains Pakistan, which is hell-bent upon annexing Kashmir.

The Kashmir problem is one of the most heavily discussed topics in the country because since it began thirty years ago, the light at the end of the tunnel has not been visible. The world has accepted India's claim that Pakistan is behind the proxy war in Kashmir. The UN has also clarified that the Kashmir issue needs to be settled bilaterally and the UN has no role in it. The Simla Agreement clearly laid down the principle that the Kashmir issue must be resolved between India and Pakistan themselves. Equally importantly, there was an unwritten understanding reached on the matter of the final settlement of the Kashmir issue between Indira Gandhi and Zulfikar Ali Bhutto. It is unfortunate that Bhutto did not keep his side of the promise after he went back to Pakistan.

Prime Minister Vajpayee gave the Kashmiris great hope when in April 2003 he unexpectedly visited Srinagar and announced that he looked forward to solving the issue with an open mind. He said that the basic parameters of the solution would be in tune with 'Insaniyat, Kashmiriyat and Jamhooriyat'. He offered the hand of friendship to Pakistan and announced a ceasefire, which held for several years. The first-ever talks between the Centre and the separatists were also held. By 2006–07 people believed that the militancy was almost over and only a handful of militants were left, confined to the four pockets of Lolab, Shopian, Tral and Kokernag in the southern part of the Valley. Pakistan, under Musharraf, perhaps put the squeeze on the ISI and dissuaded them from providing assistance to terrorists. Unfortunately, the Vajpayee government lost the election in 2004. The talks again started between Dr Manmohan Singh and Musharraf but were inconclusive because Musharraf was also gone by August 2008. As a result, this promising decrease in the militancy between 2006 and 2008 was lost without any advantage being drawn from it.

From 2010 onwards started a period of discontentment, stone pelting and people coming out on to the streets. Burhan Wani's death in 2016 led to a period of mass rage. The education system was crippled. Hurriyat became irrelevant and the control of the militancy shifted to the hands of the youth. A kind of rejection of governance became the focal point. The coalition of the BJP and the PDP was also perhaps one of the major causes of this rejection. The people in the Valley felt that it was a sell-out and an unholy alliance. The rejection was obvious as the then chief minister in the coalition, Mehbooba Mufti, came a distant third in the 2019 Parliamentary elections.

David Devadas, author, journalist and expert on politics, has written a book on Kashmir titled *The Generation of Rage in Kashmir*. He had carried out an extensive survey in 2010–11 based on a sample of 7,000 students in schools and colleges. Some of the conclusions are important and relevant even today. The bulk of the students gave priority to peace, stability and economic prosperity rather than a regime change. The first three factors still remain their preference. Almost 48 per cent believed that the militancy was a jihad while a roughly equal number, 46 per cent, said no to that. Also, 84 per cent rejected suicide attacks and did not consider these to be a part of Islam. The aspirations of 22 per cent included freedom, over 21 per cent gave preference to employment and a small 6 per cent blamed corruption.[1] From this one could conclude

---

1 David Devadas, *The Generation of Rage in Kashmir*, p. 70.

that almost half the number, which is silent, would be happy if peace returned.

Post 5 August 2019, Prime Minister Modi announced to the world that India was committed to building a 'New Kashmir', which would be prosperous and modern.

The Fallout of the Reorganization Act

For several decades, Article 370 had created and maintained a separate identity for Kashmiris, which prevented them from feeling one with the rest of the country. It isolated the Kashmiris and, at the same time, for them it became a matter of honour to retain the separate identity.

Pakistan and radicalization are the other factors that did not allow the situation to improve. There was also an ever-increasing friction amongst the three regions of the erstwhile state, which further vitiated the environment.

It was obvious that there was no chance of the situation improving in due course, on its own. Some drastic action was required to put matters on the right track. For a transient provision, which Article 370 was, seventy years was too long a period for it to be in force, and it had to go. The price that the nation was paying was too high. So, the Government of India rightly acted. The die has been cast and there cannot be any going back.

What is now important is to analyse the impact of this action and how it has changed, or not changed, certain important aspects that have a direct bearing on peace in Jammu and Kashmir. Certain questions need to be asked and answered to take intelligent stock of the situation.

To What Extent Has the Abrogation/Dilution of Article 370 Resolved the Kashmir Issue?

The Positives That Have Emerged

The single biggest positive outcome of this development is that it has removed all uncertainty with regard to the future of Jammu and Kashmir. Henceforth, there can be no talk of freedom or separation. Their destiny is now irrevocably linked with that of India. They are as much a part of India as UP or Rajasthan or Tamil Nadu or any other state in the Union is. They will now work for the country and enjoy all the benefits of a progressive country. Kashmir will cease to be the fiefdom of a few families who are perceived to be involved in rampant corruption. Out of the three major regions of the erstwhile state, two, i.e. Jammu and Ladakh, are very happy with this development. Only the Kashmiris remain unhappy with the change, that too primarily because of being under the influence of Pakistan and radicalization.

This development will also provide the opportunity to rectify the relationship amongst the different regions of the state. This problematic relationship must be analysed and all imbalances removed. The responsibility will devolve on the leaders of both union territories to identify and explain their own special needs. The central government can then look at these rationally and act accordingly.

The world has accepted India's action in J&K. Except for Pakistan, no other country has questioned India's right to act on an internal matter on its own. So all these huge positives have accrued.

Aspects That Remain Unresolved

The people of Kashmir, who are central to the problem, remain alienated, angry and frustrated. However, this is likely true of 30–40 per cent of the population. The rest are probably either fence-sitters or perhaps are satisfied that they are seeing the end of this dark era.

The worry has now perhaps shifted from the aspiration of azadi to a bigger worry that India will change the demography of Kashmir. They fear that over a number of years, the government will alter the demographic profile of the region by bringing in settlers from the rest of India, just like China has done in Tibet and Xinjiang. They are now very worried that they will be reduced to a minority in their own area. The grouping of Kargil with Leh and Jammu with Kashmir is conceived to be part of the plot to counterbalance and reduce the Muslim majority. The India–Pakistan territorial issue still remains, but the dimension of the issue has changed vastly. The old LoC had de facto acquired the status of an international border, especially after the Simla Agreement. But India's claim has now firmly shifted to PoK and Gilgit-Baltistan, in accordance with the resolution of the Indian Parliament in 1994.

Pakistan, for whom Kashmir has always remained a core issue, has been reduced to the status of a helpless onlooker, now defending PoK and Gilgit-Baltistan. They will go to any extent to create major problems in Kashmir, because that is the only trump card they possess. No wonder they have started talking of a nuclear war.

The Islamization of Kashmir and the dangerous fallout of that remains a major issue of concern for India. The Pakistan deep state will not let up on that effort under any circumstances.

For Kashmiris, another great setback has been that not only has their state been bifurcated but it has also been reduced to a union territory, with no certainty as to when statehood will be restored.

The mainstream leadership of Kashmir is also likely to turn hostile and even become separatists. But this is not going to be a simple proposition, and I do not believe it will be easily possible because they understand well that Pakistan offers them no better option.

So overall, despite the positives, certain basic problems remain and the law and order situation continues to remain complicated.

Can India and Pakistan Ever Be Friends?

When the two-nation theory was floated by the Muslim League, they were very hopeful of getting a Muslim Pakistan that would be somewhat of an equivalent of India. The British were complicit in this, because they had visualized that there would be a Hindustan, a Pakistan and a Princestan (princely states that would remain independent). When that did not come to be, Jinnah said in exasperation that he had never imagined that they would get such a 'moth-eaten Pakistan'. The second partition of Pakistan by way of the creation of Bangladesh was another great setback. The existential problem in the leftover Pakistan has become even graver as they feel insecure that India has not reconciled to the Partition, and some day they will gobble up Pakistan. But that is not true. India has accepted Partition as a reality and moved on. From the time I was a young officer in 1962, the teaching in the army has always been that a stable and prosperous Pakistan is in India's interest. This approach has never changed. It is Pakistan that is still stuck in the old groove. It is sad that Pakistan and India have had no shared vision or dreams since Partition.

At the time of Partition, Pakistan got roughly 19 per cent of the population, approximately 19 per cent of the finances but 30 per cent of India's army. Such a big and cohesive army (heavily officered by Punjabis) with full armament for a much smaller country was always going to be a problem. To ensure that they did not lose their importance and budget, the Pakistani army had to invent a threat, and the Kashmir issue became that threat. The Pakistani army will thus never let the problem of Kashmir be resolved.

Even though Kashmir has been afflicted with serious radicalization, the jihadis of Kashmir are not part of the global jihad. They are controlled by Pakistan's ISI, except for one small faction of the Ghazwat-ul-Hind, to which Zakir Musa belonged. This is an Islamic term mentioned in some hadiths (some scholars question this), predicting a final battle with India in which Muslim warriors will conquer the whole Indian subcontinent. Kashmiri jihadis will always be controlled by the ISI because their finances, armament and training remain dependent on the ISI. Geography, by way of the contiguous border between India and Pakistan, also facilitates that. So they will always be exploited by Pakistan. That is Pakistan's greatest advantage.

To illustrate the impact of finances, the revelations of a sting operation by the India Today TV channel in October 2019 are relevant. Nayeem Khan, a separatist leader (now president of the Hurriyat), revealed that Rs 450 crore (USD 70 million) had been spent to keep the agitation going in the wake of Burhan Wani's death in 2016. Finances are provided under the guise of charitable donations from the Saudis and from a reportedly Rs 150–200 crore budget of the Pakistan deep state. Imagine a poor country like Pakistan spending so much money on terrorism.

Elites within the system on both sides (Kashmir and Pakistan) have huge vested interests in the conflict. They keep pushing the younger generation into the conflict, while their own wards are safely studying or working abroad. They are thus thriving on a conflict economy.

Thus, unless enlightened leadership takes over in Pakistan and has a firm grip, there is no chance of India and Pakistan moving on the path of friendship. However, with 'terror petrodollars' drying up, Pakistan may eventually be compelled to shun their enmity with India.

How Has Pakistan Reacted to the Changed Status of J&K?

Pakistan was caught unawares by the abrogation of Articles 370 and 35A, as evidenced by their reaction. They had become complacent as a result of the meeting between President Trump and Prime Minister Imran Khan in late July 2019, wherein Trump had offered to mediate on the Kashmir issue.

Following the abrogation of the two articles and the reorganization of the state, Imran Khan has indulged in uncontrolled and unwise rhetoric, often talking of the possibility of a nuclear war. However, the world has looked at this nuclear brinkmanship with the degree of disdain it deserves.

As we have seen, Pakistan's efforts to raise this issue in the UN Security Council met with little success. The discussion in the UNHRC also went unfavourably for Pakistan. India deplored Pakistan's 'repeated misuse' of the UNHRC platform to peddle its fabricated narrative on Kashmir. India also advised Pakistan to look into its own acts of discrimination and intolerance committed against the ethnic minorities in PoK, that is, Khyber Pakhtunkhwa, Balochistan and Sindh. Pakistan's effort to have a resolution on Kashmir admitted in the forty-seven-member UNHRC also did not fly as it failed to garner even the minimum support required from sixteen nations for admission of the complaint. In September 2019, Pakistan took up the case in the UN General Assembly, but Imran Khan's nuclear rhetoric was heavily criticized and was taken as proof of Pakistan's immaturity.

His speech was in high contrast to the Indian prime minister's, who did not even mention Pakistan in his speech.

Sadly for Pakistan, even the OIC did not support their complaints.

On a tactical level, as expected, Pakistan filled up all launch pads to aid the infiltration of the maximum possible hardcore terrorists into the Valley. The LoC became hot and Pakistan resorted to firing to draw international attention. However, the possibility of Pakistan going to war with India by itself remains low because Pakistan knows it cannot take on India conventionally, and the world has rejected their nuclear bluff and blackmail. However, on 25 February 2021, on the initiative of General Bajwa, chief of the Pakistani army, India and Pakistan released a joint statement announcing a ceasefire along the LoC. This was formalized in a meeting of the DGMOs of the two countries. This ceasefire is more or less holding for now.

Another issue that Pakistan must be seriously worried about is that India could now openly assert its claims on PoK and Gilgit-Baltistan. The military understands that that is a sure path to destruction.

So, overall Pakistan is in a difficult situation because they seem to have lost the plot, at least for the time being. India's only serious concerns could be about a major incident similar to the Pulwama attack taking place in Kashmir or anywhere in India, to which it may be compelled to react. It is also possible that this attack may be launched by Pakistani terrorists coming from Nepal or Bangladesh and not from within Pakistan's borders, which could cover Pakistan's tracks.

Also, the possibility of jihadis getting control of a low-yield nuclear device in connivance with rogue officers cannot be ruled out. That could pose a dangerous situation.

However, India should not be overly concerned about incidents of violence as these have remained part of the pattern for the last thirty years. They will not disappear in a hurry. India will have to remain on guard as before for quite some time.

What Has Hurt the Kashmiris the Most?

Sheikh Abdullah had accepted the much-reduced autonomy of Jammu and Kashmir when he signed the 1975 accord with Indira Gandhi. Psychologically, however, Article 370 was deeply embedded in the Kashmiris' psyche, and its removal has shaken them badly.

The loss of statehood has further added to their loss of self-esteem. They feel that this will result in the loss of the liberties and constitutional rights that their own Constitution had guaranteed them. This perception or misgiving can only be addressed through dialogue.

The Kashmiris' biggest worry today is how seriously their Muslim identity is threatened in a Hindu majority state. They are stunned by the prospect of their being reduced to a minority in Jammu and Kashmir.

The current phase of violence in Kashmir has gone beyond the political narratives of azadi and self-determination. It has turned into a battle between deeply radicalized Kashmiris, especially the youth, and non-believers of the Indian state.

The question that remained of prime concern was to see how they would react after the restrictions on the internet were lifted. Would they follow the path of sanity and take up the government on its offer of prosperity, employment and education for their children? Would they realize that Pakistan cannot do very much for them except use them as pawns in their own selfish games? Or would they once again engage in a losing battle in the long term?

The 4G internet services have now been restored but no change has been observed in the pattern of violence.

Has the Kashmir Issue Become Internationalized?

The Indian government has been able to persuade the world that the change in Kashmir's status is an internal matter for India and not a matter of international concern. However, a clamour has developed against this development from three categories of people, namely, old foreign policy conservatives; indigenous Modi critics; and the West (especially left liberals such as Bernie Sanders in the US and Jeremy Corbyn in the UK). Malaysia and Turkey have also raised discordant notes, but those pale in comparison with the acceptance from the rest of the world.

India has since released the mainstream leaders and also lifted the excessive restrictions in the Valley. This will further remove this issue from the focus of the world.

There have been a few positives on the international front following the Reorganization Act. Indeed, because of India's growing economic potential, the world has reacted to the recent developments in a far more muted manner as compared to 1990–91.

The 'Howdy Modi' event in Houston in September 2019 was a grand spectacle and raised the stock of Indians the world over. President Trump was committed to India, to the extent that a personality like Trump could be depended upon. This was evident during his visit to India in February 2020, which was called 'Namaste Trump'. This grand spectacle left Trump and his family tremendously impressed and put India and US friendship on an even firmer footing. The Joe Biden administration remains equally friendly with India and has not shown any shift from the policy and is treating the Kashmir issue as a bilateral matter between India and Pakistan.

Further, any terrorist activity from Pakistan will draw a strong reaction from the FATF and IMF, as Pakistan is in the limelight for being a hub of international terrorism.

The Development Process in Kashmir

Haseeb A. Drabu, who was the finance minister in Mehbooba Mufti's government in J&K till he was sacked because of differences of opinion, gives a good insight into the minds of the Kashmiris. He feels that the Kashmiris view the abrogation of Articles 370 and 35A and the reorganization of the state as Kashmir being conquered and the Kashmiris vanquished. They feel that the Government of India erroneously thinks that by dispensing largesse, the people's attention will be diverted from their disenfranchisement and disempowerment.

- Unfortunately, the Kashmiris have been used to looking at life through a narrow and self-centred prism and have never given a second thought to their other state mates, the Jammuites and Ladakhis. That will now not work. The prime minister has promised that Jammu and Kashmir will become a model state and the government has also decided to nurture and strengthen the state machinery from the bottom up. To this end, the government has planned several activities and initiatives. A remuneration package – the highest in the country – for urban bodies has been given to mayors, deputy mayors, and councillors of Kashmir. Anganwadi (government-run rural childcare centres) workers received a salary hike of 25 per cent, while village-level workers received a 500 per cent hike in allowances.

- The honorarium to 30,000 policemen and officers has been increased and their hardship allowance raised. An additional 40,000 personnel have been enrolled as old-age pensioners.
- About 4,000 teachers have been recruited, and 30,000 Rehbar-e-Taleem teachers have been regularized. (This is despite the fact that in J&K the student teacher ratio is 16:1, far better than the national average of 24:1. Bihar has a ratio of 57:1).
- Massive enrolment of youth (almost 50,000) is planned to be carried out in the police and CRPF at the earliest. This will provide a big avenue of employment. Past experience has shown that huge numbers always appear for these recruitment drives.

The critics, as well as many from within Kashmiri society, feel that there is no development angle related to this problem. Despite all these efforts, the Kashmiris will become more insular economically and ultimately more vulnerable. They further claim that the government's hidden agenda is to give money to every stakeholder and buy their acquiescence and ironically turn Kashmiris into pampered stone-pelters.

The point that is missed or overlooked is that the central government has numerous welfare schemes and that all the schemes that are now being introduced in the erstwhile state are a part of those schemes. They are now covered under them and are no longer ineligible because of Article 370.

The prime minister has repeatedly said that 'we want to embrace all Kashmiris to create a new Kashmir. Development of every Kashmiri is the government's pledge and commitment'.

David Devadas gives another twist to this process. He feels that to Kashmiris, azadi denotes a nebulous idea of rights, which could mean a sense of security regarding Muslim practices and of getting state largesse without paying special taxes. I agree with him. In my experience, whenever one tries to probe a Kashmiri's mind regarding his interpretation of azadi, he appears to be quite confused.

Needless to say, while it may be necessary to create jobs, introduce schemes, improve infrastructure and provide substantial finances to the region, these should be given as evenly as possible to Jammu and Kashmir and Ladakh according to their needs. The fair distribution of resources is imperative.

New Factors in Jammu and Kashmir and Their Impact

In 1994, the Indian Parliament passed a unanimous resolution that India would strive to reacquire the lost territories of PoK and Gilgit-Baltistan from Pakistan and Aksai-Chin from China.[2] More recently, Home Minister Amit Shah in his speeches in both houses of Parliament reiterated that India retains its claim on these areas. This issue needs some examination. All such decisions bring with them their own repercussions, but India has more than enough experience to handle such matters. Some relevant factors to keep in mind in this regard are that India's claim on PoK and Gilgit-Baltistan is genuine and legal because the Instrument of Accession signed by Maharaja Hari Singh on 26 October 1947 included

---

2 The 22 February 1994 resolution of the Indian Parliament with regard to Jammu and Kashmir declared that the state of Jammu and Kashmir has been, is and shall be an integral part of India and any attempts to separate it from the rest of the country would be resisted by all necessary means. India had the will and capacity to firmly counter all designs against its unity, sovereignty and territorial integrity and demanded that Pakistan vacate the areas of the Indian state of Jammu and Kashmir that it had occupied through aggression. Further, all attempts to interfere in India's internal affairs would be met with resolutely.

all these areas, as they were very much a part of the Jammu and Kashmir state at that time. Having said that, for India, the time frame within which these areas will be merged with it is not that important and hence is not a dictating factor. It will be quite acceptable even if this goal is attained in the distant future.

Further, India's claim on these areas does not necessarily denote that these will be acquired by force. The muscular approach could be one important option out of several others. These other options could include encouraging and supporting the ongoing freedom movement in these areas. Development and consequent prosperity in Jammu and Kashmir is likely to further add to the vigour of the uprisings in PoK and Gilgit-Baltistan, which have been brewing for quite some time now.

India has the option to take a proactive approach rather than remain on the defensive as it has always been. However, India must decide on its long-term strategy and refine it before it acts; there are likely to be consequences for every action that will be taken, and these must be well war-gamed and analysed beforehand.

Whether India adopts a muscular option, or a non-muscular alternative or a combination thereof, there are a few aspects that will have a bearing on whatever action is taken and must be planned for. If India chooses a kinetic option, the additional troops that will be required to capture this area will have to be brought in over a period of time. Subsequently, the troops to retain the additional areas of PoK and Gilgit-Baltistan will have to be built into India's overall requirement of troops. These will become part of the rationalization of troops for the entire theatre of J&K and Ladakh and the PoK and Gilgit-Baltistan areas.

This action will pitch India face-to-face with the Chinese in the CPEC area, which will have its own dynamics. This may be worrying the Chinese, and hence their pronouncements on Kashmir are becoming shriller. The Chinese have added 36,000 guards in the CPEC region to protect their assets. This adds to the magnitude of the challenge.

Pakistan and China will have no contiguous border once PoK and Gilgit-Baltistan merge with Jammu and Kashmir. This will remove all anomalies with respect to the length of India's border with China. China keeps floating two sets of figures with regard to the border length between India and China, putting it between 2,000 km and 4,000 km. If Kashmir is part of India then the length of the border is 4,000 km, otherwise it is just 2,000 km.

Now let us look at Pakistan's plight. If Jammu and Kashmir is off the negotiating table, Pakistan has no trump card left up their sleeve. Terrorism has been the only state policy for them. Pakistan appears to have lost their balance and is thus indulging in rhetoric such as a bloodbath will ensue, war will be the only option and it may lead to a nuclear war.

Also, if Pakistan is forced to stop promoting terrorism because of pressure from FATF and IMF, then they are likely to have major security threats within their own country at the hands of terrorist groups such as JeM and LeT who would not like to be restricted from their terrorist activities.

India must also redouble its efforts to choke the terrorist support and financial networks.

Finally, the most important task is to gradually bring Kashmir back to normalcy. As a matter of fact, this is India's greatest challenge at present. In the long run, the union territory of Jammu and Kashmir has to be elevated to the status of one of the most progressive states in the country.

Equating the Palestine and Kashmir Problems

Some misinformed elements are suggesting that the Kashmir situation is heading the Palestine way. They perhaps believe that it will drag on unendingly. This comparison is not very convincing due to the obvious dissimilarities between the two. The only common factor is that one of the affected parties in both the cases are the 'Muslims'.

However, before I dwell on the comparison between the two issues, it would be desirable to understand the background to the Palestinian conflict.

Briefly, Palestine is a small region of roughly 2,400 square miles, but it has played a prominent role in the ancient and modern history of the Middle East. Violence has defined much of its history as it has been the site of constant political and operational conflicts. The history of the Israeli–Palestinian conflict dates back to the communal violence that began in Palestine between the Israelis and Arabs in 1920 and eventually erupted into full-scale hostilities in the 1947–48 civil war. Earlier, steady Jewish immigration into the area and British colonial rule had led to the 1936–39 Arab revolt in Palestine. At this time, the Zionist movement, seeking a homeland for the Jews, was burgeoning and reached its peak following World War II and the Holocaust.

At this stage most nations of the world were sympathetic to the Jews, who had been persecuted throughout the world and had faced terrible persecution and slaughter during World War II. Before Israel was declared a nation state on 14 May 1948, the majority of people dwelling in this region were Arabs. In 1947, the UN accepted the idea of partitioning Palestine into a zone for the Jews (Israel) and another for the Arabs (Palestine). With this proposal, the British withdrew from the region and Israel was created on 14 May 1948.

As a consequence of the 1967 war, Israel absorbed major areas of Palestine, as well as additional territory from Egypt and Syria. By the end of the war, Israel had expelled 3,00,000 Palestinians from their homes, including 1,30,000 who were displaced in 1948, and gained territory that was three and a half times its size.

Present Palestine theoretically includes the West Bank (a territory that divides Israel and Jordon) and the Gaza Strip (bordering Egypt and Israel). Today, most of the West Bank is majorly administered by Israel, though 42 per cent of it is under varying degrees of autonomous rule by the Al-Fatah-run Palestinian Authority. The Gaza Strip is currently under the control of Hamas.

In 1982, as a result of the Israel–Egypt Peace Treaty of 1979, Israel withdrew from all of the Sinai Peninsula except the contentious territory of Taba, which was returned after a ruling by a commission of arbitration in 1989.

So, are there any similarities between Palestine and Kashmir? The answer is an emphatic 'No'. Kashmir is considered an integral part of India while the Israelis do not claim Palestinian territory as a part of Israel and call Palestinian areas as 'occupied territories'.

- Kashmiris are full and equal citizens with all the rights and privileges enjoyed by all other citizens of India whereas Palestinians do not enjoy any of the rights and privileges enjoyed by the citizens of Israel.
- Palestine has been a cause célèbre for the Islamic world, which considers it an issue of Muslims. Only Pakistan has treated Kashmir as a Muslim issue, and this stance has found little resonance in the rest of the Islamic world. Even in India, Muslims do not look upon it as a Muslim issue.

- There are no restrictions on Kashmiris with regard to travelling or settling anywhere in India, nor are there any restrictions on their occupying any positions in the military, bureaucracy and government. Palestinians need special permits to enter Israel and there are restrictions on their settling or working in Israel.
- Palestinian territories are no longer claimed by any of the other countries in the region. The issue is of Israel ending its occupation and a Palestinian state coming into existence. In Kashmir, part of the territory of the erstwhile princely state has been occupied as an act of aggression or has been illegally occupied by regional players, namely, Pakistan (PoK and Gilgit-Baltistan) and China (Shaksgam Valley and the Aksai-Chin area).
- Broadly, the Palestinian struggle is not communal. Palestinian Christians and Muslims are both part of the struggle for statehood and for putting an end to Israel's occupation. In Kashmir, the separatist movement is a thinly disguised Islamist movement. While it hides behind a veneer of ethnic nationalism, Kashmiri separatism is underpinned by Islamism. As a matter of fact, radicalization has become a major part of the problem.
- Legally, Kashmir's accession to India is unquestionable and based on the Instrument of Accession duly signed by Maharaja Hari Singh. In Palestine, Israel's occupation has no legal justification.
- After the abrogation of Articles 370 and 35A, there is a fear in Kashmir of a demographic invasion in Kashmir, but this is misplaced because the forcible changing of the demography of a region is not a policy of the Government of India (unlike China and certain other parts of the world). Also, other states in India have not seen a demographic transformation.

In Palestine, the fear is of the Palestinians changing Israel's demography if they are given citizenship. Also, the issue in Palestine is of Israel making settlements in Palestinian territory and forcibly annexing those areas. This has never happened in Kashmir and even when the authorities planned to make colonies for the police and civil servants, these colonies were only for erstwhile 'state subjects' and very different from the settlements in Palestine territory.

- It should be clear from the foregoing that there are no similarities of any consequence between the two disputes. In the case of Kashmir, there was dithering for a long period over terminating the temporary/transient provision that was Article 370. Now that a decisive step has been taken, this problem should head towards a resolution in a certain time frame, as discussed subsequently. There is no such hope in the case of the Israel–Palestine conflict.

The Road Ahead

The Kashmir imbroglio was primarily the outcome of the Pakistan-sponsored proxy war, and their greatest success has been in deeply radicalizing the somewhat confused and disillusioned people of the Valley. Radicalization in the Valley is a critical, perhaps the most critical, factor now. These Kashmiris are, however, the same people who welcomed the Indian forces in 1947 with open arms and friendly slogans such as '*Hamlawar hoshiar, hum Kashmiri Hindu, Muslim, Sikh taiyar*' (Attackers beware, we Kashmiri Hindus, Muslims, Sikhs are ready). Also, they are the same people who gave early warning about the intrusions by Pakistani forces in 1965 and 1971 and even during the Kargil war in 1999.

Once they see the economic progress and prosperity in the state, the better quality of education, better job opportunities, and the constant dialogues going on with them, including with religious teachers (maulvis), and they lose faith in Pakistan's ability to help them, they are likely to be more rational and amenable to a balanced solution and turn positively towards India.

The biggest priority and challenge before the central government will be to re-establish law and order, get the routine of daily life restarted and provide a first-rate administration. When the time is opportune, elections must be organized at the earliest. As the mainstream parties are likely to lose their erstwhile hold on Kashmiri politics, it is essential to identify and help establish the second rung of leadership to fill the gap.

Pakistan, till very recently, was labelled a problem state and a hub of terrorism. However, Prime Minister Imran Khan's visit to the US in July 2019 resulted in a new bonhomie in the bilateral ties between the two countries and a belief that they could do more in areas of overlapping interests. For India, these overlapping interests meant Pakistan promising that it would bring the Taliban to the negotiating table and help facilitate the US pull-out from Afghanistan. In return, the US restarted military aid to Pakistan. It approved $125 million to provide Pakistan with technical support for its fleet of F-16 aircraft after Prime Minister Imran Khan's first official visit to Washington in September 2019. Trump also, in misplaced enthusiasm, offered thrice to mediate between India and Pakistan on the Kashmir issue. India, of course, flatly refused such an offer in accordance with their principle that Kashmir is a bilateral issue. On being prodded by the US, the IMF has also approved a $6 billion loan to Pakistan to help resuscitate its ailing economy, though only $2 billion have been released so far in three tranches due to tough preconditions attached to the loan.

There is no doubt that Trump, in 2019, despite his so-called friendship with Prime Minister Modi, spared no effort to please

Pakistan as long as Pakistan could deliver on its promises. The US–Taliban deal was finally signed in February 2020. Its provisions include the withdrawal of all American and NATO troops from Afghanistan, a Taliban pledge to prevent al-Qaeda from operating in areas under its control, and talks between the Taliban and the Afghan government. However, the Taliban made it very clear that they would come to the negotiating table only after the US pulled out of Afghanistan. Further, they do not recognize the Constitution of Afghanistan and want an Islamic Constitution. The Taliban claimed during intra-Afghanistan talks that they were committed to peace talks, adding they wanted a 'genuine Islamic system' in Afghanistan that would make provisions for women's rights in line with cultural traditions and religious rules 'under Shariya'.

US–Taliban Accord and Impact of the Security Situation in J&K

As Afghanistan lurches towards greater instability with US forces moving out, India's core concern continues to be that the Taliban or al-Qaeda could be used by Pakistan to target India (especially J&K) once again. Minister of External Affairs S. Jaishankar had told the UN Security Council on 22 June 2021 that Afghanistan needed a 'genuine double peace', that is, peace within Afghanistan and peace around Afghanistan. It requires harmonizing the interests of all. There are many facets of consequence in the war in Afghanistan but here we will focus primarily on India.

The question which is uppermost in every Indian strategist's mind is whether Pakistan will be in a position to use its obvious advantage in Afghanistan to gain an upper hand in J&K, like it tried in 1989-90. The most common perception is that when the Taliban returns to power, the ISI will be in a position to recruit 3,000 to 5,000 Taliban fighters and induct them into J&K.

There can also be no doubt that Pakistan's intent remains unchanged: the creation of turbulence and mayhem in J&K to keep the proxy war alive. It would like to believe that a mix of Afghan, Pakistani and local Kashmiri terrorists may be difficult for Indian security forces to effectively neutralize.

Because of its perennial perceptional short-sightedness, the Pakistani deep state will not be able to appreciate that the situation in J&K is not even remotely akin to 1989-90. India now has thirty years of experience and very strong, multi-layered security grids comprising the Indian army, RR, CRPF and the state police forces, backed by an efficient intelligence system and a responsive UT administration, post the reorganization of August 2019. They will be in a position to handle even much more heightened proxy war challenges. The Indian capability to limit infiltration is intensely strong today, with the anti-infiltration fence having undergone multifarious improvements. Most importantly, the local ecosystem, which would have been the greatest support to such hybrid warfare in Kashmir, has been more or less neutralized over the years. However, India must prepare for the worst possible situation and initiate necessary measures now.

Such an effort on Pakistan's part, should it hypothetically succeed, is likely to bring about some increase in violence and slow down the financial development and social outreach programmes of the government. If there is a civil war within Afghanistan post US withdrawal, it is likely to fuel the rise of Islamist politics across the region and it would be unrealistic to believe that Kashmir could be somehow kept aloof from this adverse development. The Afghanistan National Army, which was highly demoralized because of poor leadership at both the military and political levels, has fully collapsed and no resistance from it can now be expected. As per credible information, Pakistan has already shifted some militant camps to Taliban-controlled Afghan areas, which are likely to emerge as safe havens for all kinds of jihadist groups. Al Bader is one such terrorist group of the 1990s which is being shifted and it has strong ties with the Haqqani Network. It is also very likely that Pakistan, in order to create turbulence in India, will induct some jihadis in areas where Pakistan may already be having some sleeper cells. These together may try to create chaos and disturbance. But, fortunately, India has strong internal cohesion and unity in its diversity. We must continue to maintain a lot of emphasis on this aspect and increase our vigilance in the hinterland to defeat this possible menace.

There is no doubt that in any new power equation that may emerge, Pakistan and China will certainly be the beneficiaries. China also needs Afghan support to ensure that Uyghur militants are not allowed in its Xinjiang region. In return, China will provide the Taliban government recognition and possibly some financial help, but it can never match the American contributions. Russia is also expected to lean towards Taliban and this troika may emerge to support the Taliban government. The Afghan situation thus continues to be in a flux. It needs to be watched very carefully and all possible contingencies catered for.

Recommended Solutions

I have personally had numerous interactions at all levels with both Hindus (including Kashmiri Pandits) and Muslims across Jammu and Kashmir and also with the planners and drivers of the Kashmir policy at the state and national levels.

These discussions have also included exchanges with Dr Karan Singh, the former Sadr-i-Riyasat of Jammu and Kashmir, the first governor of the state and Union cabinet minister for a long period. I have also had the opportunity to discuss this issue with Narinder

Nath Vohra, who served as governor of the state for ten years, from 2008 to 2018. He had a successful tenure during some of the most difficult periods in the state.

The recommendations given subsequently are based predominantly on my own long experience in the affairs of the state, enriched by these very useful interactions.

Basically, there are five major dimensions of the Kashmir issue that have to be dealt with, namely, the external dimension, intra-state issues, constitutional aspects, humanitarian aspects and development, and deradicalization and engagement with the youth.

External Dimensions

The Jammu and Kashmir problem has an external dimension because out of a total area of 2,22,236 sq. km, 78,114 sq. km is today a part of PoK. In addition, Pakistan ceded 5,180 sq. km to China in Shaksgam Valley for the Karakoram Highway up to Gwadar port. Also, China illegally captured 13,297 sq. km of the state territory in the Aksai-Chin area in 1962. The Indian Parliament passed a resolution on 22 February 1994 that Pakistan must vacate those areas of J&K that they had occupied through aggression in 1947 and also the area that they had ceded illegally to China.

The settlement of the J&K problem with Pakistan thus has three aspects. Firstly, now that J&K stands fully integrated with India, the LoC stands as a de facto international boundary between India and Pakistan, provided both governments are agreeable to this and until a final settlement is reached. All the same, in effect, it does not change India's external borders. This part has been settled and is not open to negotiations.

Secondly, there is the issue of the 78,114 sq. km occupied by Pakistan as a result of its aggression in 1947. India has categorically restated its claim on these areas, which rightfully belong to it.

Finally, there is the issue of the area illegally ceded by Pakistan to China in Shaksgam Valley, which needs to be settled.

It has always been India's stand, reiterated in September 2019 in the US by External Affairs Minister Dr S. Jaishankar, that

> India has no problem in talking to Pakistan but it has a problem in talking to terrorists. The dialogue can also be only on the pending issues now and not on issues which have already been settled. Islamabad has created an entire industry of terrorism to deal with the Kashmir issue. In these talks Pakistan will have to provide India, as said earlier also, verifiable, irretractable and credible proof of their sincerity and honesty of purpose. They will have to first dismantle the terror network inside Pakistan before the next step is taken by us of a discussion with them.

Intra-state Issues

There have long been sharp differences amongst the three regions of J&K – Jammu, Kashmir and Ladakh – on virtually all accounts. The Jammu and Ladakh regions have felt that they have been under the shackles of the Kashmiris and have always been dealt with unfairly in the distribution of jobs, the provision of educational and administrative facilities, and the allocation of finances. As a matter of fact, both Jammu and Ladakh have always harboured aspirations of separating from J&K.

Fortunately for Ladakh, it has now been turned into a union territory, with Kargil grouped with it. That makes it a geographically homogenous and viable entity. As a union territory, it will be administered directly by New Delhi and will have no problem with resources as the Centre would like to turn Ladakh into an attractive tourism hub. Also, there is an abundance of mineral resources in this area, which will help it develop into an affluent region. However, the people in Ladakh will have to ensure that they maintain good relations with the Shia Muslims of Kargil and also be fair to them in the distribution of resources.

Even though people in Jammu would have liked to be separated from Kashmir, it was a wise decision to retain Jammu and Kashmir as one political entity. Jammu provides the necessary glue for Kashmir to be part of India. Here I must sound a word of caution. Everybody has been talking of the development of Kashmir, with hardly any mention of the Jammu region. It is of paramount importance that the shares of both Jammu and Kashmir in all aspects are divided strictly in proportion to their population and area profile. With Jammu and Kashmir now a union territory, new procedures and systems are already in the process of being evolved and are at a fairly advanced stage. This is thus the right time for the people in the Jammu region to ensure that they get their rightful share of resources. If they waste this opportunity, they will have only themselves to blame.

Once the internal issues of the erstwhile state have been resolved, the terror situation has been stabilized and the Valley is quiet, an environment conducive to dialogue will emerge. At that stage, the central government must commence multi-pronged dialogues to resolve all irritants. These should be with all cross-sections of society, but all within the framework of the Indian Constitution. It is essential that the people become partners in guiding their own destiny. When the security environment is right and all systems have fallen into place, the Centre should consider restoring statehood to Jammu and Kashmir at the earliest.

It will also be a great help if the Muslim leaders in India raise their voice against terrorism in the Valley and exhort the people of Kashmir not to fall prey to the ISI's machinations.

Constitutional Aspect – Delimitation in J&K

The Centre, in March 2020, constituted a delimitation commission, with former Supreme Court judge Ranjana Prakash Desai as chairperson. The delimitation has to be carried out based on the census of 2011. The commission was given an extension of one year and is likely to submit its report by March 2022. This would be the first major step to ensure equitable representation in the state assembly from both Jammu and Kashmir. Currently, it is skewed in the favour of Kashmir.

The table below illustrates the demographic profile and existing allocation of seats in the state assembly.

Region	Population*	Percentage of state population	Area percentage	Seats
Kashmir	69,07,623	55.04%	15.73% (least area)	46
Jammu	53,50,811	42.63%	25.93%	37
Ladakh	2,90,492	2.33%	58.33%	4 (no more part of this exercise)

Details of demography based on 2011 census

Here, a background to the delimitation process in India will be in order. In India, the main basis for allocation of Lok Sabha seats to various states is the population of a state. The division of each state into territorial constituencies is readjusted after the completion of a census so that a uniform population-to-seat ratio is maintained within the state and throughout the Union. So, the purpose of delimitation is the rationalization of the structure and composition of the electoral constituencies on the principle of 'one vote and one value'. Separate delimitation commissions were set up in India in 1952 (based on the 1951 census), 1962 (based on the 1961 census), 1972 (based on the 1971 census) and 2002 (based on 2001 census). The Forty-Second Amendment Act, 1976, had put a ban on any further delimitation of the constituencies till 2000. So, the total number of seats in the Lok Sabha and Rajya Sabha had remained the same from 1976 to 2002. This ban was imposed mostly on account of the apprehension that a few states, in order to get more seats in the Lok Sabha on the basis of a large population, may not take much interest in family planning programmes. In July 2002, a delimitation commission was constituted to carry out delimitation based on the 2001 census. The commission had submitted its recommendations, but they were initially not acted upon. In December 2007, the Supreme Court, on a petition, issued a notice to the central government, asking for reasons for non-implementation. On 4 January 2008, the Cabinet Committee on Political Affairs (CCPA) decided to implement the recommendations of the Delimitation Commission. The recommendations of the commission were approved by the president on 19 February 2008. The Eighty-Fourth Amendment Act, 2002, froze further delimitation till 2026, that too until the relevant figures for the first census taken after 2026 are published. That means delimitation can only take place after the census of 2031. This decision was based on the calculation that India would be able to stabilize its population by 2026.

The last time that the boundaries of constituencies were redrawn in Jammu and Kashmir was in 1995. It was based on the 1981 census. Due to the insurgency and terrorism situation, a census could not be held in 1991 in Jammu and Kashmir. The Constitution provides for delimitation every ten years. Hence, the next delimitation of assembly constituencies in J&K should have taken place in 2005. However, in 2002, when Dr Farooq Abdullah was the chief minister, the state government arbitrarily amended the Representation of People Act of 1957 and Section 47(3) of the Constitution of Jammu and Kashmir and froze the delimitation till 2026, based on the logic of trying to follow the Indian pattern.

The minister of state for home affairs, G. Krishan Reddy, said in a written response in the Lok Sabha in a debate on delimitation in July 2019 that in the 2002 delimitation exercise in India, Jammu and Kashmir was not included within the purview of the Delimitation Act of 2002, as Article 170 of the Constitution of India, which deals with the delimitation of constituencies of state assemblies, had not been extended to the state. 'Delimitation of legislative assembly constituencies in Jammu and Kashmir is carried out under Section 47 and 141 of the Constitution of J&K.' The Jammu and Kashmir state should have constituted a delimitation commission under its own powers, like the rest of the country, in 2002. But they did not do so, perhaps deliberately. It was obvious that Farooq Abdullah's action was with a view to retain power in the Kashmir Valley, as the Kashmiris would thereby have maximum representation in the state assembly.

This has been starkly unfair, like so many other systems in the state. There are many factors that are connected to a delimitation exercise in the state but have not been taken into account while carrying out this exercise. For one, the Kashmiri Pandits, who number over 4 lakh, have been exiled from the Valley; most of them are now settled in the Jammu region. Also, refugees from West Pakistan who migrated in 1947 and settled in the state have not been given voting rights. This has been a very unfair deal and needs to be rectified. The Gujjars, Bakarwals and Gaddis, who were given scheduled tribes status in 1991 and form 11 per cent of the state's population, are settled in different parts of the state. They still do not have political reservation.

The state BJP has also been demanding that one-third of 24 seats reserved for PoK should be de-freezed and allotted to the refugees settled in Jammu for more than 70 years, besides three seats for Kashmiri Pandits, Scheduled Castes, Scheduled Tribes and other neglected people.

It is true that the politicians from the Valley and the separatists are not happy with the idea of a fresh delimitation, citing the freeze in delimitation till 2026. They are advocating that this freeze has been accepted by the J&K High Court and the Supreme Court, which have turned down the representation on this account by the Jammu and Kashmir National Panthers Party. However, all these objections have became irrelevant after the promulgation of the J&K Reorganization Act 2019.

The Centre's initiative is fair because the delimitation should take into account the latest census data and also a few other factors, which have been enumerated above. The objective of the central government is to correct the alleged inequity and regional disparity with regard to Jammu (and Ladakh – now not applicable) and also to provide representation to all reserved categories in the state assembly. To be fair and transparent, the delimitation commission is headed by a retired judge of the Supreme Court, Justice Ranjana Prakash Desai, with two members, that is, the central election commissioner and the state election commissioner. In addition, it has invited five associate members (ex officio MPs from J&K) nominated by the speaker. They include Dr Jitendra Singh, Jugal Kishore Sharma, Dr Farooq Abdullah, Mohammad Akbar Lone and former justice Hasnain Masoodi. When completed, the delimitation will bring the state on a par with the rest of the country and also help lessen the intra-regional tensions.

Following the J&K Reorganization Act 2019, the number of seats for J&K has increased from 107 to 114, including 24 reserved for PoK. The Jammu region has demanded that the number of seats be decided based on topography, terrain and size of the region. The Kashmiris, on the other hand, have advocated for the population and density of the area to be the main deciding factors.

The final call for the distribution of the additional seven seats will be taken by the Delimitation Commission. Also, the acceptance or otherwise of the demand for other categories of seats being recommended by different parties will fall within the purview of the commission.

Humanitarian Aspects and Development

However much the Kashmiris may be misguided and radicalized through Pakistan's efforts, they are India's people. The Kashmiri Pandits had to leave the Valley because the state could not provide them security, which was a huge state and national failing. People from the Jammu region have also suffered.

The Kashmiri people must understand that the deeply radicalized approach that is now rampant in the Valley runs against their basic nature. They should also remember that Sheikh Abdullah, their very own Sher-e-Kashmir (Lion of Kashmir), in his speech to the Constituent Assembly had said:

> Looking at the matter too from a more modern political angle, religious affinities alone do not and should not normally determine the political alliance of States. We do not find a Christian block, a Buddhist block or even a Muslim block, about which there is so much talk now a days in Pakistan. These days economic interests and a

community of political ideals more appropriately influence policies of States.

The real character of a State is revealed in its constitution. The Indian constitution has set before the country the goal of secular democracy based upon justice, freedom and equality for all without distinction. This should meet the argument that the Muslims of Kashmir cannot have security in Kashmir where the large majority of the population are Hindus. Any unusual cleavage between religious groups is the legacy of imperialism, and no modern state can afford to encourage artificial divisions if it is to achieve progress and prosperity. The Indian constitution has amply and finally repudiated the concept of the religious State which is the throwback to medievalism, by guaranteeing the equality of rights of all citizens irrespective of their religions, colour, caste and class.

I am convinced, based on all my experience in this matter, and with my own intimate knowledge of the state where I grew up, that the future of Kashmir lies with India just as that of the 204 million Muslims (estimates of 2019) in the rest of India. They live in harmony in India, and India's peaceful existence, despite its great diversity, is a matter of great appreciation and envy all over the world. Prime Minister Modi said at the 'Howdy Modi' event in Houston on 23 September 2019 that Indians were not only proud of their 'unity in diversity but we celebrate our diversity'. Similarly, the Kashmiri Muslims are also likely to be satisfied over a period of time, like the rest of the Muslims in the country. But for that, India first needs to set in motion a process of development in the region.

The erstwhile state has tremendous potential for development. Tourism is one of the biggest sources of income; handicrafts, horticulture, the apple trade are other sources. During relatively peaceful interludes, 10–15 million tourists have visited the Valley in a year, which includes the 4–5 million devotees visiting the holy Amarnath shrine. This number can go up manifold in more stable, peaceful conditions. Similarly, Jammu has over 10 million devotees visiting the Vaishno Devi shrine in a year. Once better road and rail connectivity are developed, tourism, trade and employment opportunities will increase significantly, and things are likely to improve considerably. That will also be the time when corporate houses can be encouraged to set up industry in the region.

Similarly, the areas of Ladakh and Kargil are made for tourism. Their mineral resources are also a great treasure in themselves.

Deradicalization in the Valley and Engagement with the Youth

The success of the Pakistan-sponsored proxy war lies in the fact that in the last few years, Jammu and Kashmir has generally witnessed a fast rise in the levels of radicalization and violent extremism. The recruitment of locals into the militancy, after showing an increase post 2008, basically due to the limited infiltration by foreign militants, is now coming down after 2019. Of the 121 militants killed in the Valley in the first six months of 2019, 82 per cent were locals. This clearly proves that the youth are becoming deeply radicalized. What is even more worrisome is that some of the well-educated and employed youth have also fallen prey to the ISI's psychological machinations.

Even though I have covered this aspect earlier in this book, it is so important that it merits more emphasis and to be listed as one of the five major areas of concern that need to be tackled.

Radicalization is the product of protracted psychological conditioning of the mind; it has no quick fixes. The unemployed and idle youth are easy prey for the persistent efforts of Pakistan and the constant propaganda from the mosques. This multipronged strategy has resulted in bringing in a staunch Wahabi culture in the Valley. This is despite the fact that this fierce Islamism is at odds even with the rest of the Indian Muslims.

Bashir Assad, in his book *K File*, says,

> The current phase of violence in Kashmir has gone beyond the political narratives of Azadi and self-determination. Azadi does not have the potential to transform a whole generation of youth as rigidly as the current generation. It is the Islamist ideology that is producing the dead men walking in Kashmir who love and seek death the way we seek life.

Journalist Tavleen Singh, in her Sunday column in the *Indian Express* on 3 November 2019, said that 'the kind of Islam spreading slowly but surely for many, many years in Kashmir has changed the objective of the armed insurgency from azadi to establishing an Islamic State governed by the Shariat'.

Apologists from both within Kashmir and outside try and portray that this movement is against the oppression by the state and the security forces. Nothing could be further from the truth. The fact is that Pakistan's deep state, separatists and the misguided youth have oppressed the people of Kashmir. Unfortunately, the peaceniks and human rights promoters in India have also contributed to the state's efforts being undermined and the sacrifice of the people, police and the army being taken lightly or even ignored.

Even though 'political conflict' remains at the centre stage, the issue is far more complex. There is today a whole generation of youth in the Valley that has gone crazy and is yearning to embrace death for the glory of Islam. They aspire to establish an Islamic caliphate in the Valley. We would recall that post Burhan Wani's death in 2016, the separatists and other leadership were pushed to the background and youngsters, many between 12–15 years of age, assumed leadership.

The maulvis and theologians have mercilessly pushed their youth towards a radicalized Islam based on the models of the Wahabi and Deobandi sects. These maulvis, mostly from UP and Bihar, are the root cause of the problem. They must be weeded out of the state and replaced by much-better educated maulvis.

There are a few factors that help in understanding the gravity of the situation. For one, people in the erstwhile state talk about Islam all the time, regardless of whether they follow it or not. Then, the mullahs are the ones spearheading the narrative of *'Azadi ka matlab kya'* (What does freedom denote), 'Nizam-e-Mustafa' (Islamic rule), and *'La ilaha il allah'* (There is no god but Allah). This implies that non-Muslims are infidels and they have no right to exist.

Further, a common narrative in the Valley is that 'Islam is in danger'. The easiest story to sell is that the present BJP government in New Delhi has umbilical links with the radical Hindu cadre of the RSS, and they are out to uproot Islam from the state.

Mullahs are the ones spreading the narrative of *'azadi matlab kaya, la ilaha il allah'*. Common Kashmiri children are being charged emotionally and readied for martyrdom.[3]

Women are the most vulnerable section of Kashmir's society. They are the real victims of this conflict as they lose their sons in

---

3   Bashir Assad, *K File: The Conspiracy of Silence* (New Delhi: Vitasta), p. 99.

this militancy. Traditionally also they have always been the main agents of transformation of society. Women comprise the largest natural institution which influences the children.

In Kashmir, the set of grievances against the Indian state were catalytic in the quick spread of this ideology that killing and attacking them (Indians) was legitimized. Women in Kashmir are pivotal in constructing this narrative. Soon it was accorded social sanction.[4]

Thus, the biggest challenge that India faces today in the Valley and even in the rest of the erstwhile state is in countering this degree of fanaticism. There is no doubt that an enduring strategy has to be devised that focuses not just on targeting the external factors that fuel radicalization but also puts equal emphasis on the process of deradicalization within the Valley. Employment has to be provided to the unemployed youth, who are mostly educated. Idle youth become ready fodder for turning into religious fanatics.

It is gratifying to note that there are some state police organizations that are working on deradicalization programmes in other parts of the country. The Aurangabad (Maharashtra) police are one such example. They have already enrolled over 120 men, women and students who were involved in suspicious activities in this programme. They are put through a psychometric test that has 240 questions about the personal traits and activities of the individual. The effort is to pull people back from the edge. Legal action is taken only against those who are deeply involved. At least five states – J&K, Punjab, Karnataka, Madhya Pradesh and Gujarat – want to start a programme on the model of the one in Maharashtra.

---

4   The given paraphrased views are of Bashir Assad in his book *K File: The Conspiracy of Silence* (New Delhi: Vitasta, 2019), pp. 191–92.

In addition to the ongoing security operations, the process of deradicalization will require the coordinated deployment of the political, diplomatic, economic, social and perception management systems. It is likely to be a slow and long-drawn process, stretching over perhaps the next 5–6 years. It cannot be rushed. Thus, deradicalization has to be worked on, governance will have to be improved and corruption weeded out from the state to pull people out of this delusion. The perception management initiative must aim at cementing the mental and emotional bonding of the people, especially the youth, with the rest of India.

I am not an expert on Islam. Whatever little that I can claim to know was learnt during the course of my profession and from literature that I have studied out of interest in the subject. However, here I am again taking the help of the writings of Bashir Assad. He has claimed that in today's Kashmir, 'it is a war between Dar al-Islam (House of Islam) and Dar al-Harb' (the rest of the world outside the domain of Islam is collectively called Dar al-Harb). It is generally believed that no truce between them could exceed a duration of ten years (a precedent set during Muhammad's lifetime).

As a strategy, there is a need to muster the help of reputed Muslim bodies in India that are moderate. The Muslims in India have merged well into the shape and structure of the country and they are amongst the peace-loving people of the world. They must be persuaded to come forward to bring our brethren in Kashmir back on the right track through close interactions and exchange programmes.

One such reputed Muslim body, which I have known intimately from my tenure as director of the Vivekananda International Foundation, is Jamiat Ulema Hind. We ran a series of deradicalization seminars with them and other similar organizations such as the one in Ajmer Sharif Dargah. Jamiat Ulema is one of the leading organizations of Islamic scholars belonging to the Deobandi school of thought. They openly declare that any separatist movement is unacceptable to them. Inimical forces are bent upon destroying Kashmir, which they believe is an integral part of India. They support the philosophy that 'we do not want a country based on religion and we make no compromise on national security and integrity of the nation'. We must fight and educate the extremists of the Valley with the active help of these saner voices of Muslim scholars in the mainland. They can indeed be potent tools and there are plenty such organizations in the country.

In the ultimate analysis, the youth of Kashmir must be brought to a level of positivity wherein they start looking at religion in terms of moderation and Sufism, just like in the rest of India. But along with that it is essential to provide them good education and employment. India should deliver on her promise of building a *naya* Kashmir in the face of the challenge posed by radicalization.

Pressure Points India Should Apply on Pakistan

There are certain issues that India can take advantage of to end Pakistan's meddling in Jammu and Kashmir.

India's objective should be to raise the cost to Pakistan of waging a proxy war against India to a prohibitive level over a period of time.

The aim of Indian diplomacy should be to isolate Pakistan in the international community and work towards having it branded as a terrorist state. FATF and IMF are two important forums that can be used to achieve this. Pakistan is required to effectively implement targeted financial sanctions against all terrorists designated under UN Security Council resolutions 1267 and

1373 and those acting on their behalf, including preventing the raising and moving of funds, freezing assets, and prohibiting access to funds and financial services. Pakistan can be downgraded to the blacklist should they continue to be involved in terrorism or any of these activities. Pakistan's financial condition is so bad that the loans they are taking are primarily being utilized to service the debt interest. In fact, Pakistan's prime minister stated in his address to the UN General Assembly on 27 September 2019 that half of his country's GDP was being utilized to service their debts. Thus, Pakistan has a huge dilemma before them: they must either stop terrorist activities or be financially ruined.

On another front, India's vocal support of the long-oppressed people of Balochistan and Gilgit-Baltistan has galvanized their movements and caused active embarrassment to Pakistan. This effort should be increased manifold.

India should also consider supporting Afghanistan's stand that the Durand Line is no longer relevant and the boundary between Afghanistan and Pakistan should be considered afresh.

India must at the earliest make arrangements to ensure that they fully utilize their quota of water from the north Indian rivers, a large part of which are flowing unharnessed into Pakistan.

Afghanistan has not been able to fully utilize its share of water of the Kabul river and its tributary, the Kunar river. Now that India has successfully completed and handed over the Salma dam to Afghanistan, it should offer to build dams on both these rivers, the waters of which flow into the Indus river. This will have serious implications for Pakistan. However, this thought process will have to be put on the backburner or shelved for the present.

Finally, India should consider redeveloping their capability for covert operations against Pakistan, which were discontinued when Inder Gujral was the prime minister of India in 1997–98.

India's Policy of Strategic Restraint Stands Tweaked

Pakistan has always followed a strategy of aggression against India for multiple reasons, which have been explained earlier in this book. They fought three wars against India. After their defeat in the 1971 war and the ensuing division of Pakistan, Bhutto swore to develop nuclear bombs even if they had to eat grass. Post Bhutto, General Zia-ul-Haq evolved a strategy of bleeding India through a thousand cuts. They infiltrated militants and regular J&K militia troops into the Dras, Kargil and Batalik areas many months before May 1999 in General Musharraf's time, soon after Prime Minister Vajpayee's peace mission to Lahore and the Lahore Declaration on 21 February 1999. Where and when have they proved themselves to be trustworthy?

Neither after all these provocations nor after the attacks on the Indian Parliament in 2001 and in Mumbai on 26 November 2008 did India choose to inflict punishment on the perpetrators of terrorism operating from various bases in PoK and even from within mainland Pakistan.

India exercised extreme strategic restraint by limiting the reactions to within their side of the LoC. It has only been in the last two years that India has conveyed a message to Pakistan that they will from now on hit its bases not only along the international border in J&K (erstwhile LoC) but even deep inside its territory, such as in the case of Balakot, if need be. India's days of passive restraint are over.

Another angle to this new approach by the Modi 2.0 government is that they went ahead and revoked Article 370, which in any case was meant to be a temporary and transient arrangement.

India's foreign minister, while speaking on the revocation of Article 370 in New York on 27 September 2019, made India's new approach very clear. He said that for 'far too long we had done the same but to no good, that is why we decided to act differently [tweaking the strategic approach], but with no change affected in our international borders. So it should not worry anyone.'

India will continue to supplement its counter-proxy-war operations with strikes inside Pakistan against their terrorist organizations such as the JeM and LeT, whom they unashamedly call strategic assets.

Imposing an Unbearable Economic and Military Cost on Pakistan

India has always been very considerate towards Pakistan despite all their follies and imprudence. But the time has now come to generate international pressure and economic costs that choke Pakistan's economy. Only then will Pakistan realize that they cannot afford the economic burden of waging a proxy war against India, irrespective of how low-cost an option it may appear to be to them.

The Pakistani army has insisted on maintaining a large force of over 6,50,000 personnel against an imaginary threat from India. Yet, in the four wars that they have fought against India, they have been the aggressors. In not even one case did India start the war. How then do they conceive a threat from India? So why does Pakistan, a country one-seventh the size of India, have to maintain such a large army? Obviously, it is because of aggressive designs against India.

It is only when the Pakistani army begins to hurt and bleed that the Pakistani deep state will realize the futility of its nefarious designs towards India. India must start building up and maintaining pressure against Pakistan from all directions from hereon.

Dealing with Pakistan

Pakistan will not easily abandon their obsession with Kashmir or outgrow their existential fears. For the Pakistanis, the contrived fear about their security and existence will remain as they are aware of their weaknesses and precarious financial position.

Also, their army, out of self-interest, will try its best to ensure that there is no movement towards peace with India. In the final analysis, the internal dynamics of Pakistan, its army and the fundamentalist terror groups located and operating from within Pakistan are the main regressive factors.

India's foreign minister, S. Jaishankar, has stated that Pakistan has to accept that the model built by them no longer works. They cannot use terrorism as a legitimate state instrument. He gave food for thought when he said that 'Bombay is not a part of Kashmir; then why was it attacked with their support?'

A dialogue with Pakistan may be commenced when India considers it to be an opportune time. But India must first insist that Pakistan stop the promotion of terror. Remember that even during the height of the World War II, the Germans and the British kept a dialogue going. Mao Tse-tung famously said, '*Ta ta, tan tan*', which means, fight fight, talk talk. India should not allow dialogue to cease but that will depend on Pakistan's behaviour and intentions. A backchannel dialogue may also be considered alongside a formal dialogue or even independently of that.

India should also be very clear that a single surgical strike or the destruction of a terrorist training centre inside Pakistan cannot force them or the terrorists to change their attitude. The Balakot strike, however, did serve as a stark warning to them. After this strike, it is likely that they have been forced to reconsider their tactics of promoting a proxy war inside Jammu and Kashmir. They may thus be evolving options that are less risk-prone, ones that will not invite a strong Indian response that could result in an escalation on the ground, something a rational Pakistan would neither want nor risk.

Another aspect that India needs to consider is whether the Pakistani army should be engaged in a dialogue in some form or the other, as no resolution or peace process with Pakistan is likely to be successful without the Pakistani army having an important say in the matter. There are a number of think tanks in India that are involved in regular dialogue with senior retired armed forces officers of Pakistan. It would be worthwhile to get an understanding of the mindset of the Pakistani army through the medium of these think tanks and also convey India's viewpoints to them for discussion. This may greatly help in progressing any talks with Pakistan.

India's dialogue with Pakistan should be holistic and not only aim at engagement. India must extend the scope of these talks to cultural and commercial constituencies within Pakistan. India should also leverage other instruments of power such as its excellent relations with the US and countries such as France, England, Germany as well as several Islamic countries.

India Emerging as an Economic Giant

India is a fast-developing economic power. It aimed to become a $5 trillion economy by 2024, which would get pushed back by a few years due to the Covid-19 pandemic's adverse impact on the economy. A former CEO of the Wipro Group had assessed that by 2030 India would be a $10 trillion economy, which would be the third-biggest economy behind the US and China. By 2050, according to an assessment by PricewaterhouseCoopers (PWC), China is likely to be a $58 trillion, India is likely to be a $44 trillion and the US is likely to be a $34 trillion economy. The World Bank's assessment is that by 2050, China will be a $70 trillion economy, the US is likely to be a $40 trillion economy and India will be the third-biggest economy in the world at $35 trillion. Presently, an economic slowdown is emerging in India (primarily due to Covid), but eventually it will be a big economic power and almost twenty times stronger than Pakistan. India would have thus moved far ahead of them. Pakistan could gain immensely by having a flourishing trade with India, if better sense prevails.

Terrorist Funding and Saudi Complicity

Pakistan's ability to promote terrorism in Kashmir will become limited over time unless it is heavily supported by Saudi petrodollars. Their own capacity to direct any money towards promoting terrorism will become increasingly limited, given their economic situation.

Even though Saudi Arabia has a quarter of the world's oil resources, they are not infinite. Already in 2019, the per capita income of Saudi nationals had dropped from $18,000 to $7,000. Even though their oil resources are likely to last for over seventy years, the demand for oil is going to steadily decrease.

An important factor that will reduce the demand for oil appreciably is the large-scale production of shale gas by the US. The COVID-19 pandemic is another factor that has reduced the demand for oil and the cost per barrel to an all-time low. The oil-producing countries are not likely to come out of this shock for quite some time to come.

Also, climate change is causing great concern to all the countries in the world. As a result, the world is fast moving towards an electric transportation system. The revolution in the car industry is being led by Tesla, General Motors and Volkswagen, and they are hoping to trigger a paradigm shift. It is expected that in the next ten years or so, 90 per cent of the cars in the developed world will be electric cars. In the developing world, this shift may take another 10–15 years.

Drone attacks on Saudi oil wells in recent years have brought to light the increasing vulnerability of oil availability and also the matter of pricing. These factors are also driving the effort towards electric transportation systems.

Also, with better engines, the demand for fuel oil is expected to drop by approximately 4.3 litres per 100 km. Overall, over the next 15–20 years, the oil requirement is expected to drop by over 21 per cent.

Efforts are also on to reduce the cost of gas and when the cost falls below USD 1 for 60 kWh in the not too distant future, more and more heavy vehicles will shift to gas as a source of energy.

Because of these developments, most countries whose economy is driven by oil and gas are looking for other avenues of income. Saudi Arabia is leading this effort; their crown prince, Mohammed bin Salman, had announced in 2016 that the Saudi vision was to reduce their dependence on the oil economy and diversify.

All these details have been given to explain that this source of money from the Islamic world, which is being misused for promoting terrorism, will be limited in the near future.

It is a truism that a terrorist network can survive only with assured funding. Money is needed to pay the salaries of the recruits and to purchase armament. The US has been leading a war on terrorist funding to dismantle these networks. This is the strategy they have primarily adopted, besides other measures, to contain terror. With the US effort, USD 140 million have been frozen till date in 1,400 banks around the world. This is despite the fact that terrorists have become experts at eluding the legal machinery.

One of the biggest sources of terrorist funding is donations through charities. These provide the reservoir of funding. Charities based in Saudi Arabia constitute the most important sources of funding. The Government of Saudi Arabia has taken many steps to disrupt this funding, with some success. In the Islamic world, there are tens of thousands of such channels, as Robert O. Collins, co-author of *Alms for Jihad*, explains. 'Zakat' is a pillar of Islam (compulsory giving of a portion of one's wealth to charities to spread Islam). Some of these charities contribute directly to terrorist networks and some donate to spread Islam but can be co-opted by terrorists, who then divert these funds. The dropping of their incomes from countries such as Saudi Arabia will limit their capacity to donate.

Drug money and hawala transactions are another major source of terrorist funding. For Pakistan, one simple and easy source of money is the poppy trade in Afghanistan. In his book, *Illicit*, Venezuelan journalist Moisés Naím explains how terrorist organizations raise funds and transfer them.

In another book, *Chasing Dirty Money*, Peter Reuter and Edwin M. Truman explain that financial crime is so widespread that almost 10 per cent of the global GDP is laundered money. Hawala transactions are amongst the commonest and easiest forms of money transfer in our part of the world. The modern financial system is so vast that getting any information on these illegal transfers is like finding a needle in a haystack.

An *India Today* team carried out a number of sting operations on 30 September 2019 in Chandni Chowk Bazar, old Delhi, under the codename 'Operation Kashmir Almonds'. They reached out to some almond merchants to transfer some money to Srinagar. Any amount was acceptable to these merchants on a premium of 1.3 per cent, meaning transfer fee of Rs 1,300 per lakh of rupees to be transferred. The merchants complained that it had become difficult to carry out hawala operations under new law but they would definitely manage. Till the government puts a complete and ultra-tight lid on this racket, the money will keep flowing for stone-pelting operators in the Valley, though these have drastically been reduced. (These live operations were shown on India Today channel on 30 September 2019.)

It has been found that old Delhi continues to be the centre of hawala transactions and it is fairly easy to send money to Kashmir through these means. What is of equal concern is that senior politicians and big businessmen of Kashmir are believed to be the nerve centre of this trade. This system has to be busted to ensure that these money transfers are stopped. Even though the NIA is doing a good job, it is primarily an investigative agency and not a preventive one. For taking on the additional responsibility of tackling the hawala network, this organization would have to be substantially strengthened, which must be considered a priority. There is a long way to go before India attains this capability, but the sooner it attains it, the better it will be.

12
Conclusion

'The fault lines are shifting from the boundaries of nations into the web of our societies and the streets of our cities. And terrorism and extremism are global forces that are larger than their changing names, groups, territories and targets.'

– Narendra Modi

Today, the scenario as it emerged after 6 August 2019 has no resemblance to the last thirty years of the proxy war.

The biggest change that has come about is that India has taken a conscious call that it would not do more of the same. India has got rid of a defensive mindset and switched to a proactive strategy. Let us put all the pieces of the jigsaw puzzle together and contemplate whether or not they will be able to generate a force multiplier effect.

The erstwhile state of Jammu and Kashmir has been bifurcated into union territories and the subjects of law and order and administration have thus come directly under the control of the

Centre. The government has concentrated the requisite quantum of paramilitary forces to deal with the civil population and handle the militancy and law and order situation in the Valley. The army will guard the border, especially against BAT/rogue actions, block infiltration of militants and operate along the exterior lines (area between the population centre and the LoC). The RR will continue to maintain the permanent counter-militancy grid and guard the exterior lines, and assist the army. India is also maintaining a high state of vigil across the country and has prepared itself to counter any possible terrorist actions anywhere in the country, of which there is a real threat.

India has made it clear to Pakistan that the erstwhile LoC, with the abrogation of Article 370, should be treated as an International Border. It is thus no longer on the table for discussion. The topics of dialogue, if and when any talks take place between India and Pakistan, will be confined to terror, PoK and Gilgit-Baltistan. These are the areas that Pakistan illegally captured in 1947-48 from the state of J&K, which had legally acceded to India in totality. Also open for discussion will be the Shaksgam Valley, which Pakistan illegally ceded to China. With the creation of Kargil and Ladakh as a separate union territory, China feels that India is keeping the issue of Aksai-Chin alive.

Pakistan had long deterred India by carrying on with their proxy war under the umbrella of nuclear blackmail. By responding to the Uri and Pulwama incidents offensively through strikes inside PoK and the Pakistan mainland, India shattered the bogey of Pakistan's 'strategy of full spectrum deterrence'. This will force Pakistan to reconsider its brinkmanship.

India has also shed their past inhibitions and taken its case forcefully to various world forums to expose Pakistan's duplicity and the fact that they are a hub of global terrorism. The 'Howdy

Modi' forum in Houston on 22 September 2019, where President Trump also joined Modi, as well as discussions in the UN Security Council closed-door meeting and at the UN Commission on Human Rights have shown to Pakistan that the world is not going to barter their economic relationship with India for an antiquated and non-existent issue such as Kashmir. They have accepted in principle that Kashmir is an internal matter for India. They are only concerned with the human rights aspects, in which India has had an impeccable record in the past, and which India will do its best to enhance in the days and months to come. Except for Malaysia and Turkey, no other Muslim country has supported Pakistan. The European parliamentary delegation that visited the Valley, Ladakh and Jammu regions in October 2019 went back satisfied. Their only suggestion was that the restrictions imposed in the region following the abrogation of Articles 370 and 35A should be lifted at the earliest. There have been two more such delegations which visited the valley, the last being on 18 February 2021. Virtually all the restrictions, including on 4G and internet, have been lifted. The US state department has even gone to the extent of advising Pakistan to also talk of the human rights of Muslims in Xinxiang rather than of only those in Kashmir.

India has over 204 million Muslims, living peacefully. This is the second-highest Muslim population in the world. The world is aware of the fact, as Prime Minister Modi said in the US, that, 'diversity is not only India's strength, but Indians celebrate diversity'. The world admires India for this.

As for China, the pro-democracy movement in Hong Kong has picked up momentum. With China's past record in Tibet and Xinxiang, they are in no position to advise India on human rights, irrespective of how much they may like to support Pakistan.

Added to all these factors is the pressure that is being applied on Pakistan by the IMF and FATF. It may be recalled that at the FATF meeting held in Paris in October 2019, Pakistan's actions were found to be satisfactory on only five counts out of a total of twenty-seven. They found Pakistan's record of taking concrete steps to curb their factory of terrorism to be dismal. As a result, Pakistan has been retained on FATF's greylist for the time being. They have, however, been given time to improve their standing. If they do not show definite improvement, Pakistan will be downgraded to the blacklist. This will make it very difficult for them to get financial assistance from global institutions. Pakistan's foreign minister, Mahmood Qureshi, warned his country on Pakistan TV that being put on the greylist itself had resulted in a loss of over USD 10 billion in one year.

So, Pakistan's ability to promote terrorism in Kashmir is going to come under increasing scrutiny and pressure. Financially, it will cripple them and they will become unsustainable.

Another major instrument for promoting terrorism has been petrodollars, but they too are shrinking by the day. In another 5–6 years, this source is also likely to be severely curtailed. Without financial support, terrorism cannot prosper.

The biggest bastion of resistance in Kashmir is likely to be the Islamic extremists, who are looking to establish an Islamic caliphate. However, their staying power will be severely hampered in the absence of all other supporting elements. Moreover, the radicalization factor is predominant only in the southern part of the Valley. At least 40 to 50 per cent of Kashmiris are fence-sitters and more or less okay with the Indian state, especially the Paharis, Gujjars, Bakarwals, Rajputs, Sikhs, Pathans and Shias.

India is attacking militancy simultaneously from all directions. They are trying to build a strong administration in Jammu and Kashmir from the bottom up. The panchayat and block-development elections that were conducted after October 2019 saw 98 per cent voting. Further, the first elections in the UT of J&K took place between 28 November and 19 December 2020 in the form of by-elections to District Development Councils (DDC) and municipal and panchayat-level bodies after the central government amended Jammu and Kashmir's Panchayati Raj Act 1989 to establish DDCs in all districts. Around 70-75 per cent of the electorate voted. India must also restart the process of political engagement as soon as the security situation is conducive to that. Some violence in the process will be inevitable and must not discourage the effort. This would be in tune with India's own democratic traditions and international image. The Centre must also allow peaceful protests because these are a democratic articulation of grievances.

The militancy will have to additionally withstand pressure from a concentrated dose of development, falling unemployment, investments by the corporate sector to promote industry in Jammu, Kashmir and Ladakh. These developmental activities will start having an impact in another 3–4 years. This is a crucial period and must be optimized in order to attain the goal of a 'New Kashmir'.

Militancy Unlikely to Survive for Long

I am convinced that the momentous developments of 5 and 6 August 2019 dealt a death blow to the militancy in Kashmir. From an aggressive position, Pakistan and the separatists have been reduced to scurrying and fending for themselves. Also, as a result of the abrogation of Articles 370 and 35A, new dilemmas have arisen for the Kashmiris.

They have lost their special status. This had always made them think of themselves as different from the rest of India. Now, they fear that they will be reduced to a minority in their own home state.

Further, the state of Jammu and Kashmir has been broken into two parts and they have been relegated to the status of a union territory. They feel this will result in the loss of the liberties that were ensured within the dispensation of their own Constitution under Articles 370 and 35A. The big question that looms large in front of them now is whether the statehood of J&K will ever be restored. I think Kashmiris view the bringing of security directly under the Centre as an instrument of denying them their liberties. They worry that Indian domination will be complete from here on.

If India recovers PoK and Gilgit-Baltistan from Pakistan, then they will also have to share their prosperity with the poor and neglected people of these areas.

Pakistan has been reduced to a hopeless situation by India. It has become quite clear that Pakistan is no match for India in any field, whether diplomatically, economically or militarily. The Kashmiris' dependence on Pakistan was perhaps a big mistake for which they have paid the price. Indeed, their desire to join Pakistan or become independent has become a lost hope.

Added to this is the financial mess that Pakistan is heading towards at the hands of the FATF, on account of promoting terrorism. How then will Pakistan be in a position to continue to help the Kashmiris?

All these factors put together will surely make the Kashmiris have a serious rethink about their approach and aims for the future. What should they do? Should they still dream about independence or should they try and recover what they have lost? Can they really take on India with the assistance of a hopeless Pakistan? The answer is an emphatic 'No'.

It looks likely that after the first 2–3 years of resistance, the militancy will start crumbling gradually in the Valley. Because of the extreme radicalization in the region, they may manage to hold out for another 4–5 years at the most. Thus, in a period of 8–10 years, the militancy in Jammu and Kashmir is likely to be brought to an ineffectual state.

By then, Pakistan would possibly be in such a financial mess that they would be forced to look towards India, which will be on the way to becoming an economic giant, possibly the third largest in the world. Around this period, the inflow of petrodollars from Saudi Arabia and other sources to Pakistan would have also dropped drastically, thereby severely restricting their ability to assist the Kashmiris.

India may well then extend a hand of friendship towards Pakistan to promote better relations with them. At such a stage, Pakistan may readily accept India's offer for their own survival. India should at that stage adopt a supportive attitude towards Pakistan and make them a part of the regional economic integration. Perhaps that will be the time when peace will slowly return to the Valley.

The Idea of India

The idea of India is not based on religion. India has believed in cohesiveness and inclusion for centuries. That is what Mahatma Gandhi and Rabindranath Tagore taught India. Swami Vivekananda, the great Indian philosopher, in his famous speech at the World's Parliament of Religions held in Chicago in 1893 said that he was proud to belong to a religion (by implication, country) that had taught him tolerance and universal acceptance. All the great leaders of the country advocated the same during India's struggle for independence.

I would like to quote here from an article in the *Indian Express* dated 12 October 2019, titled 'Unworthy Nations – Why India Must Not Reject Gandhi and Imitate Pakistan'. The article is even more relevant because the author, Khaled Ahmed, is a Pakistani citizen who is a consulting editor with *Newsweek Pakistan*. The thrust of his article is that 'in Pakistan nobody in pursuit of knowledge sets much store by that'. The reason is that 'an ideology based on religion does not brook revision'. Mahatma Gandhi taught inclusive faith, which believed in Hindus and Muslims living together. That is why the author exhorts India to acknowledge Gandhi and reject Pakistan.

That is precisely why a 'Kashmir based on religion' does not fit into the philosophy and idea of India. Kashmiris have to change, become inclusive and merge with India. They have got the opportunity to do so now and they should not miss it. They have already wasted seven decades since Independence.

In the interim, till Pakistan's capacity to promote terrorism is appreciably degraded, India should aim to keep violence in the Valley under control and focus on developmental activities. To this end, it should concentrate on deradicalization in the Valley and engagement with the youth, which should be a priority. This will pose the biggest challenge.

Ensuring better administration and the economic development of Jammu and Kashmir and delivering a new Jammu and Kashmir and Ladakh, as Prime Minister Modi announced from the ramparts of the Red Fort on 15 August 2019, are the important tasks ahead.

Also important will be keeping multipronged dialogues going within the state till solutions that are to everybody's satisfaction and contribute towards the national interest are found. This will also help settle the intra-regional frictions within the union territories, especially between Jammu and Kashmir.

The central government has announced a people-friendly approach wherein they intend to take care of the families of the terrorists and try to bring them back into the mainstream. However, terrorism itself should be dealt with an iron fist.

The government should also work towards holding assembly elections in Jammu and Kashmir as soon as the security situation improves and the proposed delimitation has been carried out. Restoring the democratic process at the earliest must remain a priority.

Bringing the Kashmiri Pandits back to their homeland in Jammu and Kashmir will be a litmus test of the success of India's Jammu and Kashmir policy.

Finally, full statehood must be restored to Jammu and Kashmir (less Kargil and Ladakh) in a reasonable time frame.

There is no doubt that the time will come in the not-too-distant future when peace will return to the Valley and the state. Eight to ten years is not a long span of time in a nation's history. Kashmir will once again be a paradise on earth!

Epilogue

When an early draft of the manuscript of this book went to the publishers in November 2019, it already included the post 5 August 2019 developments and the abrogation of Articles 370 and 35A and, with that, one era of the Kashmir story had ended. However, by the time this book is published, it will be over two years since the Government of India altered the special status of the state and split it into two UTs. A new era in this story has thus begun. I have updated the narrative in the preceding chapters up to August 2021, besides adding this Epilogue.

Over two years ago, the BJP government did what no one in Kashmir had ever thought anybody could do – let alone would do – namely, abrogating Articles 370 and 35A. No political party in India worth its name has disagreed with the Government of India's initiative. With this momentous decision, the government seemed to have closed all options for any negotiated settlement on Kashmir with the separatist parties in Kashmir and also with Pakistan.

New Delhi's reading of the situation was governed by the fact that Articles 370 and 35A were two constitutional provisions of a temporary and transient nature, which provided Jammu and Kashmir a special status within the Indian Constitution for an interim period until J&K's status was finally settled. Even Pandit Nehru – as did all subsequent leaders such as Indira Gandhi – called and considered it a temporary measure. But Kashmiris somehow thought of it as a fundamental right of exclusivity, which kept alive the idea of J&K either becoming independent or seceding to Pakistan.

There were many opportune times for India to do away with these special provisions: first in the aftermath of the historic victory in 1971 over Pakistan and the consequent Simla Accord; and second, when the Indian parliamentary resolution of 22 February 1994, with full consensus, stated clearly that all territories that were under the erstwhile Maharaja of Jammu and Kashmir before the signing of the Instrument of Accession to India on 26 October 1947 belonged to India and that India would aspire to regain all these territories. Unfortunately, India could not take advantage of these opportunities and generate consensus within the country due to various considerations, including dithering on the part of the governments of the day and their desire to have the full support of the Kashmiris, which in any case would never have been forthcoming.

Historic Decision of 5 August 2019

Since 1952, no central party has stood by these articles in their entirety. All governments, including those of the Congress, diluted various provisions of Articles 370 and 35A from time to time. The BJP showed decisiveness and finished the long-pending agenda. Some political analysts such as Shekhar Gupta called it a continental shift in the Government of India's approach, which included 'international, political, diplomatic, strategic, tactical, moral and cartographic dimensions'.

The BJP government was convinced that the situation in J&K had only worsened and encouraged separatism and terrorism. It was also of the view that 'two families' (the Abdullahs and the Muftis) had taken advantage of their positions and were not siding forcefully with India. Also, corruption was rampant and despite huge funds being pumped in by India, the state was not progressing at the desired pace. It also assessed that the time had come to clip the wings of Pakistan, whose sole agenda was to destabilize India and the state of J&K. Pakistan had also ceded large parts of Indian territory in Shaksgam Valley illegally to China and was posing a grave strategic threat to India in collaboration with China. This assessment proved right when, from May 2020 onwards, India was confronted with a serious face-off with China in eastern Ladakh, and Pakistan had also concentrated over a division in Gilgit-Baltistan. Jointly, both China and Pakistan posed a serious threat to all of eastern Ladakh, including Daulat Beg Oldi (DBO) and Siachen Glacier.

India thus wanted to deal with this problem not only politically and administratively but also strategically. Policymakers in New Delhi were convinced that this problem would persist till Pakistan possessed the means to pursue its strategy of proxy war, which it had started in 1989. The high-profile terrorist attacks in Pathankot, Uri and Pulwama had further enhanced the determination of the Government of India to bring about a total 'strategic transformation'. The Balakot operation by India on 26 February 2019 gave a distinct glimpse of the firm approach the Modi government would follow in the days to come.

The Government of India, post 5 August 2019, also promptly published two maps of J&K showing Pakistan-occupied Kashmir, Gilgit-Baltistan and Aksai-Chin in Ladakh as territories within Indian boundaries. All this was done with such finesse that nobody got a whiff of it and Pakistan was not able to react effectively to these developments.

A notable and wise aspect of India's action was to keep Jammu and Kashmir together as one UT. Jammu is a glue to bind Kashmir to India and keeps both regions economically viable as their economies are largely inter-independent. Similarly, another was to fulfil Ladakh's long-standing demand and aspiration for a separate identity. It also left no doubt in the mind of China that India still has a claim over Aksai-Chin. Bifurcating the state into two UTs – Jammu and Kashmir, and Ladakh – has given the Government of India the opportunity to take the law and order and administration of the UTs under its direct control, thus eliminating the political machinations of local leaders and the chain of corruption. Now is the time to bring about decisive development in all three parts of the erstwhile princely state, to prove to the Kashmiris that the Government of India genuinely means them well.

No well-informed opinion would have perceived these actions as the end of the J&K problem. It was quite clear that this conflict would persist till the elephant in the room, Pakistan, possessed the means to pursue its proxy war and the radicalized elements within the Valley retained the network to operate in cahoots with Pakistan.

The Aftermath

To get a fair assessment of the impact of the decision, we must consider a variety of aspects, including the international dimension, the internal security situation, governance of the UTs including the promised development status, and the attitude of the people.

Overall, the aim should be to gain credibility and trust through actions on the ground and the involvement of the local population. Lt Gen. Ata Hasnain, a keen watcher of Kashmir, has rightly pointed out in one of his writings that these 'transformational decisions by themselves cannot become game changers, they also need solid national backing against the counter forces that exist internally and internationally, to attempt to reverse the trends'.

The International Dimension

The Government of India's stand is clear that the nullification of Articles 370 and 35A is an internal affair. India's constitutional changes in J&K do not affect their external boundaries, be it the LoC with PoK or the LAC with China in Ladakh. Both Pakistan and China thus have no grounds to protest as, importantly, nothing has changed along the borders with both these countries.

Most countries have treated the abrogation of Articles 370 and 35A as an internal matter of India. The then US State Department spokesman Morgan Ortigas had said, 'We are closely following the events in Jammu and Kashmir. We have taken note of the announcement by India, of revising the constitutional status of Jammu and Kashmir and India's plan to split the state into two union territories. We call on all parties to maintain peace and stability along the Line of Control.' Similar views have been expressed by Ned Price, the State Department spokesperson of the Biden administration: 'I want to be very clear that there has been no change in US policy in the region.' The response of all European countries has been along similar lines. The Quadrilateral Security Dialogue (QSD, also known as the Quad) countries have also treated this action as an internal matter of India.

The UAE, which has emerged as a key partner of India in the Gulf region, has also taken note of India's move to declare Jammu and Kashmir as a UT. Saudi Arabia has refused to back Pakistan on the Kashmir issue, and this has rattled Pakistan. Even the OIC – to Pakistan's dismay – had nothing negative to say and treated this action as an internal matter of India.

The effort by China to take up the matter in the United Nations Security Council remained only transactional in nature and thus inconsequential. So, the Indian government largely succeeded in keeping the matter away from international scrutiny.

However, the prolonged detention of mainstream leaders for almost a year, and the non-availability of internet facilities, especially 4G, drew unfavourable comments from the international community. India's security establishment at that stage felt that the restrictions on 4G and the internet were essential for some time to disrupt militant activities. The US took a nuanced approach and expressed concern over widespread detentions, including those of politicians and business leaders. They called for a resumption of the political process.

The Government of India reacted when it was confident that the security situation was stable. Farooq Abdullah and Omar Abdullah were released on 13 and 24 March 2020 respectively. Mehbooba Mufti was released later, on 13 October 2020, after fourteen months. A large number of other leaders were also released in this time frame. 4G was reintroduced, initially in two districts on an experimental basis in late August 2020 and then fully restored in February 2021 on the improvement of the security situation. Of all the decisions, the non-availability of the internet had drawn maximum criticism and almost led to the internationalization of the Kashmir issue. The counter argument, which had its own logic, was that the suspension of the service virtually brought the ISI and the terrorist network to a standstill, thereby seriously disrupting their activities.

Epilogue

Pakistan's Reaction

Pakistan refers to Kashmir as its 'jugular vein'. The options for it have become nightmarish since India rescinded Kashmir's semi-autonomous status on 5 August 2019. Most strategic analysts opine that Pakistan has 'limited options' to respond to India's decision on J&K as Islamabad has 'little credibility' on the issue, given its long history of covertly supporting militant groups and fostering terrorism in the state since 1990. The US Congressional Research Service, in its second report on Kashmir in 2020, stated that 'Pakistan's ability to alter the status quo through military actions has been reduced in recent years, meaning that Islamabad will have to rely primarily on diplomacy'.

But this report does not take into account the nexus between Pakistan and China on both the diplomatic and military fronts. A possible reason for China's face-off with India in eastern Ladakh is to not only meet its own strategic objectives against India, but to also incidentally help its ally, Pakistan, find remedies to its problems in Kashmir.

On the political front also Pakistan has run into some very rough weather. To condemn India for changing the status quo in Kashmir, Pakistan approached Saudi Arabia to convene a session of the OIC, but the request was turned down. The subsequent remarks by Pakistan's foreign minister, Shah Mehmood Qureshi, that 'if you cannot convene it, then I will be compelled to ask Prime Minister Imran Khan to call a meeting of the Islamic countries that are ready to stand with us on the issue of Kashmir and support the oppressed Kashmiris', created quite an embarrassing situation for Pakistan. This greatly miffed the Saudis, who not only rebuffed the Pakistani army chief, who was sent to Riyadh to meet Crown Prince Mohammed Bin Sultan and assuage Saudi tempers, but did not even grant him an audience with the royal. The visit did not produce any fruitful results, and on the contrary the news came that Pakistan was returning the aid that it had received from Saudi Arabia – $1 billion out of the $6.2 billion pledged – after borrowing the amount from China. Interestingly, this three-year financial package to Pakistan also seems to have reached an end within just a year. This comes against the backdrop of the 'threat' by Pakistan's foreign minister to Saudi Arabia that Pakistan would pull out its allies from the OIC and arrange the meeting itself. This would have another adverse side effect in terms of the substantial aid that Pakistan was getting to promote fundamentalism in Kashmir also perhaps being cut off. The biggest setback for Pakistan perhaps was when Saudi Arabia termed India's decision an internal affair.

Thereafter, Pakistan got together with Turkey and Malaysia to convene a summit of Islamic countries – a kind of parallel OIC – which turned out to be a flop. Pakistan is now trying to get support from countries like Turkey, Malaysia and Iran, but so far nothing concrete has emerged.

There is huge pressure on Imran Khan and the deep state to do something substantial. Pakistan was hoping to create severe challenges for India in the domains of internal security, a hot LoC, information and psychological warfare and also generate a 'two-front threat'. But now, Pakistan's only satisfaction could be by way of a face-off between India and China in eastern Ladakh. In all other areas it has not met with any meaningful success.

Pakistan's only trump card in Kashmir has been the infiltration of hardcore jehadis into J&K, which provided the backbone to the militancy. Pakistan's first efforts in 2020 to infiltrate terrorists into J&K commenced in early April after a severe winter. However, the infiltration was reduced appreciably due to effective Indian military operations and the anti-infiltration grid along the LoC.

Recruitment of local Kashmiris has gone down by 40 per cent. The deep state is now wondering if it will run out of resources soon. Pakistan may thus be forced to commence infiltration from different locations (the Jammu–Kathua routes) and attempt one or more Pulwama-type terror acts, but there is a huge risk in that for them given the strong Indian reaction to such an attack in the past. This finally leaves them with the only option of an active LoC and employing Border Action Teams or attempting shallow objectives, for example, of the Pathankot and Nagrota type, if at all militarily possible due to the heightened Indian military vigilance. However, this too seems to have failed because Pakistan was forced to accept a ceasefire along the LoC in February 2021 due to prohibitory retaliation by the Indian army and global pressure, especially from the FATF and IMF.

Khaled Ahmed, consulting editor of *Newsweek Pakistan*, aptly summed up Pakistan's dilemma in his article in the *Indian Express* on 5 September 2020. He said, 'Imran Khan's past anti-US and pro-Taliban rhetoric doesn't make him too acceptable to the world outside.' Khan's reference to Osama bin Laden as a 'martyr' of Islam has disappointed many who admired him for his honesty in financial matters. But his mishandling of foreign policy has made his supporters regret that they were led astray by his rhetoric. He has thoroughly mishandled the Kashmir issue by listening to 'Muslim' leaders such as Recep Tayyip Erdogan of Turkey and Mahathir Mohamad of Malaysia to challenge Pakistan's Arab friends for not 'uniting against India on Kashmir'.

Maulana Fazlur Rehman, a hardcore right-wing politician and president of the Jamiat Ulema-e-Islam, showed the degree of despondency in Pakistan while addressing his supporters in Peshawar on 18 August 2020, when he said, 'India revoked Kashmiri's special status and tactically announced the region as an integral part and we were pushed downward [...] Yesterday we were thinking how to take Srinagar, today we are thinking as to how to save Muzaffarabad'.

And finally, another headache for Pakistan is that it is under the close watch of the FATF, which retained Pakistan on the Grey List in its meeting held from 21 to 25 June 2021, as it took note of Pakistan's inability to take appropriate action against UN-identified and listed terrorists such as JeM chief Masood Azhar and 26/11 mastermind Hafiz Saeed. Pakistan continues to be in the high-risk category of the Basel Institute on Governance's independent, data-based index of risk of money laundering and terror financing around the world and is currently ranked twenty-eighth with a score of 6.3. Another headache for Pakistan is that it has just come to light that Syed Salahuddin, the head of Hizb-ul-Mujahideen, the main terror group operating in Kashmir, is on the payroll of the ISI. This establishes the direct complicity of Pakistan with terrorists and terrorism in J&K. So far, Imran Khan's government has been unable to get any bills against terrorism-related money laundering approved in the assembly, which would be required to prove that Pakistan is serious about curbing terrorism.

Currently, Iran and North Korea are on the FATF's Black List. Even if Pakistan is not there yet, that sword of Damocles will always be hanging over its head. It will be very difficult for them to get any loans or financial assistance if they are not removed from the Grey List. This is precisely why it will be unwise for them to get involved in any high-profile terrorist acts in J&K.

Internal Security

Contrary to all apprehensions of a rebellion or mass civil disobedience post 5 August 2019, reasonable peace prevailed in J&K. This was a big achievement on the part of the J&K administration under the close watch of New Delhi. As Lt Gen. Ata Hasnain says, '[...] the eco-system of terror so deftly manipulated by ISI, directed by the separatist leaders and led in the streets by younger men and some women just could not get going. It needed leadership, along with the network activation but it failed to deliver'.

This was because of good planning and preparation in the run-up to the important announcement of 5 August 2019. The over-ground worker network was seriously dented in the preparatory stage as most of them were taken into preventive custody. These included hundreds of low-profile workers besides the prominent ones. The plan had been put into motion since the removal of the BJP–Mehbooba government. The separatists were also isolated and their hold over the system had weakened. Another big achievement was the tightening of the noose around clandestine terror funds. As a result, stone-pelting in the streets came to a virtual stop, and it remains so even presently, up to August 2021.

Infiltration has also reduced due to the army's increased security vigilance along the LoC. Only 50 militants were able to infiltrate as against 138 in 2019. An even bigger sign of a shift is the 40 per cent decline in the enrolment of youth in terror groups in the past year, with fresh recruitment being abysmally low. Only 100 local boys reportedly went into the terrorist fold in 2020 as compared to 172 who joined in 2019.

The forces neutralized 157 terrorists in 2019. In 2020, 221 terrorists were neutralized in more than 100 counter-terrorist operations. Terrorists could initiate only 244 attacks in 2020 as against 592 in 2019 (a fall of 62 per cent). The number of security forces personnel killed in action declined by 28 per cent, with 62 personnel in 2020 as against 80 in 2019. The biggest successes were in terms of better intelligence inputs, close cooperation amongst the army, paramilitary forces and police, and the elimination of virtually the entire terrorist leadership. Understandably, there was a rise in ceasefire violations, totalling 5,133 in 2020 as against 3,479 in 2019, an increase of 48 per cent, as per a written statement in the Rajya Sabha. However, the ceasefire has since been accepted after talks at the DGMO level in February 2021 and is holding.[1] Poonch bore the maximum brunt while Kathua saw the highest rate of truce violations.[2]

Drones – A New Dimension to the Proxy War

A new dimension was added to the proxy war when a drone-based attack was launched by terrorists (the Pakistan deep state) on 27 June 2021. Explosives were dropped on the Jammu air force station in an effort to destroy and damage property and cause loss of life. We are aware that drones have a deadly all-terrain, all-mission combat capability and phenomenal endurance. They can carry variable loads of about 10 to 15 kg and can operate undetected. They have accurate target acquisition capability based on technical data or programming. Unlike human resources, drones don't face problems of crew fatalities, combat fatigue or motivational blues.

It is likely that this mode of warfare and destruction will be increasingly employed in the future to bolster and keep alive the faltering militancy despite the Pakistani army's assurance of a ceasefire.

More than 300 drone sightings have been unofficially reported since August 2019, though so far no damage of consequence has occurred. Therefore, India needs to nip the trouble in the bud and develop speedy detection and destruction capabilities. India has already placed equipment with anti-drone capability in Jammu.

---

1 According to a statement made by Minister of State for Defence Shripad Naik in the Rajya Sabha.
2 Data from the *New Indian Express* and some other sources.

We may also consider responding offensively at a strategic level to such provocations.

Radicalization

One of the major causes of worry in Kashmir has been the increase in radicalization and fundamentalism. Mosques and madrasas have been the breeding grounds for these trends, attracting the idle youth, who are educated but jobless. Sadly, this is in the same Kashmir that has a culture of Sufism and Kashmiriyat. Now is the time for the administration to lay special emphasis on this aspect and take corrective action. Radicalization is perhaps the most negative and retrograde factor that needs to be eliminated through a combination of means including development, job opportunities, fair governance, and cleaning up the system in mosques and madrasas. A lot has already been written on this issue in earlier chapters. Radicalization remains a big challenge in the long term. Fortunately, this wave has not spread as seriously in north Kashmir as compared to south Kashmir.

Political Activity

It is important to restore political activity in J&K to involve the people and political parties in managing their own affairs. The perception that panchayati raj would be able to replace mainstream political activity is likely a case of misplaced optimism.

With the release of mainstream leaders, finally on 22 August 2020, six of the main political parties broke their silence and reaffirmed their commitment to the Gupkar Declaration of 4 August 2019. The declaration was signed just a day ahead of the annulment of J&K's special status. The signatories included the leaders of the National Conference, Peoples Democratic Party, Congress, People's Conference, Communist Party of India

(Marxist) and Awami National Conference. Their announcement stated that 'all political activity would be subservient to the sacred goal of reverting the status of J&K to as it existed on 4 August 2019'. This means that they wanted the restoration of Articles 370 and 35A, of the constitution of J&K and of statehood, with Ladakh once again a part of J&K. They considered the measures taken as amounting to disempowerment and a challenge to the basic identity of the people of J&K.

The Gupkar Declaration made by the leadership of the six main parties in the region stated that:

- all parties would be united in their resolve to protect and defend the identity, autonomy and special status of J&K against all attacks whatsoever;
- the modification or abrogation of Articles 35A and 370, and the unconstitutional delimitation or trifurcation of the state would be an aggression against the people of Jammu, Kashmir and Ladakh;
- the parties participating were resolved to seek an audience with the president and prime minister of India and the leaders of other political parties to apprise them of the current situation and appeal to them to safeguard the legitimate interests of the people of the state under the constitution of India; and
- finally, all the political parties were resolved to remain together and stand united in their struggle to safeguard the identity, autonomy and special status of the state.

Interestingly, Farooq Abdullah in his own statements had said, 'nothing about us without us'. He also reacted sharply to Pakistan's statements by saying, 'Pakistan has always abused mainstream political parties of J&K but now suddenly they like us. Let me make it clear that we are not anybody's puppets, neither of New Delhi, nor of anyone across the border.' This was a significant statement because if they are prepared to discard Pakistan, India could consider having a dialogue with political leaders from the UT.

But the problem for all the mainstream parties such as the NC and PDP, which have spun their politics around autonomy, is that any departure from this stand would question their relevance in Kashmir's politics.

Even though they have managed to revive a joint strategy to counter the public pressure and New Delhi's unrelenting mood, they must be less than hopeful in their own assessment. The main reasons for this would be Pakistan's proven inability to swing any meaningful action in the state. Pakistan has already lost four wars to India. Its thirty-year proxy war has only resulted in mass destruction and deaths and has not been able to shake India's determination regarding Kashmir. Even the funds have dried up. Another main reason, as Haseeb Drabu, the former finance minister of J&K, says in his article in the *Indian Express* (7 August 2020), is that 'there is no alternative view on Kashmir. The view that was the dominant one till not so long ago has dissipated overnight. It would appear that, for the first time in history, domestically there is complete consensus on Kashmir. There are thus no supporters left for them in India.'

When you discuss this issue with the Kashmiri public at large, their main worry is that they have lost their statehood, which is a great humiliation for them. The domicile rule that was recently introduced is another great cause of worry and the fear of being outnumbered in their own state is haunting them. They are also not very sure of the effect of 'delimitation' on the political scene when it is finalized. And lastly and most importantly, they have lost faith in the value of their own leadership vis-à-vis the powers of the central government. This is where they stand as of today. One can perhaps say that the people have generally lost the appetite to revive a full-fledged agitation against India.

So, what is the roadmap of the political parties? For the present, the parties are displaying unanimity, but they have a tough path ahead and only time will tell how matters unfold.

Breaking the Ice: A Welcome Political Initiative

Prime Minister Narendra Modi initiated the political process in J&K when he held a meeting with fourteen leaders from all political parties in the region on 24 June 2021. He set the tone for the meeting when he announced that it was to remove '*dil se doori aur Dilli se doori*' (bridging the trust deficit and bringing Delhi and the state closer).

The talks were held in a congenial environment with all participants being given a chance to express their views. Ghulam Nabi Azad, a former chief minister, presented five key demands: restoration of statehood at the earliest, Vidhan Sabha elections at the earliest, guarantees to local people on government jobs, careful implementation of the domicile law so that J&K is not flooded by outsiders, rehabilitation of Kashmiri Pandits and release of all political prisoners.

Significantly, Article 370 did not prove to be a negotiation killer and no political party talked of violent protests. Most parties felt that it would be appropriate to wait for the outcome of the case which is presently being heard by a constitutional five-judge bench in the Supreme Court.

The Kashmir-based parties felt that delimitation was not needed at this stage when it was scheduled for the rest of the country in 2026. They questioned why J&K should be treated differently. Farooq Abdullah emphasized that when statehood is restored, J&K

should not be a truncated state and the J&K state civil cadre and the IAS cadre must also be restored.

Mehbooba Mufti said that the people of the Valley were angry about the way in which Article 370 had been abolished. This was a question of their identity and it was given to them by Pandit Nehru and Sardar Vallabhbhai Patel. She also emphasized that India should talk to Pakistan just as it was talking to the Taliban and China.

In brief, all parties generally agreed to consider participation in the delimitation process and the subsequent assembly elections. This was probably an imperative so that they do not lose their political space to the BJP, as they did at the time of the Block Development Office elections. However, many of them suspected a hidden motive behind the decision to have the delimitation process at that stage.

All participants were appreciative of the prime minister's having taken this step to break the ice. Prime Minister Modi assured the participants that his government was committed to reviving the democratic process through assembly elections and to the restoration of statehood as early as possible and sought their participation in the delimitation process.

Separately, Union Home Minister Amit Shah promised a review of the release of political prisoners through a committee under Lieutenant Governor Manoj Sinha.

The initiative was expected to attract favourable attention in the West and to be welcomed by the Biden administration in the US. An important point to consider also was whether the process was part of behind-the-scenes contact between India and Pakistan, which had earlier resulted in the February 2021 ceasefire announcement by General Bajwa. Another significant point was the fact that National Security Advisor Ajit Doval and his Pakistani counterpart Moeed Yousuf, at the meeting of the Shanghai Cooperation Organization on 23 June 2021, agreed to cooperate in the joint fight against the threats of international terrorism and religious radicalization.

Both countries are taking care to tone down the political rhetoric. Overall, talks with the state leadership and the initiatives with Pakistan may be of great consequence, even though it may be too early yet to make a firm prediction about the future course.

Governance

The Government of India has reposed a lot of hope in corruption-free and efficient governance, bringing about positivity among the people in the UTs. Unfortunately, in the past two years, not many significant signs of improvement have emerged. Perhaps this is too short a span of time to judge. Covid-19 has also slowed down several initiatives. A new lieutenant governor, Manoj Sinha, who is a politician, has been placed in J&K with the hope that he will be able to start the political process and a few people-friendly activities. The hope that good governance will become an important driver for the future narrative has yet to significantly materialize on the ground. However, reports indicate that the new lieutenant governor is quite active.

The mood of the people in Kashmir is of disappointment and of being let down. The administration will have to regain their faith with efficiency and work on the ground. All three provinces – Jammu, Srinagar and Ladakh – have their own separate aspirations and goals. These must be understood and worked upon. Unless that is done with sagacity and sincerity, we will remain in a state of struggle. The finest administrators, with people-friendly attitudes, need to be posted to each district and the central secretariat to achieve the goal of all-round progress. Only a 'whole of the government approach' will work. Jobs, opportunities in India and education facilities should remain on the top of the agenda. As of now, it would be a stretch to say that the Centre has won the confidence of the people with its development agenda.

As Lt Gen. Ata Hasnain has said, '[…] this is a domain where greater credibility will need to be generated for better national and international endorsement'. Electoral activity can only be revived after the delimitation process. So, the chances of a popularly elected government taking charge appears to be a distance away. The electoral process will itself be the biggest indicator of normalcy being established. We will have to wait and watch while development proceeds apace.

Pakistan and China – Collaborators in Perfidy

Even though Ladakh is situated in a remote corner of J&K, it is essential to examine this stand-off between India and China as this confrontation has all the possibilities of spreading throughout J&K, up to the extremity of India's eastern sector. This development has serious implications and is thus relevant to this narrative of the state of J&K.

China and India – the two most populous countries in the world and both nuclear-armed – are now engaged in the most dangerous border crisis since they fought a war in 1962. Pakistan, the third nuclear power in the region, has also joined this possibly pre-planned scenario by reportedly deploying a division in Gilgit and Baltistan. In all probability, one of the reasons why this face-off has been instigated is to help Pakistan counter India's 5 August 2019 initiative in J&K.

The direct action by the Chinese in Ladakh militates against their standard approach, which has been to treat the Kashmir issue as a bilateral matter between India and Pakistan, even though they have been sympathetic to the Pakistani cause. Even on 6 August 2019, after the revocation of Articles 370 and 35A, in a written statement for China's foreign ministry, their spokesman Hua Chunying termed this issue the 'legacy of history between India and Pakistan'. Expressing serious concern he said, '[...] the parties concerned should exercise restraint and act with caution. We call upon the two sides to peacefully resolve relevant dispute through dialogue and consultation and safeguard regional peace and stability'.

When China has always treated the Kashmir issue as a bilateral matter, what then has provoked them to create a serious situation in Ladakh? Ambassador Shyam Saran, one of India's most distinguished foreign secretaries, clearly articulated his views on this in an interview with Karan Thapar (25 August 2020) for *The Wire*. He said, 'China has chosen this time because the world is pre-occupied with the COVID-19 pandemic. China believes that in terms of its own economic and military capability it is in a very strong position. It sees itself as a pre-eminent power in Asia. They want to put India in its place and convey the message clearly that India is not in the same league as them and thus cut India down to size. China is also concerned with the development of infrastructure by India in Ladakh and other border areas and wants India to stop, which cannot be accepted as it will put India at a great disadvantage.'

This assessment by Ambassador Shyam Saran is supported by many strategic analysts. Similarly, S.D. Muni has written in the *Indian Express* (25 August 2020):

> China is not interested in any strategic equilibrium being promoted, as suggested by our Foreign Minister, with any

of its Asian neighbours, least of all with India. Its efforts are clearly to build a hierarchical Asian order, with itself at the top. Beijing wants India to occupy a slot in such a hierarchy commensurate only with its power status. It is very well aware of India's economic and military strength, which it knows well, that they are well behind the Chinese potential and might. China is ruthlessly resisting India's entry into any world bodies like UN Security Council and Nuclear Suppliers Group (NSG). It is encircling India strategically and economically through various corridors like CPEC [China-Pakistan Economic Corridor] and Bangladesh-China-India-Myanmar (BCIM) and the trans-Himalayan connectivity network.

Another distinguished diplomat, Ambassador G. Parthasarathy, who has been India's High Commissioner to Pakistan, has said in *India Today* (21 September 2020): 'China has taken us for a ride since 1962; they never defined the LAC, using each time to their advantage [...] each stage they gained a bit.' In spite of all the summit meetings at Wuhan, Ahmedabad and Mahabalipuram, China does not seem to be in a mood for reconciliation. Their dialogues only seem to be a strategic ploy to buy time.'

One could also argue that China's military intrusion into Ladakh is not directly related to the problem in Kashmir. However, the fact is that this offers China and Pakistan a very good opportunity to fight together for several complementary objectives. This serves the cause of both countries well and takes care of their strategic objectives such as 'providing depth to the Aksai-Chin Road, Shaksgam Valley and CPEC' for China. Similarly, for Pakistan, it secures the Gilgit-Baltistan area and gives them an opportunity to try and take Siachen Glacier and take possession of Nubra Valley, besides helping China to capture Shyok Valley and Daulat Beg Oldi.

It would not be correct to link the recent statements of some of our leaders reasserting India's claims over PoK, Gilgit-Baltistan, Aksai-Chin and Shaksgam Valley with this stand-off, as they are in accordance with the Indian Parliament's unanimous resolution of 1994. So, there is nothing new in these statements to alarm either China or Pakistan.

As on 9 September 2020, the situation on the ground was that China had made appreciable ingress in the Depsang area, which has long been a bone of serious contention and thus a legacy issue (18 km west of LAC and 30 km southeast of DBO). Both sides have withdrawn from the Galwan area – where a bloody skirmish took place on 14–15 June 2020, and India lost 20 soldiers in hand-to-hand combat and the Chinese many more – with a buffer zone in between. The Chinese are still holding the areas of Hot Springs and Gogra. In Pangong Tso, the Indians initially held positions up to Dhan Singh Thapa post and a few dominating heights, with the Chinese a couple of hundred yards below them. The Chinese continued to hold the areas from Fingers 5 to 8.

There were many rounds of talks between the two sides, starting from the level of battalion commanders to brigade commanders and corps commanders, but they did not produce any fruitful results. The Chinese continued to hold the same positions that they occupied in early 2020, except Galwan, from where there has been a mutual withdrawal.

On the night of 30 August 2020, the situation changed dramatically. The Indian army, accompanied by Special Forces (Special Frontier Force composed of Tibetan volunteers), occupied five major features along a ridgeline on Kailash Range, south of

Epilogue

Pangong Tso, that is, Magar Hill, Gurung Hill, Mukhpari, Rezang La and Rechin La. These tactically critical features are at heights of between 17,000 and 18,000 feet and they are on the Indian side of the LAC. They provide security to Chushul, which serves as a gateway to Leh. The Indians have rightly claimed that through this surprising and bold manoeuvre, they have thwarted China's intentions to alter the ground situation. The army has an official term for this, that is, 'quid pro quo', defined as an action to grab territory in exchange for a settlement. With all these dominating heights held by our troops, armour movements were not possible for the Chinese as they were squarely under the observation of the Indian infantry and armour. The much-touted Spanggur Gap was thus well covered from the Indian positions. These heights also opened up avenues for offensive options by India. Incidentally, all these features were the sites of bloody battles in 1962. These included the epic battle of Rezang La, where a company of the 13 Kumaon battalion, under Major Shaitan Singh, fought to the last man; 114 out of 123 men were martyred. Major Shaitan Singh was awarded the highest military decoration for gallantry, the Param Vir Chakra (Posthumously).

Based on the number of troops amassed by them, the Chinese were not in a position to carry out any meaningful offensive action. For that, they needed to build up at least three to five times more strength, which looked to be unlikely at that stage. Overall, the Chinese army is in the process of 'shaping the battlefield and creating firm bases', from where they can commence their operations in the next phase, which could be at any time in the next one to three years.

A conflict in this area is likely in the future. That could spread to an all-out conflagration. In such a scenario, China is likely to violate the territory of Bhutan (both in western and eastern

Bhutan) to turn the flanks of our defences in the eastern sector. India must prepare for this contingency at this stage itself.

For China, the areas that they feel could be threatened by the Indians are the Aksai-Chin Road, Shaksgam Valley and CPEC, in which they have invested USD 62 billion. This provides them with a critical axis to Gwadar Port. Similarly, Pakistan is looking for any opportunity to capture Siachen Glacier and then, with the Chinese on the other side in a contiguous flank, assist them to capture DBO and provide security to Gilgit-Baltistan and the Aksai-Chin area.

It must be remembered that this is the only area in the western sector that provides complementary objectives to China and Pakistan, where they can fight side by side and assist each other. It goes without saying that the LoC will definitely be activated by Pakistan, and India will be confronted with a two-front scenario, which is a difficult situation for any country to handle. However, India is prepared for it.

Let us visualize how the battle could progress. On the Pakistan side, Siachen Glacier takes them very close to Shaksgam Valley. Siachen is also located on the immediate flank of the critical Indian position of DBO. An infantry-led operation by Pakistan through Siachen could access the relatively unguarded and somewhat indefensible Nubra Valley and then the thrust could head for DBO. If they succeed, a continuous swathe of territory on the Karakoram Range could fall to Pakistan. This could broaden Pakistan's boundary with China and offer the two adversaries of India the ability to conduct operations in collusion to capture the entire Nubra and Shyok valleys. However, Siachen Glacier is difficult for Pakistan to capture and will be crucial to the success of this operation. It will be almost impossible for Pakistan to crack the Siachen defences, and this operation could stall at this stage. China could also put pressure on DBO from the Depsang area, and India is likely to be confronted with a difficult situation. That is why Depsang is so important. However, India has a strong hold in DBO, and it will be difficult for the Chinese to make a dent in these defences.

Ideally, the ultimate objective for China and Pakistan would be to force the Indian army to pull back to the Ladakh Range, but that is possible only if both the western and northern flanks of Ladakh are occupied. The Indian army's defence of Ladakh resting only on Ladakh Range will be an unacceptable contingency. Leh, the capital, would have in that case only one mountain range to provide it depth. However, India could reoccupy all the dominating heights in Chushul (Kailash Range, which are our own areas) and with that China will have no chance of succeeding in this area.

The scenario given above is purely hypothetical, but it is a possible one. The Indian army would never allow it to succeed. On the other hand, it offers Pakistan and China a fruitful option, which they would not like to miss. Hence, a war in the near future is not unlikely, and India needs to remain prepared.

The Indian army is already preparing for a conflict in this sector. Both Pakistan and India have almost mirror-like deployments in this area. Both sides have concentrated over 50,000 troops each in the region. Thanks to the proxy war by Pakistan, the Indian army is combat-hardened and ably led by commanders at all levels. High-altitude warfare also comes naturally to them as they have been deployed in Siachen Glacier since 1984. Facing such live situations as in Ladakh is nothing new to them and they have already adapted well to combat in these altitudes.

The Indian air force has built up significant strength in this area and is already flying numerous combat sorties. Air Chief Marshall

R.K.S. Bhadauria, in an interview on 4 July 2021, mentioned that the Chinese, even though they have withdrawn from the forward areas, are strengthening their infrastructure and air power in a big way in the immediate depth areas. The Indian navy has also gone into operational mode. Another major development has been the opening of the Atal Bihari Vajpayee Tunnel (previously known as Rohtang Tunnel) from Manali to Leh, which will enable the movement of heavy vehicles round the year, thus significantly increasing India's logistic capabilities. With all these developments, I am certain that India will give a very good account of itself should a war take place. We, however, need to prepare for it in a systematic manner and at an intense pace.

On the diplomatic side, on 5 September 2020, there were inconclusive talks between Defence Minister Rajnath Singh and his Chinese counterpart on the sidelines of the SCO meet in Moscow. On 10 September, similar talks were held between the two foreign ministers at the SCO summit. Some decisions were arrived at to de-escalate the situation. But the follow-up will naturally come with many problems. The trust deficit between the two sides is so complete that the uncertainty will remain until the Chinese show their honesty of purpose on the ground. The principle of the LAC as the basis for peace has failed and can no longer be relied upon. The ultimate solution lies in reaching a border settlement with China.

Confidence-building measures have not helped in the past, nor are they likely to help in the future. The Chinese have already opened fire on several occasions. The real question is whether China wants peace with India, or if it is ready to sacrifice its friendship with India on the altar of its goal to become the premier power in Asia and the world.

Defence Minister Rajnath Singh made a strongly worded statement in the Lok Sabha on 14 September 2020. He repeatedly named China for violating all border agreements with India and refusing to accept customary and traditional boundaries. He blamed China for attempting to unilaterally alter the status quo of the LAC and said that while India wanted to peacefully resolve the ongoing military confrontation, it was fully prepared to deal with any situation. He also emphasized that no one should doubt India's determination to safeguard its borders, as it believes that mutual respect and sensitivity are the basis for peaceful relations with neighbours. Lastly, the amassing of troops by China goes against the 1993 and 1996 pacts. Respecting and strictly observing the LAC is the basis for peace and tranquility in the border areas.

However, post the diplomatic efforts and corps commander level talks, the last being on 24 January 2021, a decision was reached that in phase one of the process, in the area on the north bank of Pangong Tso, India will hold positions up to Dhan Singh Thapa post (near Finger 3) and China will withdraw up to east of Finger 8. India will also vacate and pull back troops from the Kailash Range. I feel that in their anxiety to get India to vacate the heights along Kailash Range, the Chinese pushed for this agreement in phase one. Ideally, India should not have agreed to this pull back from the Kailash Range, since it is in our area and provided us with great operational leverage. However, both countries have pulled back troops in accordance with the agreement regarding the area of Pangong Tso.

In another round of diplomatic talks held on 25 June 2021 of the Working Mechanism for Consultation and Coordination on India-China Border Affairs (WMCC), both sides agreed to maintain dialogue and communication to reach a mutually acceptable solution for complete disengagement from all friction points along the LAC in eastern Ladakh to enable progress in overall bilateral ties. After the twelfth round of military talks between the corps commanders, disengagement from another friction point, Gogra, was carried out and all temporary structures dismantled on 4-5 August 2021. The two remaining friction points now are the Hot Springs and Depsang areas. The Ministry of External Affairs has clarified that it was agreed upon, in the interim, that the two sides will continue to ensure stability on the ground and prevent any untoward incidents.

The Quest for Peace and Prosperity

It is to India's credit that the momentous decision of 5 August 2019 received tremendous support within the country from different shades of people and political parties. Even internationally it was accepted as an internal matter of India. Yes, the confinement of the mainstream political leadership and the removal of internet facilities for a prolonged period drew some sharp adverse reactions. However, now with the release of all political leaders and full restoration of 4G and internet facilities, the situation has improved considerably. To cap it all, the prime minister's meeting with all mainstream political parties of J&K on 24 June 2021 brought a glimmer of hope in the union territory. Of course, everyone understands that this meeting was just a beginning and many more will have to follow.

The relative peace, reduced local recruitment and fall in militant activities in the Valley are all signs that the people have not rejected the Indian initiative altogether. This provides the government with an ideal ground to shape a peaceful and prosperous Jammu and Kashmir in the future.

The best way to that route will be to sincerely implement the prime minister's slogan of '*Sabka Sath, Sabka Vikas, Sabka Vishwas*' (development for all, with everyone's trust and cooperation). This will bring in homogeneity and a sense of brotherhood among the people in the two union territories. It will also help reduce radicalization and revive the region's old culture of Sufism and Kashmiriyat.

But this will require hard work backed by efficient administration in the two union territories. The perennial problem of lack of development must be solved. The introduction of job opportunities, excellent education facilities and infrastructure, as well as provisions to extend their trade in India as never before, will help immensely. Unfortunately, the pandemic has slowed down the process considerably, even though the Government of India has appreciably enhanced the annual budgets of the UTs.

All three provinces – Jammu, Kashmir and Ladakh – have their own aspirations. These will have to be identified, understood and worked upon with sensitivity and maturity. This will also bring them all closer to one other, because favouritism would hopefully have been eliminated.

The political process has already been revived and differences of opinion have been respected. Politicians, when sincere, have the capacity to arrive at workable solutions and consensus. The intent must be honest and visible to integrate J&K fully with India through the political, social, economic and psychological domains. The statehood of the UT of J&K must be restored at the earliest and at an opportune time. This has already been promised by the prime minister as well as the home minister during the all-party meeting of 24 June 2021.

Militancy in the region is not likely to disappear in a hurry. It may take eight to ten years, but the intensity is likely to decrease over time, as Pakistan's ability to create mischief will also reduce, as discussed in the book in the earlier chapters.

The Government of India must set a goal that Jammu and Kashmir will become a paradise on earth, as always dreamt by the people. That will be the road to peace, prosperity and our success!

Appendix A

Instruement of Accession of J&K State

INSTRUMENT OF ACCESSION OF ...J A M M U...A N D...KASHMIR STATE

WHEREAS the Indian Independence Act, 1947, provides that as from the fifteenth day of August, 1947, there shall be set up an independent Dominion known as INDIA, and that the Government of India Act, 1935, shall, with such omissions, additions, adaptations and modification as the Governor-General may by order specify be applicable to the Dominion of India;

AND WHEREAS the Government of India Act, 1935, as so adapted by the Governor-General provides that an Indian State may accede to the Dominion of India by an Instrument of Accession executed by the Ruler thereof:

NOW THEREFORE

I Shriman Indar Mahandar Rajrajeshwar Maharajadhiraj Shri Harisinghji Jammuu Kashmir Naresh Tatha Tibbet adi Deshadhipati Ruler of ...JAMMU...AND...KASHMIR...STATE............... in the exercise of my sovereignty in and over my said State Do hereby execute this my Instrument of Accession and

1. I hereby declare that I accede to the Dominion of India with the intent that the Governor-General of India, the Dominion Legislature, the Federal Court and any other Dominion authority established for the purposes of the Dominion shall, by virtue of this my Instrument of Accession, but subject always to the terms thereof, and for the purposes only of the Dominion, exercise in relation to the State of JAMMU AND KASHMIR (hereinafter referred to as "this State") such functions as may be vested in them by or under the Government of India Act, 1935, as in force in the Dominion of India on the 15th day of August 1947 (which Act as so in force is hereinafter referred to as "the Act").

2. I hereby assume the obligation of ensuring that due effect is given to the provisions of the Act within this State so far as they are applicable therein by virtue of this my Instrument of Accession.

3. I accept the matters specified in the Schedule hereto as the matters with respect to which the Dominion Legislature may make laws for this State.

4. I hereby declare that I accede to the Dominion of India on the assurance that if an agreement is made between the Governor-General and the Ruler of this State whereby any functions in relation to the administration in this State of any law of the Dominion Legislature shall be exercised by the Ruler of this State, then any such agreement shall be deemed to form part of this Instrument and shall be construed and have effect accordingly.

5. The terms of this my Instrument of Accession shall not be varied by any amendment of the Act or of the Indian Independence Act, 1947 unless such amendment is accepted by me by an Instrument supplementary to this Instrument.

6. Nothing in this Instrument shall empower the Dominion Legislature to make any law for this State authorising the compulsory acquisition of land for any purpose, but I hereby undertake that should the Dominion for the purposes of a Dominion law which applies in this State deem it necessary to acquire any land, I will at their request acquire the land at their expense or if the land belongs to me transfer it to them on such terms as may be agreed, or, in default of agreement, determined by an arbitrator to be appointed by the Chief Justice of India.

7. Nothing in this Instrument shall be deemed to commit me in any way to acceptance of any future constitution of India or to fetter my discretion to enter into arrangements with the Government of India under any such future constitution.

2

8. Nothing in this Instrument affects the continuance of my sovereignty in and over this State, or, save as provided by or under this Instrument, the exercise of any powers, authority and rights now enjoyed by me as Ruler of this State or the validity of any law at present in force in this State.

9. I hereby declare that I execute this Instrument on behalf of this State and that any reference in this Instrument to me or to the Ruler of the State is to be construed as including a reference to my heirs and successors.

Given under my hand this......2.6.16..........day of ~~August~~ OCTOBER, Nineteen hundred and forty seven.

Harisingh

Maharaja Dhiraj of Jammu and Kashmir State

I do hereby accept this Instrument of Accession.

Dated this..twenty-seventh..day of ~~August~~ October, Nineteen hundred and forty seven.

Mountbatten of Burma
(Governor-General of India)

Appendix B

The Ten Commandments Issued by the Chief of Army Staff, Based on Directions of the Supreme Court

1. Competence in platoon/company level tactics in counter-insurgency operations.
2. No meddling in civil administration.
3. Willingly carry out civic action with innovations.
4. Develop media interaction.
5. Respect human rights.
6. No rape.
7. No molestation.
8. No torture resulting in death or maiming.
9. No military disgrace.
10. Only fear God, uphold dharma and enjoy serving the country.

Appendix C

Kashmir - A New Chapter Begins

Presidential Proclamation Post,
5 August 2019

A New Chapter

In a momentous decision that should mark the beginning of a new chapter in Kashmir's history, the President of India issued the following notification this morning (August 5, 2019) which was placed in both houses of the Parliament:

MINISTRY OF LAW AND JUSTICE

(Legislative Department)

NOTIFICATION

New Delhi, the 5th August, 2019

G.S.R .551(E).— the following Order made by the President is published for general information:—

THE CONSTITUTION (APPLICATION TO JAMMU AND KASHMIR) ORDER, 2019

C.O. 272

In exercise of the powers conferred by clause (1) of article 370 of the Constitution, the President, with the concurrence of the Government of State of Jammu and Kashmir, is pleased to make the following Order:—

1. *(1)* This Order may be called the Constitution (Application to Jammu and Kashmir) Order, 2019.

    (2) It shall come into force at once, and shall thereupon supersede the Constitution (Application to Jammu and Kashmir) Order, 1954 as amended from time to time.

2. All the provisions of the Constitution, as amended from time to time, shall apply in relation to the State of Jammu and Kashmir and the exceptions and modifications subject to which they shall so apply shall be as follows:—

    To article 367, there shall be added the following clause, namely:—

    "(4) For the purposes of this Constitution as it applies in relation to the State of Jammu and Kashmir—

    (a) references to this Constitution or to the provisions thereof shall be construed as references to the Constitution or the provisions thereof as applied in relation to the said State;

    (b) references to the person for the time being recognized by the President on the recommendation of the Legislative Assembly of the State as the Sadar-i-Riyasat of Jammu and Kashmir, acting on the advice of the Council of Ministers of the State for the time being in office, shall be construed as references to the Governor of Jammu and Kashmir;

    (c) references to the Government of the said State shall be construed as including references to the Governor of Jammu and Kashmir acting on the advice of his Council of Ministers; and

    (d) in proviso to clause (3) of article 370 of this Constitution, the expression "Constituent Assembly of the State referred to in clause (2)" shall read "Legislative Assembly of the State".

RAM NATH KOVIND.

Index

Aam Aadmi Party (AAP), 223
Abdullah, Farooq, 88–89, 91–92, 97, 106–8, 191, 213, 223, 321–22, 354, 363, 365; advocacy, 108; all-party conference at house of, 223; coalition government of, 92; and dismissal of government, 92
Abdullah, Omar, 121, 354
Abdullah, Sheikh Mohammed, 24–25, 31–33, 35–41, 44–45, 51, 64, 78, 86, 88, 96, 107–8, 131, 213, 218, 301, 323; against plebiscite, 32; arrest of, 38, 40, 88; as chief minister, 39; death of, 88; Mullik on, 32; as prime minister of Jammu and Kashmir, 27, 41; release of, 88; speech at United Nations, 40; speech to the J&K Constituent Assembly, 41; visit to Rawalpindi, 64

accession of Kashmir, 26, 28, 36, 41, 65–66, 310; *see also* tribal aggression/invasion; Jammu and Kashmir War
Aerostats, 262
Afghanistan, 5, 8, 11, 14, 16–17, 66, 85, 91, 93–94, 106, 114, 157, 173, 184, 236–38, 258, 265, 312–13, 331, 338; American pullout from, 259, 313; Salma dam to, 331; Wakhan Corridor of, 11
Afghanistan National Army, 314
agitations, 15, 37, 119–20, 123, 125, 138, 161, 164, 298; of 2008, 164; as sponsored, 123; terrorism of, 165
Agra Summit, 133
Ahl-e-Hadith school/factions, 148, 161
Ahmed, Aziz, 77
Ahmed, Khaled, 347, 357

Index

Ajmer Sharif Dargah, 329
Akbar, and occupation of Kashmir, 4
Akhnoor, 70–71
Alam, Masarat, 220
Al Badar, 126
Ali, Chaudhry Muhammad, 60
alienation, 10, 126, 147, 187–88, 191–93, 215, 295
All Jammu and Kashmir Awami Action Committee, 98
All Jammu and Kashmir Plebiscite Front or Plebiscite Front, 39, 88–89, 105
All Parties Hurriyat Conference (APHC), 105–6, 118–19; and ISI, 162
Alms for Jihad, by Collins, 337
Alston, David, 137
Amarnath shrine, 324
Amarnath Shrine Board land dispute incident, 164
Amarnath Yatra, 103, 116, 120, 126–27, 165, 218, 222; attack on, 163
Anan, Kofi, 65
Anantnag, 138, 185
Andrabi, Asiya, 220
Anglo-Sikh wars, 2, 5
Anglo-US resolution, 57
Ansar Ghazwat-ul-Hind, (AGuH), 126, 239
anti-India elements, 123, 125, 143
anti-infiltration grid, 127, 158, 163, 357
anti-national elements, 119, 126, 141
anti-Shia riots, 15
Arab Spring, 125, 141
Armed Forces Special Powers Act (AFSPA), 99–103, 121, 123, 161–62, 187–88, 282, 285; and withdrawal option, 284
armed insurgency, 122, 326
army: attacks on camps of, 122, 163, (*see also* attacks; suicide attacks); operations, 161, 165, 283, *see also under separate entries*
Article 35A, abrogation of, xiv–xv, 44–45, 99, 184, 190, 194, 212–19, 221–25, 227, 229–31, 233–34, 241–42, 250–52, 257, 264, 275, 299–301, 303, 310, 341–42, 344–45, 349–50, 353, 362, 368
Article 170, 321
Article 356, 42, 215
Article 367, 232–33
Article 370: abrogation of, 39–42, 44–46, 87, 123, 169, 184, 190, 212–15, 218–19, 223, 225, 230–33, 237–38, 242–43, 245, 276, 294–95, 301, 304, 311, 332, 341, 349, 362, 365; Jagmohan on, 46; Nehru on, 46
Arunachal Pradesh, 45
Ashoka, Emperor, 3
Assad, Bashir, 273, 325, 328
Assam Rifles, 159
assassinations, 98
assembly elections, 88, 118, 191, 348; 2014, 191; of 1996, 118; of 2002, 118, *see also* elections; by-elections; civic body elections
asymmetrical warfare, Dershowitz on, 86
Atal Bihari Vajpayee Tunnel, 374
attacks, 22, 24, 58, 70–71, 103, 112, 114, 116, 121–22, 124, 126, 149, 163–64, 177–78, 189,

220, 263, 300, 332; on army camps, 122, 163; on police stations, 167, see also suicide attacks
Averell Harriman, W., 129–30
Awami National Conference, 362
Ayub Formula, 129–30
Azad, Ghulam Nabi, xvi, 364
azadi, 105, 126, 161, 173, 187, 239, 274, 296, 301, 304, 325–27
Azad Jammu and Kashmir (AJK), 7, 9–10, 12–13, 23, 58, 113, 132, 134, 205–6, 211; Council, 10, 206; Force, 69; Interim Constitution Act, 1974, 9; Legislative Assembly election ordinance, 207
Azad Jammu and Kashmir Act, 1970, 9
Azad Kashmir Constitution Act 1974, 13
Azhar, Masood, 114, 177, 182, 230, 358; declared as global terrorist, 182; release of, 114

backchannel: dialogues, 266, 268, 334; politics, 136, 268–69
Baglihar project, 260
Bahujan Samaj Party (BSP), 223
Bajaj, Pandit, 46
Bajwa, Gen., 236, 300, 366
Bakarwals, 88, 321, 343
Balakot air strike, 179, 181, 183, 249, 261, 332, 334
Balochistan, 299, 330
Baltistan, 6, 12–13, 55, 129, 206
bandhs (shutdowns), 138, 164
Bangladesh, 75, 78, 227, 235, 297, 300; creation of, 75, 235, 297
Bangladesh, Bhutan, India, Nepal (BBIN), 260;

Bangladesh-China-India-India-Myanmar (BCIM), 369
Banihal Pass, 222
Baramulla, 21–22, 26, 47, 69
Batalik areas, 109–10, 331
Batamaloo revolt, 162
BAT/rogue actions, 341
battle of Asal Uttar, 71
Beg, Mirza Mohammad Afzal, 39, 86
Belt and Road, see One Belt One Road initiative
Bengal Initiative for Multi-Sectoral Technical and Economic Cooperation (BIMSTEC), 260
Bhadarwah, 104, 222, 285
Bhadauria, R.K.S., Marshall, 374
Bharatiya Janata Party (BJP), 37, 81, 107–8, 123, 126–27, 166, 169, 190, 218–19, 224, 272, 293, 322, 327, 349–51, 365; and PDP, 166; withdrawing support to PDP, 126, 169, 190, 359
Bhartiya Jana Sangh, see Bharatiya Janata Party (BJP)
Bhimber, 2, 8
Bhutan, 227, 260, 372
Bhutto, Zulfikar Ali, 63, 73, 76–84, 94, 206, 208, 236, 292; and Lahore lobby, 79; and nuclear capability, 85, 331
Biden, 228, 366
bilateral agreements, 66, 76, 82, 226, 267, 292
Bin Laden, Osama, 357
bin Salman, Mohammed, 337
Bin Sultan, Mohammed, 356
Bloeria, Sudhir, 194, 205
Border Action Teams (BATs), 357
border, fencing of (see also counter insurgency (CI) grid), 115–17,

158, 163, 184, 187, 254, 262, 264, 296, 343
Border Security Force (BSF), 104, 187
BRICS (Brazil, Russia, India, China and South Africa)–BIMSTEC outreach summit in Goa, 261
Brown, William, Maj., 12, 47
Buddhists, 1, 16, 88
Budgam, 138, 185
Burke, Edmund, 128
Bush, George W., 212
by-elections: 2006, 118; 2018, 118, 191, *see also* elections

car bombs, 186, 246
ceasefire, 48, 76, 113, 115, 126, 292; of 1949, 9, 49; of 1971, 75, 79; in 2003 by Pakistan, 115; Dar declaring, 113; during Ramadan, 126
under UN auspice, 47
Central Reserve Police Force (CRPF), 104, 172, 176–78, 188, 221–22, 245, 248, 283–84, 304, 314
Chandni Chowk Bazar, as 'Operation Kashmir Almonds,' 338
Chasing Dirty Money, by Reuter, 338
Chenab, 55, 116, 187
Chennai Vision, 228
Chhamb–Jaurian sector, 70
Chhamb sector, 70
Chibal, 2
China, 7, 11, 15, 51–52, 63, 68, 73–75, 80, 85, 139, 182, 208, 210–11, 228–29, 237, 258, 265, 267, 287, 296, 305, 310, 335, 342; and border, 307; capturing areas in Aksai-Chin area, 316; ceded to, 67; human rights violation in, 226–27; and Pakistan, 16, 48; Pakistan ceded Shaksgam Valley to, 8, 316–17, 341
China–Pakistan Economic Corridor (CPEC) or Belt and Road, 8, 15–16, 210, 229, 237, 307, 369–70
China war, 1962, 63
Chitral Scouts, 47
Chittisinghpura massacre, 113
Churchill, Winston S., 20, 49
citizenship, 43
civic body elections, 164
civil administration, 100, 125, 151–52, 160–61, 165, 169
civilians, 103, 116–17, 119, 126, 149, 241, 248, 283; death of, 125, 164, 241, 283; terrorists victimising, 241
claymore mines, 111
climate change, 336
Clinton, Bill, 111
Clinton, Hillary, 156, 266
Collins, Robert O., 337
communalism, 27, 38
conflict, dimensions of, 143–44
Congress party, 88–90, 108, 115
corruption, 251–52, 275, 279–81, 328
counter-infiltration grid, 104, 109–10, 162–63, 166, 187, 238, 248
counter-insurgency (CI), 104, 109–10, 112, 152, 156–60, 163, 189, 284; operations, 156–60; warfare school, 158

counter-proxy-war operations, 332
counter-radicalization, *see* deradicalization
Covid-19 pandemic, 231, 246–47, 277, 335–36, 366, 368; and oil shock, 336
crowd dispersal, equipment for, 289–90
Cuban missile crisis, 268
Cunningham, George (Sir), 23
curfews, 138, 240, 247, 252
cyberspace, 139, 142, 147–48, 150, 155, 254
cyber warfare, 152, 154, 192

Dal Lake, 4, 122
Dar, Adil Ahmad, 112–14, 177, 189
Dark net, 140, 154
Daruwala, K.N., 207
Datta Khel, 13
Daulat Beg Oldi (DBO), 351
Davidson, Michael, 33
deception, 143; cyber, 140, *see also* cyberspace; cyberwarfare
Delhi Agreement, 1952, 27, 44
Delimitation Act of 2002, 321
demilitarization, 56, 59
democracy, 12, 26, 90, 137, 170, 203, 257, 291
demonetization, 263
Deo, Ranjit, 1–2
Deobandi sects, 114, 142, 150, 326, 329
deradicalization, 272–75, 316, 325–30, 347
Dershowitz, Alan, 86
Desai, Ranjana Prakash (J), 319, 322
Devadas, David, 171, 293, 304

Devasher, Tilak, 236
development: humanitarian aspects and, 323–25; socio-economic, 276–78
Development Process, 303–5
Dhaka, fall of, 75
Dhar, D.P., 82
Dhar, P.N., 77–78, 81–83
dialogues, 132, 136, 143, 190, 212, 248, 251, 256–57, 261, 264–66, 272, 301, 317–18, 334, 341; with Pakistan, 264–67; within state, 271–72
Diamer-Bhasha Dam, 15
Didda, Queen, 4
Diplomat's Diary, A by Kaul, 80
'disturbed areas,' 11, 99–100, 161
Disturbed Areas Act, 1976, 99
Dixon, Owen, Sir, 54–56, 128–29
Doda, 104
Dogra, Prem Nath, 37
Dogra rule, 5, 17
Doval, Ajit, 221, 223, 366
Dras, 47, 109–10, 331
drones, 239, 247, 262
drug money, 338, *see also* hawala transactions
Dulat, A.S., 18
Durand Line, 331

East India Company, indemnity to, 2
East Pakistan, 74; military crackdown on, 73; revolt in, 73
education, 126, 277, 301, 311
Eighty-Fourth Amendment Act, 2002, 320
Eisenhower, Dwight D., 130, 134, 218
e-jihad, 150

elections: 1983, 88; 1987, 89–91,
98, 113; 1996, 107; 2009
General, 119; rigging in 1986,
91, 161; in state, 106, 115;
voting patten in, 138
Emergency, 77
employment issue, 44, 146, 224,
251, 272, 293, 301, 304, 328,
330
Enforcement Directorate (ED), 220
European parliamentary delegation
visits Kashmir, 342
extra-judicial killings, 102
extremism, 142, 144, 162, 166,
220, 273, 325, 329, 340; Hilary
Clinton on, 156; Islamic, 343

Faesal, Shah, 119
fake: encounter, 119; money, 189
fanaticism, 327
Farooq, Mirwaiz Umar, 88–89,
98, 106, 119; house arrests of,
221
Farooq Abdullah–Rajiv Gandhi
Accord, 88–92
Al-Fatah-run Palestinian Authority,
309
Fateh, Zafar Abdul, 114
Fazl-ur-Rehman, Maulana, 358
fear psychosis, 99, 144
Financial Action Task Force
(FATF), 183, 229, 238, 303,
307, 330, 343, 345, 357; Black
List of, 358
floods of 2014, 122–24, 166, 204,
252, 280
foreign terrorists, 105–6, 166,
184–86, 188–89; *see also* global
terrorism

Forty-Second Amendment Act,
1976, 320
Frank, Katherine, 83
Frequency-hopping radio, 111
fundamentalism, 19, 97, 177, 242,
256, 292, 356, 361; Islamic, 97;
Rushdie on, 176

G-7 meeting in Paris, 227
Ganderbal, 185
Gandhi, Indira, 45, 74, 76–81,
83–84, 88, 292, 301
Gandhi, Mahatma, 28, 31, 291,
346–47
Gandhi, Rajiv, 89
Gauhar, Altaf, 111
Geelani, Syed Ali Shah, 113, 119,
162, 170
Generation of Rage in Kashmir, The,
by Devadas, 293
Geneva Protocol, 82
Ghani, Ashraf, fleeing to UAE, 259
Ghaznavi Force, 69
Ghazwat-ul-Hind, 298
Gilani, Pir Maqbool, 38
Gilgit Agency, 11, 55, 129
Gilgit-Baltistan-GB (as Northern
Areas), 2, 6–8, 11–15, 47,
55, 129, 193–94, 203, 205–6,
208–11, 229, 235, 264, 267,
296, 300, 305–7, 310, 330,
341, 345, 351, 368, 370, 372;
acquisition of, 16–17; central
rule from Islamabad in, 208;
general elections in, 16; protest
in, 13, 210; resolution for
province of Pakistan, 12; self-
governance in, 209; as status of
full province, 12

Index

Gilgit-Baltistan Council, 209
Gilgit-Baltistan Empowerment and Self-Governance Order 2009, 208
Gilgit-Baltistan Legislative Assembly, 209
Gilgit-Baltistan Order of 2018, 209
Gilgit Scouts, 12–13, 47
Gilgit Wazarat, 55, 129
Goel, A.K. (J), 232
Governor's Act, 96–97
Governor's rule, 92, 96, 104, 127, 169, 204, 219; on 19 June 2018, 219
Gracey, Gen., 22
Graham, Frank, 57–58
Grant, Ulysses S., 156
Gross State Domestic Product (GSDP), 277
Gujjars, 88, 321, 343
Gujral, Inder, 331
Gul, Mast, 105
Gulmarg, 22, 38, 69
Gupkar declaration, 362
Gupta, Sisir, 27, 29, 50
Gurez, 47
Gurmani, Mushtaq Ahmed, 206
Guru, Abdul Ahmed, assassination of, 98
Guru, Mohammed Afzal, hanging of, 121
Gwadar Port, 316

Hajipur Pass, 71
Haksar, 77, 82–83
Haqqani, Husain, 134, 315
Harkat-ul-Jihad-i-Islami (HUJI), 106, 114
Harkat-ul-Mujahideen (HUM), 106, 111, 114
Hasnain, Ata, 215, 273, 353, 359, 367
Hasnain, Syed Ata, Lt. Gen., 214–15, 273
Hassan, Gul, Lt. Gen., 75–76
hawala transactions, 145, 263, 338–39
Hazratbal mosque, 162; hair of Prophet Mohammed at, 103; loss of Holy Relic from, 38, 68, 105; terrorists in, 103, 105
Hazrat Sheikh Noor-ud-Din shrine, terrorists in, 105
hijacking/hostages of Air India flight IC 814, 114, 163, 177
Hindu–Brahmanical order, 3
Hindus, 4, 19, 26, 36, 88, 95, 98, 105, 311, 315, 323, 347
Hiranagar, army camp attack in, 122
Hizbul Mujahideen/Hizb-ul-Mujahideen (HM), 91, 103, 106, 111–14, 124, 169–71, 220, 239, 266, 358 killings in Azad Kashmir, 113
Hong Kong, 226; pro-democracy movement in, 342
Howdy Modi event, 302, 324, 341
Hua Chunying, 368
human bombs, 246, *see also* suicide attacks
human intelligence, need of, 245
human rights, 15, 105, 342; abuses, 119, 165; action against violation of, 172; activists, 241; of Muslims in Xinxiang, 342
Huntington, Samuel, 16

Hurriyat, 123, 165, 220, 240, 253, 293, 298
Hussain, Abid, 60
Hybrid warfare, 93, 192, 314

Ibrahim, Sardar Muhammad, 206
Ikhwan-ul-Muslimeen, 111–12, 157
Illicit, by Naím, 338
improvised explosive devices (IEDs), 106; explosion in Katra village, 115
India: national flag of, 39, 87; relations with Afghanistan and Iran, 258; and US friendship, 302; withdrawing Pakistan's most favoured nation status, 182
India-China War 1962, 129
Indian Air Force, 69, 179–80, 222, 374
Indian army, 22, 52, 70–71, 75, 102, 109–10, 115, 156, 158–60, 163, 266, 282; as part of the United Nations peacekeeping forces, 102
Indian Constitution, 35–36, 38, 44, 131, 318, 323
Indian National Congress, 36, 123
Indian Naval Ship (INS) Arihant, 262
Indian Ocean Rim Association (IORA), 260
Indian Parliament, 44, 57, 121, 177, 296, 305; resolution for PoK, 305, 316; terrorist attack on, 115, 332
Indian Peace-Keeping Force (IPKF), 159
India–Pakistan 'composite dialogue,' 115
India–Pakistan war of 1971, 49

Indira, by Frank, 83
Indira Gandhi, the 'Emergency' and Indian Democracy, by Dhar, 77
Indira Gandhi–Sheikh Abdullah Kashmir Accord, 39–40, 45, 86–88, 89, 215
Indo-Bangladesh Joint Command, surrendering to, 78
Indo-China war 1962, 68
indoctrination, anti-national, 143, 286
Indo-Pak Dialogue, 62–64
Indo-Pakistan war: of 1965, 64; of 1971, 45, 64, 86
Indo–Soviet Treaty of Peace Friendship and Cooperation, 74
Indo-Sri Lanka Peace Accord, 159
Indus Waters Treaty of 1960, 68, 259–60
infiltration, xix, xxi, 23, 70–72, 96–97, 105, 109, 115–17, 122, 143, 158, 161–63, 166, 185, 187, 189, 192, 222, 238–39, 243, 248, 300, 314, 325, 331, 341, 357, 359
information engagement, 150
information warfare, 174, 188
insaniyat, 137, 257, 292
Instrument of Accession, 7, 25, 27, 193, 235, 305, 310
insurgency, 72, 98–100, 109, 112, 142–43, 149, 152, 154, 157–58, 160–61, 163, 193, 270, 320; Pakistan-sponsored, 91
Integration of Indian States by Menon, 25
intelligence, 70, 139, 143, 188–89, 211, 245, 247, 270
intelligence agencies, 104, 106, 114, 122, 140–41, 177, 188–89, 211, 254, 270

Index

International Monetary Fund (IMF), 229, 238, 303, 307, 312, 330, 343, 357
international reaction for abrogation of article 370, 225, 231
Internet and Mobile Association of India (IAMAI), on internet users, 139
internet maulvis, 287; *see also* indoctrination
Inter-Services Intelligence (ISI), 85, 91, 93, 95, 97, 106–8, 112–14, 117, 139, 162, 211, 265–66, 292, 298, 325
Inter-Services Public Relations (ISPR), 150, 168
intra-regional tensions, 322
Intra-state issues, 317–22
IORA summit, 261
Iran, 17, 93, 184, 258–59, 356, 358
Iran-Iraq war, 93
irregular warfare, 93, 192
Islam, Salafi, 286
Islam, Wahabi, 85, 142, 148, 150, 189, 239, 255, 263, 278, 286, 325–26
Islamic, Jihad, 84–85, 94
Islamic State in Kashmir, 239
Islamic State of Iraq and Syria (ISIS), 126, 138, 166, 326
Islamism, 241, 310, 325
Islamist: ideology, 273, 326; radicals, 150, 154
Islamization, xxi, 85, 256, 296; *see also* radicalization
Islamophobia, 256
Ismailis, 6
Ismay, Lord, 21
Israel, creation of, 309
Israel–Egypt Peace Treaty, 309
Israeli–Palestinian conflict, 308
Ittehad-e-Millat, 148

Jagmohan, 46, 91, 215
Jahangir, Mughal gardens by, 4
Jaishankar, S., 313, 317, 333
Jaish-e-Mohammed (JeM), xxi, 114, 126, 177, 179, 182, 188, 230, 266, 283; camp at Balakot, attack on, 179; resolution to ban, 182
Jamaat-e-Islami, 105, 148, 168, 220
Jamaat-ud-Dawa (JuD), 182
jamaitis (hardliners), 240
jamhooriyat, 137, 257, 292
Jamiat Ulema-e-Islam, 358
Jamiat Ulema Hind, 329
jammaitis (fundamentalists), 145, 240
Jammu and Kashmir, 1–3, 5–8, 11, 13, 15–16, 27, 39, 41–46, 49–50, 56, 76, 88, 119–20, 125–26, 135–36, 138, 191–92, 207–8, 212–13, 215–18, 223–25, 233–35, 271–72, 274–76, 278–80, 294–95, 301, 305–7, 315–16, 317–21, 344–48; 2015 earthquake in, 15; accession of, 50; delimitation in, 319–22; languages of, 6; as, Muslim predominant state, 41; bifurcation of, 223, 340; as 'complex unitary system,' 145; constitution of, 42–43, 321; dispute, 27–40; history of, 1; Islamization in, 85; mainstreaming, 275–76; people in, 318; police, 184, 186–87; preferential treatment to, 204; as princely state, 27; revocation of special status of, 226;

strategic importance of, 16; as union territory, 318; zones of, 6
Jammu and Kashmir Awami League, 112
Jammu and Kashmir National Panthers Party, 322
Jammu and Kashmir Reorganization Act, 2019, 214, 240, 294–95, 302
Jammu and Kashmir War 1947-48, 46–47
Jammu Kashmir Liberation Front (JKLF), 98, 103, 111
Jammu Praja Parishad, 37
Jammu province, 47, 55, 89, 104, 115, 118, 122, 129, 164, 191, 272, 285, 317–18, 321, 323, 342
Jammu–Samba sector, 71
Jammu–Srinagar sector, 70
jazia, 230
Jhangar, 47
jihadis, 139–40, 147–48, 154, 166, 173, 182, 230, 298, 300, 315
Jinnah: for liberating J&K, 22; on Pakistan, 297; M.A., 94
J&K Reorganisation Act 2019, 97, 286, 322
Jones, Terry, 120
Juvenile management, 288, *see also* youth

Kachru, Dwarka Nath, 33
kaffirs, 166
Kailash range, 371, 376
Kamraj plan, 38
Kandahar, 114, 177
Karachi Agreement 1949, 13, 205
Karakoram Highway, 8, 316

Karakoram Range, 373
Kargil, 8 Mountain Division to, 110
Kargil Misadventure and Continuing Terrorism, 163
Kargil sector, 8–9, 13, 17, 47, 55, 71, 90, 109–11, 129, 163, 173, 214, 216, 223–24, 248, 271, 278, 296, 317–18, 325, 331, 341; Pakistan infiltration in, 163
Kargil–Tangdhar, 71
Kargil war, 95–96, 107, 108–11, 157, 174, 179, 268, 311
Kartarpur Corridor, 230
Kartarpur Gurudwara, 230
Kashm, separatism of, 162, 215, 310
Kashmir, 5–6, 47, 54–55, 64, 72, 98, 118, 120, 122, 124–26, 129, 156, 302–3, 316–30; and 1971 war, 76; as bilateral issue, 227–28, 235, 257, 312; in Buddhist–Brahmanical order, 3; Buddhist monasteries in, 3; freedom movement, 162, 166, 168; history of, 3–7; imbroglio, 164, 311; Muslims of, 19, 34–35, 148, 173, 255, 323–24; narrative, 253; Pakistan-sponsored proxy war in, 114, 158; province, 191, 317; Ranjit Singh invading, 5; resolutions, 65; return of Bollywood to, 121
Kashmir: A Study in India–Pakistan Relations, 6, 22, 26, 50, 59–60, 129
Kashmir Conspiracy Case, 38
Kashmir in Comparative Perspective, 90

Index

Kashmiri Pandits, 19, 95, 98, 103, 145, 251, 255, 315, 321–23, 348, 365; fleeing of, 98; return of, 103, 251
Kashmiris/Kashmiriyat, 17–19, 26, 28, 31–33, 50, 52, 71–72, 97, 121–23, 134–35, 137, 139, 164, 172–73, 190–91, 194, 215, 241–42, 251, 255–57, 274–75, 277–78, 286–88, 292, 294–96, 301, 303–4, 309–11, 317–18, 343–47; Devadas on, 301; fear of, 296; perceived victimhood of, 301; unrest over killing of innocent, 164
Kasuri, Khurshid Mahmud, 48, 72, 133, 135
Kathua, 285
Kaul, T.N., 80
Keran, 47
K File, by Assad, 273
Khan, Akbar, Maj. Gen., 22
Khan, Asghar, ACM, 75–76
Khan, Ayub, Gen., 39, 62–63, 68–69, 72–73, 130, 134, 206, 208
Khan, Imran, 184, 236, 265, 299, 312, 355–58; visit to China, 228; visit to US, 236, 299
Khan, Liaquat Ali, 58
Khan, Mirza Hassan, 13
Khan, Nayeem, 298
Khan, Sardar Muhammad Ibrahim, 58, 205
Khan, Yahya, 75–76, 206
Khemkaran–Valtoha, 70–71
Khrushchev, Nikita, 269
Khunjerab Pass, 16
Khurshid, K.H., 206
Khyber Pakhtunkhwa, 8, 11, 15, 299
killing, 86, 99, 111–13, 115, 121, 124, 167, 185, 221, 288; in Christchurch, 256; of panchayat members, 121; of terrorists, 117, 121, 186
Kishanganga project, 260
Kishtwar, 55, 104, 222
Kissinger, Henry, 74, 269
Kokernag, 292
Kotli, 47
Krishan Reddy, G., 321
Krishna Menon, V.K., 61
Kuka Parray, *see* Parray, Mohammad Yusuf as Kuka Parray
Kulgam, 138, 185

Ladakhis, xiv–xviii, 2, 5–7, 9, 11, 13, 55, 108–9, 129, 131, 135, 138, 191, 214, 216, 223–25, 256–57, 271–72, 303, 305–6, 317–19, 341–42, 344, 347–48, 351–53, 355–56, 362, 367–69, 373–74, 376–77
Ladakh region, 2, 5–7, 9, 11, 13, 45, 55, 90, 108–9, 129, 131, 135, 173, 191, 210, 214, 216, 223–25, 237, 248, 257, 271, 295, 305–6, 317–18, 322, 325, 341, 344, 347; Aksai-Chin, xiv, 7–8, 210, 227, 305, 310, 316, 341, 352, 370, 372
Lal, Pyare, 31
Lalitaditya, 4
Lashkar-e-Taiba (LeT), xxi, 47, 106, 111, 114, 164, 230, 239, 266, 307, 332
Lawrence, Walter Roper, 17
legislative assembly elections 2014, 122

Leh, 13, 47, 278, 296
Liberation Tigers of Tamil Eelam (LTTE), 159
Lieutenant General Philip Campose Committee, 263
Life in Diplomacy, A, Rashgotra, 82
Line of Actual Control (LAC), 237, 353, 375–76
Line of Control (LoC), xvii, xxi, 76, 78–79, 81–84, 94–97, 109, 111, 113, 115–17, 122, 158, 161–62, 166, 168, 179–80, 184, 187, 189, 222, 248–49, 262, 264, 282, 284, 296, 300, 332, 341; as international border, 82, 341; terrorist crossing over, 105
Lockhart, Robert Gen., 22–23
Lok Sabha parliamentary elections of May 2019, 218
Lolab, 292
Lone, Abdul Ghani, 91
Lone, Mohammad Akbar, 322

Madhok, Balraj, 6
Madodi, Maulana, 98
madrasas, 150, 173, 286–87
Malaysia, 229, 253, 273, 302, 342
Maldives, 227
Malik, Akhtar Hussain, Maj. Gen., 69
Malik, Yasin, 220
Mandela, Nelson, 128
Manekshaw, S.H.F.J. FM., 68
Mangat Rai, E.N., 72
Mangla Dam, 10
Mao Tse-tung, 334
Martin, Kingsley, 53
Masoodi, Hasnain (J), 322
Mass Non-Violent Civil Disobedience Movement, 244

mass rebellion, 244–46
maulvis, 142, 286–87, 312, 326
McNaughton, Andrew, Gen., 54
Mecca Grand Mosque, 93
Mendhar–Rajauri, 69
Menon, V.P., 22, 24–26
militancy in J&K, 92–93, 95–96, 100, 104, 106–8, 110–11, 117–18, 124, 127, 138, 142, 160, 163, 169, 172, 174, 184–86, 188–89, 192, 216, 220, 238–40, 243, 247–48, 281, 287–88, 291–93, 341, 343–44, 346
Militancy Post, 127, 169
Mirpur, 8, 47, 210–11; as mini Bradford, 210
Mirza, Iskander, Gen., 60–61
Mishra, Brajesh, 18
Mishra, R.K., 268
Mission Kashmir, 217–25
Mizoram, 45, 158–59; civil–military synergy, 159
mobile network, 240, 279
mob protests, 119
Modi, Narendra, 45, 214, 218–19, 223, 227, 234, 265, 280, 294, 324, 332, 340, 342, 351, 364; on development for Kashmir, 347; on diversity, 342; meeting Trump, 227; for 'New Kashmir,' 294; visit to Russia, 226
Mohamad, Mahathir, 357–58
Mohammad, Bakshi Ghulam, PM of J&K, 38, 62
mosques, 103, 143, 150, 173, 189–90, 273, 286, 325
Mountbatten, Louis, Gov. Gen., 21, 24–25, 31, 65–66
Mufti, Mehbooba, 126, 219, 293, 303, 354, 365

Mughal empire, 1, 3–5, 17
Muhammad, Ghulam, Gov. Gen., 59–61
mujahideen, 110
Mukherjee, Syama Prasad, 37, 218; Shah on, 219
Mukti Bahini, 74
Mullik, B.N., 32
Mumbai terror attack, 164, 332
Muni, S.D., 369
Munshi, K.M., 31
Musa, Zakir, 138, 167–68, 170–72, 239, 242, 256, 272, 298; elimination of, 171;
Musharraf–Manmohan Singh formula, 267
Musharraf, Pervez, Gen., 14, 48, 65, 111, 115, 133–34, 210, 264, 292–93; 331; four-point formula of, 134; JeM attempts on, 266
Musharraf–Vajpayee formula, 267
Muslim League, 94, 112, 297
Muslim population, 31, 173–74, 274, 342
Muslim United Front's (MUF), 90
Muzaffarabad, xvi, 8, 22, 26, 47, 63, 117, 165, 211, 358; capital of PoK, 8
Muzzafrabad-Uri, 21
My Frozen Turbulence in Kashmir, by Jagmohan, 46, 90–91, 215

Nagaland, 158
Naik, Niaz A., 268
Naím, Moisés, 338
Nariman, Rohinton (J), 232
narratives, 12, 38, 80, 112, 141, 149, 153–54, 164, 168, 171, 237, 240, 242, 253–54, 299, 327, 349, 366, 368
National Conference, 6, 22, 24–25, 33, 37, 62, 78, 88–90, 92, 97, 106–7, 115, 123, 362; first election win of, 33; winning 1977 election, 88; winning 1996 election, 106
National Conference –Congress alliance, 89
National Democratic Alliance (NDA), 106
National Investigation Agency (NIA), 220, 280, 339
national security strategy, 250
Naushera, 47
Naya (New) Kashmir, 212–13
Nazaria-i-Pakistan, 235
Neelam Valley, 8, 47
negotiations, direct, 59–64
Nehru, Jawaharlal, 24, 30, 32, 38–41, 44, 46, 52–53, 57–59, 62, 64–65, 130–31, 133, 213, 218, 350; death of, 39; and Kashmir, 31; and plebiscite, 31; on proposals of Pakistan, 28–29; and Sheikh's anti-India activities, 38; speech of Independency day, 217; on Western powers, 63
Neither A Hawk Nor A Dove, by Kasuri, 133
Nekowal, border clash at, 60
Nepal, 227, 300
New Industrial Development Scheme, 277
Nicholon, Emon, 15
1947-48 war. *See* Jammu and Kashmir War
Nissar, Qazi, 98

Nixon, President, 269
Noon, Feroze Khan, 61–62
Noorud-Din, Hazrat Sheikh, 105
Noor-ud-Din, Sheikh as Nund Rishi, 19, 105
normalcy, 103, 106–8, 112, 154, 157, 163, 307
Northern Areas, 7, 11, 13–14, 47–48, 54, 134; *see also* Karachi Agreement 1949
Northern Areas Legislative Council (NALC), 14
North Korea, 184, 267, 358
nuclear doctrine, of 'no first use,' 261
Nuclear Suppliers Group (NSG), 369
nuclear war, 230, 237, 296, 299, 341
nuclear weapons, 75, 94, 249, 262
Nund Rishi, *see* Noor-ud-Din, Sheikh as Nund Rishi

OGW network, 359
One Belt One Road initiative, 8
Operation Parakram, 115
Operation Pawan, in Sri Lanka, 159
Operation Sadbhavna, 151–52, 162–63, 254, 278
Operation Vijay, 110
Organisation of Islamic Countries/ Cooperation (OIC), 174–75, 227, 229, 258, 300, 354, 356; Swaraj as guest of honour at, 174
Over Ground Workers (OGWs), 127

'Pak-American Pact,' 217
Pakistan, 189, 229–30; 1965 War, 68–73, 130; 1971 War, 73–76, 84–85, 94, 331; areas ceded to Cina, 316–17; debt of, 229; army, xxi, 22, 47, 63, 66, 73–74, 93, 96–97, 107–9, 115, 139, 183, 211, 236, 249, 265–66, 298, 333–34; Eastern Wing of, 73–74; economic and military cost and, 332–33; F-16 jets near Rajouri area, 180; on FATF's grey list, 343; 'full spectrum deterrence' of, 181; IMF loan to, 312; India and, 330–31; invasion of Kashmir, 7; ISI of, 93, 193, 282, 298; ISPR (Inter Services Public Relations) of, 150; and militants, 140; military coup in 2001, 111; as Muslim State, 34; occupation by aggression, 316; Operation Badr of, 109, 111; Operation Gibraltar of, 69–71; Operation Grand Slam, 70–71; Operation Gulmarg, 22; Operation Topac, 95–96; practice of breaking agreements, 30; as problem state, 312; propaganda of, 125, 164, 166, 216, 237, 253; sponsored cyberspace, 142; sponsored terrorism/proxy war, 123, 137, 158, 160, 178, 263, 311, 325; strategic relationship with China, 48, 85; strategy of, 71, 96, 110, 172–75, 184, 261; and terror groups, 182, 258, 300; training camps, 117; training Kashmiri youth, 161; and Tulbal project, 260; and United States, 72; unrest over 1996 Legislative Assembly Elections, 207; Ziring on, 236

Pakistan and China, 307, 315, 353, 355, 367–76; nexus, 16; boundary agreement, 68
Pakistan-occupied Kashmir (PoK), 6–12, 15, 69–70, 76, 79, 81, 83–84, 111, 113, 117, 131–32, 135, 161–62, 178–79, 181, 193–94, 203, 205–8, 210–11, 229, 353, 235, 237, 264, 267, 296, 299–300, 305–7, 310, 316, 341, 345; and Gilgit-Baltistan, 15, 193–211, 229, 235, 264, 267, 296, 300, 306, 310, 341, 345; legislative assembly elections in 1996, 207; unrest in, 207, 210
Pakistan Peoples Party (PPP), 14
Palestine: Arab revolt in, 308; conflict in, 308–9; vs. and Kashmir Problems, 308–11
panchayat elections, 118; in 2005, 118; in 2018, 191, 220
Pandita, Rahul, 177
Pant, K.C., 108
paramilitary forces, 104, 159–62, 172, 183, 271, 288, 341; see also under *separate entries*
parliamentary elections, 118, 191, 218, 293; in 1996, 106, 118; in 1998, 106, 118; in 1999, 118; in 2004, 118; in 2019, 191, 293
Parray, Mohammad Yusuf as Kuka Parray, death of, 112
Parthasarathy, G., 86, 369
Partition (*see also* transfer of power), 3, 6–7, 16, 39–40, 49, 55–56, 67, 78, 94, 128, 132, 173, 235, 255, 297
Pascal, Blaise, 176
Pashtuns, 14; in Rohilkhand, 14

Patel, Sardar Vallabhbhai, 21, 31, 33, 365; Singh on, 42
Pathan campaign, 53
Pathankot, 351, 357
People Next Door, The, by Raghavan, 75, 134
Peoples Conference, the CPI(M), 362
Peoples Democratic Party (PDP), 106, 115, 124, 166, 219, 272, 293, 362
perception: management, 137, 139–40, 144, 144–49, 151, 152–255
Permanent Indus Commission, 260
Pervez Musharraf–Manmohan Singh Formula, 134–36
petrodollars, 263, 343, 346
physical connectivity, 278–79
pilgrims, 103, 118, 120, 126, 222, 230
Pir Panjal Range, 5–6, 69, 104, 164, 270, 272
plebiscite, 24, 26, 31–32, 47–52, 54–55, 59–60, 62, 65–66, 72, 129–31, 267; and Mediatory Efforts by UN, 64–67; Mullik on, 32; Pakistan demanding for Kashmir, 130; and UN, 48–59
Plebiscite Front, *see* All Jammu and Kashmir Plebiscite Front
police, 98, 118, 120, 123, 152–53, 156, 162, 169, 171–72, 221–22, 245, 248, 270–71, 278, 281, 304, 311, 326, 328; security of, 281
Policy of Strategic Restraint, 331–32
political prisoners, 29, 288–89
Poonch, 2, 6, 8, 21, 23, 47, 55, 71, 90, 116; rebellion in, 21

post-Burhan Wani's elimination, 186
Power, Jonathan, 135
president's rule, 43, 215, 233
Print media, 148, 233
propaganda, 72, 125, 139, 142, 144, 150, 248, 253, 257–58, 286–87; through Social media, 144
pro-Pakistan forces, 89
prosperity subsystem, 146–47
Proxy War, xx, xxii, 87, 89, 92, 94–97, 105, 107, 109–11, 114–15, 141, 143, 157–58, 160–61, 174–75, 181, 183, 204, 216, 249–50, 252, 254–55, 264–65, 267, 289, 314, 333–34, 340–41, 351–52, 360; 1993-96, 103–6
public interest litigations (PILs), 102
Public Security Act (PSA), 286, 288
Pulwama, 351; attack, 138, 176–84, 185, 188–89, 219, 239, 249, 257, 283, 300, 341
Punjab, 2, 5, 85, 93, 156, 160, 210, 230, 328; anti-militancy campaign in, 160; British annexed, 5
Puri, Mohinder, Lieutenant General, 110

Al-Qaeda, 114, 126, 168, 171, 229–30, 239, 313
Quadrilateral Security Dialogue (QSD as Quad), 353–54
Quran-burning controversy 2010, 120
Qureshi, Fazlul-Haq, 113
Qureshi, Hashim, 208

Qureshi, Shah Mehmood, 227, 343, 355

radicalization, 92, 95–96, 123, 137–40, 142–43, 145–48, 161, 166, 173–74, 177, 184, 186–90, 192, 239, 242, 255–56, 272–73, 281, 287, 294–95, 298, 301, 310–11, 323, 325–26, 328, 330, 343, 346, 361; countering, 150–51, 255–56; of youth by ISIS, 138
radicals, 150, 154, 166, 184, 273
radio-controlled IEDs, 111
Rage of Kashmir, by Devadas, 171
Raghavan, T.C.A., 75, 134
Rajagopala, Chakravarti (Rajaji), 130–31; (*see also* Rajaji-Abdullah Formula); to Shiva Rao, 132
Rajaji–Abdullah Formula, 130–33
Rajiv–Farooq Accord, 89, 92
Rajouri–Poonch sector, 69–70, 88
Raj to Swaraj, by Sinha, 26
Ramana, N.V., 233
Ramnagar, 2
Rao, Shiva, Rajaji to, 132
Rasgotra, M.K., 82
Rashtriya Rifles (RR), 110, 157, 222, 248
Rashtriya Swayamsevak Sangh (RSS), 108, 217–18
Rather, Abdur Rahim, 97
Rathore, Mumtaz Hussain, 207
RDX, 177, 189
Reagan, Ronald, 86
recruitments, 127, 139–40, 147–48, 166–67, 184, 192, 239, 243, 304, 325, 357, 359, 377; of local militants, 127; by terrorist

Index

organizations, 127, 139, 147–48, 166–67, 184, 192, 239, 304, 325
Rehman, Mujibur, 73; arrest of, 74
Reorganisation Act, 97, 233, 286
reorganization, 7, 250, 299, 303
Representation of People Act of 1957, 321
Research and Analysis Wing (RAW), 18
Resettlement Act, 96–97
resistance, 171, 343, 346; *see also* protest
Rohtang Pass, 109
Rushdie, Salman, 176

Sadhbhavna (Good Intentions) to Yakeen (Trust, 151
Sadiq, G.M., 215
Sadr-i-Riyasat, 27, 41–42, 87, 215, 315
Saeed, Hafiz, 220, 230, 266
Salafi, 85, 166, 255, 286
Salahuddin, Syed, *see* Shah, Mohammad Yusuf
Samba, 285; army camp attach in, 122
Sandys, Duncan, 129
Saran, Shyam to Thapar, 368
Sardar Patel: Unifier of Modern India, 25, 43
Saudi Arabia, 93, 227, 258, 336–38, 346, 354–56; Pakistani troops in, 93
Sayeed, Mufti Mohammed, 98, 106, 112, 115, 123–24
Sayeed, Rubaiya, kidnapping of, 98
Scheduled Castes and Tribes, 322
Security Forces in J&K, xvii, 100, 102–7, 112, 117, 119–22, 124, 126, 138, 140, 145–46, 150, 153, 160, 160–69, 172, 178, 183, 186, 188, 220, 241, 245, 249, 257, 269, 283, 288–89, 314, 326; attacks against, 126; seige to shrine, 105
separatism, 174, 281, 287
Shah, Amit, 217, 219, 223, 231, 366; visit to J&K, 191–92
Shah, Ghulam Mohammad, 89
Shah, Ghulam Mohiuddin, 90
Shah, Javed Ahmed, 112
Shah, Mohammad Yusuf, 91, 113–14, 220, 358
Shah, Shabir, 220
Shah, Syed Mohammed Yusuf, 90
Shah Jahan, Chashme Shahi gardens by, 4
Shaksgam Valley, xiv, 8–9, 210, 227, 310, 316–17, 341, 351, 370, 372–73; Pakistan cedeint it to China, 8
Shamshabari Range, 5
Shanghai Cooperation Organization, 366
shariah/shariya law, 168, 170–71, 239, 242, 313
Sharif, Raheel, Gen., policy of a 'thousand revolutions,' 174
Sharif, Nawaz, 111; dissolving PoK government, 207
Sharma, Jugal Kishore, 322
Sherwani, Maqbool, 22
Shias, 5–6, 14, 88, 173, 216, 318, 343
Shimla Accord, 66
Shopian, 90, 138, 185, 239, 292; rape and murder case, 119
Shourie, Arun, 264

Shri Amarnathji Shrine Board, transfer of forest land to, 118, 191
Siachen Glacier, 8, 17, 109, 115, 351, 373
Siachen operation, 96
Sibal, Kanwal, 184, 237
Sikandar, 4
Sikh militancy in Punjab, 85
Sikh rule, 5
Sikhs, 1–2, 17, 26, 103, 113, 230, 311, 343
Sikkim, 45
Simla Agreement, 49, 64–65, 76–84, 94, 267, 292, 296, 350
Singapore, 274
Singh, Amarinder Capt., 230
Singh, Dhyan, 2
Singh, Duleep, 2
Singh, Ghansara, Brigadier, 12, 47, 193
Singh, Gulab, 2–3, 5
Singh, Hari, Maharaja, 3, 20, 24, 26–27, 31, 41, 235, 305, 310; elected as Sadr-i-Riyasat, 41
Singh, Jitendra, 322
Singh, Karan, 31; as Sadar-i-Riyasat of Jammu and Kashmir, 27, 41, 315
Singh, Manmohan, 1, 136, 264, 293; and All Party Hurriyat Conference discussion, 118
Singh, Pratap. Maharaja, 18
Singh, Rajinder, Brig., 21; martyring of, 22
Singh, Rajnath, 262, 375
Singh, Ranjit, Maharaja, 2, 5
Singh, R.N.P., 25, 33, 42–43
Singh, Sardar Swaran, 63
Singh, Suchet, 2

Singh, Tavleen, 326
Sinha, S.K., Lt. Gen., 26, 286–87
Skardu, 6, 12–13, 47
smartphone users, 139
Snedden, Christopher, 19
Social media, 124–25, 138–42, 144, 146–50, 153, 165–66, 168–69, 174, 186, 188, 252, 254, 279; Alston on, 137; Arab Spring and, 141; 'asymmetric operations' and, 140; Internet and Mobile Association of India (IAMAI) on usage of, 139; Ukraine-Russia conflict and, 141
social media platforms, 139–41, 144, 148, 150, 166; Facebook, 139–40, 144; LinkedIn, 140; Skype, 148; Twitter, 139–40; WhatsApp, 144, 148; YouTube, 140, 144, 169
Sopore, 22, 112, 114, 121; as liberalized zone, 161
South Asia Terrorism Portal (SATF), 127
Southeast Asia Treaty Organization (SEATO), 66
south Kashmir, 98, 113, 124, 138, 168–70, 173, 176, 185, 239, 246, 273
Soviet Union, 62–63, 72–75, 173; invasion of Afghanistan, 93; withdrawal of Afghanistan, 93
Special Forces battalions, 188
Special Operations Group (SOG), 112, 162
Special Task Force (STF), 162
Sri Lanka, 134, 156, 158–59, 227
Srinagar, 3, 24, 26, 68, 70–71, 90, 113, 117–18, 135, 137, 153,

170, 176–77, 185, 191, 221, 225, 257, 278, 287, 292; by-elections 2018, 191
Standstill Agreement, 21
state assembly elections 2014, 166
State Autonomy Commission's report, 107
statehood, restoration of, 296, 345, 348
sting operation, 298
stone pelting, 119, 123, 164, 167–68, 172, 188, 190, 220, 246, 283, 286, 293, 338, 359; and social media, 165–69
street turbulence, 174, 241, 246; *see also* stone pelting
Subrahmanyam, B.V.R., 219
Sufism, 17, 95–96, 142, 148, 150, 164, 251, 255, 274, 329, 361, 377
suicide attacks, 111, 116, 186; on CRPF convoy, 176; J&K legislature complex, 177; in Kaluchak, 115; in Sunjuwan army camp, 115
Sunnis, 4, 88, 173
Supreme Court, xv, 10, 13, 42, 101, 121, 208, 225, 231–33, 282, 285–86, 322
Surankote, attack on village defence committee, 116
surgical strike on terrorist training centre, 263, 334
Swami, Gopal, 33
Swami, Parveen, 113
Swaraj, Sushma, 175
Sweatshirt, Earl, on communication, 137

Tagore, Rabindranath, 346

Taliban, 114, 230, 259, 266, 312–13, 315, 357, 365
Tangdhar sector, 71
Tehreek-e-Jihad-e-Kashmir (TJK), 113
Tehreek-ul-Mujahideen, 126
Tellis, Ashley J., 228
Telugu Desam Party (TDP), 223
terrorism, 92, 95, 112, 116, 120, 143, 145–46, 162, 165, 167, 178, 182–83, 212, 216, 236, 240, 243, 257–61, 264, 266, 307, 312, 317–18, 320, 330, 332, 335–37, 343, 345, 347–48; attacks of, 186; Bush on, 212; countering, 248–90; cross-border, 111; funding of, 220, 229, 263, 298, 335, 337–38, (*see also* hawala transactions); Gandhi on, 291; global/international, 303, 341, 366; grid against, 162, 187; Hillary Clinton on, 266; measures against, 127; Modi on, 340; Reagan on, 86; and Saudi Arabia funding, 335–39; Singh on, 1
terrorists: inside Pakistan, 178, 181; leadership, elimination of, 186; network, 263, 337; organizations, 111, 140, 239, 249, 332, 338; radicalization of, 147; tanzeems, 161, 168; using steel bullets, 186
Thackrey, Bal, 108
Thakre, Kushabhau, 108
Thapar, Karan, 368
Tibet, xvi, 226, 296, 342
tourism, 12, 15, 102, 121, 126, 165, 251, 324–25

Track II diplomacy, 136
training camps, 165, 178, 187, 249, 267
Tral, 169–71, 292
transfer of power, 3, 259
trans Himalayan connectivity network, 369
Trans-Karakoram Tract, 7–8
Treaty of Amritsar, 2, 5
Treaty of Lahore, 5
tribal aggression/invasion, 23, 25, 37, 52, 57, 61, 65–66, 163, 218, 305, 310, 316, 331
Truman, Edwin M., 338
Trump, 227, 236, 265, 299, 302, 312, 342; on India, 227; for mediation, 219, 299, 312
Turkey, 229, 253, 302, 342
two-nation theory, 297; *see also* Partition

Ude Desh Ka Aam Nagrik (UDAN) scheme, 279
Udhampur, 55, 285
Ulemae-Deen or Mushaikh, 9
UN–Dixon Partition Plan, 128–29
unemployment, 123, 147, 328, 344
Unified Headquarters, 104, 153, 165, 269–71, 284
union territories, 214, 223, 234, 250, 271–72, 275–76, 282, 295–96, 307, 317–18, 340, 345, 348; bifurcation as, 214
United Nations, 15, 29, 65, 128
United Nations Commission for India and Pakistan (UNCIP), 48, 53, 129
United Nations General Assembly, 129, 253

United Nations Human Rights Council (UNHRC), 253, 299
United Nations Security Council (UNSC), 29–30, 48, 51–54, 56, 58, 61–62, 63–65, 129, 182, 226–29, 253, 266, 299, 313, 330, 342, 354, 369; China and, 51; India approaching, 29; resolutions, 61, 330
United States, 33, 40, 73, 76, 129; 52, 57, 61, 63, 65, 68, 74–75, 93, 111, 114, 120, 129, 134, 182–83, 218–19, 226–27, 229, 258–59, 265–67, 287, 289–90, 302, 312–14, 317, 335–37, 342, 353–54, 357, 366, 372; Congressional Research Service, 355; Operation Rhino, 269; Pakistan as ally of, 114; Seventh Fleet into Bay of Bengal, 74; and Taliban Accord, 313–15
Unlawful Activities (Prevention) Act, 220
unmanned aerial vehicles (UAVs), 262
unrest, 94–95, 100, 138, 149, 160, 164, 190, 203; of 2008 and 2010, 164; after death of Wani, 167
uprising in 2016, 167
Uri sectors, 5, 21, 47, 69, 71, 177, 341, 351; incident in, 341
Uttarakhand, 45
Uyghur militants, 315

Vaishno Devi, 116, 120, 324
Vajpayee, Atal Bihari, 18, 108, 133, 137, 190, 257, 264, 266, 268, 292

Vande Bharat Express, 279
Varthaman, Abhinandan, Wg Cdr, repatriation of, 180
Versailles Syndrome, 82
violence, 126, 138, 149, 190, 216, 224, 239, 241, 246, 273, 275, 283, 301, 308, 325, 344, 347; in 1990, 92, 99; in 2013, 121; during 1983 election rigging, 89; during 2016-19, 124–27; in Kashmir, 122, 126, 148, 301, 325; return of, 124–27
Vivekananda, Swami, 346
Vohra, Narinder Nath, 315–16
Voice over Internet Protocol (VoIP), 148

Wani, Burhan/Burhan-ud-din-Wani, 138, 167, 169, 171, 185, 190, 221, 272, 288, 293; death of, 138, 149, 167, 169–71, 185, 189–90, 221, 246, 272, 288, 293, 298, 326; elimination of, 124, 169, 171
wars, 2, 16, 23, 46–47, 58, 70–72, 74–78, 81–82, 84–85, 94, 110, 115, 129, 132, 142, 154, 157, 178–79, 238, 255, 264, 300, 307, 309, 329, 331, 333, 337, (*see also under separate entries*); Grant on, 156
weapon snatching, 167
welfare measures, 165
Western powers, 63, 65
Widmalm, Sten, 90
Wilkinson, Paul, 234

Will the Iron Fence Save a Tree Hollowed by Termites? by Shourie, 264
women, 44, 119, 167, 283, 327–28
Working Mechanism for Consultation & Coordination on India-China Border Affairs (WMCC), 376
Wuhan, 228, 370

Xi Jinping, visit to India, 228
Xinjiang region of China, 11, 296

Yazdani, Assad, 113
Years of Renewal, by Kissinger, 269
youth, 97, 120–21, 137–38, 140, 143, 145–47, 150–51, 154, 166, 169, 171, 188, 192–93, 224, 239, 246, 251, 256, 272–73, 279, 287–88, 293, 301, 304, 316, 325–26, 328–29, 347; joining the e-jihad, 154; Kashmiri, 138, 143–44, 150, 154, 166, 169, 251, 274; killed in conflict, xvii; as self-radicalized, 138; as tanzeems, 168; for training in PoK, 161

Zafar Chaudhary, M., 194
Zain-ul-Abedin, 4
Zardari, Asif Ali, 11
Zia-ul-Haq, Mohammad, Gen., 14, 93–95, 173–74, 207–8, 331
Zionist movement, 308
Ziring, Lawrence, 236
Zojila Pass, 47, 109, 116, 173, 187

Acknowledgements

As I rose in the service hierarchy of the Indian army, it had always been in my mind to write a book or two to share my experiences – relating to my profession of arms and the nuances in planning and decision-making in the higher echelons of the army and the government in the areas of national security and nation building.

However, these thoughts had to be put on the back-burner, because immediately after my superannuation from the army, in January 2005, I was called upon to raise the National Disaster Management Authority (NDMA), as founder Vice Chairman, which occupied me full-time up to 2010. Thereafter, I became a member of the Vivekananda International Foundation (VIF) in New Delhi, an internationally renowned think tank, till I finally handed over my charge as Director in October 2017. Both these assignments needed full-time commitment and thus left me no time to write a book.

After becoming free from my role with the VIF, some friends suggested that I write a book about Jammu and Kashmir. This theme was of specific interest as it encompassed my in-depth knowledge of the subject due to close involvement with the affairs of J&K while holding higher appointments in the army. I was fortunate that I was the Director General of Military Operations (DGMO) during the Kargil war from May to July 1999. As Vice Chief of the army from October 2001 to December 2002, I saw Operation Parakram unfold after terrorists of the LeT and JeM attacked the Indian Parliament on 13 December 2001. As Chief of Army Staff from 31 December 2002 to 31 January 2005, I dealt with the militancy in the state when it was at its peak. So, I had experience with the J&K issue at the highest decision-making levels in the army over a long period of time and thus had the opportunity to work closely with national and state leaders.

In light of the aforesaid and after due consideration, I decided to undertake this project, primarily because I had substantial personal experience of the subject. Additionally, I felt that not many senior officers from the armed forces had written on J&K despite the army's close involvement with the proxy war since Independence.

Another important factor which drew me to the subject was that both my wife and I belong to the state and have been in touch with the unique traditions, culture and dynamics of the land. I vividly recall witnessing, even as a ten-year-old, the spontaneous agitation that broke out in Jammu after the death of Syama Prasad Mukherjee, founder of the Bharatiya Jana Sangh, on 23 June 1953 in the state prison. It is this personal knowledge of the region which enabled me to rationalize that even though Jammu and Kashmir are one political entity, its three main constituents, that is, Jammu, Kashmir and Ladakh, are geographically, culturally and linguistically poles apart. These regions have always nurtured their

Acknowledgements

own aspirations but militancy did not allow them an opportunity at any given time to align their interests and viewpoints.

I felt that this book would be valuable only if it was the outcome of an honest reproduction of one's assessments, wide-ranging consultations with military and civil organizations, and a detailed study of the extensive literature on the subject. I do feel that growing up in the state and witnessing events at close quarters gave me a good insight into the topic.

I would like to acknowledge that I depended enormously on my friends and colleagues from the army and also on the interactions with relevant functionaries from the civil polity. It is not possible for me to include the names of all of them, but I would like to express my deep gratitude and thanks to all those on whom I depended heavily to contribute to the ideas and knowledge for this book. I wish to specifically mention the names of the late Lt Gen. S.K. Sinha, former Governor of Assam and J&K; Air Chief Marshal Shashi Tyagi, former air chief; Lt Gen. Ravi Sawhney, who was Director General Military Intelligence (later Deputy Chief of the Army) during the Kargil operations; Lt Gen. Richard Khare, who commanded a Rashtriya Rifles force HQ in Rajouri Sector (later DGMI and Military Secretary); Lt Gen. Nirbhay Sharma, who commanded 15 Corps in the Valley (later Governor of Arunachal Pradesh and Mizoram); Lt Gen. Mohinder Puri, who commanded the all-too-important 8 Mountain Division, which was involved first in counter-insurgency operations in the Valley and then was responsible for the recapture of Kargil with great glory (later became Military Secretary and Deputy Chief); Lt Gen. Davinder Kumar, Signal Officer-in-Chief; Lt Gen. Ata Hasnain, who commanded 15 Corps in the Valley with great elan (later Military Secretary); Lt Gen. Mohinder Singh, who had commanded a brigade in the Valley (later Adjutant General); Maj.

Gen. A.K. Narula, who had commanded a force HQ in South Kashmir; Brig. (later Maj. Gen.) V.K. Lalotra, who commanded a brigade in Rajouri Sector; Brig. Anupam Bhagi, who was Senior Instructor at the College of Defence Management; and Col. Vijay Kumar, who was part of the Chief's Secretariat as my Deputy Attaché.

From the civil organizations and community, I deeply acknowledge some very valuable suggestions from K.M. Singh, who as a senior IB officer had spent over a decade in Kashmir (later on, he was DG, CISF, and member of NDMA); C.D. Sahay, Secretary Research and Analysis Wing; Dr Sudhir Bloeria, who belongs to Jammu and was also the chief secretary of the state; Ambassador Kanwal Sibal, former foreign secretary; Ambassador Satish Chandra, former ambassador to Pakistan and also Deputy National Security Advisor; Ambassador G. Parthasarathy, former ambassador to Pakistan; Ambassador Prabhat Shukla, formerly in the Prime Minister's Office during the Kargil war and later India's ambassador to Russia; Tilak Devasher, former special secretary in the Cabinet Secretariat; and Sushant Sareen, a strategic affairs analyst.

Further, I was fortunate to attend countless seminars, especially during my inning with the VIF, with large participation from the civilian population of the state, which gave me a real understanding of the minds of the common people. Similarly, my visits to the various army formations during my tenures in different assignments from 1999 onwards gave me a deep insight into the thinking of the people, their needs and their aspirations at the ground level. This greatly facilitated my thought process in framing the structure and conclusions of this book.

Acknowledgements

The manuscript was shared with some of the friends mentioned above at different stages and I am immensely grateful to them for their most constructive suggestions.

I am also thankful to my publisher, HarperCollins India, especially Krishan Chopra; Siddhesh Inamdar, who was my editorial anchor; and Shreya Lall. The suggestions from them with respect to the structural and editorial aspects of the book were very useful. They were immensely cooperative and provided beneficial inputs.

My deepest appreciation to my wife, Rita, our son, Nalin, and our daughter-in-law, Mannerath, for encouraging me to write over the three years that it took me to compile this account.

Here, I must convey my deepest appreciation for the contribution and sacrifices made by our soldiers, ever since Independence, to ensure that India's territorial integrity remains intact.

This book would be incomplete without my grateful thanks to Dr Karan Singh, who kindly wrote the Foreword to this book. Truly, no one else has as unique a perspective on J&K as Dr Karan Singh, who was the Sadr-i-Riyasat from 17 November 1952 to 30 March 1965 and Governor of the state from 30 March 1965 to 15 May 1967.

Finally, my heartfelt thanks to all my friends and colleagues for making this work a reality. In the end, it is not an official recount and I own sole responsibility for all assessments and errors if any in the book.

About the Author

General N.C. Vij was commissioned in the Indian Army on 11 December 1962 and was its Chief from 31 December 2002 to 31 January 2005. He was also Chairman of the Chiefs of Staff Committee at the time of the Indian Ocean tsunami in December 2004 and was responsible for organizing a massive response by the armed forces, including assistance to Indonesia, Sri Lanka and Maldives.

As Director General Military Operations, he dealt with the coordination and execution of Operation Vijay to address the Pakistani military intrusion in Kargil in 1999. Subsequently, he also handled the coordination and execution of Operation Khukri, which involved the rescue of 224 Indian soldiers and 11 military observers, who were part of a United Nations contingent, from the custody of rebel forces in Sierra Leone on 13 July 2000.

He has the rare distinction of commanding two corps, a strike corps and a corps in insurgency operations in the east. His tenure as the Chief of Army Staff is remembered for many a path-breaking operational and welfare project. The most notable one was the conceptualization of a strategy to lay a 740-km-long fence along the Line of Control from the Chenab River to Zojila Pass in J&K to curtail infiltration to a great extent. He handled militancy when it was at its peak in J&K for six long years, from 1999 to 2005. The South Western Command and 9 Corps were also raised during his tenure with the aim of improving the operational posture. The Ex-Servicemen's Contributory Health Scheme for veterans was also started by him.

On superannuation, he was appointed the founder Vice Chairman of the National Disaster Management Authority on 28 September 2005 for a tenure of five years. Subsequently, he became a member of the Vivekananda International Foundation, an internationally renowned think tank. He laid down his responsibility as its Director in October 2017.